DISLOCATING CHINA

To Liko

DRU C. GLADNEY

Dislocating China

Reflections on Muslims, Minorities, and Other Subaltern Subjects

The University of Chicago Press

The University of Chicago Press, Chicago 60637
C. Hurst & Co., London, England
© Dru C. Gladney, 2004
All rights reserved. Published 2004
Printed in Hong Kong

12 11 10 09 08 07 06 05 04   1 2 3 4 5

ISBN: 0-226-29776-4 (cloth)
ISBN: 0-226-29775-6 (paper)

Library of Congress Cataloging-in-Publication Data

Gladney, Dru C.
    Dislocating China : Reflections on Muslims, minorities, and other
subaltern subjects / Dru C. Gladney.
    p.cm.
  "First published in the United Kingdom by C. Hurst & Co. ...
London" - T.p.
Includes bibliographical references and index.
    ISBN 0-226-29776-4 (cloth : alk. paper) - ISBN 0-226-29775-6 (pbk. :
alk. paper)
    1. Muslims—China—Ethnic identity. 2. Ethnicity—China. I. Title:
Reflections on Muslims, minorities, and other subaltern subjects. II.
Title.
DS731.M87 G527 2003
305.8'00951—dc22
                        2003015853

⊗ The paper used in this publication meets the minimum
requirements of the American National Standard for Information
Sciences—Permanence of Paper for Printed Library Materials,
ANSI Z39.48-1992.

CONTENTS

v

Part II. REPRESENTATIONS

Part III. FOLKLORIZATIONS

Part VII. POLITICIZATIONS

PREFACE AND ACKNOWLEDGMENTS

This book follows from my *Muslim Chinese: Ethnic Nationalism in the People's Republic* (1996 [1991]). In that work, as Prasenjit Duara noted in a 1992 review, I sought to 'restructure the study of China inwards from the margins'. Ostensibly about the people known as Hui, the book sought to challenge the way in which China and Chineseness were generally understood, as privileged on a central tradition, a 'core' culture, which tended to marginalize or peripheralize anything that or anyone who did not fit that essential core. The Hui Muslim Chinese demonstrated that one could be an integral part of Chinese society and yet challenge many of our assumptions about that society itself. For that reason, they and other so-called 'minority' ethnics had generally been ignored by Western scholarship.

Since I completed my PhD dissertation in 1987, there has been a rash of publications, conferences, and research projects that have suggested a growing interest in ethnicity and minorities in China. However, I am still concerned that there is a general tendency in much of this scholarship to replicate the portrayals of minority society that they seek to evaluate. Indeed, the very terms 'minority peoples' and 'periphery studies' suggest that understanding of China continues to accept the same dichotomies of majority/minority, center/periphery, and primitive/modern that I sought to question. This volume seeks again to displace that dominant view, to suggest that China and China studies need serious dislocation. Taking inspiration from subaltern studies in South Asian scholarship and studies in cultural criticism, it asks why we have yet to accept studies of identity, ethnicity, and nationality as mainstream to our understanding of China.

The impetus for this volume stemmed from a heated conversation over dinner during an informal Friday evening 'China anthropologist' gathering at an annual Asian studies meeting. I found myself sitting among some of the leading senior China anthropologists in academia when the discussion turned to the Han as a nationality, a *minzu*. I suggested that while I believed Chinese culture and civilization had a long history and many kinds of continuities (as well as serious discontinuities and ruptures), the Han as a nationality was a construct of 20th-century discourses of nationalism that had entered China via Japan in the late 19th century. Not only were these foreign derivative discourses, but they displaced and intermingled with other, more indigenous Chinese notions of identity like person (*ren*), people (*renmin*), place (*tudi*), family (*jia*), clan (*zu*), and locality (*ben di*).

One anthropologist became so incensed at this idea that the volume of his disagreement caused one of the others present to relocate his seat to the other end of the table. I shall never forget his shouting in my ear: 'The Han certainly are a *minzu*, a juggernaut, rolling over everyone in their path!' Another more senior scholar strenuously agreed, although less noisily, pointing out that China was a structurally and socially integrated society, with a long history of cultural and social unity. A group of younger anthropologists, recently returned from their field research in China, sat mute at the other end of table. Later, one of them came up to me and said, 'I would have helped you out but there was no way to get a word in edgewise'.

What would cause such vehemence from a semantic disagreement over the question of the Han as a nationality (*minzu*)? I was treated to yet another display of the importance of this issue when I presented a paper at a UNESCO-sponsored conference on the maritime Silk Route in Quanzhou in February 1992. (I suggested to a public gathering of Chinese and foreign scholars that the multicultural nature of Quanzhou harbor, known to Ibn Battutah as Zaytun and described in Polo's writings as the largest harbor in the world, along with the genealogical record of a large foreign presence in the region since the Southern Song (12th to 13th centuries), including a Muslim harbormaster Pu Shougeng under the Southern Song and later Mongolian Yuan (13th to 14th centuries) dynasties, suggested that the people known today as Han (a category, instituted by the Mongol Yuan administration, that included

all northerners, even Koreans, but specifically excluded southerners) should be considered indicative of citizenship or residence in
China, not cultural or ethnic uniformity.) After I presented these
ideas, one woman social scientist stood up and, with tears literally
streaming down her face, declared: 'I am a Han nationality, I am
nothing but a Han nationality!' (*Wo shige Hanzu, wo jiu shige Han
minzu!*) This vehemence was matched by a Hakka schoolteacher
I once met on the streets of Fuzhou who shouted at me: 'Even
though we call ourselves in Hakka "Tang people" [*Tang ren*], we
are members of the Han nationality. Hakka are not members of the
minority backward peoples [*luohou de shaoshu minzu*]!'

Clearly, being a minority in China is not something many Han
wish to admit to, despite there having been a record number of
reclassifications in the late 1990s (see Chapter 2). But why should
Western scholars become so worked up about this as well? Perhaps
their own sense of China would be displaced, dislocated, or called
into question by such an idea. It is difficult to imagine South Asian
scholars becoming so committed to notions of Indian homogeneity (despite strong commitments to core philosophical and
textual traditions), or discounting studies of Muslims, Christians,
or other marginals as somehow less relevant to an understanding
of Indian society. Perhaps it is the recognition of and tolerance
for heterogeneity in China that has meant that while subaltern
scholars have an influential impact in India (see Duara 1995:6),
almost no similar movement has been produced in China. The
subaltern–studies movement has drawn together a diverse group of
South Asian scholars, including Giyatri Chakravorty Spivak, Ranajit Guha, Dipesh Chakrabarty, Partha Chatterjee, Homi Bhabha,
Gyanendra Pandey, Shahid Amin, and Akhil Gupta, to name but a
few, who share a common commitment to writing post-colonialist
studies of Indian society. As Edward Said notes in his introduction
to the now classic 1988 Guha and Spivak collection, under the
editorship of Ranajit Guha, the first volume of *Subaltern Studies:
Writings on South Asian History and Society* appeared in 1982 with
the claim that 'hitherto Indian history had been written from a
colonialist and elitist point of view, whereas a large part of Indian
history had been made by the subaltern classes, and hence the need
for a new historiography' (Said 1988:v).

In China a full-fledged 'subaltern scholarship' has yet to
emerge. While there is a growing dissident and women's literature,

particularly from Chinese intellectuals living abroad, there is very little written from the perspective of minorities or other disadvantaged and dispossessed groups. Women's studies and the study of women in Chinese society have begun to give voice to a wide range of opinion hitherto rarely heard (see Honig and Hershatter 1988). These studies have begun to look at Chinese society through a multitude of eyes, many of which have been suppressed or ignored. The collection *Engendering China* (Gilmartin *et al.* 1994) has sought to open up a wide variety of perspectives on Chinese society, demonstrating that cultural constructions of gender influence not only how engendered subjects act in that society, but also how we see them. Rey Chow (1990) has argued that China itself becomes the gendered feminine other for the West, leading to a lack of interest in the workings of gender difference and articulations within that society. Again, homogenization of China, either as 'woman' or as 'monoculturally Han', has led to the silencing of a wide variety of subaltern voices.

In their collection *China Deconstructs* Goodman and Segal (1994) indicated how monolithic models of Chinese society are crumbling. Yet none of their chapters gave voice to the peoples and subaltern subjects caught in the middle of that fragmentation. By employing the concept of 'regionalism', this and other, earlier studies continue to rely upon center/periphery models that downplay China's long-term social, cultural, and political diversity. There have been few studies giving voice to those subalterns who have independent histories and cultural memories that cry out for understanding on their own terms, rather than being placed in a peripheral, subregional, or 'subethnic' position.

Of course, because of political realities, critical scholarship is still produced largely from outside China, and this has yet to produce such a subaltern movement within China. In addition, it must be noted that few of the so-called 'subalterns' in South Asian scholarship themselves come from these classes, having benefited from a largely colonialist, Western, and elitist educational system. Nevertheless, by writing about such subjects and subjectivities (including minority groups, underclasses, and other marginalized communities), this group of scholars has forced a rethinking of Indian studies, initiating a post-colonialist and post-orientalist scholarship. Similarly, I hope that by focusing on these groups and the questions they raise I might further a subaltern critique in China studies.

For this study 'subaltern subjects' are the very groups, individuals, and subjectivities that continue to be regarded as somehow less authentic, more peripheral, and further removed from a core Chinese tradition.

Perhaps more to the point, reluctance to advance the notion of Han heterogeneity might be due to a reluctance to call into question the generalizability of field studies conducted among Hakka in Taiwan or Fujianese in Southeast Asia (see Gladney 1996a:107–11). For the most part, Western scholarship on Chinese society until the 1980s had been conducted in regions under Western colonial and post-colonial influence or domination (for example, Taiwan, Hong Kong, and parts of Southeast Asia). Indeed, most of the China anthropologists who confronted me at the Asian studies conference dinner table had built their anthropological careers upon studies of 'Chinese culture' from such places outside of 'China proper'. It was important for these studies, and their largely US and British funding agencies, to demonstrate that research on the Chinese culture in Thailand and Taiwan was just as relevant as studies in China were to understanding Chinese culture on the mainland, because *the Chinese were all the same*. Rarely did these studies pause to ask what is meant by 'China', or why people outside of China proper could be considered equally as Chinese as those on its so-called peripheries, without reference to any essential qualities. Maurice Freedman, in his 1969 address 'Why China?' (cited in Skinner 1979:407–24), was one of the few China anthropologists to raise this question, but subsequent scholars unfortunately attempted to locate the essence of Chineseness in reified traits or qualities such as lineage, family, or religion, rather than seeing these in their great variety and localized contexts, both inside and outside of China.

More recently, the myth of Han cultural and racial homogeneity has been advanced by at least one leading China economist to explain why China will never break apart, unlike the former USSR. Nicholas R. Lardy, China economist at the Brookings Institution, has argued:

While one can not rule out the possibility of China fragmenting into autonomous or quasi-autonomous regions, for several reasons the prospects for such disintegration seem low. Above all, China is not divided by historical, religious, racial, and other cleavages that have been so important in the disintegration of the Soviet Union and Yugoslavia. China is populated overwhelmingly by those of the Han race. (Lardy 1994:25)

While Lardy does go on to stress the long-term contributions of central planning toward economic integration in China, I find it remarkable that an economist would offer such a cultural and even racist explanation for contemporary and future geopolitical realities. Certainly 'racial' similarity, if one admits to such a thing, has neither helped Korea or Yemen come together, nor kept much of Eastern Europe from falling apart. Lardy's emphasis upon racial homogeneity, in the end, is not too different from Huntington's (1993b) 'civilizational' homogeneity (critically evaluated in Chapter 6). What is it that drives contemporary social theorists to posit homogeneity – cultural, civilizational, racial, or otherwise – as necessary to continuity? Is it perhaps due to the influence of the modern bounded nation-state in determining how scholars *and* politicians think about history, culture, and social organization? We must also remember that Sovietologists were equally pessimistic about the great Russian empire (Huntington's 'Slavic-Orthodox civilization') ever disbanding, but few offered such racist explanations.

This volume certainly does not suggest that China is about to fall apart, or that it ever will (although if the past 100 years are taken into consideration, one wonders if Lardy has been reading the same histories of China as I have). It does, however, call into question our reasons for believing why China will stay together, and what the various peoples, regions, and individuals might have to do with or say about that.

Acknowledgments

I would first like to express my appreciation to my colleagues and students in the Asian Studies Program at the University of Hawai'i at Manoa, for their support and encouragement during the many challenging times when this book took me away from the classroom and the island. Eric Harwit was especially encouraging during our many encounters with schedule-juggling during the co-teaching of our course, 'China's Ties to Central Asia'. I am especially indebted for many suggestions, comments and ideas that came out of a three-year collaboration with members of the Collaborative Research Network of the American Council of Learned Society (see http://acls.org/crn/crnhome.htm), which involved a large group of scholars who had much to do with this volume, and who cannot all be listed here, but include David A. Bell, Laurent

Dubois, Eduard Ponarin, Peter Sahlins, James C. Scott, Tylor Stovall, Janet Sturgeon, Ronald Suny, Wang Jianmin, Xu Jianchu, Yang Shengmin, Chayan Vaddhanaphuti , and, especially, Andrzej W. Tymowsky for keeping us working and networked. Appending a long list of the many friends and supporters who took the time to critically interact on many of the issues presented in this volume could not do justice to the depth of gratitude I feel for their support, but I would like to thank a few individuals who made special contributions, particularly Arjun Appadurai, Kahar Barat, Ildikó Bellér-Hann, Carol Breckenridge, Susan Brownell, Todd Carrell, Nancy Chen, Norman Diamond, Frank Dikötter, Prasenjit Duara, John Esposito, Andrew Forbes, Clifford Geertz, Julia Huang, Mark Juergensmeyer, Ablet Kamalov, Charles Keyes, Kaiser Kuo, Satu Limaye, Liu Xin, Rosey Ma, Ma Shouqian, James Millward, Pál Nyíri, Emiko Ohnuki-Tierney, Barbara Pillsbury, Gerard Postiglione, Charles Salmon, Yitzhak Shichor, Ingvar Svanberg, Ricardo Trimillos, Bulag Uradyn, Frederic Wakeman, Wang Haixia, and Andrew Watson. To the boys at Sleeps, *mahalo nui loa* for the many late evenings and early mornings of krill-slipping that helped keep my sanity throughout this project. In what has been a truly global endeavor, I would especially like to thank David Brent at Chicago University Press and Michael Dwyer of C. Hurst & Co. in London for jointly encouraging me to persevere with this volume despite many delays and diversions, as well as David Barrett, copyeditor extraordinaire, who endured many last-minute emails from my island in the heart of the Pacific to his in the heart of Australia. The editors at the *Journal of Asian Studies, Central Asian Survey, History and Anthropology*, and *Public Culture* have kindly allowed me to use revised versions of previously published material and for that I am grateful. And lastly, I would like to express my appreciation to my colleagues and new friends at the Max Planck Institute for Social Anthropology, especially Chris Hann and Günther Schlee, for allowing me some additional time and space to make the last of many corrections to this volume. I am all too aware that there are many other items and issues yet to be corrected, and this is my responsibility alone.

Halle, Germany   Dru C. Gladney
2 July 2003

1

INTRODUCTION

LOCATING AND DISLOCATING CULTURE IN CONTEMPORARY CHINA

Taking as its inspiration Homi Bhabha's call to locate culture not in any essential core qualities, but on the margins or boundaries of assumed authenticities – in the nexus of power, class, and social difference – this book seeks not to locate China and Chinese culture in any essential 'Chineseness' that is unchanging, continuous, and predetermined. Rather, it attempts to understand Chinese culture from its broad and diverse social history and contemporary multicultural complexity, to know China from the liminal others, the subaltern subjects that usually do not fit our notion of Chineseness and China. As Bhabha has written at length:

It is in the emergence of the interstices – the overlap and displacement of domains of difference – that the intersubjective and collective experiences of *nationness*, community interest, or cultural value are negotiated. How are subjects formed 'in-between', or in excess of, the sum of the 'parts' of difference (usually intoned as race/class/gender, etc.)? How do strategies of representation or empowerment come to be formulated in the competing claims of communities where, despite shared histories of deprivation and discrimination, the exchange of values, meaning and priorities may not always be collaborative and dialogical, but may be profoundly antagonistic, conflictual and even incommensurable? ... This interstitial passage between fixed identifications opens up the possibility - of a cultural hybridity that entertains without an assumed or imposed hierarchy ... Increasingly, 'national' cultures are being produced from the perspective of disenfranchised minorities. (Bhabha 1994:2–6)

This book seeks to understand how disenfranchised groups and other subaltern subjects (whether they be Muslims, minorities, students, or gendered others) might enhance our understanding of 'nationness' and Chineseness in the context of China. Racialization,

1

as evidenced by the discussion of Lardy (1994:25) in the Preface of this book, seeks the homogenization of Chinese culture at the expense of these so-called peripheral peoples (see Dikötter 1997). Others have attempted to define and redefine China's 'quest for a national identity' in various essentializing terms, including: Confucianism or neo-Confucianism (that is, recent suggestions in the political economy literature that it is Confucian culture that led to the rapid industrial successes of the East Asian economies of Japan and the 'four little dragons' – Taiwan, South Korea, Hong Kong, and Singapore), language and script (the popular notion that if one speaks and reads Chinese they are Chinese), Han Chinese sedentary agriculturalism (contrasted with 'minority' nomadism; see Fei Xiaotong 1989), the geophysical space of the country occupied by the People's Republic of China (*Zhongguo*, the Central Kingdom, centered in the territory of China; see Thierry 1989), or a biogenetic, neo-racist notion of pan-Chinese Yellowness (as Su Xiaokang's 1989 television series *River Elegy* seemed to suggest). A more fruitful approach, and one I believe more faithful to China's multicultural history (see Hershatter *et al.* 1996), is to seek to understand China from the external and internal limits of its 'geo-body' (Winichakul 1994). Only by examining notions of who is considered purely Chinese and who is 'hybrid' or not true to the essence of Chineseness can we begin to understand the dynamics of Chinese society and culture.

It must be noted, of course, that by invoking Bhabha's 'interstitial' approach, one falls into the problem of essentializing whatever is presumed to be at either end. Just as Robert Young (1995) has criticized the notion of 'hybridity' as presupposing the very same racist notions it seeks to critically evaluate (for one cannot have 'mixed' notions of biogenetics if there is not some presumed pure gene pool), suggesting the subjects of this volume are subaltern or liminal supports the idea of the 'pure' majority opposite. Studies of China's 'civilizing mission' (Harrell 1995), it seems to me, appear to be in danger of doing just that: positing a core Chinese civilization at the very same time as they criticize the civilizing mission among the 'peripheral' peoples. Its seems that in China studies we cannot get beyond the core/periphery or heartland/frontier mentality. Perhaps that is why China (*Zhongguo*) is translated as 'Central Kingdom'. But it must be remembered that this term originally referred to only one among many equal kingdoms or states, and gains meaning only in terms of its relation to those other entities (see Chapter 11). It is also largely forgotten that China's greatest expansion came at times when it was dominated by conquest dynasties from that so-called periphery.

While this book has been influenced by post-colonial studies, as found in the subaltern studies approach and in post-orientalist approaches that recognize Edward Said's critique of Eurocentric constructions of the Asian other, it should be noted that China studies has been less influenced by these approaches precisely because China has never been colonized successfully by the West. In a rather awkward and far-fetched effort to comply with post-colonial approaches, many scholars have begun to speak of China as a 'semi-colonial' state. This not only does injustice to Chinese history – in my opinion, attempting to fit it into Western critical trends (much as national histories have sought to do, as Duara has reminded us) – but also does a worse injustice to those members of the Chinese state who see themselves as having been colonized, if not repressed, suppressed, and administered in the most severe Foucauldian fashion. In this volume, I shall describe this process by reference to Michael Hechter's theory of internal colonialism. For many of China's subaltern subjects, there is nothing 'semi' about their colonial experience.

In Chapter 2, I examine the general background of cultural and ethnic nationalism in China. Influenced by Kosaku Yoshino's (1995) profound analysis of cultural nationalism in Japan – a country also regarded as completely homogeneous – I have sought to examine the contours of cultural taxonomization in China. For example, how was it that groups like the Wa, She, and Hezhe, become recognized nationalities, when other cultural and ethnic groups of much larger populations and influential histories, such as the Hakka, Cantonese, or Subei people, did not become recognized? And why do some of them wish not to be categorized as minorities? On the other hand, I seek to analyze why recognition as a minority nationality is becoming increasingly desirable in 21st-century China, to the extent that minority population numbers have grown three times as fast as the majority, primarily due to reclassification of nationality status. These kinds of cultural nationalisms in China may be influencing national trends toward a greater Chinese nationalism.

In Chapter 3, I examine how those nationalisms are mapped and displayed in China. Following Thongchai Winichakul's (1994) brilliant analysis of the Thai nation's geo-body, I have argued that much of China's cultural terrain is being mapped through the expansion of museums, increased sales of ethnic art, and, in particular, the rise of popular theme parks. Using Partha Chatterjee's notion of derivative discourses, I show how one theme park in Beijing was based directly upon the Mormon-owned-and-operated Polynesian Cultural Center in Hawaii. This leads directly into Chapter 4, where I argue that majority/minority objectifications are commodified in the Chinese public sphere, reifying certain notions of minority primitivity in order to establish majority modernity. The next chapter seeks to analyze the display of the minority other in the Fifth Generation films of contemporary Chinese cinema, with particular reference to Tian Zhuangzhuang's film *Horse Thief*. Interestingly enough, while the film's exoticized and naturalized subaltern subjects are the Tibetans, I argue that Muslims are portrayed in an even less favorable light, despite the film being based on a story by a Hui Muslim author, Zhang Chengzhi.

The intermixing of Chinese and Muslim cultures is taken up in Chapter 6, where I argue that this hybridity is the perfect counterpoint to Samuel Huntington's widely circulated theory of the 'clash of civilizations'. Muslims and non-Muslims have clearly clashed in Chinese history, but they have just as often intermarried, converted each other, and lived intermingled peaceful lives, fighting more often among themselves than between each other over the course of the 1,200-year history of Islam in China. In Chapter 7, I argue that Muslim orientation toward Mecca, and the forces of globalization and transnationalization have paradoxically contributed to certain kinds of localization. Following Arjun Appadurai's suggestion to look for localization amid transnational interactions and diasporic flows, I examine the role of tombs and their surrounding folklores in rooting Hui Muslims locally, and in connecting them to the broader national and transnational Muslim world.

In Part IV I discuss the contradictory nature of Muslim hybridity, suggesting that essentialized and static theories of identity, ethnicity, and nationality fail to take account of simultaneous selves and the oppositional shifting of highly politicized identities. I propose that instead of the biogenetic metaphor of race/ethnicity/nation, the telecommunication analogue of shifting cable channels and scrambled signals is a more fruitful means of attempting to understand shifting but regulated identities in the modern nation-state.

The role of the state in channeling identities, and local resistances to those state-defined histories, is taken up in the next part, 'Indigenizations'. Here I examine in more detail the role of indigeneity in shaping Uyghur ideas of land, history, and Islam, despite many state-sponsored attempts to contain those ideas and suppress the people that maintain them. Chapter 11 suggests that the state-supported 'nationalization' of the Uyghur people has fostered a 'cyber-separatist' movement that has increased political relevance for Turkic émigrés in China, even in their new diasporas far from their imagined homeland, East Turkestan. The next part, 'Socializations', argues that despite a centralized educational system that has sought to educate and acculturate China's subalterns along predetermined paths, other traditions of knowledge transmission have maintained parallel kinds of knowledge and histories. The essay on 'prosperity' suggests that Muslim notions of wealth not only run parallel to Chinese ideas, but also have not been held back by Chinese suspicions of mercantilism and class hierarchy.

The final two chapters, in Part VII, 'Politicizations', analyze the ways in which different subaltern subjects respond to world events, the 1991 and 2003 Gulf wars in the case of Muslims, or the end of the Cold War in the case of the students massacred in Tiananmen Square. In both cases, these subaltern groups were caught up in global events larger than themselves, and their various responses to those events met with overwhelming state response. At the same time, these highly politicized events also demonstrate that China's subalterns are no longer cut off from the world and its media, and that China's treatment of them will no longer be ignored by the outside. In very different ways, these two events, the rather conflicted Muslim response to the Gulf wars, and the student protests in the heart of Beijing, indicates that China's subaltern subjects, like Chairman Mao's peasant masses, have stood up. The entire world is now watching.

The issues raised in the following chapters seek to give voice to the subaltern subjects that are rarely heard in sinological studies, but ones that are increasingly challenging our dominant views of China. While this volume does not presume speak for China's subalterns, I hope it will eventually help to create a space for them to do so, among the interstices of Chinese society.

Part I
RECOGNITIONS

2
CULTURAL NATIONALISMS IN CONTEMPORARY CHINA

Ethnic identity in China

China is a multicultural and ethnically diverse nation-state, with tremendous cultural, geographic, and linguistic heterogeneity among its dispersed population. Yet is not usually thought of as a multi-ethnic country, but rather as one nation with one majority population, the Han, and a few inconsequential minorities on its border areas.[1] Discussions of China generally take cultural uniformity for granted, and China is often portrayed as a homogeneous nation-state. This chapter takes exception to this conceptualization of China and its population. I argue not only that there is tremendous ethnic diversity among its 'official' minority nationalities, but also that there are equally important cultural differences among China's majority population, identified as the Han people. Cultural and ethnic diversity will be seen to be of increasing importance and vibrancy in the post-Cold War era, with a rising politics of cultural difference. Cultural nationalisms, among the so-called minorities and majority, must be taken seriously if we are to understand China in the 21st century. Discussions of 'national identity' (Dittmer and Kim 1994) and 'Chinese nationalism' (Unger 1996) have tended to regard nationalism and national identity as monolithic, rather than examining the wide variety of nationalisms in China, and the nationalization of various cultures. Here I take

1. Eric Hobsbawm (1990:66) repeats this widely accepted idea of Chinese mono-ethnicity in his classic work *Nations and Nationalism since 1780*: 'China, Korea, and Japan ... are indeed among the extremely rare examples of historic states composed of a population that is ethnically almost or entirely homogeneous'. He continues: 'Thus of the (non-Arab) Asian states today Japan and the two Koreas are 99% homogeneous, and 94% of the People's Republic of China are Han' (Hobsbawm 1990:66 n.37).

cultural nationalism to refer to ways in which aspects of culture are taken to represent the identity, history, and aspiration of a people defined as a nation. Culture, as aspects of culture, such as language, religion, and physical or racialized representations, is naturalized to represent a nation as revealed in the historical development and social expression of a people (see Duara 1995). As such, cultural nationalism is that process by which perceived aspects of culture become utilized for nationalist goals, either by the nation-state or by peoples contained therein.[2]

The People's Republic of China comprises fifty-six official nationalities. These include a total population of 91 million official minorities, living in every province, region, and county, speaking a wide variety of languages that belong to four of the world's largest language families: Sino-Tibetan (for example, Mandarin, Tibetan, Kam-Tai, Miao-Yao), Turkic-Altaic (for example, Kazakh, Uyghur, Mongolian, Manchu-Tungus, Korean), Austro-Asiatic (for example, Hmong, Vietnamese), and Indo-European (for example, Tajik, Russian). These groups have always been important for China's domestic and international relations (see Pye 1975). The significance of these official nationalities has increased dramatically since the 1990s, now that China is confronted with several new nations that have significant similar populations on both sides of the border, and ethnic separatism is a major concern to leaders in Beijing.

In addition to the official minority nationalities, the state-recognized majority nationality, known as the Han, which in 1990 made up 91 percent of the total population, comprises a wide variety of culturally and ethnically diverse populations, including eight mutually unintelligible linguistic groupings (Mandarin, Wu, Yue, Xiang, Hakka, Gan, Southern Min and Northern Min). There is also marked linguistic and cultural diversity even among these Chinese language subgroups. Within the Yue language family, for example, speakers of Cantonese and Taishan are barely intelligible to each other, and among Southern Min-speakers it is equally difficult to communicate across Quanzhou, Changzhou, and Xiamen dialects. The North China dialect known as Mandarin was imposed as the national language in the first part of the

---

2. For an excellent discussion of the notion of cultural nationalism, particularly as it is applied to Japan, see Yoshino (1995).

20th century; it has become the lingua franca most often used by these peoples to communicate with each other, and it still must be learned in school. Yet as any Mandarin-speaking Beijinger will tell you, buying vegetables or radios in Canton and Shanghai is becoming increasingly difficult due to growing expressions of pride in the local languages of these areas, with non-native speakers always paying a higher price. Despite strong restrictions and discouragement from the state government, the appearance and resurgence of local languages such as Cantonese in film, radio, and television is just one indication of this increasing interest in cultural difference.

Despite growing awareness of the enormous cultural and ethnic diversity within China, most introductions to the study of China have devoted themselves primarily to the larger issues of state and society, especially economics, politics, religion, family, and the arts, with little attention to the impact of cultural diversity on any of these issues. When cultural differences have been noted, they generally have been explained as 'regional' and not important for our understanding of national identity in China. When ethnic identity is addressed, it usually has been devoted to the study of the official minorities, who generally are marginalized to the geographic and sociopolitical borderlands of Chinese society (see Dreyer 1976; Heberer 1989; Ma Yin 1989). Although the official minorities are certainly important in terms of their overall estimated population of 91 million, and groups such as the Tibetans, Mongols, and Uyghur have gained international attention, their comprising only 9 percent of China's total population has made them inconsequential to most studies of China's overall economy, politics, and society. Discussions of ethnicity in China have been restricted generally to these official minorities, and because they are such a small proportion of China's population, there has been little attention paid to ethnicity outside the official groups. This chapter will introduce further aspects of ethnic identity and cultural nationalism in China, and explore some of the reasons we have neglected in the past to focus only on official ethnicity, and why it is no longer possible to do so in the 21st century. This chapter will suggest that the study of minorities in China must not be divorced from our understanding of ethnic and national identity in general, and from the increasing importance of the politics of cultural difference throughout China.

The politics of ethnic identification

Shortly after the founding of the People's Republic of China, state planners in Beijing sent teams of researchers, social scientists, and Communist Party cadres to the border regions of the country to identify and recognize groups seeking to be registered as official nationalities, or *minzu*, a generic term with a complex and relatively recent history in China, that has been translated in English as 'nation', 'nationality', 'ethnicity', or 'people'. Although more than 400 separate groups applied to be recognized, only forty-one nationalities were listed in the first census in 1953. The 1964 census included fifty-three nationalities, and the 1982 and 1990 censuses identified fifty-six separate nationalities. What happened to the nearly 350 other groups that applied to be recognized? Some of them are still trying. At least fifteen groups are officially being considered for nationality recognition, including the Sherpas, Kucong, and Chinese Jews. Significantly, the 1990 census revealed that there were still 749,341 individuals 'unidentified' and awaiting recognition. This means that these people were regarded as ethnically different, but did not fit into any of the 'official' nationality categories recognized by the state.

The majority of the groups that were not recognized were either considered to belong to the Han majority or grouped with other minorities with which they shared some similarities. While there has not been much written about exactly how some groups were recognized or others excluded, Professor Fei Xiaotong, China's pre-eminent social anthropologist, revealed that the nationality categories employed by the Soviet Union in its identification programs were also influential in China. The 'four commons', as Joseph Stalin called them, included 'a common language, a common territory, a common economic life, and a common psychological make-up', what Stalin (1953:349) later generalized as a common 'culture'.[3] As an example of this process, Fei Xiaotong (1981:76–7)

3. Perhaps in facetious response to Stalin's emphasis on the 'four commons', Julian Huxley and A.C. Haddon (1936) noted: 'A "nation" has been cynically but not inaptly defined as a society united by a common error as to its origin and a common aversion to its neighbors'. For an excellent discussion of current anthropological approaches to ethnicity and nationality, see Williams (1989). In this study, *ethnicity* will be used to mean the self-perception of cultural difference and collective identity, whereas *nationality* will refer specifically to those groups recognized officially by the state.

discusses the case of the 'Chuanqing Blacks' in Guizhou, noting that although they had a close relationship with the Han in the region, they possessed unique features in language, locality, economic life, and psychological make-up that would warrant recognition according to Stalin's criteria. Upon more detailed study by government researchers, however, it was determined that according to linguistic and historical analyses the Chuanqing were not a separate nationality after all, but descendants of Han garrison troops who intermarried with the local population after they were sent to the south to conquer remnant forces of the preceding regime during the Ming dynasty. Apparently, however, this conclusion was not accepted by the Chuanqing, because in the late 1970s they were among more than eighty groups, totaling 900,000 people, who petitioned for recognition in Guizhou alone (*Guizhou Minzu Yanjiu* 1981 3:70 *ff.*, cited in Heberer 1989:37–8).

Other groups, however, have been more successful. The Jinuo, who live on the border of northern Burma and southern Yunnan Province, were the most recent group to be officially recognized. They were granted official minority nationality status in 1979.[4] In 1978, even though they no longer practiced Islam, approximately 30,000 Fujianese who were able to prove descent from foreign Muslims were recognized as members of the primarily Islamic Hui nationality. In this case, their genealogical proof of descent from foreign Muslim officials and traders who settled on the south coast between the 9th and 14th centuries was sufficient for recognition. This led the way for many groups to begin to press for nationality recognition based on historical records of foreign ancestry alone, even though they may lack any cultural markers of ethnicity, such as language, locality, economy, or religion.[5]

4. Ma Yin's discussion of the Jinuo does not indicate how they were recognized in 1979, but he does reveal why it was perhaps useful to recognize them, because they fit nicely into the Marxist evolutionary scheme of 'primitive' minorities. Ma Yin (1989:334) writes: 'The Jino [Jinuo] matriarchal society gave way to a patriarchal one some 300 years ago. But the Jinos were still in the transitional stage from primitivity to a class society at the time the People's Republic was founded in 1949'.
5. On the southeast coastal descendants of foreign Muslims who were recognized as Hui, see Gladney (1996a: Chapter 6). Other groups that culturally resemble the Han they live among, yet who have attained official minority nationality status, include the Manchu, She, Tujia, Zhuang, and Mongols in Huhehot.

Why would anyone want to be recognized as an official minority nationality in China, and why would the government want to recognize them in the first place? The answer may lie in the history of the Chinese Communist Party (CCP) and the influence of the Long March of 1934–35, the Party's 10,000-kilometer escape from the threat of annihilation by Chiang Kai-shek's Kuomintang forces. During the Long March, the Chinese Communist leaders became acutely aware of the vibrant ethnic identity of the many diverse peoples they encountered on their arduous trek from the southwest to the northwest. The march led them through the most concentrated minority areas of China, where they encountered peoples not always sympathetic to the Communist cause. Edgar Snow (1938) graphically described the desperate plight of the Long Marchers, harried on one side by the Japanese and the Kuomintang, and on the other by the 'fierce' barbarian tribesmen. The Party was faced with the choice of extermination or making promises of special treatment to the minorities, specifically including the Miao, Yi (Lolo), Tibetans, Mongols, and Hui, should the CCP ever win national power. Once the Long Marchers reached the relatively safe haven of the mountain caves of Yanan, they had to come up with a plan to appease the numerous Mongols in the north and Hui Muslims to the west, and their powerful warlord Ma Hongkui of Ningxia. One solution was to promise recognition of the Hui as a separate nationality and establish the first minority autonomous region in Tongxin, southern Ningxia. These pledges of recognition and autonomy, in exchange for support for the Communists, were just a few of many promises made to minorities prior to the establishment of the People's Republic in 1949.

From the beginning, the CCP followed the Soviet policy of offering the possibility of true secession for its minority republics, a policy that ultimately resulted in the dissolution of the USSR in 1991. China, however, did not maintain its commitment to a secessionist policy after the founding of the People's Republic. Before coming to power, Chairman Mao followed and frequently referred to Article 14 of the 1931 CCP constitution, which clearly stated that the Party 'recognizes the right of self-determination of the national minorities in China, their right to complete separation from China, and to the formation of an independent state for each minority' ('Constitution of the [Chinese] Soviet Republic', 7 November 1931, cited in Brandt, Schwartz and Fairbank 1952:220). This policy was supported right up to the establishment of the PRC. In 1948, Liu Shao-ch'i (1968:127–8) stated that the CCP 'advocates the voluntary association and voluntary separation of all nations'.[6]

Once the PRC was founded, however, all real possibilities of secession were revoked as no longer necessary. Instead, maintaining the unity of the new nation at all costs was stressed, as revealed by the following cable of 21 October 1949, issued by the Central Party Propaganda Office of the New China News Agency to the Northwestern Branch Office (cited in Gladney 1996a:89–90):[7]

Today the question of each minority's 'self-determination' should not be stressed any further. In the past, during the period of civil war, for the sake of strengthening the minorities' opposition to the Guomindang's [Kuomintang's, or KMT's] reactionary rule, we emphasized this slogan. This was correct at the time. But today the situation has fundamentally changed. The KMT's reactionary rule has been basically destroyed and the party leaders of the New China have already arisen. For the sake of completing our state's great purpose of unification, for the sake of opposing the conspiracy of imperialists and other running dogs to divide China's nationality unity, we should not stress this slogan in the domestic nationality question and should not allow its usage by imperialists and reactionary elements among various domestic nationalities … The Han occupy the majority population of the country, moreover, the Han today are the major force in China's revolution. Under the leadership of the Chinese Communist Party, the victory of China's people's democratic revolution mainly relied on the industry of the Han people.

Aside from the strategic enlistment of a 'united ethnic front' in support of China's precarious new nation, there was another issue at stake in the formulation of the minority identification policy: the nature of the Chinese nation itself. Since early in the 20th century, Chinese reformers, whether Kuomintang or Communist, had been concerned that the Chinese people lacked a sense of nationhood, unlike the British, Germans, and Japanese, and even

6.   I am grateful to Walker Connor for his excellent discussion of this issue and the role of 'minorities in the creation of the Chinese People's Republic'; see Connor (1984:67–101).

7.   See also a Communist Party cadre's frank analysis of the revocation of 'self-determination', 'A Discussion of the National Question in the Chinese Revolution and of Actual Nationalities Policy (Draft)', in Chang Chih-i (1966). To understand China as an affirmative-action state, compare T. Martin (20001:27–35).

the Tibetans and Manchu. In the poignant words of Dr Sun Yat-sen (1924:2, 5):

The Chinese people have shown the greatest loyalty to family and clan with the result that in China there have been family-ism and clan-ism but no real nationalism. Foreign observers say that the Chinese are like a sheet of loose sand ... The unity of the Chinese people has stopped short at the clan and has not extended to the nation ...

The identification of certain groups within China as minorities and the recognition of the Han as a unified majority played a fundamental role in forging a unified Chinese nation. For the Kuomintang, this reformulation of the national identity of China as one people with one history helped to galvanize a sense of identity not only *vis-à-vis* China's internal ethnic peoples, but also toward the foreign nations encroaching upon China's soil.

This idea of Han unity became fundamentally useful to the Communists, who incorporated it into a Marxist ideology of progress, with the Han people at the forefront of development and civilization. In the Communists' portrayal, the Han were placed in the 'vanguard' of the people's revolution. The minorities were induced to follow the Han example. The more backward, or 'primitive', the minorities were, the more advanced and civilized the so-called Han seemed, and the greater the need for a unified national identity.

The politics of Han nationalism

While research on the rise of Russian nationalism has been popular since the 1970s in Soviet studies, by foreign and Russian scholars (see Dunlop 1983; Yanov 1987), as yet no larger studies of the creation of Han nationalism have emerged – mainly because it is assumed, by scholars trained in the dominant tradition of sinology, that 'Han' is generally equal to 'Chinese' – a tradition maintained by the current regime. With the dismantling of the Soviet Union, and the rise of significant ethnic nationalisms in the new states on Russia's borders (and the emergent ones within), Russianization paradigms have been discarded and attention has turned more seriously toward the politics of difference within and around the former Soviet Union. This has not been the case for China studies. In China, preoccupation with Sinicization has paralleled the Russianization assimilationist discourse, revealing an interest only in how much the so-called minorities and other foreigners in China's midst have been absorbed into the dominant Chinese civilization, a civilization dubbed 'Han'.[8]

Since the 1990s there has been an outpouring of scholarly interest in Chinese nationalism and China's 'quest' for a national identity. However, most studies have continued to conflate the issue of the creation of the Han majority with larger questions of Chinese identity.[9] Few have questioned how the Han became the 91 percent majority in China, merely accepting the Han as representative of the Chinese in general.

The notion of *Han ren* (Han person) has clearly existed for many centuries; the descendants of the Han dynasty (206 BC to AD 220) that had its beginnings in the Wei River valley. However, the notion of *Han minzu* (Han nationality) is an entirely modern phenomenon, which arose with the shift from Chinese empire to modern nation-state. While the concept of a Han person certainly existed, it probably referred to the subjects of the Han empire, just as 'Roman' referred to the subjects of the Roman empire (roughly concurrent with the Han). This tells us little about their 'ethnicity', however, and we would be hard-pressed to determine who was Roman today. The Han are still thought to be around, though. The notion of a unified Han 'nationality' gained its greatest popularity under Dr Sun Yat-sen. The leader of the republican movement that toppled the last empire of China in 1911, Dr Sun was most certainly influenced by strong currents of nationalism in Japan during his long-term stay there. The Chinese term *minzu,* is taken directly from the Japanese term *minzoku,* and does not enter the Chinese language until the start of the 20th century. Sun argued that the ruler–subject relation that had persisted throughout China's dynastic history would need to be fundamentally transformed if a true nationalist movement were to sweep China and engender support among all its peoples. More practically, Dr Sun needed a way to mobilize all Chinese against the imperial rule of the Qing, a dynasty founded by a northeastern people who became known

8. The classic formulation of the 'Sinicization' hypothesis, that all foreign groups entering into contact with the Chinese were quickly and inexorably assimilated, is found in Ch'en Yüan (1966); see also Lal (1970).
9. For typical examples, see the collections Befu (1993), and Dittmer and Kim (1993).

as the Manchu. By invoking the argument that vast majority of the people in China were Han, Sun effectively found a symbolic national countermeasure against the Manchu and other foreigners, and to which the vast majority of the diverse peoples in China would surely rally.

Dr Sun advocated the idea of the 'Five Peoples of China' (*wuzu gonghe*): the Han, Man (Manchu), Meng (Mongolian), Zang (Tibetan), and Hui (a term that included all Muslims in China, now divided into the Uyghur, Kazakh, Hui, and so on). This recognition of the Five Peoples of China served as the main platform for his republican revolution, which overthrew the Qing empire and established the first Republic of China. The notion of the peoples of China became key to the success of a people's revolution. The critical link between Sun Yat-sen's Five Peoples policy and his desire to unify all of China is made crystal clear from his discussion of nationalism, the first of his Three People's Principles (*sanmin zhuyi*), which he argued was a prerequisite for Chinese modernization.

It is also not surprising that Dr Sun should turn to the use of the all-embracing idea of the Han as the national group, which included all the diverse peoples belonging to Sino-linguistic speech communities. Sun Yat-sen was Cantonese, raised as an overseas Chinese in Hawai'i. As one who spoke heavily accented Mandarin, and with few connections in northern China, he would have easily aroused traditional northern suspicions of southern radical movements extending back to the Song dynasty (AD 960–1279). The traditional antipathy between the Cantonese and northern peoples would have posed an enormous barrier to his promotion of a nationalist movement. Dr Sun found a way to rise above deeply embedded north–south ethnocentrisms. The employment of the term Han *minzu* was a brilliant attempt to mobilize other non-Cantonese, especially northern Mandarin-speakers, and the powerful Zhejiang and Shanghai merchants, into one overarching national group against the Manchu and other foreigners then threatening China. The Han were seen to stand in opposition to the 'internal foreigners' within their borders, the Manchu, Tibetans, Mongols, and Hui, as well as the 'external foreigners' on their frontiers, namely the Western imperialists. By identifying these 'internal foreigners' in their midst, the Nationalists cultivated a new, broadly defined identity of the Han. In Benedict Anderson's (1991:87) terms, Dr Sun was engaged in helping to construct a new 'imagined community' of the Chinese nation, by 'stretching the short tight skin of the nation over the gigantic body of the empire'.

The Communists stretched this skin even further, following the Soviet model, by identifying not five, but fifty-five nationality groups, including the Han majority. For the Nationalists and the Communists, it was not only the political necessity of enlisting the support of the ethnics on their borders that led them to recognize minority nationalities, but also the desire to unify the nation against the outsiders, by de-emphasizing internal difference. Now that China no longer faces an external threat, internal differences must be considered if we are going to understand the full complexity of local politics and identity in contemporary China.

The best analogy today may be that of the new Europe and the ancient Roman empire. Lucian Pye (1993:130) has observed that 'China today is what Europe would have been if the unity of the Roman Empire had lasted until now and there had not been the separate emergence of the separate entities of England, France, Germany and the like'. Yet one rarely thinks of the Cantonese and Shanghainese as being as different as the French and Spanish. Modern linguists might agree with this novel idea, however. Chinese ethnolinguists such as John DeFrancis and Jerry Norman have demonstrated that there is as much diversity 'among the Chinese dialects as … among the Romance languages … To take an extreme example, there is probably as much difference between the dialects of Peking and Chaozhou as there is between Italian and French; the Hainan Min dialects are as different from the Xian dialect as Spanish is from Rumanian' (Norman 1988:187; see also DeFrancis 1984:54–7).[10] As Fred Blake (1981:7) notes in his study of ethnic groups in southern China, 'Cantonese, Hakka, and Hokkien (Fujianese) with their common root in ancient Chinese are as diverse from one another as are French, Italian, and Spanish with the Latin taproot'. Much like Latin in the Middle Ages, these diverse language groups are all served with one standard writing system, Chinese ideograms (which do vary in some styles, such as Cantonese), although the speech communities are mutually exclusive. What has held these diverse communities together has been the power of the Chinese state, and the fear of foreign domination. Now that China

---

10. The best discussion of minority languages in China and their relationship to Chinese is in Ramsay (1989).

is not threatened externally, and economic reforms have given in-creased autonomy to local regions, age-old internal divisions along 'official' and 'unofficial' ethnic lines may become one of Beijing's greatest concerns as it enters the 21st century.

The politics of ethnic separatism

On 17 June 1993 two bombs exploded in the Oasis Hotel in Kash-gar, a large market town in southern Xinjiang, killing three people and ruining the entire front of the hotel. A group agitating for an independent 'East Turkestan' claimed responsibility for the explo-sion, convincing Beijing that its fears regarding Uyghur separatism and the increasing influence from the new independent Turkic states on its borders were well-founded (Kristof 1993:1). The long-standing struggles of Tibetan independence movements have also been well-documented, although 1993 was quieter than previous years (see Goldstein, M. 1990). However, until then most China scholars had dismissed the possibility of separatism as remote and the violent incidents as minor, on the periphery of China's great land-mass, and of no serious threat to the central authority. The Uyghur, Kazakh, Tajik, and Mongols, and even the Tibetans, were still felt to be marginal minorities that were expected to go the way of the Manchu and others, who were thought to have been long-assimilated into the Chinese mainstream. While I am not predicting or advocating the disintegration of China, it is impor-tant to recognize that there may be a link between recent events among the Uyghur in Kashgar and growing southern nationalisms in Canton and elsewhere, to the degree that they reflect the grow-ing salience of ethnic difference in China.

China's fifty-five official minority nationality groups include ten Muslim nationalities located primarily on China's borders with Russia and the new Central Asian states, whose majority popula-tions are mainly Muslim. With a total Muslim population of at least 20 million (greater than that of Saudi Arabia, Iraq, Libya, or Syria), China is among the nations with the largest numbers of Muslims. In 1991 Xinjiang became linked directly to Kazakhstan by rail, and overland roads to Pakistan, Kazakhstan, Tajikistan, and Kyrgyzstan are becoming much more open to cross-border travel. Weekly flights leave from Ürümqi, the capital of Xinjiang, to Istanbul, Saudi Arabia, and Central Asia. Through cross-border trade and increased foreign trade relations with the Middle East, involving significant exchanges of cheap Chinese labor, consumer goods, and weaponry, China has become closely tied to the Muslim Middle East. To maintain close ties with the Muslim world, China has had to pay closer attention to the treatment of its Muslim minorities.[11] The recognition of China by Saudi Arabia in 1990 and increasing numbers of Muslim pilgrims from China to Mecca indicate improving relations. Yet these relations will be jeopardized if Muslim, especially Uyghur, discontent continues over such issues as limitations on mosque-building, and restrictions on childbearing, and mineral and energy development in Muslim minority regions, without concern for local issues.

Protests by Uyghur and other Muslims in the past have covered a wide range of religious, family, and environmental issues. These issues have been exacerbated by increasing income disparities between the coastal regions of the southeast and east, and the primarily Muslim areas of the north and northwest (see Christofferson 1993). As contact increases between Central Asian Muslims on both sides of China's northwestern border, moves for local autonomy and even independence may need to be balanced against the desire for economic growth. Xinjiang's Muslims are well aware of the ethnic and political conflicts in Azerbaijan and Tajikistan, and that many of them are better off economically than their coreligionists across the border. The challenge to the state is to convince northwestern Muslims that they will benefit more from cooperation than from resistance.

In the south, there are nearly 12 million Kam-Thai speaking Zhuang people on the Vietnam border, and more than twenty-four separate minority groups in Yunnan Province alone, where cross-border relations with Myanmar (Burma), Cambodia, and Thailand have increased dramatically in the past few years. Weekly flights connect Yunnan's capital, Kunming, with Bangkok and Chiang Mai, and increased overland traffic has led to a rising problem of smuggling and drug trade across the Chinese border. Settling of disputes in Cambodia, Vietnam, and highland Burma have continued to be a high priority for state planners in Beijing, perhaps because of the significant potential for ethnic wars to spill over China's southern borders.

11. For a survey of Sino-Middle East relations, see Yitzhak (1989).

The importance of the minorities to China's border areas and long-term development is disproportionate to their population. Although they are only 9 percent of the total population, minorities are concentrated in areas rich in minerals and natural resources, and spanning nearly 60 percent of the country's land mass. In many border counties of Xinjiang, Tibet, Inner Mongolia, and Yunnan, minorities exceed 90 percent of the population.[12] The state has recognized the importance and distinctiveness of the minorities by creating ascending levels of minority autonomous administration. In minority-populated areas, there are five autonomous regions, thirty-one autonomous prefectures, ninety-six autonomous counties and banners, and countless autonomous villages. 'Autonomous' primarily means there is more local control over the administration of resources, taxes, birth-planning, education, legal jurisdiction, and religious expression. It does not mean that true political control is in minority hands. Whereas most minority regions and districts have minority government leaders, the real source of power is in the Communist Party, which in all of these areas is dominated by the Han majority, reflecting China's active watch over these so-called autonomous areas. As a result, these autonomous regions actually come under closer scrutiny than other provinces with large minority populations, such as Gansu, Qinghai, and Sichuan.[13]

Nevertheless, while autonomy seems to be not all that the name might imply, it is still apparently a desirable attainment for minorities in the PRC. Between the 1982 and 1990 censuses, eighteen new autonomous counties were established, with three new counties in Liaoning Province for the Manchu alone, who previously had no autonomous administrative districts of their own. The majority of the earlier autonomous districts were set up shortly after the identification programs were completed in the late 1950s.

---

12. For an excellent graphic representation of these densely populated minority areas, see Population Census Office of the State Council of the People's Republic of China and the Institute of Geography of the Chinese Academy of Sciences (1987).
13. I know of only a few minority first party secretaries in minority autonomous regions: Ulanfu, in Inner Mongolia from 1 July 1947 and to December 1966; Wu Jinhua, a Yi minority from Sichuan, who was Party Secretary in Tibet from 1982 to 1987; Yang Jingren, a Hui Secretary of the Ningxia Hui Autonomous Region from 6 February 1964 to 1967, and again in the 1980s; and Wei Guoqing, a Zhuang, in Guangxi in the 1960s and 1970s.

While it is clear the government is trying to limit the recognition of new nationalities, there seems to be an avalanche of new autonomous administrative districts. In addition to the counties and numerous autonomous villages, whose total numbers have never been published, there are at least eight new counties scheduled to be set up.[14] The establishment in the late 1980s and 1990s of more autonomous districts reflected a real desire for increasing independence from central jurisdiction. No matter how circumscribed that autonomy is in reality, it is clear that many want it.

Population politics: 'coming out' in the 1990s

The increase in autonomous administrative districts and minority population reflects what may be described as an explosion of ethnicity in contemporary China. While the Han population grew a total of 10 percent between 1982 and 1990, the minority population grew 35 percent overall. Significantly, Muslim populations grew by an average of 30 to 40 percent. The Manchu, a group long thought to be assimilated to the Han Chinese majority, not only added three autonomous districts, but grew a total of 128 percent, increasing their population from 4.3 to 9.8 million. Indeed, it has now become popular, especially in Beijing, for people to 'come out' as Manchu or other ethnics, admitting that they were not Han all along.

The Tujia, a group widely dispersed throughout the southwest, more than doubled their population from 2.8 to 5.8 million between 1982 and 1990, and will secure five of eight new autonomous counties scheduled to be set up. Even more remarkable is the case of the Gelao people in Guizhou, whose population grew an incredible 714 percent in just eight short years. Clearly these rates reflect more than mere fecundity, and extensive use of minority exception to the national one-child-per-family birth restriction. Such large population increases reflect 'category-shifting', where people redefine their nationality either from Han to minority, or from one minority to another. Children of mixed parents due to

14. The new autonomous counties (ACs) scheduled to be set up are: in Qinghai Province, the Datong Hui-Tujia AC, the Minhe Hui-Tujia AC; in Sichuan Province, the Qianjiang Tujia-Miao AC, the Pengshui Miao-Tujia AC, the Shizhu Tujia AC, the Mabian Yi AC, the Ebian Yi AC; and in Guizhou Province, the Yuping Dong AC (Ma Yin 1989:434–48).

inter-ethnic marriages are allowed to choose their nationality at the age of eighteen; before then, the parents can decide. At the same time, people who can prove minority ancestry, as in the case of the Hui in Fujian described above, can apply for re-registration. There must have been much of this category-shifting for the total minority population in China to grow from 67 million to 91 million in just eight short years.[15] One scholar predicted that if this rate continued, the population of minorities would be 100 million in the year 2000, 131 million in 2010, 221 million in 2030, and 864 million in 2080 (Tian Xueyuan 1983:147, cited in Heberer 1989:85). China has begun to limit births among minorities, especially in urban areas, in the past few years, but can it limit the avalanche of applications for redefinition? What about the hundreds of groups applying for first-time recognition?

There are also new international pressures being brought to bear on China's domestic minority policies. I have noted China's efforts to promote a more open policy toward its Muslim minorities that would be amenable to its Middle East trading partners. By contrast, international pressure still has had little effect on China's treatment of Tibetans, perhaps due to the lack of real geopolitical support for Tibetan complaints in the United Nations and elsewhere. Of more influence will be China's growing trade with South Korea and its impact on the Korean populations in Liaoning and Manchuria. The Koreans are already the most educationally advanced of all nationalities in China, including the Han, and their local economy is booming due to South Korean investment, tourism, and abundant natural resources. International tourism and travel to China's minority areas has had a significant impact on local economies, particularly with successful Silk Road tourism to Xinjiang, and the marketing of package tours to the 'colorful' minority regions of Yunnan and Guizhou for Japanese, Taiwanese, and Southeast Asian Chinese tourist groups.

---

15. Few minorities experienced population increases between 1990 and 2000 due to migration, with notable exceptions perhaps being the Vietnamese (Jing nationality, 51 percent growth) and the Russians (Eluosi nationality, 360 percent growth). The Russian population is important to watch, because events in the former Soviet Union led to a large influx of Russians to China in the past few years, primarily for trade and employment possibilities, but some attempted to settle due to fears about latent Central Asian and Siberian hostilities toward Russians in those regions.

The most striking change in China's policy toward a single minority as a result of changing international relations has been discussions about recognizing the Chinese Jews (*Youtai ren*) as an official nationality, just after the improvement in Sino-Israeli relations in 1992. The Chinese Jews, once thought extinct, are now said to number from 2,000 to 8,000.[16] China's last active synagogue was in Kaifeng, where the members of the Jewish community mentioned by Marco Polo are thought to have eventually assimilated with the Hui Muslims in the area by the mid-19th century, because of declining population, probable persecution, and lack of contact with other Jews. Gradual assimilation to the large Muslim community in the area was not surprising due to shared dietary and religious similarities, amid a Chinese population that ate pork and practiced polytheism. The Chinese Jews were distinct from the European Jews who began arriving in the 19th century to China's northeastern and eastern coastal cities from Europe and Russia, many of whom left China when the Communists took over in 1949. The reawakened interest in the Chinese Jews of Kaifeng and their reappearance has as much to do with rising ethnic consciousness (many of them claimed to have been unwillingly absorbed by the Hui and the Han) as it has to do with international, especially American Jewish, academic interest in the 'lost' Jews of China.

Clearly, it has become popular to be 'officially' ethnic in 21st-century China. But why? One explanation may be that in 1982 there were still lingering doubts about the government's true intent at registering the nationalities during the census. The Cultural Revolution, a ten-year period when any kind of difference – whether it be ethnic, religious, cultural, or political – was ruthlessly suppressed, had officially ground to a halt only a few years before. Mosques, Buddhist temples, churches, lineage halls, and other cultural institutions were torn down in the name of destroying the 'Four Olds'. By the mid-1980s it had become clear that those identified as members of an official minority were beginning to receive real benefits in terms of the carrying out of several 'affirmative action' programs. The most significant privileges included permission to

16. See the fascinating collection of papers (Goldstein, J. 1999) from the conference 'Jewish Diasporas in China: Historical and Comparative Perspectives', held at the John King Fairbank Center, Harvard University, 16 to 18 August 1992, and organized by Jonathan Goldstein.

have more children (except in urban areas, minorities are generally not bound to the one-child policy), pay lower taxes, obtain better (albeit Chinese) education for their children, have greater access to public office, speak and learn their native languages, worship and practice their religion (often religious practices such as Shamanism that were still banned among the Han), and express their cultural differences through the arts and public culture. These have become real advantages and privileges; although rarely honored in the past, they have begun to have an impact since the mid-1980s. In the modern era, people want to be 'officially' ethnic. But what about the 'unofficial ethnics' among the so-called Han?

The politics of 'unofficial' ethnicity

There is a new feeling in China, a revalorization of ancestral and ethnic ties, especially in the south. Accompanying the dramatic economic explosion in southern China, southerners and others have begun to assert their cultural and political differences. Cantonese rock music, videos, movies, and television programs, all heavily influenced by Hong Kong, are now popular throughout China. Whereas comedians used to make fun of southern ways and accents, southerners now scorn northerners for their lack of sophistication and business acumen. Studies have demonstrated a new rising importance of the politics of ethnic and cultural difference *within* China proper (Friedman 1993; Honig 1992). Not only have the 'official' minorities in China begun to more strongly assert their identities, pressing the government for further recognition, autonomy, and special privileges, but different groups from within the so-called Han majority have begun to rediscover, reinvent, and reassert their ethnic differences.

In the south especially, there has been a rewriting of history, illustrated by a new-found interest in the southern Chu kingdom as key to southern success. Museums to the glorious history of the southern Kingdom of Chu have been established throughout southern China. Many southerners now see the early Chu as essential to Chinese culture, to be distinguished from the less important northern dynasties. In a significant departure from traditional Chinese historiography, southern scholars are beginning to argue that by the 6th century BC the bronze cultures of the Chu spread north and influenced the development of Chinese civilization, not the other way around as supposed by conventional wisdom. This supports a re-evaluation of the importance of the south to China's past, as well as its economic and geopolitical future.[17]

Rising consciousness among the southern Cantonese is paralleled by reassertions of identity among the Hakka (Kejia) people, the southern Fujianese Min (or Hokkien), and the Swatow, as well as a host of other heretofore generally ignored peoples now empowered by economic success, and embittered at age-old restraints placed on them from the north. Interestingly, most of these southern groups traditionally regarded themselves not as Han people, but as Tang, descendants of the great Tang dynasty (AD 618–907) and its southern bases. Most Chinatowns in the West and in Southeast Asia are known as and built around the 'Tang Person Streets' (*Tang ren jie*), for they are peopled by the descendants of Chinese émigrés from the mainly Tang areas of southern China. Today we may very well witness the resurgence of Tang nationalisms in southern China, in opposition to the northern Hans.

The resurgence of ethnic identities in southern China may very well be influenced by similar movements in Taiwan. An increase in traffic across the Taiwan Strait has afforded access to information about widespread debates about minority and ethnic rights in Taiwan. Liao Ping-hui (1993), a Taiwanese scholar at National Tsinghua University, reports a dramatic reassertion among the 'aboriginal' (*gaoshan*) peoples of their indigenous rights and claims upon Taiwan, particularly through the public media.[18] Age-old mainlander/Taiwanese ethnic cleavages have given way to a predominance of Taiwanese language and political figures in everyday life, as well as a host of other groups maneuvering along traditional cultural and linguistic grounds for political power.

There has also been an enormous outpouring of interest in Hakka origins, language and culture in Taiwan, which may be

17. In an important ethnohistorical study, David Faure (1989) has noted that the Cantonese people are descended from the southern Yue, who were regarded as subjects of the Song empire mainly because they paid taxes. Yue who lived in the mountains often refused to pay taxes to the Song, and they became known as the Yao, now classified as a minority nationality of China, whereas the tax-paying Yue are now regarded as Cantonese Han. Politics was clearly critical to ethnic identity even in the pre-modern period. See also Ralph Litzinger's (2000) important study of contemporary Yao identity politics.
18. For traditional mainlander/Taiwanese conflict, see Gates (1981).

spreading to the mainland. The Hakka are thought to have moved southward in successive migrations from northern China as early as the Eastern Jin (AD 317–420), according to one Hakka historiographer, or as late as the Song dynasty (960–1279), according to many Hakka, who claim to be Song people (see Lo Hsianglin 1965). They have also identified themselves as southerners and as Tang people. The Hakka, however, have been registered as members of the Han nationality, perhaps because of a desire to overcome their long-term stigmatization by Cantonese and other southerners as uncivilized barbarians. This may stem from the unique Hakka language (unintelligible to other southerners), to the isolated and walled Hakka living compounds, or to the refusal of Hakka women to bind their feet. Either due to increasing pride in Hakkaness, or resurgent stigmatizations, the popular press in China is beginning to note the Hakka origins of important political figures, and it is not unusual to hear reports that a certain leader acted in a certain way because they were Hakka (leading figures considered to be Hakka or part-Hakka include Deng Xiaoping, Hu Yaobang, and Ye Jianning, father of Guangdong's last governor). It is now widely known that all of China's CCP-led southern bases of the 1920s and 1930s were Hakka, as were their leaders (Peng Pai, Fang Zhimin, Wang Zuo, Deng Zihui). People now often praise Zhou Enlai by stressing his southern Jiangnan linkages, and even Chiang Kai-shek is lauded as a southerner who knew how to get money out of the USA.

These assertions of the politics of difference within the majority Han society argue against traditional assumptions about the 'homogeneous' Chinese and the monoculturalism of China. Local differences are becoming recognized as ethnic, whereas they were previously dismissed as merely regional and therefore less important to understanding China. This semantic shift from regional to ethnic reflects a new salience placed upon the politics of difference in the People's Republic.

Traditional China studies emphasized China as one civilization, one country, and one culture. Rarely did China studies pay serious attention to cultural and political difference, unless it concerned the 'exotic' minority border peoples, almost always regarded as marginal to power and politics in People's China. This goes against a historical perspective that notes China's long divisiveness over cultural, linguistic, and other 'fault lines', which led to ethnic feuds.

As one historian of 'race' in China noted, these feuds 'strove to "clear the boundaries" by ejecting exogenous groups from their respective territories. Such ethnic clashes could be extremely violent: a major conflict between the Hakka and Punti [locals] in 1856–67 took a toll of 100,000 victims' (Dikötter 1992:70–1).

The disuniting of China?

This historical awareness of internal conflict, and ethnic and racial difference, drives a deep-seated anxiety about the possibility of China breaking up in the future. Chinese citizens rarely take China for granted, culturally, politically, or otherwise. This is because most are all too aware of how easily and naturally China could dissolve into its constituent parts. But what are those parts? What are the fault lines that underlie and permeate the People's Republic? While we certainly know the official lines of division between the minorities and the Han, we have no idea of the other unofficial fault lines of cultural difference within China. There are no maps or statistics revealing how many Cantonese, Hakka, or Subei people there are in China. The state has not wished to count them, perhaps for very good reasons.

There was a brief moment during the 1989 Tiananmen protest when residents of Beijing became paralyzed by fear. Their fear was not that the government would crack down; most people assumed that there would be intervention, and had thought that it would have been much sooner. A more widespread rumor terrifying the general population circulated that the various army divisions called in to suppress the protest were at odds with each other over whether or not to use lethal force. It was widely believed then that the Beijing-based forces were more loyal to their city's residents and would refuse to obey the command, while other armies, such as those from the Wuhan military district, were loyal to Deng Xiaoping. At one point, heavy gunfire was widely reported to be heard on the outskirts of the city, and thought to be between the various military forces converging on the city, but this was never verified. There was also a widespread belief that forces from other military districts might not respond to the order to fire upon civilian populations, and the popular rumor that minority troops from Mongolia were being sent in because they would not hesitate to use lethal force against the Han (see Gladney 1990:22). These deep-seated fears reflected a concern that China was on the verge of spiraling into a civil disunion reminiscent of the warlord era of the 1920s, when local militarists commanded personal armies, divided along the lines of cultural, linguistic, and regional political power-bases.

In a 1993 statement to the United Nations, the Russian Foreign Minister Andrei V. Kozyrev declared that the threat of ethnic violence today is 'no less serious than the threat of nuclear war was yesterday' (Lewis, P. 1993). While most people would agree that this is certainly true for the troubled regions of the former Soviet Union, Eastern Europe, Africa, the Middle East, and much of the Americas, few would acknowledge that China is also faced with such a threat. While the former Soviet Union and Yugoslavia are now particularly seen as riddled with ethnic and nationalist strife, China is still regarded as a relatively intact monolith, dominated by a centralized power structure that is intent on maintaining its control at all costs. While there is certainly some truth in these perceptions, this chapter has attempted to illustrate some of the potential fault lines in the system, which could become more salient if China begins to become unsettled. As long as the center remains intact, and there are no more social earthquakes, ethnic fault lines in China may continue to lie submerged beneath a relatively calm surface. If we are going to detect the direction future possible rumblings may take, however, we should not ignore the new politics of cultural and ethnic difference in today's China.

3

MAPPING THE CHINESE NATION

Mapping nations, mapping peoples

This chapter suggests that nations, and the peoples that compose them, are mapped by following established paths of representation. As Thongchai Winichakul (1994:15) has eloquently argued, nations become mapped through the imposition of borders, boundaries, and categories of configuration upon previously borderless, unbounded, or uncategorized regions, peoples, and spaces, creating a national 'geo-body' by which the component parts are constituted. This geo-body then becomes constitutive in the representation, revelation, and relocation of the peoples and places therein. In this chapter I argue that it is through 'path dependence' that nationhood is created by the promotion of stereotypical representations of nations and nationalities perpetuated through national censuses, museums, folklores, and, more recently, theme parks. As Fujitani (1993:101) has argued, promulgation of the accepted 'folklore of a regime' becomes an accepted hermeneutic by which contested and convoluted tales of history and society become master narratives among several competing versions, or to follow Duara (1995:81), by which histories of resistance and *dissent* are turned into accepted lineages of national *discent*. It is this path dependence that makes the Chinese Ethnic Culture Park particularly revealing for our understanding of nationhood in contemporary China, and the discourses of nationhood that have influenced and been influenced by Chinese notions of identity, empire, and nation. Path dependence and the potential for huge revenues may be the reason theme parks are springing up all over China (Bao 1994). I know of at least two in Guangdong, one in Florida (Splendid China; see page 35), two in Kunming, and two in Beijing, including the Chinese Ethnic Culture Park and the Miao Zai (Miao Village), on the distant outskirts of the city. After examining aspects of the Chinese Ethnic Culture Park that I know best,[1] and its relation to other theme parks in China and the US, particularly the Polynesian Cultural Center of Hawai'i, I shall suggest that the sorting out and establishment of paths of nationhood amid conflicting and intermeshed cultural phenomena is the means by which modern nation-states exert hegemonic discursive control, but it is a control that can never fully mask the disorder and temporality of culture.

Path dependence: derivative discourses of nationalism

In a seminal 1985 *American Economic Review* article challenging developmental and rational-choice models of economic change, Paul David, an economic historian at Stanford, wrote about the rather anomalous establishment of 'qwerty' as the industry standard for American typewriters. David described how it is that the first six letters on the upper left of the typewriter keyboard (spelled *qwerty*) became the nationwide standard for all typewriter keyboards, despite being the least efficient of other possible models. Several later attempts at more ergonomic or efficient keyboards have failed to displace the qwerty model. It so happened that when the typewriter was first produced in the 1890s, the qwerty model was quickly adapted as an industry-wide standard simply because at that time it was the only way to physically insert all of the keys. Once this became the most widespread standard by which all beginning typists were trained, path dependence insured its survival, despite many recent attempts to produce more efficient alternatives.

Noting that competing typewriter designs 'have made as much headway as Esperanto over English', Peter Passell (1996:60–1) has argued that the persistence of the inefficient keyboard due to path

---

1. In 1994–95, I visited the Chinese Ethnic Culture Park several times: in March 1994, with a Chinese ethnologist when it was under construction; in October 1995, with a Smithsonian Museum group; and on 21 November 1995, with Gerard Postiglione, Professor of Education at Hong Kong University, as part of a study of 'Cultural Preservation in Tibet' (we had just come from Lhasa), commissioned by the Committee on US–China Relations. The last of these visits was the first time I was accompanied by an official guide. I later visited the park six times to follow up on my observations, with my last visit being in early 2000. On each visit to Beijing I also interviewed scholars, officials, and workers associated with the park, and toured it. For an ethnographic video of the Tibet trip, see http://www2.hawaii.edu/~dru/video.html.

dependence can help to explain similar failures, such as: the Apple Macintosh Computer to the IBM standard (although many would argue Mac is 'better' and more user-friendly); Sony Betamax video format to VHS format (although Sony was first, it was marketed poorly and failed to establish a 'path'); the loss of the 1909 Stanley Steamer automobile design to the more costly gasoline combustion models due to the marketing of the steam engine as a 'luxury' line; the preference of light-water nuclear reactors over less hazardous alternatives such as gas-graphite systems; and the obsolescence of high-definition television before it was ever produced in quantity. Like Thomas Kuhn's (1996 [1962]) theory of scientific revolutions, the path-dependence approach suggests that standards become established not due to any inherent reasonability, efficiency, or intrinsic value, but due to historical accident, market advantage, or the sheer 'weight of numbers' (Passell 1996:61).

While Anderson (1991), Greenfeld (1992), and Hobsbawm (1992) have helped to chart the historical rise of the nation-state as something invented and 'imagined', these theories are problematic, as Comaroff (1994) has noted, in that they assume an inherent teleology driving the process; the rise of the nation-state is coupled with a Weberian 'disenchantment' of the secular and the rise of 'modernity'. However one may wish to define modernity, the rise of the nation-state with the post-imperial order may not be due to any necessary correlation with modernity. Here may be another example of path dependence: the rather haphazard, purposeless movement down one of Greenfeld's five roads, stumbling along as if in a drunken stupor. It just as well could have been any of several possible roads. Yet recent discussions of ethnic nationalist movements around the globe have often seen them as inevitable outbursts of tribal and national urges, held tenuously in check by Soviet and other formerly hegemonic regimes. The rise of nationalism today represents not a return to tribal roots but a reaffirmation of that path dependence. This chapter suggests that these paths continue, just as accidentally, and often just as linked to global capital and international tourism, through the promulgation of iconic representations in theme parks, museums, and public media.[2]

2. For the role of international tourism and travel agents in the commodification of culture, see Adams (1984, 1995). A burgeoning corpus of studies of China's tourism industry and its relation to 'selling' minority culture in China includes Gormsen (1990) and Oakes (1993, 1995).

I am concerned here with the articulation of the multiplicities of national identities within the context of where these identities are often expressed and produced, engaging in the 'borderline work of culture' (Bhabha 1994:7) by examining the borders and paths of theme parks, museums, and other constructed national 'maps'. I argue that nationalism is not just an imagined idea, but represents certain styles of imagined representation, a mode of representation that contributes to a grammar of action now most often defined by interactions within or resistance to the nation-state. As Hobsbawm (1992:4) argues, 'Nationalism is a political pro-gramme ... Without this programme, realized or not, "nationalism" is a meaningless term'. Nationalism is not arbitrary, but neither is there any core content to it; there is no essential essence that is not shifted and redefined in internal and external, often dialogical opposition, using powerful symbols that John Comaroff (1987) has accurately described as defined by 'totemic' relationality. And, as Duara (1995) has noted, all nationalisms and ethnicities are not necessarily by-products of or contained within the nation-state construction. But today these totems increasingly are contained and exhibited within theme parks, from Hawai'i to Beijing, and back again.

The Polynesian Cultural Center: a proto-path?

People are drawn to this place. Its natural beauty overwhelms the senses. They come to play, to discover, to Hawai'i. For excitement, adventure, romance, renewal. But on the windward side of the island of Oahu, there is something more: the world of Polynesia. The way it used to be. The way we wish it could still be.

The Polynesian Cultural Center in Laie remembers Polynesia. The centuries-old lifestyles, customs, arts and crafts of the South Pacific are preserved here. The way they were before the modern world changed them forever. And you can meet the people of Polynesia.

The preceding remarks are taken from an introductory video distributed by the Polynesian Cultural Center (PCC), a Mormon-owned theme park on the island of Oahu, Hawai'i.[3] After showing natural and touristic vistas of the island of Oahu during the above

3. For loan of the video and stimulating insights into the complex world of the Polynesian Cultural Center, I wish to thank Tamara Gordon.

narrative, the video continues with cliff-diving and fire-eating males, then moves to hula-dancing, singing females. A Fijian singing group then performs the song 'Bu La Laie', and a young Fijian woman introduces herself with the following narration during the course of the song:

Welcome to my world of Fiji. '*Bu la Laie*' means, 'Hello, Laie', and Laie is where the Polynesian Cultural Center is located. If you remember, '*Bu la*' is Fiji's greeting word. But the song itself not only greets Laie, it greets other countries that are represented in the center. And it also reminds the Fijians of who they are, and it encourages them to be their best, so that they can be an asset to their nation.

The segment ends with a final 'Bu La', and then cuts to a signpost with pointed signs and arrows indicating directions and distances to various other parts of Polynesia:

Fiji [left] – 3174 miles
Samoa [left] – 2612 miles
Tonga [right] – 3715 miles
Marquesas [right] – 2340 miles
Tahiti [left] – 2746 miles
Hawaii [directly down]

The next segment begins with a fade-in to a young male with a flower over his left ear, who says: 'Alo-o-oha! My name is Keith Awai and I'm from the island of Oahu. I will be your guide today through our ancient Hawaiian village at the Polynesian Cultural Center'. The video then takes the viewer on a tour of the Center, with each site of 'Polynesia' arranged along a central canal and containing a token representation of the region's culture.

One such visitor featured in yet another video produced by the PCC was the Chinese Ambassador, who visited the Center formally in August 1995. It was one several visits. The segments recorded below are taken from the video taken of his visit that was later sent to him and others interested in a record of the visit. The video begins with Ambassador Chu winding his way up the path into the Center. He is greeted by the PCC president, hired in 1994 by the Center, who makes the following remarks:

We are very very delighted to have you all join us. We have with us our distinguished guests, the Ambassador Chu, and his wife, Madam Wang. And we and all of our friends are here to greet you and to enjoy the Polynesian Cultural Center. We have all of the leaders of our church in the Hawai'i area, and the city of Laie, and Brigham Young University, and there will be an opportunity to greet all of you a little bit later on and we'll do that as we go through the Center.

The video then follows Ambassador Chu and the delegation throughout his visit to the various sites, islands, and villages of the Center, inclusive of an elaborate lei-presentation ceremony and evening program. The evening program begins with the following welcoming remarks by President Les Smith, in which he introduces a Chinese Mormon evangelist to China:

This evening there will be an invocation by Dr Chan. And Dr Chan is working with us today as a great service. He has been set apart as a traveling elder to China for our church and it is great being with him today and to hear his wonderful knowledge.

There is then a prayer by the Reverend Chan, in which he thanks Jesus (*Yesu*) for bringing the Ambassador to them and asks for God's blessing on him, his family, and his country China. The prayer is then followed by a banquet, which is served during Polynesian performances by the students at the Center. Several Chinese students also perform, and it is revealed that in addition to more than seventy Chinese students from Taiwan, Hong Kong, and Southeast Asia, there are also twenty-three students from mainland China working and studying at the Center and at Brigham Young University. Ambassador Chu concludes the evening with the following remarks:

This is not my first visit to the Polynesian Cultural Center. I have been visiting since 1994. I always persuaded my colleagues in China to come to visit Polynesian Cultural Center if they have any chance to visit Hawai'i at all. We have a saying in China: If anybody comes to Beijing on a visit, I mean any foreign friend comes to Beijing on a visit, if he hasn't visited the Great Wall, he's not considered to have visited Beijing at all. I think the same should apply to the Polynesian Cultural Center. If anybody comes to Hawai'i [applause], and if he hasn't visited the Polynesian Cultural Center, he should not be qualified as having visited Hawai'i [applause].

I think it is true the Polynesian Cultural Center is a tourist center, but it is not only a tourist center. It is also a training center for the students who study in Brigham Young University to spend some time to learn how to serve the community, to how to serve the people ...

I think I must say that I have been here four or five times. Each time I come here I spend several hours or a whole day here. My interest in this Center has never diminished. My visit this time is as exciting as my first visit to the Polynesian Center. So I can assure you that this day will remain fresh in our memory for many, many years to come. And the friendship we have established with you will be a long-standing one. Thank you very much [applause].

The video then immediately fades to Chinese music, the screen grows blank, and then yet another introductory video begins, entitled *China Folk Culture Villages* (*Zhonghua Minsu Wenhua Cun*). The video is a Chinese-produced overview of their own theme park in Shenzhen, Guangdong Province, in which there is a remarkably similar introduction to that of the PCC, only with traditional and Chinese architecture arranged along a central river near the ocean. The narrator describes the park (in Chinese) and notes that it is sponsored by the Hong Kong China Travel Service and funded by Chinese and Hong Kong joint ventures. The video cuts to a line of women dressed in colorful minority 'costumes' in front of the Chinese sign for the *Zhonghua Minsu Wenhua Cun*.

Mixed media, blurred genres, and derivative discourses

The China Folk Culture Villages in Shenzhen are presented in this video package as directly derived from the Polynesian Cultural Center. While this is difficult to establish, the many visits between Chinese government and tourist officials to the PCC, and the remarks by the Chinese Ambassador, seem to indicate mutual influence, if not direct copying. It is clear from the Mormon packaging of the introductory Shenzhen video with the ambassador's visit that they would like to think this is so. A case of successful theme-park evangelization? This may not be far from the truth, as we shall see.

In his revealing study of the PCC, Andrew Ross (1993:89) has argued that touristic performances of native culture 'is as much an interpretation of Western aesthetic codes as it is an expression of traditional values'. Here, in both Mormon and Chinese-government representations, we see the blurring of Western, Chinese, and Marxist notions of nationalism and identity. Much of this has to do with the derivative discourses of nationalism and national identity in China, which (as I have argued in Gladney 1996a: 93–6) are derived from not only Marxist and Western discourses of nationalism *à la* Partha Chatterjee (1986), but also traditional Chinese representations of identity and peoplehood. Critics of the Chinese theme park in Shenzhen and one modeled after it, Florida's Splendid China, have questioned the Chinese government's 'right' to represent various peoples (such as Tibetans and other minority groups) in certain ways (see *Tibet Press Watch* 1994:7). Ann Anagnost (1995) has noted that Splendid China represents a vision of what the Chinese government perceives China ought to be, much as the PCC video depicts Polynesia 'as it could be'. Few have noted that by including the many *minzu* (variously translated as 'nationalities', 'nations', 'ethnicities', 'ethnic', 'people', and so on; see page 36) as part of 'China's Folk Culture' it is following an important tradition of national identification and incorporation in China strongly influenced by these derivative discourses of nationalism. The notion of *minzu* is intimately connected to the promotion of the Han as the majority *minzu* of a multi-*minzu* China.

Confucian preoccupation with order and harmony in a society held tenuously together by proper relationships may be one reason for the adoption of categories of nationality such as *minzu*, with the so-called Han in majority and the other subordinate groups as minorities. The very Confucian practice of the 'rectification of names' (*zheng ming*) is of primary concern to Chinese ethnographers: once the Han and all of the minority nationalities have been identified or named, order is restored and all is well in the world. As François Thierry (1989:78) has noted:

The importance given in China to the harmony between the thing and its name is well known: every name must agree perfectly with the profound nature of what is named. Thus the graphic classification of the name of each type of Barbarian under a radical marking his animal nature is an ontological necessity. So one finds in the ideograms designating some Barbarians the root 'reptile' (the Mo, the Wei, the Lao, etc.), the root 'worm' (the Ruan, the Bie, the Dan, the Man, etc.), and above all the root 'dog' (the Di, the Yan, the Qiang, the Tong, etc.); some may be written equally with the root 'dog' or the root 'reptile' (the Wei, the Lao).

Although these root ideograms were removed from the names of the minority nationalities after the founding of the People's Republic, the labels themselves crystallized as official designations. Some were inappropriate, for the Hani call themselves Akha, the

Miao call themselves Hmong, and some Naxi also go by Muoso, while others, such as the Hui, had a wider meaning indicating more than one nationality. These designations, then, are derived from a history of assisting the Chinese state in its traditional role of bringing order out of chaos, and the Confucian practice of rectifying names. One such name invented as the label for an entire nation (*minzu*) is that of the Han.

The notion of *Han ren* (Han person) has existed for many centuries as those descendants of the Han dynasty, which had its beginnings in the Wei River valley. However, I have argued that the notion of *Han minzu* or *Han min* (Han nationality) is an entirely modern phenomenon – it arises with the shift from empire to nation.[4]

It is significant that while the China Folk Cultural Park is based on the theme of the many *minzu* of China, the minorities as usual figure much more prominently than the Han in the performances and dances, even though the Han supposedly vastly outnumber minorities in China. Because the China Folk Cultural Park includes Han and minorities, as well as focusing on different varieties of Han culture, it is considered a *min su* (folk) park, not a *minzu* (nationality or ethnic) park. The Chinese Ethnic Park (*Zhonghua Minzu Yuan*) has *minzu* in the title because it focuses not on all of the 'folk', but mainly on the nationalities or ethnicities that comprise China. Yet folklore scholars such as Uli Linke (1990:119) have noted that the invention of folklore and folklore studies had very much to do with the nationalist projects of 19th-century German romanticists to construct a common German historical and cultural heritage. As Fujitani (1993:101) has noted, the invention of the 'folklore of a regime' is critical to nation-building and nationalist projects. *Min su* is not that far from *min zu* after all. However, it should be noted here that since the late 1990s, perhaps as a result of growing US social-science influence and declining Russian influence, *minzu* in Chinese is increasingly being retranslated into English as 'ethnic' instead of 'nationality'. In 1995 the *Guojia*

4. For example, the 1996 Unger collection *Chinese Nationalism* repeatedly and uncritically conflates the notion of Han and Chinese, with Han nationalism being synonymous with Chinese nationalism (see Townsend 1996:15). Similarly, Nicholas Lardy (1994:25) has argued that it is the 'racial' homogeneity of the Han that will keep China from falling apart (see quote from Lardy on page xvii of the Preface).

Minzu Shiwu Weiyuanhui redefined itself as the State Commission for Ethnic Affairs, in place of its former English title, the State Commission for Nationality Affairs. Thus the Beijing theme park *Zhonghua Minzu Yuan* is translated by the Chinese themselves as the Chinese Ethnic Culture Park, and not as the Chinese Nationality Park.[5]

This debate, though involving a minor translation, is important in that the translation of *minzu* as 'ethnic' and no longer as 'nationality' may involve a slight but significant semantic shift. As I have argued above, translating *minzu* as 'nationality' in English is appropriate given the Soviet Marxist influence on Chinese nationality policy in the 1940s and 1950s, and the fact that the Chinese state officially recognizes only fifty-six *minzu*. Given that the history of the term 'ethnic' in Western social science has included a strong commitment to self-identification (see Keyes 1981) irrespective of state policy, it seemed more appropriate to reserve that category for groups (even in China) who perceived themselves to have a separate collective identity even if they were not recognized by the state. Thus, as Williams (1989:439) has argued, 'ethnicity identifies those who are at the borders of the empire'. At the same time, the state hires anthropologists to map those borders, which then are taken up to divide the various exhibits of theme parks and national museums. Thus, of the 400 or more groups who perceived themselves to be ethnic in 1949 and applied for recognition, only fifty-six eventually were recognized as *minzu*, as nationalities, registered by the state, with the Han *minzu* identified as the vast majority (Fei 1981). That does not mean the unrecognized others no longer considered themselves ethnic, and groups such as the Subei people in Shanghai, as Emily Honig (1992) has argued, continue to see themselves as ethnic despite their lack of official *minzu* designation. The important point here is that the role and success of theme parks such those in Beijing, Shenzhen, Kunming, and elsewhere may lead to the transformation of various folk cultures (*minsu wenhua*) into national cultures (*minzu wenhua*), demanding recognition by the state, for profit if nothing else.[6]

5. Note that the Chinese term for 'culture' (*wenhua*) also does not appear in the Chinese title of the Chinese Ethnic Culture Park (*Zhonghua Minzu Yuan*).
6. In an article in a 1996 issue of *China Focus* ('National Identity Can Be Bought'), it was noted that people are increasingly able to simply go out and purchase their national identity: 'From September 1994 to May 1995, the nationality

Since the mid-1990s, writing on China's minorities and national identification program has begun to focus on the 'civilizing mission' of China's policy toward its 'backward minorities' (see Anagnost 1994; Harrell 1995). In state-sponsored media and publications, and public representations, the Han majority are represented as the most modern and, by implication, the most educated. The Han are frequently represented as somewhere near the modern end of a Marxist historical trajectory upon which China's minorities must journey. Much of this derives from a continued commitment in Chinese social science to the study of minorities as 'living fossils' indicating the origins of 'primitive communism'. Matrilineality, communal living and property-holding, and even extramarital sexuality among the minorities all become 'proofs' of how far the Han have come. Chinese Marxist social science has been heavily influenced by stage evolutionary theory, particularly as represented in the writings of the US anthropologist Lewis Henry Morgan (see Yang Kun 1992). Yet this representation of culture and civility has a long history in China and is certainly not new to the nation-state.

In imperial China, 'others' were frequently depicted as less 'civilized' than the imperial authorities, and portrayed often as the 'uncooked', uncultured other, 'replete with all the tools familiar from the history of European expansion into Asia, Africa, and the savage-infested New World' (Rowe 1994:423). Tang portrayals of southerners also tended to exoticize and romanticize them (Schafer 1967: 83). Here, the emphasis is not upon a qualitative difference between modern and 'traditional' China, but on a possible shift in the paths of dependence during the transition from empire to nation, from discourses regarding malleable 'civilization' and education to less malleable categories of ethnicity and nation. From tribute-bearing

---

bureau of Luchuan County in Guangxi made 798.7 thousand RMB just by selling national minority identities … Why would one want the identity of a national minority? This is because there are certain advantages attached to such an identity. For instance, if a student belongs to a minority nationality, his or her admission requirements for college are ten points lower than that of Han Students, the major nationality group in China; if both a husband and wife are members of minorities, they are allowed to have two children instead of just one child. Also cadres from minority nationalities are given better chances for promotion than Han people'.

subjects to happy voting nationalities, the trope is now one of the hegemony of the nation as dominated by the majority, rather than that of the empire under the hand of the emperor.

Mapping the Chinese Ethnic Culture Park

One enters the park on the outskirts of Beijing from a side road off the Fourth Ring Road, *en route* to the airport. It is built on land originally set aside for the failed bid for the 2000 Olympics, and next to the site of the 1988 Asian Games, which can be seen from the park. As I entered on 21 November 1995 for my third visit, I had the following videotaped conversation with the guide assigned to us, who happened to be a woman of the Yi nationality:

[Guide:] You've been to Sichuan? This is Jiuzai Valley in Sichuan, have you been there? This waterfall is a small part of Jiuzai Valley.

[Gladney:] But what about this dragon?

[Guide:] This dragon is here because China's nationalities [*Zhonghua minzu*] [think that] the 'Dragon passes on to the people'.

[Gladney:] The Han worship the dragon … But do the minorities worship the dragon?

[Guide:] Some of the nationalities worship the dragon, but not each and every one. Isn't this is the China Ethnic Culture Park [*Zhonghua Minzu Yuan*]?

[Gladney:] Are there Han nationalities in the park?

[Guide:] Yes, there are Han nationalities.

[Gladney:] Are the Han represented? Do they perform?

[Guide:] No, there are none represented now.

[Gladney:] Will there be?

[Guide:] Yes, there will be. The next time you come there will be …

[Guide:] This park preserves many aspects of culture and religious culture the best, and the [Tibetan section] preserves the religious aspect of nationality culture most completely.

[Foreign scholar:] How do they determine if they have preserved it well or not?

[Guide:] Mainly from their customs [*fengsu*]. Also if its close to their most ancient practices. This can be seen fairly well … You can't say that every nationality preserves it completely, some nationalities also …

[Foreign scholar:] For example, the Manchu; the Manchu no longer have their language.

[Guide:] No, the Manchu still have it; in some small counties its still preserved, but I can't remember which…

As we wandered along the paths through the sixteen villages of the park, a later conversation with the guide also revealed a commitment to this 'pathway' of representation about national identity. When I asked why there were no Muslim nationalities represented among the sixteen nationalities, I received the following response:

[Gladney:] Is it possible to see the Muslim nationalities?

[Guide:] I'm sorry. Right now there aren't any Muslim nationalities.

[Gladney:] There aren't any yet? No Uyghur, Kazakh, Hui ...?

[Guide:] No, none ... Don't you think the Uyghur look a lot like you people?

[Foreign scholar:] Yeah, you look so much like a Uyghur you could sell lamb shashlik!

[Gladney:] OK, but why do you still not have Muslims here?

[Guide:] We have our limitations, and we've divided it into stages, first, second, and third. In the first stage you can see what we have. In the second we will have Muslims ... Uyghur, Kazakh, uh, Tajik ... In the future we'll have them.

[Gladney:] But do you have any Han here?

[Guide:] We already have them.

[Gladney:] You do? Where?

[Guide:] Just wait until we circle over there.

[Gladney:] But the Han aren't a minority nationality?

[Guide:] Although the Han are not a minority nationality, they are still a nationality. This park is the China Ethnic Culture Park [*Zhonghua Minzu Yuan*]; its not the China Minority Ethnic Culture Park [*Zhonghua Xiaoshu Minzu Yuan*].

[Gladney:] So you have any kind of nationality. Now, what about the Hakka nationality [*Ke Jia zu*], the Hakka people [*Ke Jia ren*]?

[Guide:] The Hakka are not a nationality. They are a branch of the Miao [Hmong] nationality.

[Foreign scholar:] What about the Hong Kong people?

[Guide:] Hong Kong people are Han, aren't they?

[Foreign scholar:] But what about their cultural traditions?

[Guide:] Their cultural traditions ... because their cultural traditions have been influenced by imperialism [*shoudao zhimindi de yinxiang*].

[Foreign scholar:] Imperialist influence? What kind of influence? Oppression?

[Guide:] Not oppression! Don't call it oppression. It's that they have been entirely influenced by Western culture. And their customs are very close to Western customs.

[Gladney:] Now the Hakka have their own language and their own religion. Why aren't they a nationality?

[Guide:] This kind of thing … Shouldn't you go ask the Ethnic Affairs Commission [*min wei*]? Yeah, go ask the Ethnic Affairs Commission! This belongs to the Ethnic Affairs Commission …

While the State Commission for Ethnic Affairs is not in charge of the park – it is run by a Taiwan, Hong Kong, and Beijing Municipal joint venture – the commission had to first approve the park before it was allowed to be opened. Prior to and during the construction stage, officials and scholars from the commission, and also from the Central Nationalities University, were asked for advice on the park. During its construction in 1994, I asked one of these scholars if all the minorities and the Han would be represented, and he said: 'Of course, you have to have all the minorities and the Han, lest you offend someone'. I was therefore quite surprised when I discovered no Muslim groups in the park after it opened in 1995. When I spoke about this with a Tibetan monk, Jige, working in the Tibetan section of the park, he told me: 'People who come here are mainly from northern China, and they want to see minorities they do not normally get to see. That's why you don't see any Muslims or other northern groups'. I was puzzled, however, to find the Manchu, Koreans, and Mongols well represented in the park. And even though the guide said there were Han in the park, I could find no official Han display or performances in October or November 1995.

During the construction of the park, a selection committee was sent to southwest China to recruit minorities to work in the park. The minorities were promised they would be housed for free and paid 300 yuan a month in Beijing. They were also told there would be opportunities to go to school, perhaps at the Central Nationalities University in Beijing, where other minorities are trained, once the park had made enough money to rotate personnel. The minorities were selected based on three criteria: ability to speak Chinese; ability to sing or dance their own nationality's songs; and physical beauty. This last category is important, for as Brownell (1995:23), in her fascinating study, has shown, Chinese have very definite views of 'standardized beauty'. Perhaps as a result of these standards and the goals of the park, one Dong-nationality male worker told me that the vast majority of the workers selected were female and 'beautiful' according to these criteria (tall, slender, light-skinned, with wide eyes, and so on). For example, in the Miao (Hmong) village, eight out of the ten workers were female; in the Hani village, six out of the eight workers were female; in the Dong village, three out of the five workers were female. This follows the pathway of nationality representation I discuss in Chapter 4.

While minorities in China are no longer portrayed as barbarians, and many of the disparaging Chinese ideograms that formerly scripted their names with 'dog' and 'bug' radicals were changed in 1949, their portrayal in public media and this theme park in particular, is not only much more 'colorful' and 'cultural' than the Han, but also much more sensual. One of the favorite themes that one sees portrayed on items for sale and literature made available is that of minority women, especially the Thai (Dai), Hani, and Li, bathing in the river. As at the Polynesian Cultural Center, water figures largely in the park. It runs throughout the park, in canals, streams, waterfall, and fountains. There is also the occasional re-enactment of the famous Water Festival of the Thai and other groups from southern China. During this festival, many Han believe minority women like to bath nude in the river.

The image of Thai and other minority women bathing in the river has become a leitmotif for ethnic sensuality in China, and often appears in stylized images throughout the country, particularly on large murals in restaurants and public spaces. Schoolchildren are often encouraged to make woodblock prints of Thai bathers and other exotic representations of minorities. One of the most famous incidents regarding the public portrayal of minority nudes in China was that of the Beijing Capital Airport.[7] From these representations, I have debated that minority women in China have been troped at a popular level as the ultimate 'sexual personae' (Paglia 1990:40) for the 'Eastern eye' of the broader Han Chinese society. While it may be argued whether the images of minority women bathers are actually erotic or sensual in the eye of the beholder, they are clearly images that do not apply to Han women, who are generally represented as covered, conservative, and 'civilized' in most state publications. This is perhaps why the Han nationality would not be regarded as an attraction at such a

7. I describe the 'covering and uncovering' of the Yuan Yunsheng mural in detail in Chapter 4. On my most recent visit in November 1995, the nudes were again uncovered. The videotape upon which the airport murals are shown, and from which the above conversations are transcribed, is able to be viewed at http://www2.hawaii.edu/~dru/video.html.

theme park. Nudity is often idealized and romanticized in China as being natural, free, and divorced from the constraints and realities of modern life, yet it is also regarded as improper for Han (see Brownell 1995:270, 275). Minorities become likely subjects for such displaced romantic yearnings.

Here the audience becomes an important issue but, as is the case in any discussion of public culture, this is difficult to assess. Suffice it to note that in official public arenas, such as airports, hotels, and government offices, images of naked Han women are rarely found. Representations of unveiled minority women, however, are frequently displayed in the official public sphere, as was noted at this park, where nude minority images were widely offered for sale.

At one market area, I had the following conversation with a saleswoman of minority handicrafts and erotic representations, who turned out to be a member of the Dong minority:

[Gladney:] What nationality is this? [Holds up a batik cloth.]
[Clerk:] They are the Thai nationality [*Dai zu*].
[Gladney:] What's this drawing? Are they taking a shower? [Lifting another drawing of nude woman bathing.]
[Clerk:] This? No, this is the Water Festival. Haven't you heard of it?
[Gladney:] Oh, it's for the holiday?
[Clerk:] Exactly. Haven't you seen the Water Festival? Why don't you buy this one? [Holds up a batik of a completely nude woman bather.]
[Gladney:] I've never seen it before ... What nationality is this?
[Clerk:] It's a Dong nationality woman.
[Gladney:] A Dong nationality? How much does it cost?
[Clerk:] Let me see if we can give you a deal ... Here's a nice mask; you should buy one!
[Gladney:] What nationality are you?
[Clerk:] I'm a Dong nationality from Guizhou.
[Gladney:] You're a Dong nationality?
[Clerk:] Yes, that's correct.
[Gladney:] You came here to work?
[Clerk:] Yes. You should buy one of these masks. They are used in worship.
[Gladney:] That last drawing, the one of the bathing. Is that Dong? Is that what you do as well?
[Clerk:] Yes [makes washing motions]. Buy one, buy one of these ...
[Gladney:] Thanks, but I'll buy it next time.
[Clerk:] Next time!

Clearly, the Dong saleswoman is not reluctant to market her own people's sensuality.[8] It should be noted that minority women figure largely in Chinese anthropological literature on the rise of capitalism from 'primitive communism' and 'matriarchal' society. This belief was reflected in the following conversation I had with another Dong woman encountered in the park:

[Dong woman:] We Dong nationality worship a female god the most.

[Gladney:] Are you matrilineal [*muxi zhidu*]?

[Chinese male tourist:] No way, no way. That's a situation from several thousand years ago, several tens of thousand of years ago.

[Guide:] No way, no way.

[Gladney:] So you're no longer?

[Dong woman:] No, we're no longer. But you can come see our worship of this ancient practice at one of our yearly winter festivals …

[Foreign scholar:] Your outfit is very beautiful.

[Dong woman:] This is appliqué; it's not considered that beautiful. Hand-sewn is much more beautiful.

[Chinese male tourist:] These Dong women take their clothing very seriously. On holidays, they put on their most beautiful clothes and come out. If someone like you comes, they'll come out and dance with you …

The enticement to dance with these women and observe 'ancient' matrilineal customs during festivals by a Chinese Han tourist evidences widespread belief in the exoticized evolutionary paradigm with 'primitive' matrilinealism, represented by minorities at one end, and 'modern' patrilinealism, represented by the Han, at the other. As noted by Chow (1995), the preoccupation in China with primitivity evidences itself most conspicuously on the silver screen. The popularity of this discourse is evidenced by the films *Amazing Marriage Customs* (*Jingu Hunsu Qiguai*; literally 'Strange Modern and Ancient Marriage Customs') and *Horse Thief* (see chapters 4 and 5). In general, Muslims do not do well in Chinese films, as the film *Horse Thief* by Fifth Generation filmmaker Tian Zhuangzhuang indicated. Again, this may yet be another reason why Muslims do not figure at the park. Muslim conservatism and patrilinealism (in China at least) does not fit the primitive-to-modern evolutionary scheme. One of the reasons I was quite

8.   From the video, it is not clear if the woman is really a Dong minority, or if she is merely pretending to be so to make a sale. Later, one of the other workers confirmed that the clerk was indeed Dong.

concerned about Muslim representation is that of all of the minorities in China, the Muslims have been the most successful in their public protests over misrepresentation and stigmatization of Islam in the public media. A protest over the publication in 1989 of *Sexual Customs*, a book found denigrating to Islam, received widespread media attention and immediate government accession to Muslim demands (see Gladney 1994c), and these protests have continued in recent years. This may be yet another reason park officials are reticent to include Muslims in the park display.

Minority 'primitivity' contrasts with supposed Han 'modernity'. Minorities become a marked category, characterized by sensuality, colorfulness, and exotic custom. This contrasts with the 'unmarked' nature of Han identity. 'Han-ness' for the Chinese connotes civility and modernity, and this is perhaps why more 'educated' minorities, such as the Manchu and Koreans, are rarely exoticized as sensual or primitive. The Korean presence in the Chinese Ethnic Culture Park is presented as rural and agrarian, even though the Koreans are the most educated nationality in China, far more so than the Han (see Lee 1986).

This is also perhaps why the audience for this and other theme parks in China is largely Chinese. Although Ethnic Affairs Commission officials consulted for the theme park were told that it would be for foreigners, it has turned out that the largest audiences have been Han and overseas Chinese. One German couple I spoke with told me they found the park too 'artificial' and wished they had not gone. It is surprising, however, that the park continues to turn a profit without many foreign guests, because ticket prices are far beyond the average Chinese worker's reach (160 yuan, the equivalent of about US$18, with average incomes in Beijing around 400 yuan a month). Besides overseas Chinese, I mainly noticed some school groups and the Chinese military. In addition, I found very few Japanese in the park. Although theme parks seem to be booming in Japan, they are more on the Disney variety, not the nationality kind (see Higashino 1991).

During my October 1995 visit to the park, a Tibetan monk complained that his was the only nationality in the park without any women. 'It's not fair,' Jige said. 'Every other group has three women to one man, and we fifteen monks have no one. Its because Han are not interested in looking at Tibetan women. Only those southerners.' I asked him if this may be another reason why there are no Muslims represented, but he did not know. By my visit at the end of November, there were two Tibetan nuns working at the park. Jige had gone but another monk, Thonsur, said the women were there to study and pray like the rest. All of them had been trained as monks or nuns in Tibet, at either the Drepung or Sera monasteries. When I asked Jige if he minded working as a monk for a Chinese theme park, he said: 'This is not so bad. We get to pray as often as in Tibet, its warmer here, and we get paid 300 yuan'. Our Yi guide explained that the Tibetan section was a 'religious site' and the temple to the *mizong* Tibetan bodhisattva was a 'real religious' temple. The Tibetan monks also stated emphatically that this was not part of the park, but was an actual religious site modeled on the Jokhang Temple in Lhasa. In November 1995 in Lhasa, I asked the leading abbot of the Jokhang Temple if this was the case, but he had never heard of the theme park in Beijing.

Path dependence and the seductiveness of theme parks

Just as one is confined to set waterways and walkways in the Polynesian Cultural Center and the Chinese Ethnic Culture Park, the representation of minorities and majorities in certain ways is confined to such path dependence. To use Fujitani's (1993:87) terms, they become 'mnemonic sites' whereby notions of nationality are channeled and represented. This becomes a 'monumentalization', in Anagnost's (1994:231) terms, 'in service to the national essence'. Although Anagnost's view risks a certain essentialization about the very notion of a 'Chinese essence', I would argue that the project of defining a national essence as *Zhonghua* (China or Chineseness), with the Han nationality surrounded by primitive, colorful minorities, becomes an important way of perpetuating that discourse. Theme parks may exert a hegemonic role at a discursive level in organizing what is often conflicting and intermixed cultural space into dependable and observable paths (Bhabha 1994:6). This production is often taking place in the representation of 'minorities' and other 'national' others in theme parks and commoditized spheres of representation.

The placement of the 'nationalities' in theme parks and national censuses leads to their visibility and the invisibility of majority nationality, the Han. As Williams (1989:439) has argued, 'not all individuals have equal power to fix the coordinates of self–other identity formation. Nor are individuals equally empowered to opt out of the labeling process, to become the invisible against others' visibility'. It is this invisibility of the majority imposing order on what is visible that leads to the hegemonic gaze of the observer – for few 'minorities' bother to visit theme parks. In this, and particularly in places like China, where one's nationality is assigned at birth or adulthood and registered in one's identity card, the state plays an important role, through regulation and registration, in what nationalities become visible. Like cable-television companies, it 'unscrambles' the scrambled mess of cultural interstitiality.

Scrambling and unscrambling paths

This chapter has attempted to provide a look at nationality in China by viewing the public cultures of state-sponsored media and state-approved theme parks. Yet the highly organized and highly structured theme parks and minority performances run into the dilemma George Marcus (1994:48) aptly describes as the 'problem of simultaneity' in contemporary ethnographic writing, in which one attempts to write the 'park' without reifying it. As noted above, in the discussion of Williams' concern with the invisibility of the majority at the expense of the visibility of the displayed minority, the argument here regarding path dependence concerns the nature of hierarchy, power, representation, and relationality among these peoples of China and elsewhere. And, as Paul Rabinow (1986: 234) reminded us, representations are, or often become, social facts (tragically so, for groups such as the Bosnians and Hutu). In Chapter 9, it will be argued that 'relational alterity' characterizes important aspects of stereotypical identity constructions of the contemporary nation-state. This approach seeks to move toward a more contextualized, relational approach to identity formation and expression, in which imagination, representation, and subscription play important roles, as opposed to essentialized 'tribal' or relativized 'situational' formulations.

In using this approach, I have begun to make use of the metaphor of the 'scrambled' cable channel on television tuners as a way to describe this phenomena. The analogy might be one heuristic way of looking at the current shifting 'montage' (Marcus 1994: 45) of national identities. In many areas of the United States, cable companies 'scramble' the transmission of certain pay-channels, for which subscribers must pay an additional monthly fee to watch 'unscrambled' programs in their homes, often involving a separate cable box and remote control. Once a fee is paid, those channels can be 'descrambled', a process that is activated at viewer request.[9] Alternatively, cable customers can request that certain channels be permanently blocked to prevent viewing (perhaps by children, since many of these channels are sexually explicit or feature violent programming). Those 'scrambled' channels often appear blurred and haphazardly jammed together, allowing only glimpses and snatches of sound from what is 'really' there.

Like the cable companies themselves, without the arbitrary and often artificial policies of intervening nation-states (the 'descrambler' controlled by a distantly held remote), one would not be able to 'see' or describe the blurred and shifting identities being represented. And, like scrambled or censored channels, only discourses are detectable, narratives and dislocated shapes that give the briefest of glimpses into particular styles of identity or channels being aired (though for cable channels, these glimpses are still clear enough to have parents complain about short, 'pornographic segments' visible and audible enough to entertain attentive juveniles). Similar to linguistic code-switching in social speech forms, encoded identities are often switched depending on contexts, moving up and down stereotypical scales, or perhaps discarded altogether.

An important component of this metaphor is that of subscription: groups often are enlisted by states or elites to subscribe to certain kinds of identities (ethnic, national, racial, religious, class, ranked, and so on), but in many cases they might not choose to do so. In others, subscription is mandatory, as in government-controlled cable channels and legislated national identity cards. Anthropologists might have their own schemes, diagrams, and maps of identity; in most cases, people ignore them, or may even contest them (particularly if they deconstruct certain cherished and widely accepted social identities, such as ethnicity, gender, or class). On the other hand, not infrequently, anthropological ethnographies, and cultural representations of those ethnographies in theme parks

9.   I am grateful to Denys Lombard at CNRS, Paris, for first suggesting the scrambled cable channel as an example of modern blurred images. The extension of the metaphor to help descramble identity representation, formation, and politics is entirely my own device.

and museums, also become the accepted charters of social history. However, it is the modern nation-state – with its regulatory powers over not only cable channels, but also ethnic national identities, census categories, and even theme parks (see Cohn 1987) – that exerts a privileged role in defining the most accessible national channels, and provides the means to unscramble them. The paths followed by tourists on visits to theme parks have often been defined by anthropologies and channeled by state-controlled regulatory agencies.

Breaking path dependence

This chapter has attempted to sort out (to unscramble?) how it is that theme parks themselves become a metaphor for path dependence in the identity constructions of modern nation-states. In China, all of the nationalities portrayed in theme parks are Chinese citizens, and travel on a Chinese passport, whether they like it or not. The project then becomes not any essentialized attempt at a final definition of the meanings of these representations (that is, *what* is a Uyghur or Han), but an examination of the conditions of representation (that is, *when* is a Uyghur or Han represented in a certain way).

Such identities are particularly called into question once people move across national borders and join the transnational diaspora (see Chow 1994:99–105). The project then becomes not any essentialized attempt at a final definition of the meanings of these representations, but an examination of when they come to the fore, and with whom they are asserted. Maybe this is why theme parks such as the Polynesian Cultural Center and the Chinese Ethnic Culture Park stress the ancient, primordial, and traditional condition of the peoples displayed. It would not do to have them working as chemists or engineers in contemporary clothing.

This project also calls into question the nature of majority national identities in China and elsewhere. It is often through internal exoticization and external anti-foreignism that nationalist projects are promoted. China is not immune to these kinds of nationalist ideologies. For example, one such nationalist rallying call to unify all Chinese against a growing US threat came from none other than Zhang Chengzhi, a Hui Muslim, described as a 'proto-nationalist', the acknowledged first and self-described last Red

Guard (Barmé 1996:269). Zhang, while in Japan on 26 December 1996, wrote the following upon the occasion of Chairman Mao's 100th birthday:

But now we are in the 1990s. Following the collapse of the Socialist Bloc, and during the Gulf War, the international powers led by America and England set out to destroy the Islamic world which they perceived as being a potential enemy. The infamous Monroe Doctrine, formulated to deal with the forces of self-determination in Latin America, is an old weapon in the U.S. arsenal. The most recent example of its application was the Panama invasions. Next time will be China's turn. China, not Communist China, but the massive cultural entity of China, is next on the hit list of the New World Order. Although we are confronted by this international situation Chinese intellectuals (and here I include the majority of Chinese studying overseas) are still unashamedly pro-American. (Zhang, cited in Barmé 1996:270)

Part II
REPRESENTATIONS

4
MAKING, MARKING, AND MARKETING IDENTITY

Representing identity

The representation of the minority in China reflects an objectivizing of a majority nationality discourse that parallels the valorization of gender and political hierarchies.[1] This process reverses subject/object distinctions and suggests a number of parallels. Minorities are to the majority as female is to male, as Third World is to First World, and as subjectivized identity is to objectivized identity. The widespread definition and representation of the minority as exotic, colorful, and primitive homogenizes the undefined majority as united, mono-ethnic, and modern. The politics of representation in China reveal much about the state's project constructing, in often binary minority/majority terms, an 'imagined' national identity (Anderson 1991). Through reading the representation of minorities in China, this chapter suggests that we learn as much, and perhaps more, about the construction of the identity of the majority, who in China are known as the Han nationality.

Following the tragedy of the 1989 Tiananmen massacre, there has been an onslaught of scholarly publications attempting to define and redefine China's 'quest for a national identity' in various terms (described in greater detail in Chapter 1, page 2), including:

1. For critical their comments on earlier versions of this chapter, I wish to thank my colleagues at the University of Southern California, and participants in 'Dimensions of Ethnic and Cultural Nationalism in Asia', University of Wisconsin–Milwaukee; the Tri-University East Asia Area Committee seminar at the National Humanities Center, Chapel Hill; and the Regional Seminar of the University of California, Berkeley. I am particularly indebted to Benedict Anderson, Eugene Cooper, Thomas Gold, James Hevia, Janet Hoskins, Ira Lapidus, Nancy Lutkehaus, Gary Seaman, and Frederick Wakeman.

Confucianism or neo-Confucianism; language; Han Chinese
sedentary agriculturalism; the geophysical space of the country
occupied by the PRC; or a biogenetic neo-racist notion of pan-
Chinese Yellowness.[2]

By contrast, a burgeoning literature on the anthropology of the
self has argued for movement away from reified definitions of self
to emphases upon 'multiplicity, contextuality, complexity, power,
irony, and resistance' (Kondo 1990:43). Similarly, studies of ethnicity and nationalism have begun to move away from either culturally or primordially based formulations, to the analysis of power
relations, particularly in contemporary nation-states (Anderson
1991:16; Comaroff, John 1987; Hobsbawm 1990; Gladney 1996a;
Keyes 1981). The connection between the relationally described
identities of nationalism and gender was made most clearly in the
conference volume *Nationalisms and Sexualities* (Parker *et al.* 1992).
The authors convincingly argue that, 'like gender – nationality is
a relational term whose identity derives from its inherence in a
system of differences' (Parker *et al.* 1992:5; *cf.* Caplan 1987:10). In
this chapter, I wish to extend this argument to address the issue of
relational identity in China through the analysis of the politics of
minority/majority representation.

Perceptive China scholars have noted the colorful portrayal of
minorities in China as derogatory, colonial, and useful to the state
(Diamond 1988; Thierry 1989), but this extends to imperial times
and is not particularly new (see Eberhard 1982). Studies of modern Chinese art have also drawn attention to the important place
of minorities in the formation art history of the PRC (Chang
1980; Laing 1988; Lufkin 1990). I would like to suggest here (and
I believe that this is a new direction) that the objectified portrayal
of minorities as exoticized, and even eroticized, is essential to the

2.   For explorations of Chinese identity, see the Dittmer and Kim collection
      China's Quest for a National Identity (1993); three chapters on China in Haru-
      mi Befu's collection *Cultural Nationalism in East Asia* (1993); and two special
      issues of the journal *Daedalus* (Spring 1991 and Spring 1993). The 'Confu-
      cianist' argument has been most recently rearticulated by Samuel Hunting-
      ton (1993), and more classically by Mary Wright (1957). Interestingly, none
      of these authors has problematized the connection between 'Han' and 'Chi-
      nese', which, although historically suspicious as it will be shown, nevertheless
      still dominates Chinese discussions of majority/minority national identity;
      see Yang Kun (1992).

construction of the Han Chinese majority, the very formulation of the Chinese 'nation' itself. In other words, the representation of the minorities in such colorful, romanticized fashion, has more to do with constructing a majority discourse than it does with the minorities themselves. This minority/majority discourse then becomes pervasive throughout Chinese culture, art, and media. In her book *Woman and Chinese Modernity*, Rey Chow (1990:21) also makes the important connection between ethnicity and the construction of Chinese womanhood, but Chow's is an external argument about the Western construction of China as feminine, while I am linking internal constructions about the minority other within Chinese society. In conclusion, I also extend the argument to popular culture in general, with a reference to the interesting continuance of this discourse in the film *Ju Dou* (1989), by Zhang Yimou. Significantly – and here this study makes a contribution to those discussions that attempt to move beyond Edward Said's Eurocentric orientalist critique – the representation of minorities and the majority in Chinese art, literature, and media will be shown to have surprising parallels to the now well-known portrayals of the 'East' by Western orientalists. This 'oriental orientalism', and the objectification of the minority other and majority self in China, will be shown to be a 'derivative discourse', in Partha Chatterjee's (1986:10) terms, stitched from Chinese, Western (namely Morganian and Marxist), and Japanese ideas of nationalism and modernity.

This approach rejects the traditional center/periphery construction of Chinese society, with the so-called minorities on the distant margins of Chinese society and nationality. It also challenges the dominant idea that 'cultural change [in China] was overwhelmingly one way' (Naquin and Rawski 1987:129), or that anyone who came into China – foreigner, minority, or barbarian – was subject to Sinicization (Ch'en 1966; Lal 1970). In these more traditional configurations, Chinese culture functioned simultaneously, to quote James Hevia (pers. comm.),[3] as both 'sponge and eraser' of foreign cultures: China not only absorbed outsiders, but also

---

3. For my earlier critique of the 'marginalizing' discourse regarding minorities in China, and its reliance upon Shils' (1975) center/periphery model, see Gladney (1996a:94–6); see Appadurai (1986b:745–55) for a general theoretical critique of the model and its influence upon social theory.

dissolved them, and the few that survived on the 'periphery' were generally thought 'marginal' to the understanding of Chinese society. During my fieldwork I was often surprised to find that many of the reforms in China, whether they were in spheres related to the market economy, privatized agriculture, or religious and political freedom, were first allowed in minority areas, and these often directly influenced the nature and force of change among the Han (see Gladney 1990a). In this chapter I want to extend the argument further and show that even in the areas of popular culture, art, film, and moral value, the so-called peripheral minorities have played a pivotal role in influencing and constructing contemporary Chinese society and identity. I am addressing public culture in its often state-sponsored production and reproduction, concerning myself more with representations in nationally distributed media and film, rather than a specific field site.

I also suggest that the commodification and objectification of minorities in China represents something more than a response to Western consumer tourism, providing the state not only with hard currency, but also with important symbolic capital, to use Bourdieu's (1977:6) construction. The exoticization and representation of minorities is an enterprise that took on enhanced importance with the rise of the Chinese nation-state, and is central to its nationalization and modernization project: the homogenization of the majority at the expense of the exoticization of the minority. The so-called minorities, long confined to the margins of Western and Chinese theoretical discourse on Chinese society, are no longer marginal to our understanding of contemporary China, and perhaps never should have been.

The display and commodification of the minority other in China

One cannot be exposed to China without being confronted by its 'colorful' minorities. They sing, they dance; they twirl, they whirl. Most of all, they smile, showing their happiness to be part of the motherland. The four-hour Chinese New Year program is a yearly special broadcast throughout China to its population of 1.3 billion. And, even though only 8 percent of that population is supposed to be minority (the Han majority make up 91 percent of China's population, according to the 2000 census), fully one-half of the evening's programming is devoted to smiling minority dancers. A brief examination of the opening minutes of the program immediately reveals the crucial role minority peoples play in the contemporary construction of the People's Republic of China.

The program begins with a view of the clock tower on the Central Radio and Telegraph Building, located on Chang An Avenue, striking 8 o'clock, the time for the start of the show, which lasts until midnight. It is the most popular program on television during the New Year, carried on the CCTV Central Broadcasting System that is received throughout China, including Tibet and Mongolia, and even Taiwan and Hong Kong. During my several years of fieldwork in China, I noted that most families from Beijing to Xinjiang preferred to stay at home on New Year's Eve and watch this program, surrounded by relatives and a few close friends. During the 1991 broadcast, I sat with Chinese friends in their apartment in Beijing, and was repeatedly told to sit and watch the program with the rest of the family, even though I preferred to catch up on the local gossip. After the clock shown on the television struck 8 p.m., the doors to the elaborate stage opened to reveal a wide array of colorfully dressed minorities advancing onto the stage. After a brief introduction to the evening's program, four well-known television-personality hosts wished the audience a 'Happy New Year' and initiated the first choreographed program of the evening by stating: 'China is a multinational country, fifty-six different nationalities, like fifty-six different flowers. The many nationalities wish to extend to all of you a Happy New Year through a special Tea and Wine Happy New Year Toast!' The program follows with first Tibetans, then Mongols, Zhuang, Uzbek, Korean, Wa, Hui, and other minority dancers presenting Buddhist *hata* (scarves), other minority gifts, and cups of tea and wine to the studio audience, and singing their native songs in their native languages, with Chinese subtitles.[4] In a striking resemblance to the tribute offerings of the ancient Chinese empires, the minorities act,

---

4. It is noteworthy that although the Hui do not possess their own separate language, and are known for eschewing the 'songs and dances' by which many minorities are iconographically represented in China (see Gladney 1996a: 21–30), in this program they sing and dance just like the rest of the performers. Instead of detailed lyrics from a traditional New Year folk song (of which there is none), the Hui sing their traditional Arabic greeting, '*A'salam Alei Cum*', over and over again. The Chinese subtitles translate this formulaic greeting as '*Pengyou Nihao*' (Friend, hello).

sing, and perform ritualized prostrations as they offer their greet-
ings to the studio audience, who appear to be largely members of
the Han majority. They appear so because they are uniformly (as if
in uniforms) dressed in conservative suits with ties, Mao jackets, or
other formal, dark 'Western' attire, which is in marked contrast to
the colorful costumes of the minority entertainers. Non-minority
entertainers and hosts exclusively wear Western-style suits and
dresses. Well over half of the rest of the four hours of programming
is devoted to minority songs and dances.[5]

After the People's Republic of China was founded in 1949, the
state embarked upon a monumental endeavor to identify and recognize as nationalities those who qualified among the hundreds of
groups applying for national minority status. The question of one's
nationality, which is registered on one's passport and all official
documents, is determined by Stalinist and historical criteria that
determine if one is a member of a group that was ever linguistically, economically, geographically, or 'culturally' distinct from the
so-called Han majority population (see Fei 1981; Yang Kun 1992).
This recognition may make a considerable difference in obtaining
certain privileges accorded to minorities, in some cases including
permission to have more than one child, obtaining entrance to university, and having access to local political office, special economic
assistance, and tax-relief programs. Those who were recognized
by the state are always portrayed in the state-sponsored media as
happily accepting that objectivized identity. For example, the caption for a photograph of several minorities in traditional costume
pictured in a brochure introducing the Nationalities Cultural Palace (*Minzu Wenhua Gong*) in Beijing reads: 'The Happy People of
Various Nationalities' (*Minzu Gong* 1990:12). Significantly, Tiananmen, the Gate of Heavenly Peace, is bordered on both sides by the
slogans 'Long Live the People's Republic of the Chinese People'
(*Zhonghua Renmin Gongheguo Wansui*) and 'Working Peoples of
the World, Unite!' (*Shijie Renmin Gongren Tuanjie*). These state-
sponsored signs on public buildings and in the media repeatedly

---

5.   In her informative MA thesis, Lufkin (1990:3) observes that minority folk-
     tales, like performers, are disproportionately represented. Of the more than
     seventy folk-tales published in the magazine *Chinese Literature* from 1951 to
     1976, 75 percent were by national minorities. I am grateful to Felicity Lufkin
     for making the MA thesis available to me after presentation of an earlier ver-
     sion of this chapter.

emphasize for the Chinese populace that China is a multi-ethnic and multinational state – a point that is critical to China's representation of itself to itself, and to the international sphere. China regards itself as a multinational nation-state that must be reckoned with by other multinational, 'modern' nation-states.

As multinational, China portrays itself as democratic, claiming 'autonomous regions, prefectures, counties, and villages' based on the Soviet model, but in name only, since the Chinese constitution does not allow true geopolitical secession – something perhaps the conservative Russian right-wing now wish Stalin had thought of when he approved a Soviet constitution that allowed for political secession of the (now former) republics. The myth of democratic representation is critical to China's construction of itself as a modern multinational state, distinguishing and distancing itself from the ancient feudal Chinese empires that did not allow for representation. As Spivak (1990:105) argues, 'One of the gifts of the logic of decolonization is parliamentary democracy'. Given public criticism over China's treatment of Tibet, it is not surprising that Tibetans are often represented as the most willing subjects of Chinese 'democratic liberation'. In one state-sponsored pictorial, a Tibetan is portrayed as happily voting, as if he really did control his own destiny. The caption reads: 'Happiness Ballot' (*Nationality Pictorial* 1985:10). In another published painting, several minorities are portrayed on the Great Wall, happily proclaiming in the caption, 'I love the Great Wall' (*Nationality Pictorial* 1985:21) – though the Great Wall was primarily built to keep nomadic peoples out. It is also interesting to note that in this figure clearly geared for schoolchildren, the people on the Great Wall, with one exception, are clearly Muslim: the men wear Turkic and Hui Islamic hats, and the woman is veiled. The odd man out, strangely enough, is an African. Perhaps he is shown on the wall with the other minorities to represent their ethnic solidarity; more seriously, perhaps it is to emphasize their corporate 'primitivity' (that is, to promote the idea that China's minorities are like 'primitive' Africans), which is key to understanding the position of the minorities in the Marxist–Maoist evolutionary scheme.

The commodification of minorities is accomplished through the representing, packaging, and selling of their images, artworks, and 'costumes' in the many pictorial gazetteers, such as *Nationalities Unite* (*Minzu Tuanjie*) and *Nationality Pictorial* (*Minzu Huabao*), as well as in museum displays, such as in the Nationalities Cultural Palace, an enormous exhibition hall and conference center on Chang An Avenue, which houses a store selling minority artifacts and costumes, as well as temporary exhibitions regarding minority nationalities. It is bordered by the Nationality Hotel and offices of the State Commission for Ethnic Affairs, the ministry charged with administrating all dealings with minorities in China. In minority areas there are boutiques, open markets, tourist stores, and even 'cultural stations' (*wenhua zhan*; see Schein 2000) where minority goods are collected, displayed, sold, and modeled. Books and sets of photographic cards published by the state introduce the fifty-six nationalities of China and are widely distributed to school-children, foreign students, and tourists, and carried by officials on trips abroad as gifts to their host institutions. In baseball-card fashion, the back of the card has each group's statistics, summarizing the nationality's distinctive history, language, and culture. The nationalities are portrayed on the front by a 'representative' iconographic image, generally a picture, of that group, colorful and usually female.

It is noteworthy that of the fifty-six nationalities introduced in the state-sponsored English-language pictorial *Chinese Nationalities* (1989), only three are represented in the first picture by males. All fifty-three others are represented by a beautiful, alluring young woman in colorful 'native' costume. The minorities are almost always portrayed in natural, romantic settings, surrounded by fauna and flora. Significantly, however, the Han are represented in the same book by conservative, middle-aged women in an urban setting, with what is generally thought to resemble modern, Western-styled and coiffed hair, dressed in Western-style sweaters, and modest pants and long-sleeved outfits. This displays what the authors perhaps considered to be the Han women's modernity and, by extension, their normality, civility, and subjectivity. The authors of *Chinese Nationalities* chose that photograph to represent the Han, not one that bears any resemblance to a 'traditional' Chinese society, even though the minorities are always shown in their 'traditional' dress. Instead of being represented as singing and dancing, the Han women in one photograph are represented with single infants in strollers. The caption reads: 'Its good to have only one child' (*Chinese Nationalities* 1989:20). When minority men are portrayed, as is rarely the case, they are generally exoticized as strong and virile, practicing strange and humorous customs, or possessing extraordinary physical abilities in sport, work, or the consumption of large amounts of alcohol – much more than a typical Han (*Chinese Nationalities* 1989:16). 'To drink like a Mongol' is an often-heard compliment in China.

The state, through commodifying and representing its minorities as colorful and exotic, engages in a project familiar in the representation of colonized peoples by colonial regimes. By publishing an extraordinary collection of orientalist erotic postcards, the Algerian Malek Alloula (1986) examines French observations of Algeria, and claims to be sending the postcards back 'to [their] sender' (Alloula 1986:5), unveiling the role of the 'colonial harem' as both orientalizing the other and subjectivizing the European self. Through state-sponsored representation of the minority other as exotic, much the same is accomplished in China, only in the context of what Michael Hechter (1975) has termed 'internal colonialism'.[6]

Essentializing the Han

The representation of the Han as 'normal' and unexotic is critical for understanding the construction of present-day Chinese identity. Just as Peter Worsley has shown that the discourse of First and Third worlds helps to confirm the so-called First World's superiority (see Worsley 1984),[7] the subordination of nationalities in China leads to the clear promotion of the Han to the vanguard of the peoples of the People's Republic. While research on the rise of Russian nationalism has been popular in Soviet studies since the 1970s, by foreign and Russian scholars, as yet no larger studies of the creation of Han nationalism have emerged – perhaps because it is often assumed that 'Han' is generally equal to 'Chinese'. Few have questioned how the Han became the 91 percent majority of China. Yet in China, identity papers register one not as Chinese (*Zhongguo ren*), but as Han, Hui, Manchu, or one of fifty-six

6. For more on the theory of 'internal colonialism' and China's subaltern subjects, see Chapter 16, this volume.
7. In Aijaz Ahmad's (1992) controversial critique of the 'Three Worlds' notion, he accuses Edward Said, Fredric Jameson, and Salman Rushdie of subscribing to an essentialized 'third world' of non-Western literatures. For a response to Ahmad, see the fall 1993 issue of *Public Culture*, especially Sprinker's (1993) critical assessment.

stipulated identities. In China, national identity is not only 'imagined', it is stamped on one's passport.

Han modernity and the construction of primitivity

As discussed in Chapter 3, the Han are frequently represented as somewhere near the modern end of a Marxist historical trajectory upon which China's minorities must travel (see page 38). In his famous 1878 treatise, *Ancient Society*, Lewis Henry Morgan described in his first chapter, entitled the 'Ethnical Periods', the development of society from savagery to barbarism, and then to civilization. Tong Enzheng, a Sichuanese anthropologist and museologist, was one of the earliest to publicly criticize Chinese anthropology's heavy reliance, almost reverence, for this theory of societal evolution:

> Because of the esteem in which both Marx and Engels held [Morgan's] works, and especially because Engels, in *The Origin of the Family, Private Property, and the State*, affirmed many of his views, there has been a tendency among scholars to mistakenly equate his positions with specific positions taken by Marx and Engels, positions which themselves were mistakenly equated with the fundamental principle of Marxism. As a result, Morgan's most representative work, *Ancient Society*, has been canonized, and for the past 30 years has been regarded as something not to be tampered with ... therefore, to cast any doubt on it would be to cast doubt on Marxism itself. (Tong 1989:182, 184)

In China, minority studies became an avenue for repeatedly proving Morgan (and, it was believed, Marxist thought in general) to be correct, through the examination of minorities as representatives of earlier forms of society, living fossils of savagery and barbarism (Tong 1989:185). The Han, as representative of higher forms of civilization, were clearly more evolved, and were to lead the way for minorities to follow. As if to underline the continued dominance of this theory, Fei Xiaotong (1989), China's most revered social scientist, presented a 1988 Tanner Lecture in Hong Kong, entitled 'Plurality and Unity in the Configuration of the Chinese Nationality', which was later published in the *Beijing University Journal*. In the article, Fei traced the rise of the Han people from multi-ethnic origins prior to the Qin dynasty, and their almost unilineal descent to the present day, despite absorbing and being conquered by various foreign tribes and nations.

As soon as it came into being, the Han nationality became a nucleus of concentration. Its people radiated in all directions into the areas around it and, centripetally, absorbed them into their own groups and made them a part of themselves ... As the non-Han rulers' regimes were mostly short-lived, one minority conqueror was soon replaced by another, and eventually all were assimilated into the Han ... But as the national minorities generally are inferior to the Han in the level of culture and technology indispensable for the development of modern industry, they would find it difficult to undertake industrial projects in their own regions, their advantage of natural resources notwithstanding ... Therefore, our principle is for the better developed groups to help the underdeveloped ones by furnishing economic and cultural aids. (Fei 1989:39, 45, 47, 52)[8]

The 1992 film *Amazing Marriage Customs*, distributed by the Nanhai Film Company and the China Film Corporation, provides evidence of the popularity of the discourse of nationalism and Han superiority in China. Filmed entirely in China with government support, the film is a survey of marriage customs there, with a heavy dose of minority practices, especially in Yunnan. What is noteworthy about the film is not the typical exoticization and eroticization of minorities as described below, but the deliberate structuring of the film along stage evolutionary theory. At the beginning of the film, we are shown primeval visions of a Neolithic past and the emergence of primitive mankind. The narrator intones:

Getting married is natural, but during long period [*sic*] in history, men had no idea of 'love' and 'marriage'. From 'childhood' of human history, 3,000,000 B.C. to the end of matrilineal society in 5000 B.C., marriage history transits from group marriage, polygamy, to monogamy stage [*sic*]. Each stage has its own development, traces of which could be found, only three decades ago in China ... From 3,000,000 B.C. to 1,000,000 B.C. human society began to form. There was nothing called marriage, or it was called primitive promiscuity [*yuanshi luanhun de jieduan*; literally 'stage of primitive confused marriage']. From 1,000,000 B.C. to 100,000 B.C. human society divided into blood families [*xueyuan jiazu*]. Promiscuity existed, called consanguine group marriage. In matrilineal society, group marriage outside tribe [*sic*] started. In ancient society, nothing called marriage could be found in group marriage. The relationship was casual. (*Amazing Marriage Customs*; directed by Suen Wan and Guo Wuji, 1992)[9]

8. These excerpts from Fei's article are from the English transcript of the Tanner Lecture, which had not been published when this chapter was written.

9. The text cited here and below is taken directly from the English subtitles, with Chinese and some literal translations provided in brackets. A similar film

The film then presents a succession of minorities in various stages of transition from 'matrilineality' to 'patrilineality', including intimate scenes of marriage and mating rites among the Naxi, Dong, Bouyei, Yao, Hani, Wa (Va), Moso, Zhuang, and Miao (Hmong). Several of these groups are described as practicing 'free love' and being very open to sex'. In one scene shows Dong women bathing in the river, only barely covered by their triangular tops, and as the camera focuses on exposed breasts, the narrator states: 'The [women] take a bath in the river after work, what a lovely scene. The scenery is beautiful enough, they make it more fascinating'. In one particularly explicit bathing section featuring Miao women, the camera zooms in on a group of women disrobing completely in the river, and with long-lens shots taken through the grass in a voyeuristic fashion, the narrator notes the arrival of several men:

They've asked their lovers to come. What for? To watch! A thorough examination indeed! If he's satisfied, must do something [*sic*], in a very polite way of course. He present her a red ribbon, in a serious manner. Very happy indeed! The ribbon is a token for engagement. With this token she is somebody's. How romantic!

Following the matrilineal section, the film introduces the Uyghur Turkic Muslims of Xinjiang. 'Islam' we are told, 'respects patriarchy and husband right'. And 'women are subordinate'. The final scene begins with views of Tiananmen Square and the Forbidden City and, against a background of Han couples dating in the park, the narrator states:

The characteristic of modern marriage is freedom, monogamy, and equality between sexes. The law of marriage stipulates ... no force on

---

survey of minority marriage customs, produced in Hong Kong by the Wah Ngai Film Production and King Video, is entitled *The Inside Story of the Great Southwestern Forbidden Borderlands* (*Da Xinan Jinjing Tanmi*, 1990). In this film, there is one incident where the Bai nationality in Yunnan is described as being so 'hospitable' that the host offers his wife to the guest as a sexual partner. The 'custom' is then enacted on film. *Y Na Na: Woman of a Thousand Places* (1992), a film by Yvette M. Torell, replicates this exoticized portrayal of Thai, Naxi, Bai, and Tibetan women in Yunnan and Tibet, complete with the now mandatory Thai bathing scene. In a well-worn, inaccurate representation of the 'Naxi' matrilineality (see McKhann's excellent 1995 critique of this mistaken view), Torell's introduction invites the viewer to learn from their 'matriarchy'. It is noteworthy that these films, like minority representation in general in China, focus almost exclusively on women and sexual relations.

either side. Or a third party interfering! Love is most essential in modern marriage. Having love affairs [*tan lianai*; literally 'speaking about love relations'] is a prelude of marriage. In the countryside of Beijing you may observe this wonderful prelude.

The film then notes that in a 'modern large' city it is often difficult to find a mate, and therefore computerized dating is featured as a 'modern' solution for finding a partner. The film culminates with a grand mass wedding of 100 couples, dressed in formal Western attire, who were actually married at the Beijing Hotel as a result of successful computerized matchmaking. The narrator concludes: 'Monogamy means equality between the sexes. This harmonious union of love, marriage, and sex life notes the result of evolution in history'. By the end of the film, the viewer is left with the distinct feeling that the minorities and 'primitives' had more fun.[10]

The minorities play a very important role in China's official vision of history, nationality, and development. Their 'primitivity' contrasts with supposed Han 'modernity'. Minorities become a marked category, characterized by sensuality, colorfulness, and exotic custom. This contrasts with the 'unmarked' nature of Han identity. Han-ness for the Chinese connotes civility and modernity, and this is perhaps why more educated minorities, such as the Manchu and Koreans, are never exoticized as sensual or primitive.[11] The Han, although they supposedly comprise 91 percent of China's population, are rarely described or studied as Han per se, whereas whole research centers and colleges are devoted to the study and teaching of minorities in China. Anthropologists of Euro-American society have begun to note a similar process in the unmarked majority category of 'whiteness'. Majorities, according to Virginia Dominguez's (1986) revealing study of Louisiana Creole identity, become 'White, by definition'. It is only the so-called

10. The linkage of matrilineality with existing 'primitive' minorities is supported by descriptions of several groups in *China's Minority Nationalities* (Ma Yin 1989 – the translation of the standard text *Zhongguo Shaoshu Minzu*). For example, 'The Jino matriarchal society gave way to a patriarchal one some 300 years ago. But the Jinos were still in the transitional stage from primitivity to a class society at the time the People's Republic was founded in 1949' (Ma Yin 1989:334).

11. I would like to thank an anonymous reviewer for bringing this point about Koreans and Manchu to my attention. The Korean minority is the most educated and one of the most economically advanced groups in China.

ethnics (a term in the *Oxford English Dictionary* that comes into the English idiom as denoting 'heathen') who are marked by 'culture'. Majorities, by extension, become denaturalized, homogenized, and essentialized as 'same'. This is particularly true, it seems, of Asia, where large blocks of Chinese, Japanese, and Koreans are thought to be homogeneous. In the West, it is whiteness that is beginning to be problematized in the effort to scrutinize and come to terms with minority/majority discourses.[12]

Exoticizing and eroticizing minorities in China

Although minorities are no longer portrayed as barbarians in China, they are portrayed in public media as more colorful and cultural than the Han (thanks perhaps to Stalin, whose four criteria the Chinese state adopted for recognizing a people as a nationality included culture), and much more sensual. One of the favorite themes, that of minority women bathing naked in the river, is discussed in Chapter 3, page 42.

In her perceptive article about the popular David Henry Hwang play *M. Butterfly*, Garber (1992:123) stresses the importance of clothing in making the link between gender representation and transvestism. The link between clothing and nationality, in which minorities are generally dressed in 'costumes', while the majorities merely wear 'clothes', is clearly made in Chinese museums, popular culture, and film. The changing of clothes and the altering of a re-stricted Han self is precisely the basis for the 1985 movie *Sacrificed Youth (Qing Qun Ji)*. In this film, by the Beijing Film Studio's woman director Zhang Nuanxin, Duoli, a young Han woman from Beijing is sent down during the Cultural Revolution to the Thai minority region of Yunnan in Xishuangbanna, near the border of Burma and Thailand, where she is confronted by more 'liberated' Thai female customs. She wishes that she could be as free and, in a moment of rebellious assertion and self-transformation, exchanges her drab, blue worker's clothes for a Thai sarong, whereupon she is

12. Dominguez (1986:140 *ff.*) chronicles the 'veritable explosion' of defenses of white Creole ancestry in New Orleans once increasing polarization of white/black racial categories called attention to their identification with 'blacks' despite their physical appearance as 'whites'. For problematizing 'whiteness', see also the excellent work by Frankenberg (1993), and Stoler's 2002 book on white colonials in the Netherlands East Indies.

pronounced 'beautiful' by her Thai hosts and girlfriends. This leads her further on the road to self-criticism and the cultural critique of repressed Han identity. In this instance of retailoring the nation, to borrow a phrase from Parker *et al.* (1992:120), for Duoli cross-dressing becomes a transnational political act.

In another scene in *Sacrificed Youth*, Thai women are shown in the classic cultural trope as freely bathing nude in the river – a rare bit of soft porn for a 1985 film in China. The film's protagonist observes the Thai women swimming from a distance and wishes she was less inhibited by her Han mores so that she felt she could join them without her swimsuit. 'Later,' she declares, 'I learned to swim like they did, and I never wore a swimsuit again.' The bathing scene is prefaced by an encounter between a group of young Thai working women and men, who stop to sing antiphonal sexually suggestive songs to each other. Here too, the sent-down Han observer declares: 'I could not join them, which made me feel inhibited and culturally behind'. Admiration for minority sexual freedom and 'natural' state of being becomes the foil by which Han majority and state-supported values are criticized. Both scenes are introduced and concluded by long shots of verdant, rushing waterfalls, suggesting perhaps that it is the natural sphere, with its cleansing element of water, that transforms what the state denigrates for Han as erotic and perhaps pornographic into what is natural and unfettered.

Pornography in any form is restricted in China as illegal.[13] This includes any publication, foreign or domestic, that the state

13. I use 'restricted' here because, although prohibited as pornographic for the general populace, it is widely available, and foreign films with sex and nude scenes may be viewed in various elite universities and training institutes. In 1983 I viewed the thought-to-be-very *huang* uncensored version of *Kramer vs Kramer* at the Beijing Foreign Languages Institute with a group of Chinese English students, their spouses, friends, and several cadres of the university. Chinese colleagues frequently complained to me that literature and films regarded as pornographic and illegal for common people were readily available to elite government officials and their families. Explicit foreign films are also widely shown in the joint-venture hotels throughout China, and such access to these and other 'Western' luxuries is one reason Chinese youth envy those who can obtain jobs in such hotels. Here I must make very clear that the difference between what is erotic and pornographic in China is defined by what the state regards as legal and illegal. The point here is not about eroticism in general; it is that in China, representations of Han subjects classed by the state as pornographic would not be illegal, and thus only erotic, if the Hans were

censors regard as morally inappropriate for its broader population. Foreign visitors in the past were regularly searched upon entry for magazines, books, and videos regarded as pornographic, and there are regular police raids upon a burgeoning black-market industry of (literally) underground video parlors and markets for erotic literature.[14] While there has been a profusion of illicit pornographic material since the 1990s and it has become much more widely available in urban areas, it is still illegal and arrests may be made. In the mid-1980s a wide variety of magazines and books with sexually suggestive titles and scantily clothed men and women proliferated throughout the nation's bookstores and newsstands. Particularly popular was the *jian mei* (make, or establish, beauty) genre of athletic magazines and playing cards, which portrayed mainly Han Chinese and foreigners lifting weights or posing in skimpy bathing suits.[15] State censors prohibit depiction of total nudity, and these publications were frequently reviewed and confiscated. Yet despite this severe restriction upon and preoccupation with the

---

dressed as minorities. In China, 'erotic' is generally glossed as *xing aide*, or that which influences or encourages sexual love; whereas 'pornographic' is generally translated *se qing*, or literally 'colorful sentiment', obliquely referring to the color yellow, which refers specifically to the pornographic press.

14. Legalized 'private video rooms' (*geti luxiang yuan*) are found in most cities and towns in China, showing films imported from Hong Kong, Taiwan, and the West, which are frequently monitored by the local police. They are also known to show slightly risqué or even 'hard core' erotic films late at night, when the authorities are not around. Even in remote rural areas, where the police are fewer and farther between, these parlors are not unusual. I recall late one night in May 1985 passing by one such parlor with a long line out front, whose ticket prices had been increased from 15 fen (cents) during the day to 5 yuan (Chinese dollars, equivalent then to slightly less then US$2) due to what I was told to be the very 'yellow' (*huang*, the Chinese euphemism for pornographic subject matter) nature of the Hong Kong film. This parlor was quite popular, even though it was located in a Muslim minority area, within the Hezhou Hui Autonomous Prefecture in Gansu.

15. See Orville Schell's (1989) humorous portrayal of this burgeoning industry of sexually suggestive publications, which led in part in 1989 to a widespread series of protests by Muslims offended by their depiction in a Chinese book, *Sexual Customs* (*Xing Fengsu*). In response to what was termed China's 'Salman Rushdie' incident, the state banned and burned the book, closed the publication house, and arrested the authors (see Gladney 1996a:1–15; 1994). Many of these publications have been strictly curtailed as 'bourgeois liberalism' since 1989.

sale of nude representations of foreign and Han Chinese women, throughout China, in state-sponsored media as well as foreign and domestic tourist shops, images of nude minority women are publicly displayed, *National Geographic*-style, in various suggestive poses. Not only are nude representations of minorities displayed in galleries and public spaces like the Beijing Capital Airport, but they are readily available for sale in hotel tourist boutiques and minority crafts shops, such as the Central Institute for Nationalities Minority Handicrafts Store and the Nationalities Cultural Palace.

Scholars of traditional China are quite familiar with the long and widespread tradition of erotic art and literature, which had little to do with minorities. In *Sex in China*, Chinese sexologist Ruan Fangfu (1991:2) notes that the earliest sex manuals came from China, where one could find the classic sexological text *He Yin Yang Fang* (*Methods of Intercourse between Yin and Yang*, dated 168 BC), as well as the pre-Tang *Important Methods of the Jade Chamber*, *Book of the Mysterious Penetrating Master*, and other classical texts, which now are found in comic-book form through Taiwan and Southeast Asia, but are still restricted in China.[16] After surveying this abundant traditional literature, Ruan (1991:29) divides it into three categories: descriptions of the mystical benefits of sexual intercourse; the health benefits of intercourse if following certain theories and texts; and the inherent pleasurability of sex. Dutch sinologist Robert Van Gulik collected hundreds of Chinese erotic sex manuals that proliferated in the late Qing, and popular classics like *Dream of Red Chambers* and *On the Water Margins* are extremely explicit and rarely published in their unabridged forms.[17]

If erotic images and public portrayals of Han Chinese sexuality are an acknowledged aspect of everyday life in traditional China,

16. I am grateful to John Ollsen for directing me to this source.
17. The 1988 Exhibition of Nude Art (*Luoti Huaxiang Zhanlan*) at the Beijing Fine Art Museum was the first since the founding of the PRC to specifically exhibit nudes. Although it also included many minority nudes, it was closed after less than two weeks, despite enormous ticket sales at more than fifty times the normal price (5 yuan instead of 10 fen, equal to US$2 instead of the normal US$0.03). The state justified the closure of the exhibition by claiming many of the female models had objected to the public showing of their nude portraits as immoral. The models' husbands publicly complained of being the brunt of jokes, and claimed their wives were no longer safe from attack. The state apparently has never been worried about this problem where minority women models and their husbands are concerned.

Taiwan, Hong Kong, and Singapore, why have they been so absent, so repressed, in the Chinese mainland since 1949? George Mosse's (1985) argument linking totalitarianism and sexuality might have some bearing here. Mosse argues that unlicensed sexuality represents a threat to totalizing states. If Foucault (1980:24) is correct that the 'policing of sex' is an important component in maintaining the unmitigated power of the central state, then China's repressive prudishness is perhaps the best example of this endeavor. The policing of sex tends to also roughly coincide with radical leftist authoritarian campaigns in China; for example, the 1966 to 1976 Cultural Revolution, the 1984 Spiritual Pollution campaign, and the more recent post-Tiananmen Six Evils campaign of 1989–90, in which public sexuality, pornography, and prostitution were all condemned as 'feudalist' and thought to be an insidious part of the 'democratic' or liberal movements that led to the crackdowns. In July 1990, the Vice-President of China's Supreme People's Court, Lin Zhu, issued a new decree that traffickers in prostitution and for pornography would be subject to the death penalty (*Sing Pao Daily* 18 July 1990; cited in Ruan 1991:180). China is one of the few non-Islamic nations where prostitutes, pimps, and purveyors of pornography are routinely rounded up, imprisoned, and even, perhaps, executed under the 'hoodlum offenses' statute.[18] Slightly explicit films such as Zhang Yimou's *Red Sorghum*, and later *Ju Dou*, all proposed, approved, funded, and produced by the state during more liberal periods, are routinely banned once more radical political winds prevail.[19] In other studies, Ardener (1987:114) and

18. Ruan (1991:83, citing a *People's Daily* article of 15 February 1990) reports that a crackdown on prostitution and pornography announced by Li Ruihuan in September 1989 netted 103 prostitutes in Beijing alone between 25 November and 15 December. The Vice-Minister of the Public Security Bureau reported that by January 1990 there had been 35,000 separate cases prosecuted, involving 79,000 prostitutes and their customers. On 16 April 1993, Reuters reported a *Beijing Evening News* story that Wang Shuxiang was sentenced to death by the Beijing Intermediate Court for selling pornography and illegally trading in publishing quotas.

19. In 1992, the *New York Times* (Kristof, 13 February:A7) reported the arrest of Pan Weiming, a forty-two-year-old former chief of propaganda in Shanghai, for aiming to 'philander with woman'. A well-known pro-democracy advocate, Pan was arrested in 2001 and handed a four-year sentence for soliciting a prostitute in Sichuan. Supporters argue it was a set-up, since the entrapment procedure involved videos in the hotel room, and long-term surveillance of

Mayer (1975:260) have shown how 'prudery' serves to reinforce, and even invent, social hierarchies. In China, enforced prudishness and controlled fertility among the Han, as opposed to represented minority sensuality, serves the state's national project of emphasizing Han solidarity, civility, and modernity.

Sex becomes one of the most public of private contested political spaces in China. In a state that regularly monitors the monthly menses of its women workers, engages in Malthusian birth-planning programs, and strictly regulates the age at which one can marry (twenty-one for women, twenty-two for men), it is not surprising that sexuality has become highly politicized. In Chapter 15, I discuss the role that liberated sexuality played in the Tiananmen Square student protest, particularly in the students' public attempt to wrest political control of their bodies away from the state. Here, I am arguing that it is the repression and control of sexuality among the Han, and its open representation among the minorities, that demonstrates the important role eroticization of the engendered minority other plays in the Han construction of self.

Painting minorities: the invention of the Yunnan School

In the early 1980s, several northern Han painters were assigned to southern China to paint minorities and other 'appropriate' subjects, leading to what has since been called the Yunnan School (*Yunnan Huapai*) of modern Chinese painting. The Yunnan School has been regarded as one of the first distinct schools to emerge in contemporary Chinese art and has had a tremendous influence on the current generation of artists in China. In the early 1980s, Jiang Tie-Feng, Ting Shao Kuang, and He Neng became known in China for challenging accepted norms of painting, particularly for their nudes with accentuated breasts in brilliant colors. This led, according to Joan Lebold Cohen, noted critic and dealer of Chinese art, to the founding of the 'Yunnan School of Heavy Oil Painting

---

his activities, with subsequent interrogation reportedly focusing more on his pro-democracy contacts than his well-known sexual dalliances. In another crackdown, the Sichuan Fine Arts publishing house was closed down for printing obscene books, and two others were cited (*Turkish Daily News* 22 April 1993:2). The reporter noted: 'Chinese authorities have a very broad definition of pornography that often includes just about any depiction of the human body that is not in a medical or scientific context'.

in 1982' (Cohen, J. 1988). It is significant that Ting Shao Kuang, one of the most prominent and successful members of the school, has stated repeatedly that there is no such organized 'school'; rather, his and other similar work represents a style of art that is new in its subject matter (mainly minorities) and style (use of heavy oil and bright colors in abstract forms). In an 11 July 1992 recorded interview with Ting Shao Kuang by the Los Angeles Chinese television station, Channel 18, Ting said: 'There is no such thing as the Yunnan Art School. We are all different artists from China trying to revolutionize the repressed mainland Chinese painting through the use of minority subjects, sexuality, and heavy oil colors, in often Western-influenced styles'. It is revealing that Ting should say this, since one of his well-known paintings is entitled *Dawn of the Yunnan Art School* (Ting 1990:11), and he has become one of the wealthiest and most successful representatives of the Yunnan School style. The Yunnan School may very well exist only in the West, where it has met with tremendous financial success. Joan Cohen (1988), claiming that the school represents a 'renaissance' in Chinese painting, suggests that the most significant event in the development of the Yunnan School was when He Neng, Jiang Tie-Feng, and Liu Sha-ohui were commissioned to produce paintings for a documentary film project, 'featuring the costumes, habits and environment of the various minority peoples living in Yunnan' (Cohen, J. 1988:5). By traveling to the minority areas, Cohen explains, the northern Han artists found that they could express many of their artistic interests through the color and style of minority representation.

Liu Bingjiang's *Nude*, shown at the Oil Painting Research Association Exhibition in Beijing 1979, is clearly a minority representation, indicative of early Yunnan School tendencies. On a colorful background, a dark-skinned female nude is realistically portrayed kneeling with her hands on the ground in a submissive posture, wearing nothing but her jewelry. Given the tapestry background, her jewelry, and, most importantly, the posture, the painting is one of the earliest works in the Yunnan School style. According to Cohen (1987:46), her kneeling position is not within the officially sanctioned 'academic painting repertoire', and thus suggests to Cohen a 'South Asian' influence. It is important to note that the bracelets worn by the nude clearly resemble shackles, and combine with the posture to evoke in the painting an air of erotic subservience and submission.

Although it is not the case with abstract Han figure paintings, it has been and still is officially acceptable to vividly and realistically paint, exhibit, and sell artworks portraying minority nudes. In another example, Chen Zhangpeng's oil of a nude is appropriately titled *Innocence*. Reflecting Western influence, especially that of Gauguin, Picasso, and even Andrew Wyeth, this painting situates the exoticized minority subject in both the past and the present. Joan Cohen's caption explains: 'Chen's sketchy study of a nude kneeling next to a tiger expresses the ancient Chinese idea that the untrammeled nature of the wild creature is innocent. Likewise, primitive people, uncorrupted by civilization, are innocent, a concept similar to Rousseau's romantic notion of the noble savage' (Cohen, J. 1987:65).

The 'innocence' of minorities in China contrasts well with representations of Han Chinese women as the modern workers of the industrialized nation, who Chairman Mao once declared, 'Hold up half the sky'. The notion that the minorities represent the beautiful 'noble savage', unsullied by Chinese political machinations and the degradations of modern Chinese society, is an important theme for China's modern artists. It may very well represent a Gauguinesque romanticization of the 'savage' in contrast to the modern alienation of Chinese urban life. It may also be viewed as a cultural critique, or rejection, of modern Han China – an accepted venue for criticizing the depersonalizing, totalitarian state.

In an interview, the Yunnan painter Xiao Jia-he, a former student of Jiang Tie-Feng, and himself the son of an intermarriage between a Han and Jingbo, stated that the reason he liked to paint minorities was, 'They are pure and beautiful. It makes me feel peaceful when I paint them'. When I asked him why seven of the ten paintings in his exhibition – with such titles as *Ancient Girl*, *Tara's Toilette*, *Summer Solstice*, *Blossoms*, *Morning Prayers*, and *Homage at the Spring* – portrayed minority women in kneeling, submissive poses, with voluptuous, scantily clothed figures, he said: 'Because I like the human body, and I think this portrays the essence of female beauty. Its also difficult to capture an entire woman's body in a small painting if she is standing' (pers. interview, 30 July 1991). It is significant that in later conversations, Xiao Jia-he explained that once he came to the United States, he was urged by American gallery owners and agents, particularly the Allen H. Fingerhut Group, which strongly promoted most of the Yunnan

Art School paintings (and published Cohen's 1988 book *Yunnan School*), to increase his use of motifs and colors popularized by the Yunnan Art School, since it sold well in the US. 'They told me to use more pastel, gold, and bright colors; to paint beautiful, large-breasted women in elongated form, and to use "ethnic" clothing. I even included a lot of African clothing because of my interest in Africa. I tried to make my art look more erotic [*xing aide*] but not pornographic [*se qing*]' (pers. interview, 30 July 1991). Although most of his artwork was popularly received, comments from viewers at one of his exhibits critical of his representation of minority women caused him to re-evaluate the Yunnan School style. 'I have since rejected the Yunnan Art School,' he told me in a later interview (29 February 1992). 'They are only interested in making money, repeating the same old saleable paintings. It is too repetitious. It is not art ... I refuse to jeopardize my artistic career just to make money.'[20]

By objectifying minority women as colorful, exotic, and erotic, robbing them of their individuality and subjectivity, these Chinese artists are engaging in an anthropological enterprise well-established by Lewis Henry Morgan, Franz Boas, and other early US historicists who posited a 'common psyche' shared by all primitives. Although Boas and later anthropologists stressed individual contributions to the construction of cultural artifacts, and through painstaking ethnographic work brought to light the individual contributions of many 'primitive artists', Boas' commitment to the notion of a common cultural determinism and psyche in artistic construction nevertheless contributed to the

20. Exhibition comments on Xiao Jiahe's works included the following: 'Your work reminds me of Gustav Klimt's gold period, Picasso's colors after Cubism, Kokoschka's hands, Miró's organic shapes, Native American Indian women ...' 'An enthralling body of works, full of magical shapes and curves, flowing like everlasting rivers. A joy to see.' 'Talented, yes! Evocative, yes! But because your main subject in this exhibition is young, nubile women (one model?), I could see you having commercial success in advertising art.' 'I feel that the two best paintings were the one of the peasant and the weaver's daughter. You unquestionably have tremendous talent, however, what distinguishes these two over the others was the subject. The beautiful young woman in each painting offers no insights into the female human being. She is more object than an exploration of the subject ...' (Handwritten comments from the exhibition 'Works by Chinese Artist Xiao Jiahe', Memorial Union, University of Wisconsin, Madison, 5 to 30 July 1991).

objectification of the minority other. In his path-breaking 1927 study *Primitive Art*, Boas revealingly wrote: 'The same motive recurs over and over again in the tales of primitive people, so that a large mass of material collected from the same tribe is liable to be very monotonous, and after a certain point has been reached only new variants of old themes are obtained' (Boas 1927 [1955]:330). It is precisely the repetitive nature of 'primitive' art construed as generic, unsigned, and anonymous that makes it so attractive to the 'modern' collector. Since primitives are all similar in their artistic representations, their artwork and thought patterns homogenized by a uniform culture, why should one piece of art need a signature? According to Sally Price, it is their anonymity and timelessness that make primitive artworks so attractive to the time-bound, modern individual: 'In the Western understanding of things, a work originating outside of the Great Traditions must have been produced by an unnamed figure who represents his community and whose craftsmanship respects the dictates of its age-old traditions' (Price 1989:56).

Significantly, the use of 'traditional' minority art, colors, and styles may be said to have paved the way for the public reintroduction of the Han nude in China, but only in a very highly stylized, Picasso-like form. Western motifs, styles, and color, with minority subjects, become a thinly veiled means of challenging traditional Chinese artistic conventions. Han female nudes, when they are officially and publicly represented at all, are generally in highly stylized forms, often in the Picasso genre, as a famous oil, *Daughter of the Sea*, by Jiang Tie-Feng demonstrates. On a brochure featuring a print of Jiang's 1988 *Playing Water*, there is an eroticized and Picassoesque portrayal of the Yunnan Thai Water Festival, including black sensuous dancing figures, with large breasts and nipples accentuated in bright reds. The back of the promotional brochure reads:

Jiang Tie-Feng is the most influential contemporary artist of the People's Republic of China. His 'Yunnan School' represents the first new Chinese art movement in 700 years, and the rebirth of artistic traditions that have been repressed since the Ming Dynasty. (Fingerhut Group Publishers, brochure, 1992; see also http://www.fingerhutart.com/jiang.htm)

The Picassoesque portrayal of Han women and the abstract representations of the minority women has become so popular now in the West that not only have Chinese artists like Jiang Tie-Feng, He Neng, and Ting Shao Kuang become extraordinarily successful and wealthy, purchasing houses in Bel Air and Beverly Hills, but also they have spawned an entire lucrative industry now sweeping the upscale art industry in China and overseas. After I visited a Shanghai exhibition of Ting's work in spring 1992, he told me that he was literally mobbed by his fans. 'If I had painted Han that way when I was in China before, they probably would have arrested me. Now I am a hero' (pers. interview, 11 July 1992).

The Austin Galleries is a series of chic art dealerships with galleries in Chicago, Detroit, San Francisco, Carmel, and Laguna Beach. At the well-appointed Chicago gallery, I was attracted in November 1991 by a large Yunnan School painting of a minority dancer, prominently displayed in the glass case fronting onto Michigan Avenue. Not only were there several Yunnan School-style paintings by a Han Chinese immigrant, Wu Jian, but also there were similar versions by a certain artist, Wong Shue, who, as I later found out, was originally from Jamaica. The gallery consultant, Bella Cipkin, explained that artworks of the genre were the bestselling in the gallery, with large paintings selling for US$8,000 to US$10,000, and that many artists were beginning to copy the flowing, colorful style. She said it was the most popular art form to have come along in years, and the fastest-selling style in all seven of the Austin Galleries. Cipkin noted: 'The mauve colors and liberating minority art in its breathtaking sensuality goes well with the furnishings in professional's homes'. She also went on to suggest that one of the reasons the art might have become more popular in the United States was that it represented minority art: 'What with the problems in Tibet and all, Americans want to support the ethnic people in China all they can'. It is important to note here that, of course, very little of the Yunnan School art is actually produced by minorities.

Marginalizing the center of Chinese film

'Minorities film' has followed oil painting in reforming the accepted norms of Chinese taste. Paul Clark (1987b:20), a noted critic of Chinese film, argues that it is the 'propensity of minorities film to explore normally avoided subjects' that made the genre so successful and influential. In a Channel Four (UK) documentary on 'New Chinese Cinema', Wu Tianming, the director of the now famous Xi'an Film Studio, where many of the influential Fifth Generation filmmakers were working (including Zhang Yimou, Tian Zhuangzhuang, and Chen Kaige), quoted a Chinese proverb – 'When there's no tiger on the mountain, the monkey is king' – indicating that it is distance from the centers of power such as Beijing and Shanghai that allowed his studio the freedom to explore. In the documentary, the young director of the new, more realistic minority films *On the Hunting Ground* (1985) and *Horse Thief* (1986), Tian Zhuangzhuang, explained why he chose to film in minority areas:

I had several reasons. For one, Beijing Film Studios wouldn't let us direct when we were assigned there ... *On the Hunting Ground* and *Horse Thief* may deal with regional minorities [literally 'minority nationalities'], but they're actually about the fate of the whole Chinese nation. (*New Chinese Cinema* 1988)

According to Paul Clark, in his analysis *Chinese Cinema*, it is the search for a 'national style' (*minzu fengge*), which was lacking among the Han, that directors found among minorities: 'Paradoxically, one of the most effective ways to make films with 'Chinese' style was to go to the most 'foreign' cultural areas in the nation' (Clark 1987a: 101). The search for a national identity in China apparently became more readily understood in opposition and contrast to minority cultures, which were thought to be more vibrant and easily objectified than that of the amorphous, invented Han Chinese self. Through the representation of minorities as sensual, liberated, and colorful, Chinese filmmakers and artists found a 'metaphorical resource' (James Hevia, pers. comm.). They were able to introduce taboo and often illegal art into the Chinese cultural mainstream. These artistic motifs then eventually influenced the broader Han-majority-accepted cultural repertoire of artistic convention, leading to the establishment of a 'national' style and identity.

Through the national medium of officially approved film, Han national identity becomes clearly objectified. In Zhang Nuanxin's *Sacrificed Youth*, there are two scenes in which there is an explicit rejection of sensual involvement by the female protagonist, precisely because she is a 'Han'. In the first instance, Duoli, the Beijing Han youth sent down to the countryside, is being cajoled while gathering firewood in the forest by her Thai coworkers to discuss a ride home in an ox-cart, which she received from a Beijing man whom she had met in the marketplace. When she protests that there is nothing between them, her Thai coworkers chide, 'Don't be afraid to tell us!' She replies: 'We are Hans you know, we don't start love affairs that young' (literally 'We are Han people; we don't talk about love that early').[21]

In the second instance, Duoli is sitting alone with the very same Han youth late at night in the dark, romantic forest, listening to the enchanting music of a distant Thai celebration:

[Duoli:] What are they singing?
[Male friend:] Can't you tell? 'My lover's hands are tender and fair.'
[Duoli:] Don't they find it embarrassing?
[Male friend:] Why should they? Isn't it better to speak out one's feelings? Unlike we Hans, always beating around the bush.
[Duoli:] Speak out yourself then, no one tries to stop you.
Male friend:] But can you?
[Duoli:] Why not?
[Male friend:] OK. What's on your mind now?
[Duoli:] I … I find … its getting cold. Let's go home.
[Male friend:] Is that all?
[Duoli:] Yes.
[Male friend, while gazing at her in her sarong:] You are a Han from head to toe [literally 'No matter what you say, you still are a Han'].

In an interview published in the journal *Camera Obscura*, Zhang Nuanxin, the female director of *Sacrificed Youth*, states that she made the film to encourage the expression of Han female subjectivity and beauty:

After I read the original short story by Zhang Manling, I felt there were many things in it that I'd experienced myself. I'd been down in the countryside, too. I'd felt that the older and less attractive clothes were [*sic*], the better. When we were very young, we couldn't make ourselves attractive, nor could we express love. (Zhang Nuanxin 1989:21)

Indeed, it is the need for self-discovery, awareness, and expression that Chris Berry (1991a:196) has argued pervades much of Women's Cinema in China. Yet it is only by going to minority areas and contrasting the repressed, bounded Han female self with the constructed minority other as unrestrained and beautiful

---

21. In this chapter, 'literally' refers to my translation of the original spoken or written text, while the translated or subtitled versions are given where available, unless otherwise noted.

that these goals can be explored on the screen. This goes against Julia Kristeva's utopian construction of the position of women in Confucianized Chinese society, and although it is framed as a Western critique, I agree with Rey Chow that it nevertheless idealizes the position of women in China to an inexcusable degree.

There are important parallels here to the *National Geographic* tradition of the sexual portrayal of the other for a conservative readership that generally regards such portrayals of its 'own' as pornographic.[22] Clearly, in both cases there is a hierarchy of self: voyeurism of the other is permissible when they are regarded as less familiar, less civilized, than one's own. As Paul Clark (1987b), the critic of Chinese film, has argued in an *East–West Film Journal* article, 'Ethnic Minorities in Chinese Films: Cinema and the Exotic', film in China from the beginning was regarded as a foreign medium, a venue for viewing the exotic and strange. When China became closed to the outside world after 1949, minorities for the first time *took the place of foreigners* as subjects of the exotic. As Clark (1987b:15–16) explains: 'Film audiences could travel to "foreign" lands without crossing the nation's borders'.

But I would go farther than Clark's emphasis on fascination with the exotic. In China there is more to it than the typical *National Geographic*-style romanticization of the primitive, which one might argue is found in almost any society. Here, the state is intimately tied to and in control of, and provides funding for, the politicized process of portraying the other. In Said's (1978) terms, the state has turned its gaze upon the internal other, engaging in a formalized, commodified oriental orientalism, which may be focused on the minorities but represents a long tradition of fascination with the outsider in Chinese society.[23] The real issue here is why the state should choose to explicitly support such an enterprise. I argue that the politics of this representation of minority other is both an extension of power-relation practices in the traditional Chinese state, and a product of China's rise as a nation–state.

22. For an excellent deconstruction of the eroticized, exoticized image of the 'primitive' in *National Geographic*, see Lutz and Collins' (1993) *Reading National Geographic*.
23. Louisa Schein (1990), in a provocative analysis, uses the notion of 'internal orientalism' to describe this project. In China this fascination with the exotic has extended not only to the minority nationalities, but also to representations of foreigners.

Contesting and coopting otherness: eroticizing (even) the Muslims

While minorities appear to have had little choice in the way they have been exoticized in the media, and Han must also conform to their *de*-exoticized essentialization, there have been several attempts at contesting that restricted space. Not only did the student democracy movement emphasize the sensual, the unique, and the individual, but films such as *River Elegy* (*He Shang*; 1988), *Sacrificed Youth* (1985), *Red Sorghum* (1988), and *Ju Dou* (1989) all represent various popular levels of contestation (see Wang, Y. 1989:32). Minorities have also attempted to voice their objections. The covering up of the nude bathing portion of Yuan Yunsheng's painting at Beijing Capital Airport was partly because of complaints from Yunnan minority cadres.[24] In Ürümqi, Xinjiang, a large group of Uyghur Muslim artists rallied in protest in 1987 over an exhibition at the Overseas Chinese Hotel of portrayals of Uyghur and other Central Asians by Han artists that they claimed denigrated them as either too humorous or too sensual. Paintings primarily by Han artists portrayed the Uyghur singing, dancing, riding donkeys, and balancing watermelons on their heads. Worse yet, many paintings portrayed Uyghur women in revealing skirts and engaged in erotic dances (for example, Ting Shao Kuang's *Silk Road* portrays a bare-breasted minority women on a background of deserts and camel caravans). For many Uyghur, these representations are particularly offensive, because they regard themselves as conservative Muslims.

While one might be prepared to allow for the fact that south-western minorities may have more 'open' sexual practices than the Han in China today, they are not the only minorities portrayed as sensual and erotic. While the Thai women did traditionally bathe in the nude (although many may fear to now), and the Nuoso as a matrilineal society may very well have allowed extramarital sexual practice at the matrilocal residence, the Uyghur and other Muslim peoples can hardly be said to be more publicly erotic or sensual than the Han in their traditional culture. Uyghur women are widely known throughout China to traditionally cover themselves with *chun purdah*, which are *purdah*-like head scarves and wraps that

24. Yuan Yunsheng's mural was covered and uncovered a number of times, and has been restored to its original eroticized form. Given the post-1989 political climate in Beijing, this may reflect another attempt to repress difference among the majority by emphasizing the erotic, exotic ways of the minority.

completely envelope their faces and hair, and extend over their hands and down to their ankles. Unlike the Middle Eastern *purdah*, where eyes and sometimes faces are exposed, Uyghur *chun purdah* cover the entire face and body. As Muslims, the Uyghur are generally much more conservative than Han Chinese in the public sexual sphere. Despite the protestations of the minorities, these eroticized representations continue, underscoring the extraordinary contrast between the Han and minority spectacle in China.

Like many tourist hotels, the Sheng Tang (Ascendant Tang) Hotel in northeast Beijing has a tile mural of a Tang-dynasty minority dancer, with accentuated nude breasts, in the center of its main dining hall. On the opposite walls, erotic stylized murals from the Dunhuang Buddhist grottoes grace the dining room. Like many public places in China, the sensual 'flying apsarases' are an officially sanctioned art subject (Cohen, J. 1987:17–20). I once asked a group of Han scholars viewing this mural if they thought the dancers were minorities or Han, and they all said minorities, even though the theme is from the Buddhist caves of Dunhuang, supposedly the cradle of *Chinese* Buddhist religious tradition. While Buddhism became transformed into a Chinese religion, its sensual representation in art and apsarases has apparently remained an attribute of foreigners and minorities, not Han.

In the Chinese tourist pictorial *A Picture Album of Turpan Landscape and Custom* (1985:16), a Han artist, Gu Shengyue, portrays the sensual images of the Dunhuang caves, with floating female apsarases and their accentuated breasts, hovering above him, almost as if to say: 'Although these Uyghur claim to be Muslim, we know what they are really thinking about when they sing and dance'. They have become yet another landscape in the national repertoire of China. In another portrait from page 18 of the same pictorial, erotic Buddhist figures are portrayed hovering above ecstatic Uyghur dancers. Central Asian dance and artistic display come to represent a metaphor of sensuality and eroticism for Han China, even though the region is now dominated by Muslims.

Extremely realistic is the figure painting *Nude with Apples* (in Cohen, J. 1987:101), by Tang Muli, a Han artist who has traveled widely abroad. With a Central Asian hat, sitting upon a Xinjiang carpet, and eating apples, often produced in China's dry, cold northwest, the full-frontal nude in this realist painting is clearly meant to portray a Central Asian minority, although the model may very well be Han. Perhaps Tang Muli knew that a Han woman could never be portrayed so vividly and realistically. Yet this is despite Muslims being the most conservative of all peoples in China.

The last painting of eroticized Muslims I shall note is also the most startling: Zhao Yixiong's 1979 oil *Awakening of Tarim*. Of this controversial painting, Cohen (1987:54) writes: 'Tarim symbolizes the beginnings of modernization on the edges of the great Takla Makan, China's most terrible desert. She awakens on a vibrant patchwork of Silk Road images: camels, mosques, oil derricks, Buddhist deities, oases, grapes, gourds, and pomegranates'. While paintings of Uyghur and other Muslims by Han artists such as Huang Zhou have had a long history in China, they were never so eroticized as Zhao Yixiong's. His painting makes clear the dramatic link between nationality, women, and modernity. By depicting his nude Uyghur female subject as 'awakening' from her traditional life to a modern world filled with oil rigs, airplanes, and nuclear installations, Zhao Yixiong perhaps suggests that it is only in throwing off the traditional minority culture of Islam, with its covered women, mosques, and caravans, that Tarim, the woman and the region, can be modernized. Depicting camel caravans and mosque minarets literally emerging from between the woman's thighs, this painting would, of course, be extremely offensive to Uyghur. Nevertheless, it was commissioned to be painted by Zhao Yixiong, who, as a painter for the Chinese Museum of Chinese History and Revolution, is employed by the state to represent the other in an orientalist fashion strikingly similar to that of Alloula's *Colonial Harem*.

Significantly, Cohen informs us that the Chinese authorities disallowed the exhibition of Zhao's striking painting. One immediately assumes this was due to its explicit, erotic nature. Yet, according to Cohen (1987:54), 'The [Oil Painting Research Association] excluded it because of the green streak on the woman's buttocks – an Expressionist gesture that was apparently thought to be offensive'. Extraordinarily, expressionistic representation was rejected as proper for minority portraiture, with explicit realism favored for public consumption. By contrast, it is often realistic representation of the Han female body that has been heavily restricted by the Chinese state. Just as the subordination of Chinese women reifies the elevated position of men, so the exoticization of minorities essentializes the imagined identity of the Han, and reaffirms Han feelings of superiority. Public, state-sponsored minority representation as both more sensual and primitive than the Han supports the state's agenda. With the proper educational and economic progress, the minorities will eventually attain the modernity that the Han have attained, and enter into the same civilized restrictions under the authority of the state as vanguard. Symbolic tribute by minorities becomes an important link with China's past, establishing their own feudal pasts, and a signal of who will lead the future. It also legitimates the state's authority to enforce homogeneity, morality, and 'civility' among the 91 percent Han majority, while difference is 'temporarily' tolerated among the 'backward' minorities. In a socialist society that claims to be post-Confucian, gender and ethnic hierarchies continue to be articulated in a discourse of morality – the proper ordering of the social universe. It is precisely resistance to that order that makes the film *Ju Dou* so controversial.

Woman as minority and other in China

The furor over the nomination of the film *Ju Dou* for an Academy Award in 1991 was primarily due to the film's offensiveness to Chinese moral and hierarchical sensibilities, according to the press (WuDunn 1991:B1). Not surprisingly, *Ju Dou* was made by a product of the Xi'an Film Studio, director Zhang Yimou, who starred in Wu Tianming's iconoclastic film *Old Well*. Ju Dou, a young bride, is physically abused for not being able to become pregnant by her elderly, probably impotent husband. She is beaten repeatedly, tied, and even pinned down by a horse-saddle on which her elderly husband sits while he sexually abuses her, in what may probably be China's first, and perhaps last, bondage-style film. To save herself (the old man had already beaten to death two previous wives), she seduces her husband's adopted son, and the resulting story of their infidelities is what the Chinese find most offensive. Just as Ju Dou is expected to accept her fate, even at the point of death, so are Han Chinese women required to restrict their sexuality in the services of the state. Similarly, minority women are allowed to be portrayed erotically because that too serves the interests of the regime. This may also be a contributing factor in the state's general exemption of most minorities from the birth-planning program.[25]

25. Until recently, minorities were allowed to have one or more extra children than the Han in their area. In my research, I found that this policy in practice

Minority women are encouraged to be fecund; their bodies are less controllable than that of the ritually bound Han women. Perhaps one metaphorical reason the state exempts most minorities from birth-planning is to preserve the notion that minorities represent uncontrolled sensuality, fertility, and reproductiveness; Han represent controlled, civilized, productivity. Yet it is primarily not women's bodies that are at issue; it is the state's (and by extension, the patriarchal male's) control of them.

In a fascinating parallel to the Thai-bathers motif pervading much of minority art, there is an critical moment in *Ju Dou* in which Yang Tianqing, the adopted son, voyeuristically observes Ju Dou bathing through a hole in the washroom wall. This scene bears striking resemblance to the voyeurism of the Miao men and film-viewers of Miao women bathers in the *Amazing Marriage Customs* film, described on pages 61 to 63. Note that in each case it is water and bathing that leads to the voyeuristic gaze and the construction of the sexual object. As the adopted son enlarges the hole for a better view, Ju Dou discovers him and covers the hole with straw from the inside of the washroom. Later, she once again finds that he has removed the straw from the inside for an unobstructed view. This time, however, in a radical departure from traditional Chinese female modesty (but more like the Miao and Thai bathers), she allows him to view her naked body, savagely marked by his adopted father's beatings. The shock engendered by her beautiful but grotesquely bruised body compels yet humiliates the viewer. Similarly, Han voyeurism of minority women, and the submission of Han women to the patriarchal social order, is what the state, for its own self-perpetuating reasons, considers proper in China.

Zhang Yimou's reversal of those roles in *Ju Dou* delegitimizes the state's authority to objectivize the other, both woman and minority, and this may be an important factor in the Chinese attempt to prevent the film's nomination for an Academy Award. By turning her gaze directly back on the adopted son, Ju Dou both humiliates him and establishes her subjectivity, resisting his use of

---

meant that in most rural areas, minorities had as many chilren as they wanted. Post-1989 attempts to institute birth-planning in Mongolia and Xinjiang have led to riots among the minorities, who argue that China's policy of encouraging Han 'assimilation through immigration' has led to excessive Han population growth in their areas.

her as an object of sexual desire. By taking affairs into her own hands, and later seducing him, she establishes her own identity and asserts individuality.

Minorities, too, by allowing the objectivizing gaze of the state-sponsored media, establish their identity and right to a voice in their own affairs, coopting and turning whenever possible these objectivizing moves to their own benefit. In this way, the maintenance and assertion of minority culture, no matter how exoticized or contrived, may be seen as a form of resistance. By participating in their 'training' by the Han Chinese state, supporting minority art and culture, they often find ways to promote values that may be contrary to the state's modernizing program. These glimpses of a more naturalized, colorful, liberated, and sensual lifestyle, which urban Han Chinese now find so alien to their own living situations, contributes to the popularity of minorities as colonized and gendered subjects (see Chatterjee 1989:624). It also might explain why minorities and their exoticized portrayal in the Yunnan Art School are extremely popular in the West, where many long for a similar naturalized lifestyle, often as a way of critiquing China's image as a totalitarian homogenizing state. Successful marketization of these images in the global capitalist economy perpetuates minority/majority discourses in China and abroad. The appearance of books, courses, and institutions devoted to the study of China's minorities within and without China reflects this homogenization – as if one could draw a clear line between the minorities and the rest of 'Han' China. This chapter has argued otherwise, attempting to directly link minority with majority discourses in the public sphere. In China and elsewhere, constructing minority identities is directly related to the identity of the majority. As Han-ness is related to 'whiteness', so the majority in China is invented as an unmarked category, courtesy of a subjugated, stigmatized, and identified minority.

Although alienated moderns may wax nostalgic over exoticized representations of imagined pasts, the belated arrival in China of Hobsbawm's (1991:163) universalized 'nationality principle', coupled with the government's expressed desire to be reckoned as a modern nation-state, indicates that the identification, and exploitation, of minorities for tourist dollars and nationalization programs will mean their continued stigmatization as exoticized subjects – a stigma that they may only infrequently turn to their own benefit. Minority cooption of these motifs may help increase their autonomy, turning the tables of representation. Yet these attempts at subjectivity and independence will always be threatening to any totalizing, objectivizing state that seeks homogeneity of the majority at the expense of the minority. It is no surprise that *Ju Dou* was banned and minorities are encouraged to do little more than sing and dance in China's Republic of Peoples.

5

FILM AND FORECASTING THE NATION

The Fifth Generation

Tian Zhuangzhuang, one of the most controversial of China's Fifth Generation filmmakers, in 1993 garnered the highest awards at both the Tokyo International Film Festival and the Honolulu International Film Festival for his film *The Blue Kite* (1993). Tian's reputation was established by two earlier films that have been described as ethnographic and documentary in nature, despite being feature films, due to their minority subjects and locations in Mongolia and Tibet. As Tony Rayns noted in his review of origins of the New Chinese Cinema, these two earlier films, *On the Hunting Ground* (*Liechang Zhasa*; 1985) and *Horse Thief* (*Daomazei*; 1986), were important departures from the earlier 'minorities films' tradition in China in that they showed 'the physical and spiritual lives of "national minorities" in Inner Mongolia and Tibet, minus the usual mediating presence of Han Chinese' (Rayns 1991:112). This chapter will suggest that the deliberate silencing of the Han Chinese voice in Tian's minorities films represents an important shift at the inception of the Fifth Generation films – a shift away from national narrative toward cultural critique. By moving their films to the geographical and national borders of China, Tian and many other filmmakers were able to effectively address critical issues gnawing at the heartland. Through filming minorities and other subaltern subjects, Tian and other Fifth Generation filmmakers contributed, perhaps unwittingly, to a forecasting of the Chinese nation: how it was mapped, conceived, and located from the borders to the heartlands.

Although Tian's 'minority' films were to become overshadowed by his award-winning *Blue Kite*, we would do well to take another look at what became known in China as the 'Chinese Westerns', precisely because they show the earlier efforts of a young, relatively unknown filmmaker to address subjects both critical of Chinese culture and society, and highly visual in nature (both *On the Hunting Ground* and *Horse Thief* were famous for their stunning cinematography, minimalist dialogue, didacticism, and narrativity).[1] Tian's films have been compared to the 'minorities films' genres that preceded them, but I will argue here that Tian's work and the role they played in influencing and helping to form the Fifth Generation represent a significant departure or, to use Gayatri Spivak's term, a 'strategic intervention' in apprising the status of the Chinese nation-state and film in China.

Tian's *Blue Kite* represents a more direct and devastating critique of the policies of the totalizing and vacillating Chinese state that led to such radical periods as the Great Leap Forward (1959–1961) and the Cultural Revolution (1966–1976) (and Tian, if I read him right, believes the state is still susceptible to similar shifts of political pendulum – which perhaps indicates why Tian is being sued by the central authorities for distributing the film abroad after it had been banned in Beijing), and the demise of Tian's three marriages. What is significant about Tian's earlier work is that he chose minority subjects to engage in a similar cultural and political critique, but more obliquely. In the political climate of the mid-1980s, it was still more acceptable to stand on the margins (literally the geographical borderlands of Tibet and Mongolia) than to criticize the state from the center. One may argue that *The Blue Kite* is still a 'safe' attempt at critical intervention, since it takes as its subject the officially excoriated Cultural Revolution. Even though Tian in almost soap-operatic style reiterates the now accepted themes about the

1.   Tony Rayns groups Tian's films with other Fifth Generation films, including Chen Kaige's *Yellow Earth* (Guangxi Film Studio, 1984), Zhang Zeming's *Swan Song* (Pearl River Studio, 1985), Wu Ziniu's *The Last Day of Winter* (Xiaoxang Studio, 1986), and Huang Jianxin's *The Black Cannon Incident* (Xi'an Film Studio, 1985). He argues they are all 'new wave' for the following reasons: 'They all minimize dialogue and trust their images to carry the burden of constructing meaning. They deliberately seek out subjects and angles of approach that have been missing from earlier Chinese films ... a distinctively Chinese cinema, free of Hollywood and Mosfilm influences alike. Most important of all, though, they stand united against didacticism. They interrogate their own themes, and they leave their audiences ample space for reflection. After three decades of ideological certainty in Chinese cinema, they reintroduced *ambiguity*' (Rayns 1991:112; emphasis in original).

mistreatment of intellectuals and the dissolution of families, it is still a topic not widely dealt with in the public sphere in China, and one that had the film banned and Tian sued by the state. By selecting such 'marginal' and 'safe' subjects, Tian clearly knew what he was doing.

Horse Thief is also worthy of another look because it represents an important, if not final, contribution of China's Fifth Generation filmmakers. The Fifth Generation is widely attributed as having created a new era of films that deliberately chose the genre of minority and rural regions as useful canvases on which to paint their larger constructions and deconstructions of Chinese society. Wu Tianming did it best perhaps in *Old Well* (Xi'an Film Studio, 1986), but Chen Kaige was most dramatic in *Yellow Earth* (Guangxi Film Studio, 1984). Zhang Yimou, possibly the most famous of the Fifth Generation, accomplishes much the same kind of distancing through moving his films to rural and, for the most part, pre-revolutionary China.[2] In similar fashion, Tian takes us to minority areas set in 1923 to paint his devastating critique of Chinese society and the roles its subject peoples play in that cultural criticism. It is significant that Tian may have been the last of his Fifth Generation to have done so. Professor Zhou Chuanji, the teacher of many of the Fifth Generation filmmakers who studied with him in the early 1980s at the Beijing Film Academy, stated that he believed *Horse Thief* was the last of the Fifth Generation films.[3] This was, Zhou argues, primarily because of the film's artistic quality, non-commercial nature, and reliance upon state funding. Later films by Zhang Yimou, Chen Kaige, and Tian Zhuangzhuang were made with substantially larger funding, much of it foreign (from Hong Kong, Taiwan, and Japan), and with a view to international distribution and profit-making. *Horse Thief*, therefore, may very well be the last of its Fifth Generation.

2. Until his film *Qiu Ju* (1993), set in rural Shaanxi, Zhang Yimou's films all took place in pre-revolutionary China, including *Hong Gaoliang* (*Red Sorghum*; Xi'an Film studio, 1988), set in the Sino-Japanese War; *Ju Dou* (1989), set in rural Sichuan; and *Raise the Red Lantern* (*Hongdeng Gaolou*; 1991), set in the early 20th century. For an excellent review of *Red Sorghum* that sets out themes often repeated in Zhang's later work, see Wang Yuejin (1989:31–40).

3. Pers. interview. I am grateful to Huang Hai-yen for arranging this meeting with Professor Zhou Chuanji during a visit to Honolulu.

Horse Thief *and its critics*

Horse Thief was very controversial in China, although not for the reasons one might expect. It was not the subject matter that most found upsetting. The faraway, exotic minority subjects in *On the Hunting Ground* and *Horse Thief* not only confused Tian Zhuangzhuang's urban audiences, but also bored them – so much so that they stayed away in droves and wondered loudly why the state supported such obscurantism. The uproar in the popular press was not over controversial content; it was that Tian's films made so little money. They were duds. Chris Berry (1991a) informs us, in his essay 'Market Forces: China's "Fifth Generation" Faces the Bottom Line', that most films in China make money not so much by box-office sales as by the ordering of prints by state-run theaters. An average film sells more than a 100 prints. Tian's *On the Hunting Ground* film sold two. *Horse Thief* did only slightly better with seven. Both films were mainly purchased by the head offices of the China Film Corporation, which were already under contract to do so. The director Zhang Junzhao (maker of *One and Eight*, *Come on, China!*, and *The Lonely Murderer*), justified his more conservative and straightforward films as necessary for political and financial survival. '*Horse Thief* and *On the Hunting Ground* lost tens of thousands of *yuan* between them, and no one went to see them,' Zhang noted. He then asked: 'Do you think the Xi'an Film Studio will dare to use him again?' (in Gao 1991:131). Zhang was apparently right, in that Tian's next film was not until six years later, and it was financed by outside sources.

Tian and, more importantly, his boss Wu Tianming, the head of Xi'an Film Studio from 1983 to 1989 and widely regarded as the father of the Fifth Generation filmmakers, argued that these were art films and deserved to be made 'for art's sake'. In Tian's defense, Wu Tianming explained: 'There are three audiences that have to be satisfied in China. One is the government, one is the art world, and one is the ordinary popular audience' (Berry 1991a:122). He goes on to say that the 'reform films' are shot for the government, the 'exploratory' films for the art world, and the 'Kung Fu' films for the popular market. Tian's work was clearly too exploratory for China's audience. In an interview with China's widely read film journal *Popular Cinema*, Tian defended himself: 'I shot *Horse Thief* for audiences of the next century to watch' (translated in Yang Ping 1991:

126). Quoting Wu Tianming, Tian says he would rather 'a film didn't sell a single copy, just so long as the quality is good'. At least Tian's *On the Hunting Ground* sold two copies. In Tian's opinion, 'the main problem was the audience' (Yang Ping 1991:126). *Horse Thief*, therefore, may mark the end of the Fifth Generation, not only due to its content, but also as a result of the post-*Horse Thief* institutional shift away from state funding dissociated from profit concerns, to films funded by transnational film corporations (in Japan, Hong Kong, and Taiwan) geared for financial success on the world market.

Minority representation in China

I noted earlier that Tian's films indicated a significant departure from earlier 'minorities films' in China. Minorities film includes a wide range of state-sponsored educational and feature films in China set in minority areas from the 1950s to the mid-1970s, which almost exclusively emphasize not only the 'color' and beauty of their 'traditional' cultures, but also their 'backwardness' (*louhou*), their oppression under the old 'feudal' system, and their 'liberation' by the Communists. As such, these films represent attempts by the state to modernize and 'civilize' not only the minorities, but also the cinematic public at large, who learn to distinguish between primitivity and modernity by viewing the 'plight' of the minorities. In the 1950s, 'documentary' films were made in minority areas, depicting strange and sometimes erotic customs, including matrilocal marriage and extramarital sex, often using minority and Han actors to act out what were thought to be primitive minority customs left over from the feudal era.[4] Clark (1987b:22–5) argues that in the 1960s, feature films depicted the 'soft' southwestern minorities such as the Yi, Miao, Zhuang, Thai, and Bai as the 'happy, smiling' natives, including *Ashma* (*Ashima*; directed by Liu Qiong, Haiyan Studio, 1964), *Third Sister Liu* (*Liu Sanjie*; directed by Su

---

4. These films are no longer publicly shown and are now located in the archives of the Chinese Academy of Social Sciences, Institute for Nationality Studies (*Zhongguo Shehui Kexue Yuan, Minzu Yanjiusuo*). They include such films as *Zouhun* (*Moving Marriage*), shot among the Naxi (Nuoso), and other films on the Yi, Wa, and Miao in Yunnan, Guizhou, and Sichuan. For an excellent overview of minorities film in China, see Clark (1987b).

Li, Changchun Studio, 1960), *Five Golden Flowers* (*Wuduo Jinhua*; directed by Wang Jiayi, Changchun Studio, 1959), and *Menglongsha Village* (*Menglongsha*; directed by Wang Ping and Yuan Xian, August First Studio, 1960). Northwestern minorities, such as the Uyghur, Tibetans, Mongols, and Kazakh, were featured in films that tended to stress 'harder' themes such as class and political struggle in harsh and exotic environments, including *Visitor on Ice Mountain* (*Bingshan Shang de Laike*; directed by Zhao Xinshui, Changchun Studio, 1963), *Red Flower of Tianshan* (*Tianshan de Honghua*; directed by Cui Wei, Chen Huaikai, and Liu Baode, Xi'an and Beijing studios, 1964), and *Son and Daughter of the Grassland* (*Caoyuan Ernü*; directed by Fu Jie, Beijing Film Studio, 1975). The disruption caused by the Cultural Revolution and the reintroduction of Western films into China in the late 1970s and early 1980s meant the decline of this traditional exoticization in service of the state. Chinese audiences could once again turn to imported films to satisfy curiosities about things foreign, and the minorities began to appear in films by Tian and others for difference reasons.

Since the setting of *Horse Thief* is Tibet, an excellent contrast illustrating this transition in minorities film is provided by another film on Tibet, the classic *Serfs* (*Nongnu*; directed by Li Jun, August First Studio, 1963).[5] In this film, as in so many others, the minorities become useful subjects for illustrating the evils of social oppression in a feudal society that the Communists liberated in 1949. A Tibetan serf, Jampa, is abused and mistreated by the son of his Tibetan landlord, who goes so far as to make him serve as his footstool, and even as his horse, with the son occasionally riding around on Jampa's back. Most of the film details this abusive relationship and the harshness and poverty of life on the Tibetan Plateau, prior to direct Chinese Communist control.

Things change dramatically when the 1959 revolt takes place and the rebels, who include Jampa's Tibetan overlords, are forced to flee (presumably with the Dalai Lama, who is leading the 'oppressors' away from the 'liberating' army). Once again Jampa is forced at gunpoint to serve as his master's beast of burden, carrying him on his back as they flee. When Jampa resists this mistreatment, literally flinging off his oppressor, his master attempts to shoot him and suddenly a People's Liberation Army (PLA) soldier intervenes, giv-

---

5.   This film is described in detail by Paul Clark (1987a:96–9).

ing his life to protect Jampa. Jampa returns to help the PLA soldiers suppress the rebellion in Lhasa, even unearthing caches of arms in a temple statue of a bodhisattva, becoming thus a metaphor for both liberated and subjugated – an unwitting servant of yet another master, this time in a PLA uniform. *Serfs*, of course, makes it clear that the green uniform is to be preferred over the saffron.

Serfs shares some key similarities with *Horse Thief*, but even more important differences. Both films exoticize the minority subjects, their lands, and life-worlds, but for very different reasons. One is in service to the state, the other in resistance to it. One represents a 'civilizing project', the other the suggestion of radical alterity, although both claim to be ethnographic.[6] Jampa turns against his oppressor, becoming subjugated to the state. The horse thief turns against his people by preying upon them, and retribution is dealt to him by his people and their system of natural justice: abandonment to an ecosystem he has violated by stealing from his people, to a nature that finally turns against him. While the first film makes religion a part of the feudal oppressive system, the second naturalizes Tibetan religious experience, making it part of the exotic and harsh nature that administers blessing and retribution among the thief's people. Both use the minorities in their quest to be politically and socially relevant to the majority audience that gazes at these minorities and their surroundings in all their exoticized splendor.

The representation of the minority in these films and other public portrayals in China reflect an objectivizing majority nationality discourse that parallels the valorization of social and political hierarchy. The widespread definition and representation of the minority as exotic, colorful, and primitive homogenizes the undefined majority as united, mono-ethnic, and modern. Thus, both *Serfs* and *Horse Thief*, though using ethnographic subjects, have little to do with Tibet or the minorities; they have much to do with the Han majority, and issues concerning their audience. The ethnic subjects in these and other minority films become useful venues for addressing controversial and sometimes taboo issues among the majority. The politics of representation in China reveals much about the state's project of constructing, in often binary minority/ majority terms, an 'imagined' national identity (Anderson 1991).

6.   I am grateful to Michael Fischer for drawing my attention to the contrast in these strategies.

Through reading the representation of minorities in China, *Horse Thief* suggests that we might learn much, perhaps more, about the construction of majority identity in China, and the state of society in general, by backtracking to the larger issues lying behind the film and the choosing of minorities as its subjects.

The background to minorities film

The genre known as minorities film has played an important role in reforming certain accepted norms of Chinese taste. According to Paul Clark (1987a), in his analysis of Chinese cinema, Chinese filmmakers used minorities to project their own concerns regarding Han national identity. Tian Zhuangzhuang defended his using minorities as important film subjects precisely because they were exotic and different. He argued that people misunderstood his film because of the 'foreign' subject: 'It's an alien culture' (Yang Ping 1991:129). In a Channel Four (UK) documentary interview, Tian Zhuangzhuang noted that *On the Hunting Ground* and *Horse Thief*, though dealing with exotic minorities, were 'actually about the fate of the whole Chinese nation' (*New Chinese Cinema* 1988).

Paul Clark (1987a:101) argues it was the search for both the exotic and a 'national style' (*minzu fengge*) that drove minorities films. Through the medium of officially approved film, Chinese national identity becomes clearly objectified in Tian's films. By going to minority areas and objectifying the constructed minority other as radically alterior, unrestrained, virile, beautiful, and at times brutally violent, the repressed, bounded Han majority self becomes subject to cultural critique.

Borderless crossing: exoticization in Chinese film

Here there are major parallels to the *National Geographic* tradition of the exoticized and eroticized portrayal of the other for a conservative readership that generally deems such portrayals of its own as too extreme or even pornographic (see Lutz and Collins 1993). But there is more here than just fascination with the romanticization of the primitive *à la National Geographic*, which is arguably present in most societies. The Chinese state is intimately tied to and in control of the politicized process of portraying the other, and funds it (or in Tian's case, attempts to sue for its financial return). But why should the state choose to explicitly support such an enterprise. As I argued in Chapter 4, the politics of this representation of minority other is not only an extension of power-relation practices in the traditional Chinese state, but also a product of China's 20th-century rise as a nation-state.

In *Horse Thief*, Tian takes us to a faraway land to reveal the moral depravity of an over-bureaucratized, urbanized Chinese core, which lacks beauty, vigor, and ritual. The pageantry, natural justice, and, in the end, brutality of *Horse Thief* sends a message to China's alienated urban populace – a message that many of them might not have been ready for. It succeeds in convincing them that their lives are less spiritual, less natural, and bound by the vicissitudes of the modern condition. Yet in the end the film also fails, precisely because its subjects become over-exoticized, too alien for its audience to understand or become attracted to. The message is too ambiguous. It was thus ultimately rejected by the broader population. Just as the singing and dancing, squeaky-clean minorities of an earlier genre failed to convince its audience that these people really were 'liberated' by the Party, and not just playing parts for a new director, so Tian's minorities films are fundamentally disappointing, in that they both break with earlier representations of minorities and simultaneously reconstitute them.

The exoticized and even romanticized images of the harsh Tibetan landscape serve as vehicles for widening the gulf between the audience and the subjects of the film. Few in China could relate to the open territory, uncrowdedness, lawlessness, and isolation of Tibet or Mongolia as they are portrayed in Tian's films. The distance between majority self and minority other is made unbridgeable; the absence of the Han in the films, and anything to which they can relate, make the films alien, and alienating, to the viewer. This is deliberate. Tian's motive is not ethnographic; he does not want his Han viewers to understand, establish empathy, or reach any commonality with his foreign subjects. His purpose is that of alterity: by contrasting naturalized, primitive, and even barbaric minority life with the viewer's domesticated, modern, and civilized existences, Tian calls into question the very basis of that contrast.[7]

---

7. Tian reveals his deliberate ethnocentrism when he justifies the horse thief's lawlessness as being part of his 'alien' nature. When his interviewer points out that 'horse-stealing is always wrong', Tian responds: 'Horse-stealing is very

By mid-1980s China, intellectuals had begun to openly readdress issues of urban alienation, democratization, sexuality, and cultural criticism that had been raised during the 1978–79 Democracy Wall Movement, leading to the 1986 and 1989 student democratic protests (Gladney 1990). The horse thief's freedom, disregard for the state and its laws, loyalty to his family and clan, and close attachment to nature call into question the primitive/modern assumptions of his viewers: Is the modernized, urbanized, civilized life any better? Only through driving the self/other wedge as deep as possible in this film can Tian begin to force these issues on his audience. He certainly could not raise them directly.

In the early minorities film genre and in Tian's use of minorities in film, the minority subjects are still just that: subjects of a colonizing regime with a civilizing project. And this project of civilization, and modernization, may be just as alien to the minorities as it is to the majority. Although Tian's film is more direct, and critical of the state, it reaffirms the minority as a colonized, orientalized subject. As in earlier films, the minorities speak Mandarin, although with a slightly Qinghai or northwestern accent. They have no 'voice', literal or otherwise, of their own. Tibetan is only spoken in song, greeting, or curse.[8] The Tibetans deal strictly in Chinese currency, language, and bureaucracy, readily accepting the Chinese administrative apparatus – the foreign overlordship of their land.

This issue, of course, is never politicized in these film genres (lest they be even likelier candidates for the censor's knife), but in Tian's

---

common in Tibet, to the point where it's almost a profession. For reasons of physical geography and lack of economic development, horses are a form of currency in Tibet, and so horse-stealing happens a lot. For me to become a horse thief would be the same as becoming a carpenter, and I wouldn't feel there was any difference' (Yang Ping 1991:130).

8. When I complained of the overuse of voiceover and dubbing in Chinese films, Zhou Chuanji said the high rate of illiteracy in China meant subtitling was not possible. Chinese characters on screen would not work because many Chinese could neither follow them, nor read them fast enough to keep up with the dialogue (even though in *On the Hunting Ground* and *Horse Thief* there is almost no dialogue). Perhaps to help correct this problem and reach a wider audience, Hong Kong films have begun to use not only English subtitling, but also Mandarin characters *and* special Cantonese characters, differing slightly from China's national script. These three lines of subtitling take up nearly one-third of the screen. One can only imagine what would be left of the screen if Tibetan or other indigenous languages were added.

film, there is no device that would even suggest it is problematic for him. In the earlier state-run minorities films and in Tian's work the minorities are merely useful subjects (compliant, like an orientalized female) in larger projects that have more to do with issues concerning the majority *watching* the film than the minorities *in* the film.

Representing Horse Thief's *minorities*

In two cameos from *Horse Thief*, we see minority representation for Tian at its best, or perhaps worst. I refer here to the scenes featuring the only other non-Tibetans in the film, in both cases involving Hui Muslim traders. Frequent travelers to Tibet have noted the extraordinary number of Muslim traders plying the Tibetan markets with their wares. These Hui merchants come from as far away as Qinghai, Gansu, Ningxia, and Xinjiang, exchanging tea, religious objects, and manufactured items from inland China for hard currency, Tibetan handicrafts, and imported goods from India that are brought in by Nepalese and Tibetan relatives in India. As elsewhere in China, the Hui become the ethnoreligious mediators, the middlemen in a small private economy that 'fills the cracks of Chinese socialism' with Muslim entrepreneurialism (see Gladney 1996a:149–60). And as one finds for Muslims throughout China, the same stereotypes apply. In case the viewer has forgotten, Tian repeats them. The film portrays the Muslims as crafty, sly, stingy, and untrustworthy, especially in the first scene, in which they sell Tibetan goods at a handsome profit. The camera focuses on the bearded Muslim in white hat clinking the silver coins to be sure they are real, indicating his lack of trust in his clients. It is also noteworthy that the Hui merchant, though Muslim, does not hesitate to sell Buddhist religious objects to Tibetans – anything for a profit.

In the second, more dramatic encounter, three Muslim traders are surprised by Norbu and his accomplice on a distant trail and robbed at knifepoint of their goods and money. After being robbed, one Muslim makes a feeble attempt at attacking Norbu with a small knife, slightly wounding him in the leg (which Norbu later describes as being inflicted by a 'dog'), and Norbu severely cuts him with his much longer Tibetan sword. Yet Norbu is compassionate in his victory, offering money to each Muslim as a means of survival, and turning the majority of the goods over to the temple as an offering. For their part, the Muslims appear weak, cringing, and vindictive. The Tibetans, by contrast, are strong and ruthless, and possess a distinctive 'honor among thieves'. In a stateless region where the police are nowhere near and all that matter are the laws of nature and clan (to which Norbu ultimately succumbs), the Tibetans are clearly the masters of their brutal environs. Norbu may be a horse thief (*dao ma zei*), Tian seems to imply, but he has more honor than these larcenous Muslims (*zei huihui*).[9] The remarkable fact that the film is originally based on a story written by Zhang Chengzhi, a Hui Muslim nationalist who is recognized as China's first Red Guard (see Chapter 2), indicates the widespread and accepted nature of this stereotypical portrayal of Muslims in China.

Majority agendas, minority subjects

Horse Thief begins and ends with close-up scenes of one the harshest realities encountered on the Tibetan Plateau: the funerary rite of 'sky burial'. In both scenes we are given an intimate look at the Tibetan ritualized practice of presenting the prepared remains of the recent dead to carrion birds to be fully consumed, hastening one's eventual reincarnation or possible escape into the afterlife. While we are not told who the victim is in either scene, the final scene implies that it is Norbu himself being consumed, after being caught a last time at stealing horses and punished by his kinsmen, and indeed, nature itself. Despite his guilt at breaking the laws of the land, it is clear the film ultimately portrays Norbu as a victim, not only of the carrion birds, but also of the harsh environment in which he is forced to steal if he is to survive and support his family.

This play between individual victimization and group survival, personal guilt and social exoneration, private attachment and public betrayal, thematically relates to a cataclysmic event intimately known by every viewer of the film in China: the Great Proletarian Cultural Revolution. Indeed, Zhou Chuanji and others have argued that it is the Cultural Revolution that has set the Fifth Gen-

---

9. This may be a play on the term for 'thief', *zei*, which rhymes with, and is frequently combined with, *Hui* (pronounced *whey*). Hence the horse thief (*daoma zei*) is more crafty (*zei*) than the larcenous Hui (*zei Huihui*) with whom he interacts in the border regions.

eration apart from its predecessors and successors. Tian joined the army during the Cultural Revolution and would have seen direct evidence of its excesses due to the use of the army to finally curb the escalating violence. Although the director was raised in a film family – both his parents were actors and later officials in China's film industry – Tian did not enter the filmic world until he trained in the army as a still photographer, and later as a cinematographer at the Beijing Agricultural Film Studio after he left the army at the end of the Cultural Revolution in 1975 (Berry 1991b:194–5). This is perhaps why his films stress the visual over the narrative. It also might suggest why the Cultural Revolution may serve as an important background to the film.

The Cultural Revolution is certainly a major theme that many of the younger directors have only recently begun to address, as in Chen Kaige's *Farewell, My Concubine* and Tian Zhuangzhuang's *Blue Kite* (both of which were banned in China). It may very well be that *Horse Thief*, which at the time could not deal with the Cultural Revolution explicitly, addresses it implicitly, serving as a grand metaphor for the brutal victimization of the Cultural Revolution, where the drastic shifts in Party politics led to the attacks not only between political factions, but also between husband and wife, parent and child, friend and friend.[10] The harshness of the ecological environment of Tibet can be mapped against the brutality of the political territory of internal China, indicating to the film's audience that victimization is a natural expediency. And indeed, the vulture scene might even indicate final exoneration. At one point during the film, one of Norbu's clan members states that Norbu is so evil that not even the carrion birds would consume his flesh. That the last scene features a sky burial, with Norbu the most likely victim, may indicate that in the end he too will experience ritual rebirth. A hidden message of hope for Chinese society in general? If so, it was too subliminal for its critics to note.

We are left with a deeply complex film that few in China attended and even fewer understood. It became thing of a cult classic abroad for its revealing location footage of life on the Tibetan Plateau, but few have noted its significance either for China or for

10. See Anne Thurston's (1987) dramatic depiction of victimization in her account of the personal experiences of several prominent individuals and their families during the Cultural Revolution.

minority representation. Minorities are represented on film much as they are exoticized and stigmatized in the public sphere. It is just that Tian's exoticization has a point: cultural intervention at the center of Chinese society. Issues such as the Cultural Revolution, alienation, criminality, identity, religiosity, and spirituality were pressing concerns in mid-1980s China, and still may be today. But at the time, to address these issues, Tian and other filmmakers, artists, and even tourists, had to travel to the margins – to distant borderlands, which, as *Horse Thief* shows us, can reveal much, even of the heartlands, of China.

Part III
FOLKLORIZATIONS

6
ENMESHED CIVILIZATIONS

Huntingtons 'clash of civilizations' in China

Many scholars have argued that, unlike the post-colonial world that was dominated by nation-states and eventually the alignment of smaller nations along a great divide of superpower polarities, the late-capitalist, post-industrial, and post-modern societies will be characterized by the diasporic condition, the dissolution of national borders, and the intermingling of identities. This chapter will examine three origin and creation stories of the people known as Hui, or Muslim Chinese, to demonstrate that these ideas of hybridity and heterogeneity mark not only their ideas of ethnohistory, but also those of many other cultures. As such, these pre-modern myths are thoroughly *post-modern* in their contemporaneity.

At a geopolitical level, Samuel Huntington has argued that there will be a clash of civilizations, not nations, in the post-Cold War world. For Huntington, culture defines the fault lines along which civilizations are bound to conflict in the modern world. He writes:

The great divisions among humankind and the dominating source of conflict will be cultural. Nation states will remain the most powerful actors in world affairs, but the principal conflicts of global politics will occur between nations and groups of different civilizations. The clash of civilizations will dominate global politics. The fault lines between civilizations will be the battle lines of the future. (Huntington 1993b:22)

In this chapter, by examining the creation and origin myths of a very hybrid group belonging to a great Chinese civilization, that of the Muslims Chinese (or the Hui), I shall argue that Huntington's view of culture and civilization is fundamentally misguided and entirely unhelpful for understanding cultural nationalism and

ethnic conflict in the modern world, and I shall thus join a growing number of critics of Huntington's thesis.[1] I shall also argue that
Muslim Chinese myths of origin, as do many creation and origin
myths, show an inherent hybridity, and do not support nationalist
or cultural absolutist claims by Huntington and others.

The case of the Hui people is particularly critical to the 'clashed
civilizations' thesis. Huntington singles out Confucian and Islamic
civilizations as being fundamentally different to each other, and as
posing the greatest threat to the West. In all, Huntington (1993b:
25) identifies 'seven or eight major civilizations' in the contemporary world: Western (including Europe and North America), Confucian, Japanese, Islamic, Hindu, Slavic-Orthodox, Latin American,
'and possibly African'. The greatest threat to the West, Huntington
predicts, will come from the Islamic and Confucian civilizations,
and the possibility of their forming an anti-Western alliance is his
greatest fear. This was spelled out most fully in an earlier article,
'The Islamic–Confucian Connection' (Huntington 1993a:19–23),
in which he argued that the fundamental differences distinguishing European, Confucian, and Islamic (often glossed as 'Arab')
civilizations will lead to inevitable conflict and misunderstanding.
Consider, for example, the following statement:

European communities, in turn, will share cultural features that distinguish them from Arab or Chinese communities. Arabs, Chinese and Westerners, however, are not part of any broader cultural entity. They consti-
tute civilizations. A civilization is thus of the highest cultural grouping
of people and the broadest level of cultural identity people have short of
that which distinguishes humans from other species. It is defined both by
common objective elements, such as language, history, religion, customs,
institutions, and by the subjective self-identification of people. (Huntington 1993a:24)

What of the Muslim Chinese, however, who claim descent
from intermarriages between foreign Muslims (Arabs, Persians,

---

1. See particularly the rebuttal issue to Huntington in *Foreign Affairs* (Fall 1993),
    which contained critical readings by Fouad Ajami, Kishore Mahbubani,
    Robert Bartley, Liu Binyan, Jean Kirkpatrick, and others. Elsewhere, Rich-
    ard Cooper (1994:9) added to the growing critique by arguing that conflict
    arises not between cultures, but between rivals for political control, which
    occurs 'within as well as between civilizations'. Liu Binyan (1994:20) notes
    the so-called Confucian civilizations on either side of the Taiwan Strait have
    many more issues dividing them than ideologies uniting them.

and Turks) and Chinese in China over the course of the past 1,200 years? This, of course, raises the subsequent question of bicultural-ism and multiculturalism. If civilizations are defined by cultures that are fundamentally different from one another, what of those caught in between; or at the interstices of culture, language, history, religion, customs, and institutions; or in the transnational diaspora moving between these so-called civilizations? If Rey Chow (1993) is correct to say that the shifting cultures of the diaspora most char-acterize the post-modern condition, and that writing that diaspora is now our most daunting challenge, then the situation described by Huntington must apply to either the modern or pre-modern condition, where one might still imagine cultures and civilizations in relative isolation from each other. In his sweeping history of the Middle East, Bernard Lewis (1996) calls Islam the 'intermediate civilization' that rose between the remote culture of the East and Europe, between the ancient world and the modern. This interme-diacy is what gave the Middle East its dynamism, before the long decline after the 16th century. Perhaps it is the 'intermediacy' and cultural hybridity of the Hui that makes study of them so impor-tant for our contemporary predicament. The case of the Hui sug-gests that the Islamic and Confucian traditions at least have been interacting for more than a millennium. Huntington's dichoto-mous view becomes problematic when we consider that many of the most recent clashes in the post-Cold War era have been *within* cultures and civilizations, rather than *between* them, particularly when we consider Islam.[2]

Indeed, most of these so-called civilizations have been interact-ing and influencing each other across the ancient routes through-out Eurasia that linked East and West through what later became known as the Silk Road. Interestingly, one folklore scholar writing in Calcutta in the 1930s, Sir Jehangir Colverjee Coyajee (1936),

2. Charles Maier (1994:10) argues that the 'Islamic challenge (will) be one that is ultimately fought within the borders of its own civilization', which, although reifying 'Islamic' civilization, admits that the potential for conflict between Muslim groups is at least as great as tensions between Muslim and non-Muslim, as the Iran–Iraq and Gulf wars evidenced. The Malay Muslim scholar Chandra Muzaffar (1994) suggests that reifying 'Islamic' civiliza-tion as unified or predominantly Arab also neglects the fact that the largest Muslim populations today are spread across the multinational populations of South and Southeast Asia.

argued the early cults and legends of Iran and China were intricately intertwined. The Kubrawiyya Sufi order in Gansu is yet another example of Persian–Chinese interaction, with Iran believing so strongly that these early Sufi's came Persia that they are supporting the study of the son of the Kubrawiyya shaykh, Zhang Hairu, in Tehran.

The Muslim Chinese and other similarly interdependent groups (and in the modern world few are not so), will evidence the need for a more developed theory of folklore and mythology that takes into account not only the heterogeneity of culture, but also the contingency of identity in the modern nation-state. This is particularly critical for the next step of negotiation, which is not between cultures or civilizations, but between nation-states in a multipolar, decentered post-Cold War world. This is precisely the step that Huntington's remarkably facile theory of cultures and civilizations does not allow us to make; it is a theory that is surprisingly essentialist and dichotomous in a world where cultures and their folklores, peoples, and policies are increasingly fuzzy, interdependent, and mutually enmeshed.

It is interesting that earlier studies of the Muslim Chinese in China also took the Huntington absolutist position: that these people had to choose between two fundamentally opposite civilizations, Islamic or Chinese. Raphael Israeli's (1978, 1984) 'if you can't beat 'em, join 'em' thesis continues to pervade much of Western thinking about Muslims in China, who due to their diasporic predicament had two choices – rebel against the Chinese order and establish their own Islamic state, or assimilate. In fact, sometimes they did both, and at other times they did neither. This chapter, through examining some of their origin and creation myths, will seek to suggest why.

Standing exactly between Muslim and Chinese civilizations, the Hui become the perfect counter-example to Huntington's thesis that civilizations are fundamentally different and generally opposed. Many Hui and descendants of Hui in Taiwan and China, who comfortably worship their Muslim ancestors, raise pigs, and fully participate in southern Min Fujianese political culture, would object to the dichotomy of East/West, Muslim/Confucian, that Huntington finds so useful. Even the most conservative of Muslims in China have been influenced by (and influenced) the broader Chinese culture, as witnessed by their unique art form that combines both Arabic and Chinese calligraphic forms to represent Islamic, Daoist, Buddhist, and Confucian contents (see Gladney 1996a:264). Muslim Chinese dialogical interactions with Islam, formal and folk Chinese religious traditions, and Central and Southeast Asian cultural and economic connections have produced a vibrant cultural identity that cannot easily be placed in any category, although they continue to be labeled as Hui by themselves, their neighbors, and, in mainland China, the state, which has identified them as one of fifty-six *minzu* (official nationalities).[3]

Creating hybridity: human and Hui origins

Origin myths are generally thought to form the basis of truth of claims about the authenticity of a religion or a people. The Pan Gu myth, the Ramayana, the Mahayana, and story of Genesis (accepted by Christians, Jews, and Muslims) all become the basis for claims about ancestry, religious truth, and rights to land. They not only substantiate deeply held truths about the origins of the world, but generally say something about the people(s) that inhabit it. The story of Abraham's descent from Adam can be used today to justify Jewish claims to the land of Israel. According to many scholars, origin and creation myths are also used as basic 'charters' of ethnic and national authority. As charters for identity, origin and creation myths provide a sense of continuity with the past and assist adaptation to the changing social present. According to Bentley (1983: 9–10), charters are those shared texts, myths, rituals, or objects that are accepted and used primordially to refer to a group's distinctive identity. Judith Nagata (1981:111) writes: 'Charters of identity that draw on a (putative) notion of common blood, origin, descent, or kinship connection as a reason for being or acting may be labeled ethnic'. Origin and creation myths become the basis for claims to ethnic purity.

Many of the newer nations are founded on alternative myths of history, indigeneity, and independence that are employed to justify separatist visions. From Mao to Milosevic, modern nation-

---

3.   The multivocal and rather unfortunate term *minzu* is very problematic, especially when translating it into English. For a lengthy critique of the derivative origins of this term from Japanese, German, English, and traditional Chinese notions of peoplehood, nationhood, race, and ethnicity (all of which can be expressed by the single term *minzu*), see Gladney (1987b, 1996).

makers have turned to national folklores to support the manifest destinies of their people. In an excellent article detailing the rise of Japanese nationalism, Takashi Fujitani has shown that this 'folklore of a regime' is one of the primary ways states legitimate claims to land and history. Folklore scholars such as Uli Linke (1990:119) have documented the 'invention' of 'folk lore', the beginnings of the search for the 'lore' of the '*volk*' with German and other 19th-century romanticist attempts to describe the unity of their nation based on a common cultural and historical heritage that was reconstructed from relics of ancient traditions in German folk customs and narratives. Linke argues that there were two kinds of folklorists: 'romantic folklorists' sought unique myths of national purity to legitimate claims of national history and sovereignty; at the same time, 'administrative folklorists' sought to enhance the governing power of single German states by introducing the systematic collection and study of comparative mythology, such as comprehensive statistical surveys of local folk culture for 'knowing' the population.

Following this line of argument is Louis Snyder's classic study of the many nationalist elements found in the Grimm Brothers' fairy tales. Alan Dundes (1965) has shown how anthropological studies of folklore have helped to influence interpretations of contemporary identities. In his path-breaking research on Chinese minority folklore, Wolfram Eberhard (1965, 1970) has documented the role of the state in collecting and shaping minority mythologies and identities. Sandra Eminov (1972) has also explored links between folklore and nationalism in modern China. In China, the folklore of the regime has helped to invent, categorize, and homogenize the many folklores of its subjects (see Miller 1994). Yet few have examined how it is that minority folklore, especially that of the Hui, helps to contest received wisdoms about national and ethnic purity.

The use of folklore by religious and ethnic nationalists, and not a few racists, to invoke and legitimate claims to land and history is well known. Yet it has rarely been argued that a cursory examination of most charter origin and creation myths shows they are stories not of purity, but of hybridity, heterogeneity, and interconnectedness. Opposites attract in almost all the world's origin myths; out of that attraction emerges a newly synthesized creation: man/woman, nature/human, human/animal, matter/non-matter, spirit/flesh, light/dark, sun/moon, heaven/earth, mineral/organic, land/water, and other dialectically interacting forces (but not all of which are defined as dualities) are the basis for most myths of the world's and humankind's origins. This is expressed perhaps most elegantly in the Chinese belief in yin and yang, but it appears in most other creation and origin stories as the interacting of perceived opposites. Even in the extremely monotheistic tradition of Islam, more mystical traditions have emphasized this hybrid interactivity. The Mevlana mystic Jalaluddin Rumi once observed:

The sky keeps wandering (revolving) about the earth, just as men go about their occupations for the sake of their wives. Now this earth acts like a wife and exerts itself to bear children and to nurse them. Consequently, oh wise men, you must consider the sky and the earth as intelligent beings. If these two lovers (the sky and the earth) do not enjoy each other, why do they stick to each other like man and wife? (in Coyajee 1936:169)

Through the examination of three creation and origin myths among the Muslim Chinese, links to other creation myths from around the world will demonstrate this intrinsically hybrid nature of human and ethnic origins. The first myth follows.[4]

Adan and Haierma [5]

It is said that at the time of creation there were no human beings in the world. There was only Allah. His four Heavenly angels emerged from fire. They still had no definite form.

Allah considered it not much fun to exist like this, day in and day out. So he sent forth his first heavenly angel to fetch soil of five colors – red, yellow, blue, white, and black ... Allah was very pleased to see [the angel] return with the soil of five colors. He added some water to the soil, and from these elements he fashioned a man, lying down. God called him 'Adan', and he improved on him every day. He admonished him not to get up by himself. Nevertheless, as time passed Adan grew tired of just

---

4.   I have decided to select three myths from the 1994 Li and Luckert collection, not because it is authoritative, but because it made accessible to English readers for the first time a wide selection of Hui folklore and mythology. The collection is problematic, however, in that little research has been conducted as to the authenticity of each story reproduced. I have selected here three myths that are well known and that I frequently heard repeated during my three years of fieldwork among Muslims in China.

5.   From 'Adan and Haierma', reproduced in Li and Luckert (1994:79–82). Originally recorded by Zhang Wenbing in Heilongjiang, 1981.

lying down. He felt strong enough to rise up by himself. Therefore, one day, while Allah was momentarily absent, Adan tried to sit up.

'Oh, now I did it!' Adan's skull cracked open and his vital energies leaked out. Some of his soul-essence reached the mountains and become minerals of all sorts – gold, silver, copper, iron, tin, and others. Some of it went up into the sky and became birds of all kinds. Some reached the ground and became various animals. Some went to the rivers and lakes and became various kinds of fishes, turtles, shrimps, and crabs. Adan realized the danger he was in. He knew that if all his soul energy escaped he would die. With his left hand he hurriedly took some mud from the middle of the sole of his right foot, and he took some from the sole of his left foot with his right hand, to seal the crack on his head with mud.

That is why, nowadays still, man has a hollow arch at the bottom of both feet – because he took mud from there to seal the crack that opened on his skull …

After some time a mysterious lump appeared on Adan's third rib. It grew larger and larger. And no one knew how long it would be before the lump would erupt and a woman would come forth. And no one knew why Allah named her Haierma (Arabic: 'Hurma', meaning 'wife').

Adan noticed that Haierma was different from himself, and a sexual passion overcame him. He implored Allah that he be given a wife – and God agreed to let Haierma be that wife. Adan and Haierma were appointed to watch over the grain-fruit garden of paradise.

[After eating the forbidden fruit] both were severely scolded by Allah. To punish them, God caused the fruit in Adan's throat to protrude, as a reminder of his sin. The fruit inside Haierma was transformed in to menses. And then God separated them and placed Adan in the east and Haierma in the west. God made them miss each other, and they could not come together.

Adan had no idea where Haierma was, nor did Haierma know where Adan was. Every morning Haierma combed her hair by the sea. A swallow carried some of her loose hair to the place in the east where Adan was. Likewise, Adan washed his face every morning. The swallow carried the beard hair, which he had washed out, westward to Haierma. Observing the direction from which the swallow flew, Adan reasoned that Haierma must be in the west. Haierma, likewise, realized that Adan was in the east. So they started to seek each other in the direction of the swallow's path. Eventually they came together. As a result of their long separation they had developed a deep longing for one another …

Adan and Haierma, and their offspring, lived together at one place. They made much noise chatting and laughing. Allah became greatly annoyed by their hubbub. He therefore drove them to a place south of

Tianshan Mountain, in Xinjiang. These are the ones who became the ancestors of the Hui people.

In this version of the traditional Adam and Eve genesis story, Adam (or 'Adan') is formed out of the soil, but it is a soil that is already multicolored: red, yellow, blue, white, and black, suggesting the multi-ethnic and multiracial nature of their future progeny. The combination of inherently different spirit and matter produces flesh. Eve (his 'wife', or 'Hurma' in Arabic), in traditional Genesis fashion, emerges from Adam's rib, and their disobedient act of eating the forbidden fruit leads to their banishment, not from the garden of Eden, but from each other. This suggests a very early division between East and West as a result of humanity's refusal to live harmoniously with God and nature's demands – an environmentally determinist explanation for Huntington's civilizational conflict between East and West! The origins of the world's fauna and flora literally out of the mind of man suggests the creativity of the creature as well as the creator, although an inadvertent creativity.

The eventual reunion of Adan and Haierma leads to many progeny, so many that they again are banished to a new land, the second time they have been displaced as diaspora. This time they end up in Xinjiang (a name that did not belong to the region until the mid-19th century, suggesting a very recent version of the story), which seems to be equidistant between East and West, in the heart of Central Asia.

The Hui thus descend from the earliest humans, Adam and Eve, who are inherently hybrid, composed of many colorful elements, and from the beginning, diasporic, displaced from their home to a new land.

Here it is also important to note that despite this myth's differences from the biblical Adam and Eve story, the parallels are striking: earthen origins, male/female essential unity, asymmetry, and mutual attraction, banishment, and eventual migration to a promised land.

Legitimating hybridity: imperial imprimatur

In the new land in which they find themselves, immigrant peoples have always had to defend their right to be there. This is often accomplished through legitimating stories of assistance provided to

the hegemonic powers that be. In this classic story, the Hui recall
that they have come to China due to an imperial invitation.

Wan Gars [6]

One night the emperor of the Tang dynasty dreamt that the roof beam of
his golden palace was collapsing. The roof beam nearly smashed his head,
but it was intercepted and pushed back by the right hand of a man. The
man wore a green robe, and a white turban was wound around his head.
He had a towel draped over his shoulder and a water kettle in his left
hand. He had deep eye sockets, a high nose bridge, and a brown face.

The next day when the officials came to pay respect to the emperor, at
his court the emperor told his dream and asked for explanations.

Xu Mao stepped forward and said, 'The man is not a Han like we. He
is a Hui from the western regions. The green robe and white turban are
worn only for prayer when one goes to the mosque. The towel and the
water kettle are used to wash one's body. The great Tang empire needs the
Hui people for its defense.'

The emperor said, 'Then let us invite some Hui people to come here.'

Xu Mao said, 'We may not be able to persuade some to come by invitation, but perhaps by trading.'

The emperor said, 'What shall we give in exchange?'

'Exchange people for people.'

'All right, it shall be done!'

Upon their arrival the Tang emperor himself went to welcome them
outside the palace gate; he addressed Wan Gars as Brother ... Moreover,
the emperor ordered his high general, Jingde, to build a mosque where
Wan Gars could pray ...

Some time later the Tang emperor thought about the fact that the Hui
men who had come with Wan Gars were all single, without family. If in
the future they died, there would be no Huis to guard the Tang empire,
and that would be a big problem. So he held a grand ceremony and permitted the Hui to choose their mates. Since that time the Hui people
have been settled in China. Even nowadays there is this saying among the
Hui, 'Hui father, Han mother!'

Wan Gars is thought by the Hui to be none other than Wahb
Abu Kabcha, the cousin of Muhammad the Prophet, who intro-
duced Islam to China and is buried in the famous Bell Tomb in
Guangzhou, which bears the inscription '*Wangesi Mu*' (Grave of
Wan Gars). There are various legends of the origin of Hui and the

---

6. From 'Wan Gars', reproduced in Li and Luckert (1994:237–8). Originally
   recorded by He Jide, Xiji and Haiyuan in Ningxia Region, 1979.

arrival of Islam in China told by Hui from Beijing to Guangzhou. The most popular account is that the Tang emperor, Taizong, was disturbed by the appearance of a turbaned man chasing a phantom in a dream. His interpreter told him, 'The turbaned man is a Hui-hui of the West. In Arabia is a Muslim king of great virtue. A great sage is born, with favorable omens' (Leslie 1986:74). The emperor was so astounded by his dream and its import that he dispatched to the Arab lands an ambassador, who returned with three Muslim teachers. Impressed with the scientific knowledge and civility of these teachers, the emperor invited other Muslims to settle, build mosques, and propagate their faith. This legend is still repeated among the Hui, who share the common belief that Islam entered China during the Tang at the emperor's invitation.[7]

The veracity of this legend and other Chinese Muslim accounts of the early origin of Islam in China are discounted by Leslie (1986:60–78) and other historians. They reason that the majority of the tales result from 18th- and 19th-century Hui attempts at legitimation through reference to imperial approval and ancient origin. Drake (1943:23) concludes:

Nevertheless, the insistence upon the arrival of Mohammedanism as early as the T'ang dynasty; the suggestion of Mohammedan troops settling in north west China; and the account of the early beginnings of Mohammedanism in Canton, all reflect, however dimly, the actual facts.

For this study of ethnoreligious origin and creation myths, the legends are important in that they continue to represent agreed-upon notions of Hui heritage.

There are also local stories told about the origin of the Hui in various capital cities, such as Beijing. The following account describes the origin of the Beijing Oxen Street Muslims and is engraved on a tablet in the Niujie Mosque:[8]

In 996 A.D. a *Shai Hai* ['shaykh', elder] named Ge Wa Mo Ding came from the Western Regions (*xiyu*). This man often had strange dreams and

---

7. This legend is found in the anonymous 17th- or 18th-century *Huihui Yuanlai* (*The Origin of the Hui*) and reproduced in several Western accounts (Broomhall 1910:61–83; Deve'ria 1895:312–29; Leslie 1986:74; Mason 1929:46–53; Parker 1910:245–51; see also Tazaka 1964:193–8). A Soviet Dungan version is also discussed in Dyer (1981–83:545–70).

8. A version of this story is given in Wang Shoujie (1930:2); and the historical background is in Yang Yongchang (1981:60–2).

gave birth to three sons. The eldest, Sai De Lu Ding, could tell the good or evil surrounding different graves. He left home with no reason for some unknown place and never returned. The second, Na Su Lu Ding, could read other people's minds. The youngest, Che Ah Dou Ding, could speak the language of birds. The two younger sons lived in seclusion and refused several official posts offered to them. They became the Imam of the mosque and settled permanently in the East. They prophesied that Beijing would become a center of prosperity where emperors would reign over great causes. As a reward for their loyalty to the emperor, they were allowed to build mosques in the east of the city [the Dongsi Mosque] and in the south [the Niujie Mosque] and were given tombs inside the compound of the Niujie Mosque.

In the southeastern corner of the Niujie Mosque are two small tombs belonging to two shaykhs who came from the west and were buried in the mosque. Inscriptions over the grave record that the first belongs to Ah Ha Mai De (Ahmed), a Persian who died in AD 1280, and the second belongs to Ah Li (Ali), a Bukharan, buried in AD 1283 (Yang Yongchang 1981:61). While these graves are not patronized like those of Muslim saints in the northwest (see Chapter 7), they do represent the foreign origins of Chinese Islam to the Oxen Street Hui. I never saw anyone praying in front of the graves, nor was there incense lit for them, but on several occasions after prayer an elderly Hui would take me back to the graves and repeat the legend about these two saints and the arrival of Islam in Beijing.[9] An erudite Hui physician in Shanghai explained: 'I know I am a Chinese citizen and my home is China. However, I also know that, before migrating here from Henan, my earliest ancestors came from the west and were Muslim. This knowledge was handed down to me from my parents and, although I do not practice Islam, I shall continue to pass it on to my children'.

The legitimacy of this hybrid and diasporic ancestry is maintained by a people who believe they were invited into China by the emperor and provided invaluable assistance to him. While their foreign origin has led many to believe that they will return, and thus the popular belief about the origins of their name (*Hui*, 'to return'), their 1,200-year history in China suggests otherwise.

9. Note that the second son, Na Su La Ding, bears resemblance to the famous Yuan-dynasty official Nasredin (also Na Su Lu Ding), the supposed ancestor of the Hui in Na village, Ningxia, and of the Ding in Chendai, Fujian (see Gladney 1996a).

Maintaining hybridity: marriage and miscegenation

A fundamental question for any immigrant community is the maintenance of identity and uniqueness in the context of being a minority population. Diaspora denies the possibility of pure endogamy and exclusivity. To survive, the community must find some way to justify out-marriage and diversity. The following story suggests one possibility for the Hui in China.

The Hui people of Lingzhou [10]

It has been said that during the reign of the emperor Tang Xuanzong, the general An Lushang rose up in rebellion. The emperor had to seek refuge in Lingzhou. At that time Guo Ziyi was the commander in chief who led the Tang army against the rebel forces. Because Guo Ziyi's army was not large enough, he had to go and borrow some soldiers from the Huihe people. The requirements put forth by the Huihe people was that Guo give ten Han people in exchange for one Huihe soldier. Guo Ziyi complied with their demands because he was in dire need. And so, three thousand Han people were given in exchange for three hundred Huihe soldiers.

The battle lasted a long time. An Lushang was finally defeated and Chang'an was recaptured. The Huihe soldiers suffered heavy casualties during that battle. Only Wan Gars and the two others were left. The Tang emperor was very appreciative toward them. He asked them to remain in Chang'an and rewarded them with high positions and handsome salaries …

One of the ministers said the Huihe soldiers would settle down only if they married some Han girls. But other ministers said that not a single Han father would agree to give his daughter in marriage to a Huihe soldier. There was only one way for them, and that was to take their brides by force. The Tang emperor thought this over and decided to let the Huihe soldiers take brides by force, during the Lantern Festival …

The emperor told the three Huihe men, 'Tonight the streets will be very much alive. Surely, there will be many pretty girls in the crowd. You may go and take them by force. Those taken by you will be your wives.'

The three men were happy to hear the emperor's words. They took to the street and there took by force whomever seemed beautiful to them. That night each of them carried away nine girls. Inasmuch as they had taken away that many girls – in accordance with his own permission – the emperor had to accept the outcome as an accomplished fact. Each of the

---

10. From 'The Hui People of Lingzhou', reproduced in Li and Luckert (1994: 240–2). Originally recorded by Na Jianggao, in Wuzhong, Ningxia, 1979.

three Huihe soldiers was permitted to have nine beautiful girls as wives so long as he agreed to settle down in Chang'an.

Here we have the other side of the coin: the violence of having emigrant diasporic communities in our midst. Only through state-sanctioned rape, this story suggests, can this community survive. In the interests of national defense, the dignity of the emperor's female subjects is offered to the Hui mercenaries. The story indicates that relations, even at the very beginning, between Hui and Han were not always peaceful. Han women did not willingly go with the foreign soldiers; they had to be forced.

The history of Muslim and non-Muslim relations in China has not always been peaceful. The 19th and early 20th centuries were marked by rebellions and violent protests. My book (Gladney 1996a) has also indicated ongoing tensions and eruptions of inter-ethnic violence (see also Lipman 1991). Indeed, most non-Muslims have very different explanations of Hui origins and they are not always kind. Many Chinese stories ridicule the Muslims for their Islamic customs, which seem strange to the Chinese, particularly the pork taboo.

Among the vast majority of urban Hui and Han I surveyed during my three years of field research in China, the primary distinction noted between the two peoples was pork avoidance. This issue, while of real concern to Hui in the northwest, is not as paramount there as it is in the city. In the northwest, Muslims are numerous. The Han are familiar with Hui customs and generally are sensitive to actions that might provoke the Hui. In most villages that are either Han or Hui the issue is almost non-existent. In Ningxia's Luo village, where there is an almost even mixture of Hui and Han, the Hui households tend to be adjacent to one another. Han are careful to keep their pigs in the yards, and while mistakes do happen, people are aware of the issue and try to be sensitive.

At the other end of the spectrum, there are southeastern Hui lineages in Fujian and Guangdong who are not very concerned about the pork issue. It only becomes an issue for them when outside conservative Hui or foreign Muslims visit their village. Suggestions have been made that they cease raising pigs, but they have been doing so for centuries and there is no easy substitute. In the southern cities, where Hui are few, there is generally less concern over *qing zhen* violations. Hui identity depends on lineage and ancestry, not on cultural maintenance. At one of the two Hui restaurants in Xiamen, which opens onto the street like most small southern cafés, I paused to look at the menu. A Han came up beside me and set down his bundle before walking in and ordering a bowl of noodles. It was only when I decided to go in and had to step over his bundle that I realized he had left a pole with large, freshly butchered cuts of pork tied to either end. This would have incited a riot in the northwest and at least an altercation in most northern cities. My local Hui friend simply shrugged his shoulders and said there was no way to avoid it.

Han often cannot understand why the Hui are so over-concerned about pork. For them, it is meat, the basic protein everyone craves. One Han said to me, 'The Hui avoidance of pork doesn't make sense. They are like vegetarian Buddhist monks, but do not obtain any merit for giving up the meat'. This misunderstanding is the subject of many ethnic tales and jibes told about why the Hui do not eat pork. I never heard these stories in the northwest, but encountered them frequently in cities when I mentioned I was studying the Hui.

The most popular is that the Hui abstain from pork out of filial respect for their ancestors, who at some time intermarried with a pig.[11] A Chengdu truck-driver once recited the following slur to me regarding Hui ancestry:

Monkey for a brother	*Hou didi*
Dog for a grandmother	*Gou nainai*
A pig for their	*Zhu shi ta de*
Ancestral tablet	*Zuxian pai*

While the PRC government has gone to great lengths to correct these traditional ethnic biases, long-held ethnic stereotypes still find their way into print. A nationwide protest of Hui was sparked in Chengdu when a local newspaper published a cartoon of a Hui bowing down next to a pig during prayer. In a brief *Youth News* article (31 December 1982), the Shanghai editor responded to a question regarding the difference between Hinduism and Islam.

11. Pillsbury (1973:273) records a Hui origin myth to which they refer in response to derogatory Han tales about Hui ancestry. Hui say that they are descended from the filial son of Adam, who did not eat pork. The unfilial son ate pork, and he is the earliest ancestor of the Han.

Hinduism, he wrote, is more glorious (*guangrong*) than Islam: 'In Islam, one hand holds the sword while the other holds the Quran'. He later noted that the Muslims revere the pig, and that is why they do not eat pork. That afternoon several calls were made to the mosque and the City Commission for Nationality Affairs (CNA). Many Hui went to the office of the publisher to complain, and letters poured in. In the next issue the weekly *Youth News* published a formal apology, and on 13 January the newspaper went to press a day early to reveal on the front page that the twenty-nine-year-old editor had been fired (a rarity in China) and the seventeen-year-old writer severely reprimanded. The article, it stated, 'hurt Muslim religious feelings, was not beneficial to nationality unity [*minzu tuanjie*] and had a very bad influence'.[12] A cadre from the City CNA explained to me that while the writers were too young to understand (*qingnian bu dong shi*), this is still unacceptable in China today. In more recent years the State Commission for Ethnic Affairs has attempted to incorporate more ethnic awareness into its elementary curriculum; in 1985 it published 'nationality general knowledge' (*minzu changshi*) materials for middle-school students, which stressed mutual respect and understanding for cultural differences.

Just as marrying Han out of necessity and against the will of the Han women to survive as Muslims in a foreign land is explained in the myth recorded above, various local Hui groups have stories to explain the times when they have been forced to eat pork against their will. In Fujian and in Taiwan, various Hui lineages have continued to maintain the pork taboo in ancestor worship when they could not do so in their daily lives. While modern Ding and Guo lineage members might not be able to read their genealogies in classical Chinese, or explain why they cannot eat or use pork on ritual holidays, they are reminded regularly that their ancestors are different, and thus so are they by maintaining ritual remembrance of them (see Gladney 1996a: Chapter 6). Pu Zhenzong in 1940 told his interviewers that even though he was no longer Muslim, he was descended from Muslims, and that 'the Pu family has had a secret custom – never offer pork in ancestor worship' (Zhang 1940:2).

12. For similar denigrating ethnic stereotypes directed toward the Hui in Taiwan, and ensuing eruptions of conflict, see Pillsbury (1974:11–14).

Ding lineage members in Fujian have maintained this taboo against pork during ancestral rituals for centuries, but they do not proscribe pork for their own consumption. They have an explanation for this in the form of an often-told legend, which was related to me as follows:

Our ancestors were very sincere Muslims. At the time of our eleventh-generation ancestor, Ding Qirui, who served during the Ming dynasty as a government secretary in the Ministry of Justice, he was accused with a trumped-up charge of attempting to usurp the throne of the emperor. Because of this the emperor attempted to exterminate the Ding family. The main mark of the Ding family was their being Muslims. In order to save their lives, the Ding family could not 'practice Islam (religion) for a hundred generations' (*Baidai Zhanyang*). Thus, at that time we began to eat pork and became assimilated to the Han (*tonghua*).

This is the same story, almost word for word, told to the investigation team that interviewed the Chendai Hui man Ding Deqian in February 1940 (Zhang 1940:2). It has become an accepted text that explains the reason for the Ding Hui leaving Islam and eating pork. In the 1940 interview, as well as in mine, the Ding members explained that the phrase 'practice Islam for a hundred generations' is taken from an inscription on a wooden tablet on the front of their lineage temple, parallel to another inscription on the temple itself: 'pacify ourselves for future success' (*suiwo sicheng*).[13] In both interviews, the Ding speakers pointed out that the structure of their ancestral temple was built in the shape of the Chinese character for *Hui*, a small square within a larger one, signifying they are of the Hui. Most Han ancestral halls have covered corridors connecting the hallways on the perimeter with the main hall in the center of the courtyard. The absence of these corridors is the one feature that differentiates their hall from most other Han lineage halls.

That so much emphasis is placed upon the legend, legitimizing the use of pork by these Hui, illustrates the ritual significance

13. Ding share the belief that they are descended from the Nasredin, the son of Sai Dianchi, the famous governor of Yunnan, Sichuan, and Shaanxi during the Yuan dynasty. They say that the third characters of both texts cited above, when put in alignment, are the characters '*zhan si*', the Chinese personal name of Nasredin (Ding Zhansi), indicating a hidden reflection of their foreign ancestry in the inscriptions over the entrance to their ancestral hall. Note that both the Na and Ding lineages claim descent from the same foreign Muslim ancestor.

that the community attaches to violation this taboo. In addition to Hui Islamic concerns, Fujianese traditions of totemic prestation may play a role. In a fascinating article, Stuart Thompson (1988) has argued that the early use of a pig's head as the central part of food prestation may indicate the primary role of pork in the elementary structures of Taiwanese ritual. I was struck on several occasions when Fujianese locals mentioned the common belief that the reason Hui did not eat pork was that their earliest ancestor had mated with a pig. One Hui from the Baiqi Guo lineage village told me another story that the Hui may have also descended from a donkey, because they also proscribed horseflesh in diet and ritual, and that early Hui 'temples' often had an image, hidden in the wall behind the altar, of a donkey copulating with a man. This fantastic tale is rendered highly suspect because the Hui who related it was a member of a branch of the Guo lineage that had converted to Christianity in the 1920s, long after they had assimilated to Fujianese folkways, and he may have had reason to want to criticize Hui Muslim practices. Nevertheless, it illustrates the common pervasive belief in the close relationship between food taboo and ancestry in the Fujian cultural region. Similarly, I have seen genealogical pictorial portfolios belonging to the She minority, native to the Wu Mountains, which illustrated their own belief that they are descended from the union of a dog and human. Many of their ritual garments contain totemic representations of the dog. This is also present among many Southeast Asian groups, including the Yao. It is not surprising that many such ethnic stories thought derisive and offensive to Hui ancestry should originate in this area.

Betwixt and between

The hybridity of the Hui, the fact that they live in China, speak Chinese, but believe in Islam, generally do not eat pork, often look different (as noted in the Wan Gars legend on page 108), and believe in a separate ancestry from the Han majority has put them in a difficult place, between two worlds, East and West, Muslim and Chinese. Owen Lattimore (1950:119 n.20) noted Hui hybridity as that which made them suspect to Muslim and non-Muslim alike: they were not considered fully Muslim nor fully Chinese by many of their Central Asian neighbors.

This hybridity has been part of the Hui history throughout their 1,200 years in China and has been legitimated in their charters of origin. The Hui myths of origin and creation have helped us to understand how one 'interstitial' minority has attempted to influence and redefine Chinese national culture. This contradicts Huntington's and other essentialist views of pure Chinese and Islamic civilizations. It incorporates Tu Weiming's (1991) notion of a greater cultural Chineseness that is multicultural, heterogeneous, and diasporic. In Professor Tu's conception, the Hui can be fully Muslim and Chinese – there need not be a contradiction.

More importantly, studies have suggested that Han identity, broadly represented as homogeneous and unified, is rapidly breaking apart along cultural and regional lines of local expression (see Friedman 1994). It is now popular to be Cantonese and Shanghainese in China, and a resurgence of local power-bases, often drawn along cultural fault lines, should give Huntington pause: not only was he wrong about Muslim homogeneity, but he is misinformed about Confucian continuity as well. Hong Kong-based triads are no respecter of their fellow Confucians in Beijing if the mainlanders refuse to cooperate with the expanding operations of the triads. Huntington was correct about cultural fault lines, however, for power often flows along them. He was incorrect to essentialize culture according to general categories of civilizations without regard for cultural redefinition in dialogic interaction with significant others in the context of the modern nation-state. The case of the Hui helps to disestablish widespread beliefs about Han and Muslim homogeneity.

Yet with the rise of Chinese nationalism, modern myth-makers have begun to again look to purists myths of descent from a 'Yellow Emperor' to unite the Chinese diaspora into one greater Cultural China. This has led to fears of Chinese nationalism and expansionism from the Taiwan Strait to the South China Sea, and beyond China's borders to Southeast Asia, Central Asia, and Siberia. China, for many political scientists in the West, has become the next 'evil empire', destined to replace the former Soviet Union, but an empire based on race and civilization, not communist ideology. Huntington's theory has begun to surface even in recent science–fiction novels that portray a Chinese takeover of the universe. As we would expect, this futurist empire involves a rewriting of historical myth:

Pan Chao! It sometimes seemed as if half the films ever made had been about Pan Chao! He was the great hero of Chung Kuo – the soldier turned diplomat turned conqueror. In A.D. 73 he had been sent, with thirty-six followers, as ambassador to the king of Shen Shen in Turkestan … bringing Shen Shen under Han control … Over the next twenty-four years, by bluff and cunning and sheer force of personality, Pan Chao had brought the whole of Asia under Han domination. In A.D. 97 he had stood on the shore of the Caspian Sea, an army of seventy thousand vassals gathered behind him, facing the great *Ta Ts'in*, the Roman Empire. The rest was history, known to every schoolboy.

Rome had fallen. And not as Kim had portrayed it, to Alaric and the Goths in the fifth century, but to the Han in the first. There had been no break in order, no decline into darkness. No Dark Ages and no Christianity – oh, and what lovely idea *that* was: organized religion! The thought of it …

In his version of events, Han science had stagnated by the fourth century A.D. and Chung Kuo had grown insular, until, in the nineteenth century, the Europeans – and what a strange ring that phrase had; not *Hung Mao*, but 'Europeans' – had kicked the rotten door of China in.

Ah, and that too. Not *Chung Kuo*. Kim called it China. As if had been named after the First Emperor's people, the Ch'in. Ridiculous!

He shrugged. 'I suppose you might call it an alternative history of Chung Kuo. Chung Kuo as it might have been had the Ta Ts'in legions won the Battle of Kazatin.' (Wingrove 1990:439–54)

However, this futurist vision of Han Chinese conquest, which pits the Han against the 'Hong Mao' (the 'red-haired' Caucasians), runs counter to myths of hybridity and diaspora as found among the Hui.

A final story reminds us that Hui and other minority communities can exist for centuries without being taken seriously by the state that rules them or the scholars who study them.

Do not listen to the Hui [14]

It was said that during the height of the Tang dynasty, the Tang emperors sent diplomatic envoys to western regions, and vice versa. They got along peacefully.

One year some Hui people were sent from the Western regions, to do missionary work. The Tang emperor permitted them to settle and to marry Han girls, in Chang'an.

---

14. Reproduced in Li and Luckert (1994:249). Originally recorded by Zhao Zhibin, Gansu, 1983.

After they had gotten married, the Hui and Han lived together happily, loving and respecting one another. When the girls returned to the home of their parents to visit, they were asked, 'How do you like the Hui people?'

The girls answered, 'The Hui people are kind, and their food is good, but their language is difficult to understand.'

Their parents said: 'As long as your husband is kind, and as long as the two of you can get along well, as far as the language is concerned you do not need to listen to him.'

So for a thousand years Hui and Han, in the north and west, have addressed each other as Aunt and Uncle. There is also a saying that spread: 'Eat Hui food; there is no need to listen to Hui words.'

Perhaps now more than ever, as the world becomes more divided along essentializing lines, leading to ethnic-cleansing campaigns and exclusivizing majorities, we need the to listen to the multicultural and hybrid mythologies of the Hui. Their notions of intermediacy, tolerance, and mutuality have much to tell us about the fullness and diversity of Chinese civilization, as well as the interconnectedness and interdependence of all human beings.

7

LOCALIZATION AND TRANSNATIONAL PILGRIMAGES

Defining the Hui

Understanding of the ethnic identity of the Hui minority, recognized by the Chinese government as the largest of ten nationalities whose traditional religion is Islam, is often distracted by approaches that, in the interest of fitting them into the larger context of Muslim studies, often leave us with little knowledge of who the Hui are and what their major community interests are. Discussion of Hui identity has often revolved around comparison and contrast with a general notion of Islam, which tends to either subsume ethnic to religious identity (the Hui as Muslims in China), or treat Islam as dependent on cultural, social, or economic variables (the Hui as Chinese Muslims). At the same time, reference to the Hui as an important part of Chinese society – living in more than 90 percent of all counties and in every major city in China – has been almost wholly absent from the anthropological literature on Chinese society.[1] This neglect has continued despite the assertions of commentators such as Dreyer (1976:3–5) and Shichor (1984) that the Hui are playing a more appreciable role in China's international relations. Pillsbury (1976:2) has suggested that this hiatus in Western literature has perhaps been influenced by the Han opinion, sometimes encountered in China, in which the Hui are regarded as merely Han who do not eat pork and, therefore, as undeserving of serious academic study – evidence of a lingering 'great Han ethnocentrism' (da Hanzu zhuyi) that is condemned by the Chinese government.

---

1. Fried's (1969) excellent ethnography of a Chinese city hardly mentions the large community of Hui who lived in the area, mainly because he was not allowed into the mosque.

In this chapter I would like to shift discussion away from considerations of whether the Hui are really Muslim or merely inheritors of a cultural tradition somewhat different from the Han majority. Instead, I propose to examine one important area of interest to Hui communities throughout China that will help lead to better understanding of their identity. Of critical importance to the Hui are the lore and events surrounding various tombs and shrines in many communities. During my nearly three years of fieldwork among the Hui in several localities throughout China, I collected data on Hui tombs that may be divided for analytical purposes into historic, Sufi, and local tombs. The activities and discourse surrounding these tombs reveal much about current Hui concerns and identity in China. Historic tombs reflect concerns that put local Hui identity in an international perspective; Sufi tombs link Hui in national networks but often divide them locally; and local tombs evoke interests that are more communal, reflecting practical concerns and personal identities. While these tombs may not be relevant to all Hui and will be interpreted differently, it is my thesis that they continue to serve as powerful frameworks for personal identity and social action, which both distinguish Hui communities from one another and provide important charters for their corporate identity.

Historic tombs and international prominence

Historic tombs are among those monuments preserved by the Chinese government's State Bureau of Cultural Relics, and generally belong to foreign Muslim or famous Hui personages buried on Chinese soil. These include the various tombs and monuments erected to the supposed Muslims who served as officials, military officers, and merchants from the Southern Song through the Ming and Qing dynasties (12th through 19th centuries), and are buried in special graveyards in southern China, especially Quanzhou, Guangzhou, and Yangzhou. Historic tombs also hold the graves of Hui who played major roles in China's development and interaction with the West, including Zheng He, Hai Rui, Sai Dianchi (Sayid Edjell), Li Zhi, and, more recently, the Panthay rebellion leader Du Wenxiu (Atwill forthcoming).

The arguments of Chinese historians over whether certain historical figures like Hai Rui or Li Zicheng were Muslims has little bearing on this chapter.[2] More important is the recognition by the Chinese government of the significant role these individuals played in the development of China, which is important for Hui self-understanding. Many Hui look to these historic figures as foreign Muslim ancestors who provide proof that they are descendants of a high religious and cultural tradition. This knowledge is also playing an important role in Hui interaction with government foreign policy and in a growing awareness of their place in international affairs (see Chapter 15).

Along the southern coast of China there are large lineages of Hui communities for whom this foreign Muslim ancestry is critical to ethnic identity. In Quanzhou, the ancient international port of Zaitun that flourished from the Tang to the Ming dynasties (7th through 14th centuries), a typical response to a question I often asked about Hui ancestry was:

Of course I know my family are descended from foreign Muslims. My ancestor was an Arab, and our name was changed to Jin in the Ming dynasty. We have our family genealogy to prove it ... We are Hui because we are descended from these Muslim ancestors. (Jin family interview, 16 May 1984)[3]

This interview was conducted in a Hui household that openly includes pork as a part of its diet and practices Chinese folk religious traditions in the worship of its ancestors. The family was only recognized in the early 1980s by the State Commission for Ethnic Affairs as belonging to the Hui nationality due to research sponsored by the local Quanzhou Historical Research Society on the collected genealogies of several Hui lineages.[4]

The historic tombs of these Arab and Persian ancestors are playing an increasingly important role in the process of interaction between Hui identity and government foreign policy. In an open bid to gain diplomatic favor with wealthy Muslim nations, the Chinese

2. For the discussion on these individuals, see Bai Shouyi (1947); Bai Shouyi and Yang Huaizhong (1988); Chen Sadong (1975); Pei Zhi (1959).
3. See Huang and Liao (1983) regarding the changing of the surnames of several Hui lineages in Quanzhou during the Ming dynasty. Bai and Ma (1958) discuss the background for this discriminatory policy.
4. For further discussion on this process of ethnic identification and manipulation among the Hui in Quanzhou, see Gladney (1995; 1996:261–92).

government in 1979 declared the Ashab Mosque in Quanzhou (founded in AD 1009–10), and the Lingshan Muslim tombs outside the city, historic monuments. Substantial funds were given by the state, provincial, and city governments for the restorations of these structures, to the extent that now the Lingshan tombs have been refurbished and rededicated with a large tract of land and a sign at the entrance proclaiming 'Lingshan Holy Islamic Tombs'.

The Lingshan tombs are primarily those of two Muslim saints, said to be descendants of the Prophet Muhammad, who were buried there before the Yuan dynasty. According to He Qiaoyun's *Minshu*, the two Muslim saints buried in Quanzhou are imams Sayid and Waggas from Medina. These were two of four foreign Muslims said to have visited southern China during Emperor Wu De's reign in the Tang dynasty (618–626).[5] Fujian provincial and local municipal publications proudly proclaim Quanzhou as the site of the third most important Islamic holy grave and the fifth most important mosque in the world.[6] With this kind of publicity and state support, it is no surprise that the new international airport in nearby Xiamen was built in 1980, largely with Kuwaiti funds. In this regard, the government policy of promoting these Islamic monuments to attract investment has been relatively successful.

Unforeseen developments have arisen, however, in the changing identity of the local Hui communities. Until 1979 the several lineages of Ding, Jin, Huang, Pu, and Guo were not recognized officially as members of the Hui nationality, even though they have claimed to be Hui since before 1949 (Zhang and Jin 1940). This refusal to recognize these lineages as Hui derived from a complex combination of state policies and traditional ideas that identified as Hui only those people who were culturally Muslim and generally abstained from pork. Based on investigations into the genealogies of these Quanzhou lineages, which demonstrated that they are indeed descended from foreign Muslim ancestors, the State Commission for Ethnic Affairs, in conjunction with the China Islamic Society,

5. Wahb Abu Kabcha is said to be buried in the Guangzhou's famous Bell Tomb. The fourth saint is buried in Yangzhou, and over the entrance to the tomb, which was being restored when I visited in May 1984, was displayed a Chinese epithet proclaiming the foreign origin of Islam: 'The Dao Originates in Western Lands' (*Dao Yuan Xi Tu*). See Liu and Chen (1962).

6. For a more detailed account of the background of these tombs, see Chen Erjin (1984); Quanzhou Foreign Maritime Museum (1983).

agreed to recognize them as members of the Hui nationality. They thus found themselves in the position of recognizing as Hui a group of people who raised pigs, knew little of Islam, and were active participants in Chinese folk religious rituals.

While this recognition is consistent with the present government policy of distinguishing clearly between the Hui ethnic group and the Islamic religion, it was an embarrassment and source of tension for many conservative Hui Muslims. As a result, the China Islamic Society authorized funds to send four trained imams (*ahongs*, from the Persian *Akhun[d]*) from the Ningxia Hui Autonomous Region as teachers and missionaries to help educate the local Fujian Hui in their proper Muslim tradition. The government supported this effort in order to avoid the difficult position of having to escort foreign Muslim dignitaries to some of the earliest Muslim communities in China, who no longer engaged in Islamic practices. Post-1979 policies of 'freedom of religion' are now even more vividly evident to visiting Muslims. The Hui in Fujian are not only free to believe, but they are encouraged to do so.

The local Hui have not been passive, but are taking advantage of this change in their status. They have requested and received large state educational, agrarian, and industrial development grants (Gladney 1985:23–6). The historic tombs at Lingshan have become a focal point in this ethnic resurgence. Significantly, the Ding clan moved its lineage graves to Lingshan Hill in 1980, claiming ancestral ties to the foreign Muslims. They received provincial and state aid for the relocation. Other Hui lineages along the southern Chinese coast from Hainan Island to Wenzhou, Zhejiang Province, have been making similar claims to descent from foreign Muslims, to the extent that the size of the Hui population in the three provinces of Guangdong, Fujian, and Zhejiang has increased far beyond 51,344, the number recorded at the time of the 1982 census ('Twenty-Nine Provinces, Cities and Autonomous Regions Population', 1984, *Minzu Tuanjie* 2:38–9; 3:46–7).

A Hui friend pointed out to me the grave of his ancestor while standing in the Hui cemetery just above the Lingshan tomb complex. He described how his original surname was changed from Pu to Huang, (or in some cases Wu) out of fear of persecution for being associated with the Muslim Pu family. Many of his ancestors inscribed Huang or Wu on the front of the tombstone and Pu on the back (see Quanzhou 1983:218). 'Our yearly rituals honoring our Hui ancestors have finally paid off ...' he noted. 'Now the government has recognized us as Hui.'

The historic Muslim tombs in Lingshan, Quanzhou, as well as in Yangzhou and Guangzhou, are important reference points for modern Hui self-understanding as descendants of foreign Muslim ancestors. The growing Muslim identity of the Fujian Hui in interaction with changing sociopolitical conditions and government policy reveals an interesting dialectical process that is the basis for ethnic change (Keyes 1981:18, 25).[7] These lineages have always maintained a Hui identity that is only now, in conjunction with recent events, beginning to take on a decidedly Islamic commitment. The historic Hui tombs take on added international significance in the government effort to make use of them in their developing relations with Middle Eastern governments. These tombs have become objects of ethnic tourism and pilgrimage by foreign Muslims, as well as urban and northwest Hui who wish to explore their 'roots'. Hui minority cadres who are Communist Party members often make a point of visiting historic Muslim tombs, such as the large monument and public park built to the father of Zheng He, south of Dianchi lake in Yunnan, which affirms the ethnic heritage from which they are descended.[8]

Sufi tombs and transnational networks

Early-20th-century missionaries and travelers who visited centers of northwest Hui Islam often reported the importance of various tombs and shrines. Claude L. Pickens writes of his visit to Ma Hualong's tomb in Zhangjiachuan, Gansu:

To say in Kansu and Ningsia that one has visited this place means much in friendship among Moslems in the northwest and most parts of China. The outstanding characteristic of this Order in its several ramifications is the reverence which its members give to their leaders, who, one might say, act as mediators between man and Allah. (Pickens 1937:416)

Misunderstanding of the meaning of these tombs to various Hui communities and the Sufi orders attached to many of them

7. See Nagata (1981:112) for the relevance of this dialectic in her study of the identity of Malay Muslims.
8. For the relevance of tourism to ethnic change, see Adams (1984); E. Cohen (1979); Grayburn (1977); Greenwood (1972); Smith (1977).

often led early observers to label these Hui to be a sect of 'tomb worshippers' and polytheists. For example, Trippner (1961), in his analysis of 'grave-worshipping cults' in China's northwest, argues that they are all Shi'ite in origin and speculates that the religious tradition of Islam in China may also have originated wholly in the Shi'ite branch of Islam. The tombs have continued to spark debate in China as to the nature and legitimacy of the various Islamic orders that either venerate or denounce them. Jonathan Lipman (1994) has demonstrated how the late-19th-century reforms of the Yihewani (Ikhwan) in China pointedly proscribed the veneration of these tombs and the practice of following Sufi saints. The conflicts surrounding the tombs and their followers reflects an ongoing debate in China over what is orthodox in Islam, evidencing an important disjunction between interpretations that lean toward 'scripturalist' or 'mystical' positions. Literature produced by Hui Muslims in China during the 17th and 18th centuries also reflects this debate (see Leslie 1981).

In a similar fashion, the study of Southeast Asian Islam has often centered on the contradiction and compromise between the native culture of the indigenous Muslims and the sharia of orthodox Islam, the mystical and scriptural, the real and the ideal (see Roff 1985:8–10). The supposed compromise of the tenets of orthodox Islam to local cultural practices has led to the use of concepts such as syncretism to somehow explain the phenomenon. Sinification (or Sinicization) has been the term used to describe this process among the Hui (Pillsbury 1974:8–20, 264–74). An alternative approach, and one perhaps more in tune with the interests of Hui themselves, sees this incongruity as the basis for ongoing dialectic tensions, which often lead to reform movements and conflicts within the Muslim communities (see Eickelman 1976:10–13; Gladney 1996a:59–62; Kessler 1978:19–20). Following Weber (1952, 1958, for example), these studies seek to understand the wide variety of Islamic expression as reflecting processes of local world construction and programs for social conduct by which a world religion becomes meaningful to an indigenous society (Geertz 1968:97; Eickelman 1978:12).

Contemporary economic and sociopolitical upheavals were important impetuses for the important movements and reforms taking place within Islam in China. The source of much of their power and effectiveness among Hui Muslims, however, lay in

internal conflicts over incongruity between the state of Islam as
it was and as it should have been in the eyes of the reformers. The
early communities of Muslims in China were descended from
the original Arab, Persian, Central Asian, and Mongolian Muslim
merchants, officials, and soldiers who settled in China in large and
small numbers from the 7th to the 14th centuries (see Ma Qicheng
1983). Generally residing in independent small communities clustered around a central mosque, they became known as the Gedimu
(from the Arabic *qaidim*, 'old'), and practiced traditional Sunni,
Hanafi Islam, in contrast to the 'new' Sufi reform movements.[9]
Different Islamic factions reflecting ethnic and regional diversity
within Chinese Islam existed from its inception.[10] However, Sufi
reform movements did not begin to make a substantial impact in
China until the late 17th century, in what Joseph Fletcher (1995)
called the 'second tide' of Islam's entrance into China. Many of
these Sufi movements developed into socioeconomic and politico-
religious institutions built around descendants of early Sufi saintly
leaders known as *menhuan*, the 'leading' or 'saintly' lineages.[11] While
the scope of this chapter does not allow for the sorting out of the
history and distribution of these Sufi *menhuan* and the tombs important to them, Fletcher's cogent introductory discussion of their
development is worth citing:

Over the course of the eighteenth, nineteenth, and early twentieth centuries a considerable number of these 'saintly lineages' came into being

9.   The misleading distinction between Islamic factions known as 'old sect'
     (*laojiao*) and 'new sect' (*xinjiao*) were unfortunate attempts by Chinese
     officials, and later Western scholars (Israeli 1978:155–80), to distinguish
     between conflicting Hui factions that were involved in the many 19th-
     century Hui rebellions, much as 'White Lotus' was used as a generic label for
     Buddhist sectarian movements of the same period (Harrell and Perry 1982:
     283–305). See Yang Huaizhong (1981, 1988); Lipman (1981:134–9); Chu
     (1955); Gao (1985:245–61); Gladney (1996a).
10. See the interesting inquiry by Chen Dasheng (1983:53–64) into Islamic
     factional disputes that led to the ten-year Isbah disturbance in Quanzhou at
     the end of the Yuan dynasty (14th century).
11. *Menhuan* is the Chinese technical term describing the socioeconomic and
     religious organization of Sufi brotherhoods linked to the 'leading lineage' of
     the original Sufi founder, extending through his appointees or descendants
     to the leader himself, and from him to Muhammad. For a more detailed
     discussion, see Gladney (1996a:41–3); Nakada (1971); Ma Tong and Wang Qi
     (1985); Jin Yijiu (1985:187–203).

in northwest China, most of them within the Naqsbandi 'path'. Typically, each saint's tomb had a shrine, or *qubba* (Chinese *gongbai* or *gongbei*), and the main shrines became centers of devotional activity. The 'saintly lineages' obtained contributions from their followers and amassed substantial amounts of property. The growth in the number and importance of the *menhuan* represented an important change, because they gradually replaced the 'old' (*gedimu*) pattern by linking together the *menhuan* adherents all over the northwest. The widening compass of social integration that resulted made it easier for the 'saintly lineages' and other leaders to harness the Muslims' political and economic potential, facilitating the rise of Muslim warlordism in that region in the twentieth century. (Fletcher n.d.:15)

Many Sufi reforms swept northwest China during the tumultuous decades of the early Qing dynasty (17th to 18th centuries). Increased communication of Muslims in eastern and western directions, during what Fletcher terms the 'general orthodox revival' of the 18th century, had great influence on Muslims from West Africa to Indonesia, and not least upon China's Hui Muslims.[12] Exposure to these new, generally Sufi ideas led to a reformulation with traditional Islamic concepts in which they became meaningful to the Hui Muslims of that time, gradually institutionalized into such forms as the *menhuan*. Of those that took root and developed into full-fledged *menhuan*, only four maintain significant influence among the Hui today. According to Ma Tong (1983), these are the Kadariyah, Jahariyah, Khufiyah, and Kubrawiyya *menhuan* (see also Pickens 1942; Mian 1981:45–117; Yang Huaizhong 1988). While these are the four main *menhuan*, they are subdivided internally into myriad smaller *menhuan* and subbranches due to ideological, political, geographical, and historical differences. The history of these divisions and alliances, if it could ever be written in any detail, would reveal the tensions experienced and new meanings created as Hui communities dealt with perceived incongruities between the Islamic ideal and changing social real.

Chronologically, the Qadiri *tarikat* (known as the Kadariyah in China) was perhaps the first to become established among the Hui through Koja Abd Alla, a twenty-ninth-generation descendant of Muhammad. Chinese Sufi records show he entered China in 1674, preached in Guangdong, Guangxi, Yunnan, Guizhou, and

---

12. For further information on this period, see Rahman's 'Pre-modernist Reform Movements' (1968:237–60).

Linxia, Gansu, and was finally buried in Guizhou in 1689 (Yang Huaizhong 1988:4). While Abd al-Kadir al-Jilani is the attributed founder of the Qadiri *tarikat*, it is not surprising to find that Abd Alla perhaps studied under the great Ibrahim bin Hasan al-Kurani (1616–1690), who was initiated into the Naqshbandi and Qadiri *tarikat*, as well as several other Sufi orders. Abu 't-Tahir Muhammad al-Kurdi (who died in 1733) and his son had innumerable students who came from as far away as Sumatra, drawn from throughout the Indo-Pakistan subcontinent, as well as East and West Africa (Fletcher 1978:28). The Qadiri path (*turuq*) became rooted most firmly in Chinese soil through one of Abd Alla's students, Qi Jingyi, Hilal al-Din (1656–1719). Known among the Hui as Qi Daozu (Great Master), he was buried in Linxia's 'great tomb' (*da gongbei*) shrine complex, which became the center of Kadariyah Sufism in China. The appeal of Kadariyah Sufism as a renewal movement among the Hui was perhaps due to its combination of a simple ascetic mysticism with a non-institutionalized form of worship, which centers around the tomb complex of deceased saints rather than the mosque. Kadariyah Sufi continue to attend the Gedimu mosques in the local communities in which they live, gathering at the tombs for holidays and individual worship. In a language familiar to the Hui in China, Confucian moral tenets, Daoist mystical concepts, and Buddhist folk rituals pervade Kadariyah Sufism, which infuses them with new Islamic content (Ma Tong 1983: 328–54).[13] Although the Kadariyah has always been less influential and politically powerful among the Hui than other orders, such as the Jahariyah *menhuan*, it set the stage for many to follow.

The Naqshbandi *tarikat* became most rooted in Chinese soil through the establishment of the Khufiyah and Jahariyah orders. Originating in an earlier Central Asian and Yemeni Naqshbandi Sufism, the Khufiyah order was permeated with an emphasis on the veneration of saints, the seeking of inspiration at tombs, and the silent *dhikr* (properly 'Khafiyya', the 'silent ones'; Fletcher 1978:38). There are now more than twenty subbranch *menhuan* throughout China, most concentrated in Linxia Hui Autonomous Prefecture,

---

13. An interesting example is provided by the Jiucaiping *menhuan*, a branch of the Kadariyah in Haiyuan County, southern Ningxia, who say their order is the 'flagpole of Ali' and venerate Fatima as '*hange laomu*' (true mother), who resembles the Buddhist Guanyin (see Mian 1981:102).

Gansu Province, with the distinctiveness of the original Khufiyah ideals in some outlying areas such as northern Ningxia beginning to lose their appeal over time (see page 141). The Jahariyah order was founded under the dynamic leadership of Ma Mingxin (1719–1781) (see Ford 1974:153–5; Fletcher 1975). After twenty years of study under Naqshbandi Sufis in Yemen and the Saudi Peninsula, he returned to China in 1744 with more militant, fundamentalist reforms, and his order became known for its use of the *jahr* (vocalization) in remembrance (from whence comes the name 'Jahariyah', the 'vocal ones'). The Jahariyah are subdivided into four main *menhuan*, with subbranches extending throughout China. Of minor influence in China is the fourth main order, the Kubrawi-yya, said to have been first introduced in China in 1370 by an Arab, Mohidin, who taught in Henan, Qinghai, and Gansu, and died in Dawantou, Dongxiang County, Gansu Province (Ma Tong 1983: 451–5; Yang Huaizhong 1988:10–11). While the populations of the various Islamic factions in China have not been published, Yang Huaizhong (1988:17) writes that of the 2,132 mosques in Ningxia Hui Autonomous Region, 560 belong to the Yihewani, 560 to the Khufiyah, 464 to the Jahariyah, 415 to the traditional Gedimu, and 133 to Kadariyah religious worship sites (some of which include mosques).

The importance and extensiveness of these Sufi orders for uniting disparate Hui communities transnationally throughout China cannot be underestimated.[14] In the 1930s Pickens and a few other missionary scholars were becoming aware of these networks that extended across the country:

> Although in East China we do not think much of the Derwish Orders yet when we get to know something of what goes on we find that even in Shanghai branches of the Djahariah [Jahariyah] can be found. From Yunnan right north to Kansu and Ningsia, even Peiping and probably Manchuria, the influence of this order is felt. (Pickens 1937:414)

Ma Tong (1983:365) lists adherents to the Jahariyah Sufi *menhuan* in several provinces – Ningxia, Gansu, Qinghai, Xinjiang, Yunnan, Hebei, Jilin, and Shandong. At the 1985 commemoration ceremony (*ermaili*) of the death of the Jahariyah order's founder,

14. The Sufi *tarikat* are an important part of the many national 'networks' that Lipman (1984b:264–5) lists as linking Hui together, as distinct from the local distinct 'patchwork' communities.

Ma Mingxin, more than 20,000 adherents gathered for three days at the site of his original tomb outside Lanzhou. The government originally was not going to play any role in the ceremony, but owing to the unexpected number of participants, the city in the end supplied sanitation facilities and food. A meeting of the Provincial Islamic Society was convened afterwards, and it was agreed to allow Ma Mingxin's tomb to be rebuilt. Two months earlier, a similar *ermaili* was held in remembrance for Ma Hualong, the Jahariyah leader who led the Hui rebellion of 1862 to 1877. An extraordinary crowd of more than 10,000 followers, from as far away as Ürümqi, Kunming, and Harbin, arrived at his grave in Dongta township, Lingwu County, demonstrating the extensive influence of this order and the important focus the Sufi leader's tomb provides for galvanizing collective action.

Social interaction is often significantly influenced by membership in various Islamic orders. While intermarriage between different factions of non-Sufi Hui is common, in stronger Sufi areas of northwest China, Hui prefer to marry within their own order. This is particularly true of the Jahariyah order, and in Ningxia, even subsidiary Shagou and Banqiao *menhuan* rarely intermarry. Members of Sufi orders often wear a six-cornered hat, sometimes black, that is different from the standard rounded white hat most Hui wear. Jahariyah Hui often shave the sides of their beards in commemoration of their founder, Ma Mingxin, whose beard they say was shorn by Qing soldiers before his execution in 1781. While these markers almost universally go unnoticed by the Han majority – for whom a Hui is a Hui – northwest Hui can easily identify in the marketplace members of the various factions that divide them internally.

The tensions and conflicts that led to the rise and divisions of the four Sufi *menhuan*, and the non-Sufi reforms that followed them, are impossible to enumerate in their complexity. They give evidence, however, of the ongoing struggles that continue to make Islam meaningful to Hui Muslims. These tensions between Islamic ideals and social realities can never be said to be fully resolved into any stable equilibrium. As Fabian (1981:212–14) suggests in his study of African religious movements, these conflicts are often never resolved. Their very dynamism derives from the questions they raise and the doubts they engender among people struggling with traditional meanings amid changing social contexts. Out of these struggles sometimes arise new movements in dialectical tension with the old. These ongoing dialectic transitions have led to the powerful appeal of Islamic movements among Hui Muslims, who are faced with making Islamic ideals meaningful in the changing Chinese sociopolitical world.[15] Many of the conflicts and issues uniting and dividing these Sufi orders revolve around the tombs built to their deceased saintly leaders.

Discussion of the tombs, in print or in person, has been rare on the mainland. In the pre-1949 Chinese literature, I found only one article that dealt with them specifically (Ma Zikuo c. 1933). Chinese authors began to refer to the tombs in only a few relatively recent publications (for example, Ma Tong 1983; Mian Weiling 1981), all of which were originally published as *neibu faxing* (for internal circulation only). The reason behind this is the unclear policy of the state with reference to the Sufi and local tombs. While permission to rebuild mosques and for free religious assembly has been fully granted to China's Muslims, the reconstruction of tombs has been a quasi-legal issue that few are willing to address. When local cadres commented to me on the policy, most have said, in effect, 'No comment'. While some have noted, 'They are still illegal', others have added, 'As long as they don't influence production they should be OK'.

The reasons behind this ambivalence are numerous. From an economic standpoint, these tombs, like many Chinese graves, were traditionally located in the middle of a field, obstructing valuable agricultural production. The vast majority of tombs were

15. The development of the Yihewani in China is an especially relevant example of this dialectic, where a conservative reformist Wahhabi movement initially critical of the non-scriptural elements of Sufi and traditional Islamic factions in China became, in the process of reform, identified more with nationalist and political causes that espoused education and modernism. See especially Lipman (1994), as well as Mian Weiling (1981:118–31); Ma Kexun (1982); Ma Tong (1983:127–54); Ye Zhengang (1981). Within the Yihewani has developed another reform movement dating from the 1930s, the Salafiyya (Gladney 1999), which stresses a non-politicized fundamentalist return to Wahhabi scripturalist ideals (see Eickelman's [1976:226–8] discussion of the Salafiyya reform movement in Morocco). In turn, in the late 1990s a controversy arose within the Salafiyya over the immanence or transcendence of Allah, with the side advocating transcendence – Allah's dwelling in a high place above the affairs of men (*gao weizhishang*) – demonstrating their position by cutting their hair short. Immanentists, by contrast, let their hair grow long, down to their collars, symbolizing God's presence in the world.

torn down or moved during the land reform and collectivization campaigns of the late 1950s. The early Communist criticisms of so-called superstitious practices of *feng shui* (geomancy), which sometimes dictated the placing of graves in the middle of fields, and the restrictions on lineage or clan temples also militated against the maintenance of the tombs. Finally, specifically Sufi-related criticism movements in the 1950s were linked to these tombs. In Ningxia, after 1958, when the leader of the Shagou branch of the Sufi Jahariyah order, Ma Zhenwu, was arrested and then in 1960 died in prison, all Jahariyah- and *menhuan*-related tombs were torn down. By the end of 1966, the high tide of radicalism during the Cultural Revolution in the northwest (the *posijiu*, 'destroy the four olds' campaign), there were only a few local tombs remaining in remote places. These tombs and shrines were, and in many cases still are, regarded by cadres as feudal vestiges, politically, religiously, and culturally backward.

As in other reforms affecting the countryside, central policy often lags behind popular local movements. Throughout Ningxia and northwest China, even as the issue of rebuilding these tombs is being debated at the various levels of government, the tombs are being reconstructed with enthusiasm. A cadre in southern Ningxia commented: 'The Hui rebuild the tombs on their own at night with their own materials and money. Who can stop them?' The local cadres have taken a hands-off approach to the entire issue, while the Hui go ahead with their own agendas. Under the present state policy of protecting and assisting minorities, most local cadres are reluctant to interfere with any ethnic activity that does not directly violate existing ordinances. The rebuilding of these tombs is tolerated as an aspect of nationality religion. The dismantling of the commune and the recontracting of the land back to the farmers under the new responsibility system has also led to more personal discretion in land use (Shue 1984). It is also significant that many of the Sufi-related shrines have begun to be rebuilt since the posthumous rehabilitation of Ma Zhenwu by the state in August 1983.

The importance of these Sufi tombs, for linking Hui adherents and for being the loci of conflicts that divide them, are illustrated by a visit I made to the main tomb of the Kadariyah Sufi order in Linxia Hui Autonomous Prefecture, Gansu Province. Known as the 'little Mecca' of China, partly as a result of its key location along important trade and communication routes, Linxia has been a center for Chinese Islam and exchange with the West since the Middle Ages. Almost every major Islamic movement in China finds its origin among Muslims who came to Linxia disseminating new doctrines after pilgrimage to Middle Eastern Islamic centers. As a result, Linxia combines the spiritual importance of Mecca and the centrality in theological learning of the city of Qum, Iran, for China's Hui Muslims (*cf.* Fischer 1980).

While most Sufi shrines in China are small monuments erected over the graves of saints, the main Kadariyah tomb in Linxia is part of a huge shrine complex of buildings at the northern outskirts of the city, which includes a mosque, cemetery, Quranic school, housing for guests and the resident religious leaders, and the 'great *gongbei*' (*da gongbei*) itself, from which the *menhuan* gets its name.[16] In one place, the complex combines the *siyyid* (saints' shrine) and the *zawiya* (brotherhood) institutions, which Geertz (1968:49) distinguishes in Moroccan maraboutism. The *gongbei* is located at the back of the complex, encircled by a low fence, with incense smoke billowing from large pots in front and to the sides. Before the silk-covered tomb were prayer mats, with a man and several young boys kneeling for prayer as we walked in. Over 8,000 followers celebrated Ramadan here in 1985. The majority of worshipers gathered were women, which is consistent with what I have heard about attendance at *gongbei* prayers in general across the northwest.

As we examined the many Islamic and Chinese inscriptions surrounding the *gongbei*, the resident saint (*morshid*) was notified of our presence. Imam Yang Shijun Ali (addressed '*Lao Ren Jia*'), eighty years old, is the tenth-generation descendant of Qi Jingyi, Hilal Al-din, the original founder of the Qimen Great Gongbei branch. Ewing (1984:107) has discussed the charismatic quality of the Sufi saint (*pir* in Pakistan), who radiates *baraka* (Allah's blessing), and the importance of his dress and manner for reflecting divine power.[17] Similarly, the appearance of the Kadariyah *morshid* was

16. Like other *menhuan* in China, it takes its name from its founder Qi Jingyi, who is entombed in the shrine, as the 'Qimen' (Qi *menhuan*) branch, and from its locality, the 'great tomb' (*da gongbei*) *menhuan* (Ma Tong 1983:329).

17. Ewing (1984:106–7) suggests that for Pakistani Sufi the personal power and dyadic relationship of the *pir* with his client is more important than membership in the brotherhood itself, as Crapanzano (1973:217) writes is true for the Hamadsha in Morocco. I would argue that for the Kadariyah in China, the power of the *morshid* is directly related to the *menhuan* he

quite striking. About 152 centimeters tall, he had a wispy beard extending to his chest, his hair was completely white, and he was dressed completely in black silk. His deep-set eyes exuded an air of authority and knowledge. Likewise, the appearance of the *halifat* (neophyte student imam) I talked to, one of fifteen in residence at the shrine, was a surprising contrast to other Hui *halifat* I have known. Unlike most Hui *halifat* of other non-Sufi factions, who are generally young and well-scrubbed, dressed in brand-new black or blue Sun Yat-sen jackets, this novitiate had on a wrinkled, long-sleeved shirt with the cuffs unbuttoned and hanging down over his hands. He was thin, with sunken cheeks and dark red, tired eyes. It is important to note here that, as distinct from several other Sufi orders in China, most Kadariyah suborders are distinguished by leadership succession through religious merit, not blood inheritance. Through dedication to studies, personal piety, and the practice of abnegation according to Kadariyah doctrines, the students are promoted to higher ranks in the order. This young *halifat* could literally have a chance at sainthood, if not in this life, then quite possibly in the next. The appearance and manner of both *morshid* and *halifat* reflect Kadariyah values of asceticism and advancement through personal dedication.

An Arabic inscription on the wall directly behind the tomb provides a crucial text for Hui Sufi identity. When I asked about the inscription, the young student (*halifat*, or *mala*) answered very reverently by first reciting the Arabic, and then translating into Chinese. When I repeated it, I failed to pronounce the Linxia accented Chinese translation just right, and the *halifat* sternly replied that I should get this exactly as he said it: 'He who sees my person of Muhammad, that person actually sees Allah' (*Kanjianle wo Muhamude de ren, neige ren dishi kanjianle Anla*).

Imam Yang Shijun quietly and reverently described how the text inscribed on the wall was originally said by the Prophet Muhammad himself, shortly before he died, to his four caliphs, Abu Bakr, Umar, Ali, and Uthman. This saying insured the proper succession of leaders. He said this is the key to the Kadariyah Sufi order and, therefore, is inscribed on the wall. On a rival Kadariyah shrine,

represents. The charismatic personality of the Kadariyah *morshid* merely authenticates his right to inherit and tap that power, as succession to leadership is based on merit, not blood inheritance (see page 137).

located in the *beishan* (north mountain) Hui graveyard on the outskirts of Linxia, is inscribed the following text, written in four parallel quatrains of four Chinese characters:

Those who wish to obtain the *Dao* must take the good medicine of the *Dao* so that you might receive what you desire, you must often follow the right rules and principles. Here are thirty rules,[18] recorded as follows:

> Honestly *tao bai* [pray at the *gongbei* to Allah through the *morshid*].
> Be completely beautiful [*mei*] and reliable [*tuo kao*].
> Follow Allah's orders and proscriptions.
> Respect the religious leader [*Dao zhang*].
> Firmly remember all of the true words.
> Follow and listen to the teacher's instruction.
> Piously worship.
> Often fast.
> Propagate the heavenly lessons.
> Be filial to your parents.
> Pray for Allah's favor.
> Fear Allah's anger.
> Be free from corruption [*qinglian jijiao*].
> Be diligent in studies.
> Do not overeat.
> Do not oversleep.

The importance of loyalty and adherence to the Sufi leader's prescripts are important recurring themes in this and many of the texts I have analyzed, as are the themes of personal piety and asceticism.[19]

The personal power of the saint derives from his authority of descent from Muhammad, which is mediated through the lineage (*silsilla*) of succession from the Sufi saints who are buried in the tombs. This was explained further to me by an *ahong* who was an important member of the Sufi Jahariyah order, Shagou *menhuan*, in Xiji, Ningxia, one of the most powerful of the four Jahariyah

---

18. While there are thirty rules inscribed on the shrine, I only had time to copy those that are translated here.

19. Space does not allow for a description of the important Daoist concepts that pervade Kadariyah Sufism in China. The rather complete and complex integration of the two mystic systems accomplishes practically what Izutsu (1983), in his ambitious comparative study, attempts philosophically – '*un dialogue dans la métahistoire*'. The history of Kadariyah Sufism in China is the working out of Izutsu's metahistorical dialogue between Sufism and Daoism in the lives of Hui adherents (see Gladney 1996a:43–6).

menhuan. He stated: 'The highest level next to Allah is the Prophet Muhammad. The next level is the *morshid*. We should therefore respect him. We can ask him to help intercede with Allah for our requests and to help us after death. We must respect him, seek [*qiu*] him, but not worship him. Whoever looks at the Prophet's *morshid*, looks at Allah'.

For Hui members of Sufi orders in northwest China, identity as Hui Muslims is inextricably linked to their understanding of their relation to their foreign Muslim ancestors and, ultimately, the Prophet, through the *morshid*, either living or entombed. Differing from the process Ewing (1984:108) describes, where the *baraka* of the saint is important for healing and the validation of his authority, in China the *morshid* and their tombs are critical primarily for their providing the ancestral and theological link.

Hui concerns with identity can be seen from the many conflicts between Sufi factions, which often center upon the building and maintenance of competing Sufi tombs. At the shrine of the *Quanyi* (Complete Propriety) *gongbei*, outside Linxia, the overseer pointed out to me the lineage of Sufi saints inscribed on the wall of the shrine. He emphasized that this documented the Jiang Yuru faction was a legitimate branch of the Kadariyah, an assertion disputed by the Kadariyah Qimen *menhuan* leaders.[20] Unlike the Hui in Quan-zhou, for whom personal genealogy and the tracing of their lineage to foreign Muslim ancestors is critical, the northwest Sufi Hui are more interested in the *silsilla* of their saintly order. Discussion of membership in the proper order based on descent is often the basis for conflict and denigration of inferior orders. Members of one Sufi branch of the Hui often said their branch was superior to a rival one because their leader was descended by blood from the original saint, whereas the other branch leader was only appointed. Conversely, a rival branch would argue that blood inheritance of leadership was inferior to appointment by merit, the passing on of the *kouhuan* (oral transmission) by the saint to the follower who possessed the most *baraka*.

A recent split among another Sufi branch has developed over the tearing down of their tomb and that of another order. Apparently

20. See Ma Tong (1983:346–7) for a discussion of Ai Liang De Ni, the reputed founder of the Jiang Yuru branch of the Kadariyah *menhuan*, and his reported pilgrimage to Mecca, with the reforms he instituted on his return.

a relative of one of the order's members who moved to Saudi Arabia before 1949 has been influenced by Wahhabi doctrines, which denounce the veneration of saints and tombs. This relative has been sending cassette tapes to his sister-in-law, telling her of the need to reform the order. She in turn has been involved in tearing down many of these tombs, including the *gongbei* built for her father-in-law. In another recent problem of succession among a Kadariyah branch in Qinghai, following the *morshid*'s death, three of his *halifat* claimed they had received his *kouhuan* and were to take his place. One of them was his son, another possessed his cloak, and the third was his star student. There are now three new orders where once there was one.

Occasionally, the participants in these disputes attempt to resolve their differences in the streets. To help settle the altercations, the regional government often brought in respected Sufi leaders from the city to help the parties to the disputes to discuss their differences. While these conflicts give the local cadres many headaches in their nationality work (*minzu gongzuo*), they have not led to any widespread serious violence that I am aware of. The conflicts seemed to have remained at the local, intrafactional level, and I have not heard of any of them being directed toward the local government or Han neighbors of the protagonists. Instead, I have witnessed the concern by local government cadres and China Islamic Society leaders to attempt to work out the differences without enforcing any rigid policies. The existence of these conflicts and the flexibility on the part of the government to help resolve them illustrates that the state policy of freedom of religion, though not without its problems, is beginning to be realized in a significant way in the countryside.

These conflicts and tensions also demonstrate the continued power of Hui Sufi saints and their tombs for mobilizing collective action. While often dividing the Hui among themselves, they at the same time unite Hui communities across China through extensive networks. They play a critical role in defining identity for Hui in their multilevel hierarchy of ethnoreligious authority. At various levels Hui can identify themselves as coreligionists of the international Muslim community, Chinese citizens of China, members of the Hui nationality, adherents to a Sufi brotherhood, and residents of a local village or lineage. Sorting out how Hui maintain and manipulate their identity amid these conflicting loyalties and incongruities reveals much about the dynamic process of north-west Hui ethnic change.

Local tombs and communal interests

My first trip to southern Ningxia in October 1983 took a circuitous route to Wuzhong city through Lingwu County. Just before crossing Xinhua Bridge I noticed a large white dome rising up from the middle of a wheat field. This was an interesting contrast to the many small mosques I had noticed appearing regularly on either side of the road. I asked the cadre accompanying me in the car what it was, but he remained silent and the car kept going. In April 1985 I was able to visit the small tomb and found out from the local Hui peasants that it was the Qi Taiye (Grandfather Qi) *gongbei*, dating back over 100 years. Like many other local *gongbei* it had been torn down in 1958 and rebuilt in 1982. Inside the white-washed dome, the simple grave was bare concrete without adornment, and present were the customary prayer mat, water pot for ritual washing, and incense. The incense had been burning when I opened the unlocked door, revealing that someone had been there recently. The locals did not seem to know much more about it.

Across southern Ningxia are small local *gongbei* (called *tu gongbei*) that have existed previously for as long as 500 years. The role and significance of these tombs for local Hui communities are to be distinguished from the Sufi-related shrines described above. Dedicated to local heroes, *ahongs*, or hajji returned from Mecca, they are often the focus of collective and individual ritual action. Small tombs standing alone in a graveyard or field with no attached shrine, they usually house only one grave of the deceased local saint. As such, the can be seen to be part of a process of 'localization', by which, according to Appadurai (1990), people attempt to construct local identities distinct from national, transnational, or global processes of interrelation.

In central Ningxia, Lingwu and Tongxin counties, these 'local tombs' tend to be white rounded domes, 1.8 to 2.4 meters tall, with a low brick base and topped with a crescent moon or some other Islamic ornament. I have never seen a shrine or prayer hall attached to these tombs, and the person who takes care of them generally lives in the village nearby. On talking with these informal overseers, I found that even the name of the saint was often unknown; they were called by titles such as *baba*, *ahong*, hajji, or *taiye*. In many cases it was only known that they were a religious leader of great knowledge (*erling*) or spirituality (*yimani*). There are several *gongbei* built to outsiders (*wailaide ahong*) who did some important work and then died in that vicinity.

These tombs were often confused with the Sufi shrines mentioned above by early-20th-century Western travelers in the northwest. However, their importance and influence at the local level was well known. In the following account, Mark Botham describes a tomb he encountered in 1922 at 'Tan-wan-tou':

> Behind closed doors was the grave of the founder of the Mohammedanism of this district, hung with silk and linen draperies, in a room whose equally beautiful tomb was in the front court ... [The caretaker] was old and nearly blind, his unseeing eyes a type of his darkened soul ... We learned that many hundred years ago there came a traveller from Baghdad to these wild mountains – in those days they were desolate and well-nigh uninhabited – and he lived an austere and holy life, and took him a wife of the people of the country who were 'aborigines' or 'Mongols,' who knows which! And the present inhabitants of all that country are (they said) his progeny ... 'Do you expect him to intercede for you?' 'We hope that he will gain for us the favour of Allah. We know nothing; we are ignorant and sinful; but he has been accorded a place in heaven, and we may go there because of him.' So it is everywhere. (Botham 1924:185–6)[21]

Many of these local tombs were rebuilt in the early 1980s when the land where they were formerly located was contracted back to the local peasants. They are visited individually day or night by locals or passers-by, and prayers are read or chanted (*nianjing*).[22] It is often the local Hui women who bring their daughters into the *gongbei* for prayer, sometimes late at night. If the death day of the grave's occupant is known, there will sometimes be a small gathering, and the local *ahong* will read the scripture. If the *gongbei* is located in a graveyard, Hui generally go first to the *gongbei* and pray before going to their own ancestors' graves.

I found nineteen of these *gongbei* in Ningxia's Tongxin County and thirteen in Lingwu County, many of which have been rebuilt.

21. This tomb perhaps belonged originally to the Kubrawiyya *menhuan* in Dawantou, Dongxiang County, Gansu Province (see Ma Tong 1983:451–4).
22. The meaning of '*nianjing*' (literally 'read scripture') differs among the different factions of Hui Islam. For the traditional Gedimu, it generally means to recite memorized passages of the Quran.

These *gongbei* are generally maintained by the Gedimu traditional-
ists, but many are former Khufiyah Sufi brotherhood tombs. While
the distinctions between the Jahariyah, Kadariyah, and Yihewani
factions are clearly maintained in Ningxia, in northern Ningxia
the difference between the Khufiyah and Gedimu has become less
distinct.[23] In many interviews with Hui in the Yinchuan suburbs
and Pingluo or Helan counties I was often told, 'We are *laogu* [Ge-
dimu], Khufiyah', combining the two factions in one breath. This
response reveals two things. First, in some areas there is no difference between Khufiyah and Gedimu, and Hui can be former Khufiyah adherents who have become Gedimu 'traditional' Muslims.
Second, in other areas they maintain the *dhikr* (remembrance) of
the Sufi Khufiyah, but do not owe loyalty to the *menhuan* saintly
leaders.[24] Interestingly, there are several tombs maintained in areas
where people predominantly follow the Yihewani, a group Lipman
(1986) has shown to oppose the veneration of tombs and saints.
The local Yihewani *ahong* told me they only oppose those tombs
'with names', which means they condemn *menhuan*-related tombs,
since the names of local saints are sometimes well remembered.

The importance of these local *gongbei* and Hui reasons for rebuilding them reveal much about their community interests. Many
Gedimu have said that the *gongbei* were rebuilt and still popular
because people attribute miraculous powers to the saints buried
within. One elderly Hui woman from Lingwu said: 'Through the
laorenjia [old master] we can have our message delivered to Allah.
He is a saint who has gone to heaven and will remember us if we
remember him. It's like using the back door [*zou houmanr*]'.[25]

Requests that are brought to the saint are often related to
childbirth and domestic problems: asking for a son, finding a mate,
having a good harvest, and so on. This woman had two daughters
and was hoping for a son, since she was from a poor desert region
and was allowed to have three children under the present birth-
planning policy. She said she often went to the local *gongbei* to ask

23. Mian (1985:203–25) provides an excellent discussion of the distribution and
history of Islamic factions in Ningxia Hui Autonomous Region.
24. For an example, see my description of the non-*menhuan* Khufiyah village of
the Na family outside of Yinchuan, in Gladney (1996a: Chapter 3).
25. Using the 'back door' is a Chinese euphemism for obtaining favors through
personal connections, most often exploited by the children and families of
important cadres.

the saint to help. Many urban Hui scoff at the thought of going to these *gongbei*, but the tombs continue to have an important place in the social landscape of the Hui countryside.

Like that of the Sufi tombs, the importance of these local *gong-bei* centers on the power of the deceased saint to provide a direct link to Hui Muslim ancestors, and by extension, to the Prophet and Allah. It is not surprising that many graveyards built around these tombs appear to adopt these saints into their lineage or community. On the fringe of the Gobi desert in Lingwu County, central Ningxia, are located a series of Hui graveyards that extend for 30 kilometers along the dunes and rocky wastelands. In one of the villages I visited, Guo Jia Jiantan (Guo family alkaline bank) of Dumuqiao township, four *gongbei* had been rebuilt between 1981 and 1984 in the local cemeteries within the space of 1 square kilometer. The *gongbei* belonged to various *ahong* who had been on the hajj: Wang West Ahong, Wang Third Ahong, Jin Ahong, and an unknown 'outside' (*wailaide*) *ahong*.[26] While I was there, a funeral began for an eighty-two-year-old woman surnamed Yang, who was buried next to the Jin Ahong *gongbei*. The woman's husband was surnamed Ma, and almost all of those buried in the vicinity of the *gongbei* were of that lineage. This was also true of the graves clustered around the other three *gongbei*.

The important role of the saint for mediating on the behalf of his adopted lineage or village is illustrated by the Arabic inscription on the unusual brick *gongbei* to Wang Third Ahong nearby. In addition to the *shahadah* and the dedication of the tomb to 'Hajji Burhan al-Din', the following three lines were inscribed on the front:

The Prophet said these scholars of religion [*ulama*] will last as long as the world lasts.

The Prophet said he who loves knowledge and the scholars, God will do away with his sin.

Think highly of the scholars because you will need them in this world and in the hereafter.[27]

26. The recurring theme of pilgrimage and completion of the hajj to Mecca is an important aspect of the status of these saints, as well as the fact that many of them were foreigners or outsiders (*wailaide ahong*). For an account of the importance of the hajj in Southeast Asian Islam, see Roff (1984).

27. It is noteworthy that although the Arabic states clearly that this is the tomb of Burhan al-Din, the local Hui, most of whom only recite Quranic Arabic

The emphasis upon the importance of this saint and the other 'scholars of God' for being models of righteousness, mediators to Allah, and dispensers of blessing (*baraka*) is of obvious importance to the one who wrote the verses. Through their authority and mediation, Hui who patronize them might also experience Allah's favor, despite their personal failure to live up to the demands of Islam. The Hui villages hope that this personal tension of incongruity between the ideal and the real is to be resolved for by these adopted saints.

Local gongbei *and ethnic folklore*

Many local legends are associated with the saints of these *tu gongbei*. These legends have never been written down as far as I know and may have little basis in history, but they are significant for our understanding the socioeconomic context and concerns of Hui life.

One legend comes from a *gongbei* in Qianhong village, Wang Tuan township, Tongxin County, south-central Ningxia Hui Autonomous Region. The story goes that 400 to 500 years ago an old hajji *ahong* lived in the lower level of the valley. He did not wish to have a wife or children, and worked just enough to be able to go to mosque and pray. In the lower valley the frost comes early and occasionally it had been known to rain large hailstones, sizeable enough to kill farm animals. This had been a perpetual plague and problem to the Hui peasants, who could barely get by in a good year with the little rainwater in that area. The old hajji was concerned about this problem and said that after he died he would ask Allah to stop the hailstones and early frost. After the hajji died the weather improved dramatically and the peasants attributed this to his influence with Allah. Consequently, they built him a *gongbei* and his death date is still commemorated. When a Hui friend paid a visit there recently and asked if there had been any hail, a local answered that it no longer hailed there because of the *gongbei baba's* influence.

Another popular story also comes from a *gongbei* in Zhang Ershui village, Wang Tuanzhuang township, Tongxin County. This

---

and cannot read or speak it, refer to the tomb as Wang Third Ahong's. Farhat Ziadeh (pers. comm.) noted that there were also several errors in spelling and syntax in the Arabic. I am grateful for his assistance with these translations.

is the *gongbei* of Niu Ke Baba, an outsider who came through the area and stayed only twenty days. After the second day there he asked the people to help him dig his grave, for Allah had told him in a dream that night his death was imminent. The next morning he went up on the mountain and dislodged a large stone, which rolled down the slope into a wheat field. He bought the field from the owner and on the spot where the rock fell they dug up the ground and found a body. Instead of a foul smell, the grave emitted a fragrant odor. The body had not decomposed and was in perfect condition. They reburied the body and gave it a *gongbei* because Allah had preserved it. When the outsider died he was buried just behind it. The *gongbei* was torn down in 1966. A local cadre told me that he went to the area on four separate occasions and asked if there were any plans to rebuild the *gongbei*, to which the local people replied no. On his fifth visit he found a beautiful new white tomb in the middle of the field. People go there often individually and in groups, but there is no organized prayer service on any certain date. Occasionally, when an important local has a funeral, they sacrifice a cow there, perhaps because its named after the *niu ke baba* ('cow guest father').

There is another popular Hui legend about a *gongbei* dedicated to 'Jin jue' (barefoot) Laorenjia, which comes from Changji Hui Autonomous Prefecture in Xinjiang Region, where I visited in May 1985. The barefoot *ahong* was so poor that he did not wear shoes, even in winter when temperatures averaged well below freezing. The power of his *baraka* kept his feet from freezing. He wandered from place to place rejecting material possessions and devoting himself to prayer and study of the Quran. One day he appeared to a group of villagers and told them that he knew of an *ahong*'s body out in the desert, and that they should go bury it. When they immediately went to the place he told them, they found that it was his corpse.

These stories often combine themes of poverty, asceticism, spiritual dedication, and reward in a language familiar to anyone who has traveled in the harsh environments where Hui are often concentrated. Until the large hydraulic works were recently developed in Tongxin County, the region was unable to receive any of the water from the nearby Yellow River, and was almost a barren wasteland. It is not surprising that many of these *gongbei* stories come from this area, where they are still popular centers of worship, despite the majority of Hui in Tongxin belonging to Yihewani and Khufiyah factions.

The stories of miraculous events and special powers emanating from Muslim tombs are common wherever Sufism is popular (Geertz 1968:48–54; Eickelman 1976). Most Hui who visit these local tombs, however, are members of the traditional Gedimu faction. They are not adherents to Sufi brotherhoods, know little about the doctrines of the Sufi factions around them, and have no exposure to Islam outside China. Despite their recognition of the efficacy of deceased saints in influencing Allah's actions on their behalf, they maintain a strict monotheistic belief. For them, the saints become extensions of their own line of Hui Muslim ancestors. Even though they might not be directly related to the particular entombed saint, Hui often feel they are related ethnically to each other, and to the foreign Muslims who came to China sometime in their distant past. '*Tianxia Huihui shi yi jia*' (All Hui under heaven are one family) was a popular saying in China before the Hui had to be careful to avoid being accused of 'local ethnocentrism' (*difang minzu zhuyi*) – in other words, had to subordinate ethnic to national concerns.

It is not surprising that most *gongbei* are located in the middle of Hui lineage and village graveyards. In contrast to their Han neighbors, Hui often build their graveyards either right next to or within the confines of their village. The local graveyard plays an important role in the daily life of Hui villagers. In one village of 723 households, I observed an average of four to eight individuals who went to the graveyards (*shangfen*) every day to pray, with thirty or more going on Friday, the main day of worship. Generally, I was told, someone from the extended household made at least one trip to the graveyard each week. Hui do not believe in ghosts and gods like their Han neighbors, and are not afraid of the graveyards at night. A popular Hui proverb says: 'When on the road the safest place to sleep is the Han graveyard; the ghosts won't bother you because we don't believe in them, and local Han bandits won't bother you because they are too afraid of the ghosts'. Desecration of graveyards and tombs was one Red Guard activity in Hui areas during the Cultural Revolution that led to major and minor confrontations throughout China.

There are also important points of similarity between the Hui and their Han neighbors with regard to cosmology. Wolf

(1978:175–80) has argued that the hierarchy of the social world is mirrored by the metaphysical realm among Taiwanese villagers. While the Hui do not have a developed theology of angels and heavenly officials, they are, of course, cognizant of their own power hierarchies at the local level. For the Hui villager who knows of the various levels of leadership in the Sufi *silsilla* hierarchies extending from Allah, through Muhammad, through the line of the *morshid*, to their appointed administrators (*reyisi*), to their students (*halifat*, *mala*), and finally to the adherents themselves, it would not seem unlikely that heaven also reflects these hierarchies. As with the village head, Allah seems to honor the suggestions of devout followers closest to him – as we have seen with the deceased saint. In any non-Sufi Hui village, the power and influence of the local *ahong* with his appointed sub-*ahongs*, administrators, and students, makes the social and spiritual hierarchy significant to the average villager. Upward mobility through religious learning is an important strategy in every Hui community, almost without parallel in Han villages throughout the northwest. And if one cannot obtain favor through Quranic learning, one can always attempt to use the 'back door' by patronizing a local saint's tomb.

Several other parallels between Hui and Han interests would be worth exploring. Stevan Harrell (pers. comm.) has suggested that the role of the *gongbei* and the powers of the saint buried there resemble those of traditional temples dotting the Taiwan countryside. Women often take their daughters to these temples, seeking otherworldly help in having sons or in resolving financial problems. Miracles also are not unknown in the vicinity of these shrines, and they influence the natural powers of the earth, bringing good weather and fruitful harvests. Local non-lineage ghosts and historic heroes may become adopted by the local community as patron deities over time (Harrell 1974). While Hui do not have any known institutionalized practice of geomancy (*feng shui*), with professionals skilled in selecting sites for buildings and graves, I have noticed that many of these tombs are placed in a similar location. Hui graves are distinguished by lying on a north–south axis, with the entrance to *gongbei* tombs almost always to the south. The body lies with the head to the north, the feet to the south, and the face turned west, toward Mecca. Many Hui graveyards and tombs follow the standard *feng shui*, placed on the side of a hill with a stream or plain below. The most notable example is the graveyard and *gongbei* at North Mountain, Linxia.

Tombs and Hui ancestral tradition

The tombs and graveyards that are important to the Hui differ significantly in their social, political, economic, and religious usage and interpretation. Their influence varies in scale from the internationally important historic tombs to the local village *tu gongbei*. In this chapter I have sought to demonstrate that the interests and issues surrounding these tombs reveal much about their identity. The historic tombs highlight conflicts between accepted popular and state definitions of the Hui nationality and southern Hui lineages who maintain an ethnic identity that is no longer Islamic in content. The tombs are meaningful because they concretely demonstrate the genealogical bond between these Hui communities and their foreign ancestors, validating their claim to ethnic minority status. Sufi tombs are important to northwest Hui because they often serve as the locus for national and transnational networks that tie Hui together, as well as linking them directly to Muhammad through the mediating power of the saints buried within. Conflicts surrounding their legitimacy and history reveal much about the daily tensions experienced by many Sufi Hui in working out the practical implications of their faith in China in the light of Islamic ideals. Assurance of the authority of their Sufi order is critical to their identity as Hui Muslims who see themselves as descended from a decidedly Islamic heritage. Local tombs and the lore that surrounds them reveal daily communal and socioeconomic concerns, ways in which Hui seek to 'localize' their identity in competition over claims for scarce resources. The tombs are powerful 'sacred symbols' (Geertz 1968:79), in that they orient the Hui in terms of local heroes, who when patronized appropriately will assist them in fulfilling the demands of Islam and preserving their identity in the field of social relations.

Given this diversity in form and meaning, how can the Hui be said to be an ethnic group? While the tombs and interpretations attached to them differ radically among different Hui communities, at one point they come together to provide a common point of reference: they give evidence of descent from a long tradition, an ethnic and religious heritage that is distinct from, and in some cases in opposition to, the dominant Han society. While Hui in various localities throughout China differ from each other linguistically, religiously, culturally, and geographically, it is this shared idea of common descent from foreign Muslim ancestors that is the root of their ethnic identity as Hui. This shared identity allows strict Sufi Muslims from the northwest to stay in the homes of non-Muslim Hui in southern China, or in urban centers, without fear of violating halal (in Chinese, *qing zhen*, 'pure and true'). It also admits Hui Party cadres from Beijing into the inexpensive hostels attached to many large mosques in the northwest without concern as to their religious belief or factional membership. This also has much to do with the great popularity of Linxia, Gansu, beef noodle restaurants among urban Hui in Shanghai and Canton.

Much that is significant to Hui interests and identity was not discussed in this chapter: the central role of the local mosque, which distinguishes Hui communities radically from their Han neighbors; the mosque clergy, who exercise considerable influence on Hui villagers, whether devout Muslims or not; the Islamic school (madrasah), where many Hui children are sent informally to learn Quranic Arabic texts – and where perhaps their non-Chinese heritage is most impressed upon them (in contrast to the state school system, where they use 'Han' Chinese names and learn the Chinese language); the Hui restaurant, which is often the locus for ethnic activity in urban areas; the marketplace, where the divisions and alliances of Hui networks in the countryside become most visible, and are most critical for prosperity; the Islamic festivals and life-cycle rituals that punctuate everyday life and regularly remind the Hui of their heritage; and the idiomatic usage of Persian and Arabic loan words by Chinese-speaking Hui, who do not have a separate language of their own, but are often easily distinguished by this form of 'Hui talk' (*Huihui hua*). All of these institutions and events, together and separately, serve to situate the Hui in terms of their ancestral tradition as they interact in multi-ethnic settings.

While tombs may not be relevant to all Hui, I chose to discuss them because of their decidedly Muslim character, which encapsulates Hui ancestral tradition most vividly. The tombs play an important part in providing a sense of continuity with the past and assisting adaptation to the changing social present. This dynamic interplay between cultural meanings and social change is the basis for ethnic identity and transformation. For many Hui, these tombs serve as powerful frameworks for personal identity and corporate action. With their surrounding lore and activity, the tombs reveal much about the divergent interests of contrasting Hui communities and, at the same time, serve as important charters that speak of a common identity.

Part IV
ETHNICIZATIONS

8
DIALOGIC IDENTITIES

Ethnic dialogues

Dialogue here is not the threshold to action, it is the action itself. It is not a means for revealing, for bringing to the surface the already ready-made character of a person; no, in dialogue a person not only shows himself outwardly, but he becomes for the first time that which he is – and, we repeat, not only for others but for himself as well. To be means to communicate dialogically. When dialogue ends, everything ends. Thus dialogue, by its very essence, cannot and must not come to an end. (Mikhail Bakhtin 1984 [1963]:252)

Upon the founding of the People's Republic of China, an interesting dialogue began between representatives of the state and those who saw themselves as belonging to the 'national minorities'. More than 400 groups who, according to Max Weber's (1978 [1956]: 389) definition of ethnicity, 'entertained a subjective belief in their common descent', applied to the representatives of the Chinese government for recognition as official minority nationalities.

After protracted negotiations that involved an enormous program of state-sponsored investigations by Chinese anthropologists, linguists, and local officials, fifty-four groups succeeded in convincing the state that they were legitimate ethnic groups. The legal ratification of their ethnic status effectively excluded up to 350 other applicant groups from recognition (Fei 1981:60). The Han were officially designated the majority group of China, now comprising 91 percent of the total population. In the fifty years since that process was begun, only one other group, the Jinuo, has convinced the state of its viable existence, and was recognized in 1979. Meanwhile, fifteen groups are currently under official application and more than 749,341 people were listed as 'unidentified' in the 1990 census (*Renmin Ribao* [*People's Daily*] 14 November 1990:3).

In a discussion of the process of 'ethnic identification' in China, Fei Xiaotong, a prominent Chinese social anthropologist, outlined the Marxist–Stalinist criteria for recognition by the state as an ethnic group. To be identified, each group must *convince* the state that it possesses a common language, locality, economy, or psychological make-up, what Stalin later glossed as 'culture'. I write 'convince' here because, as I shall demonstrate below, these so-called objective criteria for ethnic identification are inherently negotiable: they are used by both sides in the debate for legitimacy.

Fei Xiaotong's description of the process of identifying several questionable nationality groups assumes these four criteria and generally begins with the study of the linguistic history of these groups (Fei 1981:67). The main agency empowered to decide upon the granting of minority nationality status to applicant groups, the State Commission for Ethnic Affairs, summarized its reliance upon Stalin's criteria:

Stalin's nationality criteria are a universal truth [*pubian zhenli*]; they have been proved through a long period of actual investigation … After Liberation, our country in the work of nationality research and nationality identification, accurately utilized Stalin's theory, causing the nationality identification work to meet with success. (State Commission for Ethnic Affairs 1983:39)

These four criteria are still viewed as normative for defining nationalities in a socialist society such as China (Jin Binggao 1984: 67).[1] For ethnic identification in China, the state defines what traditions qualify as language, locality, and culture – no matter what the group's subjective belief in its existence as a people, or in the legitimacy of these cultural traditions. The Chinese state imagines what qualifies as cultural tradition for the communities in question, and they must respond to that depiction in terms of their own traditional notions and imaginations of identity. These often conflicting imagined identities are then negotiated in each socioeconomic setting, revolving upon symbolic representations of state, self, and other.

---

1. The 1986 publication in *Minzu Yanjiu* (*Nationality Research*) of several papers presented at the 1986 Nationalities Research conference in Shanghai, where Stalin's principles were discussed, revealed that, although the principles were beginning to be questioned for the first time, they were still held as most appropriate for China.

I shall argue in this chapter that ethnic identity in China, and I think other similar contexts, is not merely the result of state definition, nor can it be reduced to circumstantial maneuvering for utilitarian goals by certain groups. Rather, I propose that it is best understood as a dialogical interaction of shared traditions of descent with sociopolitical contexts, constantly negotiated in each politico-economic setting. This approach will also be seen to shed light on majority–minority relations in China, and the ways in which ethnic minorities are not at all marginal to the construction of Chinese national identity.

The enigmatic Hui: in search of an ethnic group

I went to China in the fall of 1983 to begin study of one of the fifty-five officially identified minority nationalities, known as the Hui. According to the official state definition, the Hui are a single minority nationality, the second-largest minority group in China, the most populous of ten Muslim nationalities, with almost half of the 20 million Muslims in China, and the most widely distributed of any minority (Huizu Jianshi Editorial Committee 1978; Gladney 1987a). The other nine Muslim nationalities in China speak mainly Turkic-Altaic (and in one case Indo-European) dialects and are concentrated in China's northwest. The Hui are distinguished from other Muslim minorities by the lack of their own language. They speak the largely Han Chinese dialects of the peoples across China with whom they live, hence they have been referred to in the literature as the 'Chinese Muslims' (Israeli 1978).

Unlike many of the other minority nationalities of China, however, the Hui are distinguished negatively: apart from lacking their own language, they generally do not have the peculiar dress, literature, music, or the other cultural inventories by which more 'colorful' minorities are portrayed. Cultural differences *between* disparate Hui communities are far wider than their distinctions from the non-Hui among whom they live.

When I arrived in Beijing, I set out to carry out my rather narrowly defined proposal: an in-depth social study of an urban Muslim community concentrated mainly in one neighborhood, totaling more than 200,000 Hui. However, it was not long before my informants and Hui advisors assigned to me said that if I wanted to *really* understand the Hui I would have to travel to where they are 'typical', such as, I was told, the northwest. During my year of fieldwork on the Hui workers in Beijing city, I went on two trips through the northwest and the southeast. I then relocated a second year to the Ningxia Hui Autonomous Region in the northwest to conduct further study of a Hui Sufi community. I later returned for three months to the southeast coast to examine another fishing lineage community, and have since made trips to other prominent so-called Hui communities in Yunnan, Tibet, Qinghai, and Xinjiang. The problem was that in all of these trips, the more I traveled, the less I found that tied all of these diverse peoples together into one ethnic group. The following vignettes are drawn from my book *Muslim Chinese* (Gladney 1996a), which seeks to go into each community in much more ethnographic detail. I present them here to illustrate the diversity found among the Hui across China, and to support my argument regarding the dialogic construction of identity in China.

A northwestern Sufi community

In Na Family Village (Najiahu), located along the upper reaches of the Yellow River in China's northwest corner, I sat among over 100 Hui Sufis as they chanted the local *dhikr*. While being swayed from side to side in my spot in the back of the room, tightly wedged between two fervent devotees, I thought to myself, 'No wonder the local Han sometimes referred to them as the fundamentalist 'Shaking head religion' [*yao tou jiao*], or 'shakers'. As members of a Central Asian Naqshbandiyya Sufi brotherhood, the Hui chanted the monotheistic formulae, or *dhikr*, according to the specific dictates of their order. Villagers respond to the call to prayer issued daily from the roof of the 300-year-old Ming-dynasty mosque around which the flat-roofed adobe houses are clustered; they regularly present alms to the mosque, and follow the advice of the imam in arranging a marriage or resolving a dispute.

Although they speak only a local dialect of Northern Mandarin and have no distinct language of their own, they make use of Islamic names within the village, recite Quranic texts in Arabic, and pepper their speech with Arabic and Persian words known as *Huihui hua* (Hui speech). As members of a strict Naqshbandiyya Sufi *tarikat* known as the Khufiyah, they rarely marry outside of their order, and never to Han or members of rival Sufi groups (see Gladney 1987b:501–7). This village was similar to many other isolated Muslim communities in the northwest, which often claimed descent from Turkish or Mongolian Muslim ancestors. In the words of Robert Ekvall, who lived and traveled throughout the northwest in the 1930s, these were still 'little Moslem worlds' amid a Han Chinese state. As one local villager explained her identity: 'I am Hui because I am a Muslim, and my parents were Muslims'. These Hui, locate their unique identity by means of a dialogue with their Islamic heritage.

A Hui community in Oxen Street, Beijing

In another context, Ma Baoguo, an unemployed youth who runs a small Hui noodle stand on the outskirts of Beijing, is one of 200,000 Hui in the capital city. As China's most urban minority (67 percent of all minorities in Beijing, 87 percent in Shanghai and Tianjin), the Hui often live clustered together around the mosque in ethnic enclaves or former ghettoes. Hui *qing zhen* (Chinese for halal) restaurants can be found in every midsize town and city across China. Young Ma differs markedly from his northwestern Hui coreligionists: he is little concerned with Islamic doctrinal issues and maintaining the Muslim religious life. He had never heard of the various Hui Islamic orders that proliferate in the northwest, and he only goes to mosque twice a year, during the Qurban and Ramadan holidays.

In constant dialogical interaction with his Han majority neighbors, he distinguishes himself from them, and is often thought by them to be different because of one thing only: Ma does not eat pork. He has taken a Han wife, which his parents initially opposed, but they acquiesced when they were assured that their child would be raised – and registered – as a Hui. Young Ma is more concerned with running his *qing zhen* private noodle restaurant. When I asked him about his Hui identity, he said: 'I am Hui because I maintain the Hui way of life: I don't eat pork and like many Hui, I am good at doing business. Although I am a secular Marxist and don't believe in Allah, I go to mosque twice a year on our official "minority nationality holidays" in honor of my ancestors, who I think came from the west [*xiyu ren*] several generations ago'.

A Hui community on the southeast coast

In Quanzhou city, a small town on the coast of southern Fujian Province, a sign above the entrance to the courtyard off a narrow alleyway reads in Chinese *Musilin zhi jia* ('Muslim Family'). Below the Islamic insignia, two faded paper traditional Door Gods still guarded the entryway, while poetic Chinese quatrains welcomed the new lunar year. As I entered the courtyard, the host gave the traditional Islamic greeting, '*A-salam 'alaykum*', as incense smoke from a shrine to a local deity rose into the air behind him. My host explained the apparent contradiction between his Hui Muslim identity and his patronage of a Chinese god by reference to descent: 'I am Hui because my earliest ancestor was an Arab [*Ahlabo ren*], and our name was changed in the Ming dynasty [14th century]. We have our family genealogy to prove it. Under the oppressive policy of the Han Chinese feudal government at that time, we Hui were forced to give up our Muslim ways, wear Han dress, adopt Han customs, and not follow Muslim dietary restrictions. But we are still Hui because we are descended from foreign Muslim ancestors. We remember our ancestors were Muslim by not giving them pork during veneration [*baizu*] with the other offerings, lest we ruin their mouths [*huai kou*]'.

This man is one of nearly 60,000 Hui thinly distributed along China's southeast coast, who, because they no longer maintain Islam like the other Hui in China, were not recognized as such in the 1950s, even though they applied and tried to convince the state they considered themselves Hui. Yet these Hui lost the debate; they did not fit the state's interpretation of the Stalinist cultural criteria at that time. In addition to folk religionists, Buddhists, Daoists, and Marxist secularists, there are among these Hui several hundred Christians, who converted in the late 1930s. In 1979, however, after highly politicized negotiations with the state, demonstrating their ancestry with genealogical proof, they were officially recognized as belonging to the Hui.

This legitimation had much to do with the visits by certain foreign Muslims to prominent archeological Islamic sites in Quanzhou, including early tombs and a mosque (Gladney 1995). Kuwaiti businessmen were impressed with the Chinese state's treatment of these early Muslim coastal communities: they heavily funded the Fujian International Airport in Xiamen and a large hydroelectric

dam project outside Fuzhou. Yet fitting into the state-imagined
notion of Hui identity for these Quanzhou lineages has led to a resurgence in those cultural, generally Islamic practices associated in
the state's mind with the Hui. The Party chairman of one lineage
suggested they would be keeping the Ramadan fast soon and obtained funds to build, next to their old lineage hall, a new mosque
(called a prayer hall, *libaisi*, because stricter Muslims objected to it
being called a mosque unless all of the Hui in the village stopped
eating pork).

Hui communities in China's minority areas

The Hui nationality also includes many groups in minority border
areas who follow the language, dress, and customs of their minority
neighbors. In one Bai (Minjia) nationality village north of Erhu
Lake, in Yunnan Province, I interviewed five Hui women who
were training to become imams. They wore traditional Bai dress
and spoke only the Tibeto-Burman Bai language, yet they were
studying Arabic and Islamic doctrine in a non-Bai Hui mosque in
southern Yunnan Province. A Malay-Austronesian-speaking fishing community I visited on the coast of Hainan Island in the South
China Sea is also registered as Hui. When speaking Mandarin, they
call themselves Hui. When speaking their own language, however,
they refer to themselves as Utsat (Pang Shiqian 1988). There are
also Tibetan Muslims in Lhasa, and Mongolian Muslims in the
Alashan Banner district of Inner Mongolia, who are recognized by
the state not as Tibetan or Mongolian Muslims, but as Hui, because
there is no other special category for them.

Hui identity and state recognition

Each of these communities differs radically from the others not
only in language, locality, economy, and 'culture', but also in their
widely divergent visions of their past and future worlds. They subscribe to totally different imagined communities, to use Ben Anderson's (1991) terms, as well as dwelling in different social worlds.
Nevertheless, they are recognized by the state as one nationality, the
Hui, and they now use that self-designation in conversations with
other Hui and non-Hui. In this chapter I argue that this masking of ethnic identity and the rise of new ethnic collectivities in

China is a function of power relations and authority in the modern nation-state. As such, it gives us an excellent insight into questions of ethnicity, religion, and rationality in China, and I think, other modern nation-states as well.[2]

Past anthropological approaches to ethnicity and religion were ill-equipped to deal with ethnic identity in the modern nation-state. Most anthropological ethnicity theory-building in the West has been generated out of rather isolated studies of tribes or groups of peoples in generally small-scale developing nations – especially Africa and South and Southeast Asia. Most of these theories have been found to be cumbersome for the understanding of ethnicity in large, centralized, authoritarian nation-states like China and the former USSR, or even pluralist societies like those of the US and Western Europe. Yet it is precisely in these areas that the resurgence of ethnic identities and inter-ethnic conflict has become most pronounced in recent years – that is, the Tibetan problem in China, the violent disintegration of Yugoslavia, and the Muslim (and recent Azerbaijani–Armenian) tensions in Central Asia.

One of the reasons for the limitations of traditional ethnicity theories in the West is that they have been mired in what Carter Bentley (1987:25) described as 'antinimous posturing' over the primordialist–circumstantialist debate – sparring over whether ethnicity was either purely cultural or expressly situational. While it is clear that the Hui cannot be identified as an ethnic group according to cultural traits of language, locality, or even religion, as the case of the Quanzhou Hui demonstrates, a purely socioeconomic or politically motivated situationist approach, as found in the work of Fredrik Barth, Immanuel Wallerstein, Abner Cohen, and others, cannot account for why the Hui and other ethnic groups continued in dysfunctional situations. Particularly during the radical periods of recent Chinese history, such as the Cultural Revolution, I can find no instances where the Hui rejected their ancestry: if anything their identity became more pronounced, leading to several large-scale uprisings.

Most theorists now conclude that ethnicity cannot be reduced to a means–end calculus or primordial attachment, but must involve

2.   This is particularly characteristic of totalitarian regimes in which authority and identity infuse every aspect of identity and discourse, Claude Leforte argues in his powerful *Political Forms of Modern Society* (1986).

a combination or dialectical interaction of the two main aspects of ethnicity: culturally defined notions of descent, and sociopolitical circumstance (Keyes 1981:28). An important consideration for understanding ethnic change is the role of the state in defining the context and content of modern ethnic tradition.

Ethnicity and the nation-state

E.K. Francis (1976:114), in his lengthy and profound *Interethnic Relations*, was one of the first to argue that the rise of ethnic identities and inter-ethnic conflict was a phenomenon of the modern nation-state – as nation-states were built on the ashes of former empires, decidedly ethnic identities became more salient for social interaction and discourse. David Maybury-Lewis (1984:221), in his discussion of ethnicity in plural societies, has argued that the French Revolution's ideal of equality and participation in governance formed the basis of the idea of the modern nation-state. Rousseau would have opposed the recognition of ethnic groups for fear that they would interfere with individual representation, but 'the social pact' that he argued 'established equality among all citizens' (Rousseau 1968 [1762]:49) allowed for its possibility. Hobbes' (1962 [1651]:141) famous dictum, 'Nature hath made men so equal ...', was couched in the awareness of the differences separating men, which he encouraged the state to resolve without the need for war as a final means to adjudicate inequity and exploitation. The recognition of equality rests on the admission of difference.

Lloyd Fallers, one of the few anthropologists to analyze the 'anthropology of the nation-state', notes, 'The logic of populistic nationalism ... encourages scrutiny to discover and eradicate diversity and thus exacerbates diversity' (Fallers 1974:3). 'Since sovereignty in the modern nation-state is vested in the people, rather than in a monarch legitimated by descent or religious charisma', Charles Keyes (1984:15) perceptively argues, 'the subjects of the modern nation-state must be integrated into the people'.[3] Indeed, Ernest Gellner (1983:55) proposes that 'nationalism engenders nations, not the other way around'. It is culture – or I would argue, cultural expression – that is manipulated and invented, for the sake

3.   This is taken from the English version of the original conference paper that subsequently has been published in Russian (Keyes 1984).

of nationalist interests, those either of the state or of the community in question:

Dead languages can be revived, traditions invented, quite fictitious pristine purities restored. But this culturally creative, fanciful, positively inventive aspect of nationalist ardour ought not to allow anyone to conclude, erroneously, that nationalism is a contingent, artificial, ideological invention, which might not have happened, if only those damned busy-body interfering European thinkers, not content to leave well alone, had not concocted it and fatefully injected it into the bloodstream of otherwise viable political communities. The cultural shreds and patches used by nationalism are often arbitrary historical inventions. Any old shred and patch would have served as well. But in no way does it follow that the principle of nationalism itself, as opposed to the avatars it happens to pick up for its incarnations, is itself in the least contingent and accidental. (Gellner 1983:56)

This may be going to the extreme. If culture did not exist, Gellner seems to suggest, nationalist movements would have had to invent it. As I shall argue below, these 'inventions of tradition' (Hobsbawm 1983a:4) are better understood as negotiations over, and reinterpretations of, symbolic representations of identity – an unceasing process that becomes particularly salient when the nation-state takes upon itself the task of legislating national identity.

National identity becomes particularly critical during modern state-incorporation, where citizenship may be imposed rather than sought. In this case, participation in the government process is not so crucial as *the idea* that it should take place in the modern nation-state. The precise nature of the group becomes a matter for negotiation and genesis. In the modern era, it is often the nation-state with which ethnic groups find themselves in dialogical opposition.

The dialogical nature of ethnic identity

I propose that the formation of ethnic identity in the modern nation-state is a process of dialogical interaction between self-perceived notions of identity and sociopolitical contexts, often defined by the state. In each of these examples of ethnogenesis we see at least two levels of discourse, articulated internally and externally. I return to Bakhtin, whose study of Dostoevsky posed fundamental questions of self and society, identity and ideology:

The endlessness of the external dialogue emerges here with the same mathematical clarity as does the endlessness of internal dialogue ... In

Dostoevsky's dialogues, collision and quarrelling occur not between two integral monologic voices, but between two divided voices (one of those voices, at least, is divided). The open rejoinders of the one answer the hidden rejoinders of the other. (Bakhtin 1981 [1963]:253–4)

In the composition of ethnic discourse and identity, we find an internal dialogue between the ethnic actors over their traditional interpretations of ancestry, no matter how that is marked symbolically, and an external dialogue with those with whom the group is in significant opposition: other ethnic groups or the broader state as it is represented at the local level. As the dialogue at each level changes, so do the self- and other-definitions of the ethnic groups. This dialogue is a 'prolonged conversation', as Jean Comaroff noted in a very different context – continually revived and altered during the course of shifts in discursive power. What is unique in the modern era, however, is that groups are now not only in dialogue with, and in opposition to, other groups, tribes, ethnicities, or whatever you wish to call them, that have always existed; now the group confronts and is confronted by the state, whose general policies are articulated by its representatives at the local level.

I suggest that the process is one of dialogue and interrelation, not dialectics, in that identities do not always emerge antithetically to the old: new identities may surface, old ones may be reinvented, and each will be in constant dialogue with the other. Dialectical change implies a negation of the prior subject with the resolution of a new synthetic form. Strict Hegelian dialectics invoke notions of unidirectional change and progress. However, ethnic identity and change is often a convoluted process of dynamic interaction with prior notions of identity and environment – a setting in constant flux due to migration, power relations, and state policy. This dialogical process is seen especially in light of Hui ethnogenesis and the emergence of a higher-order collectivity. The question of state interaction and incorporation is particularly relevant to the emergence of the modern Hui people – the creation, or reinvention, of their traditions by the Chinese nation-state.

Ethnogenesis of a Muslim minority: from Huijiao to Huimin

Official histories and minority nationality maps to the contrary, before their identification by the state in the 1950s the Hui were not a united ethnic group in the modern sense of the term. Like many other groups, the Hui only emerged in the transition from empire to nation-state. The people now known as the Hui are descended from Persian, Arab, Mongolian, and Turkish Muslim merchants, soldiers, and officials who settled in China from the 7th to 14th centuries and intermarried with Han women. They largely lived in isolated communities; the only thing that some, but not all, had in common was a belief in Islam. Until the 1950s in China, Islam was simply known as the 'Hui religion' (*Huijiao*) – believers in Islam were *Huijiao* believers. Until then, any person who was a believer in Islam was a 'Hui religion disciple' (*Huijiao tu*). When necessary, some of these were further described as Hui who wore turbans (*zhuantou Hui*, referring to the present-day Uyghur), Hui with colored eyes (*semu Hui*, meaning Central Asian Turkic peoples), and other various local ethnonyms. This derives from Chinese attempts to generalize about the Central Asian peoples on its northwestern borders; one settled oases-based kingdom with which the Tang dynasty had most interaction called themselves Uyghur, and the term in Chinese became *Huihe*, or *Huigu*. By the Yuan dynasty all Muslims were referred to in Chinese as *Huihui* (Leslie 1986:195–6). The specific official labels for the Hui people and the other nine Muslim minorities were only legally established after the founding of the People's Republic.

Djamal al-Din Bai Shouyi, a famous Hui Marxist historian, was the first to argue persuasively that 'Islam' should be glossed in Chinese as *Yisilan jiao* (Islam), not the Hui religion (*Huijiao*) (Bai 1951).[4] He noted that the Hui believed not in their own religion, but in a world religion of Islam, and therefore are Muslims in religious terms. In ethnicity they are the Hui people, not Hui religion disciples. In Marxist terms, he identified a process of the indigenization of a world religion, in this case Islam, to a local context, studied by Weber and later followers of his method, which for the communities now known as the Hui had been going on for 1,200

---

4.   Bai Shouyi literally made the closing argument to an internal debate, which had been taking place throughout the Nationalist period, about whether the Hui should be known as *Huimin* or believers in *Huijiao*. This took place when many Hui intellectuals traveled to Japan and the Middle East and were caught up in the nationalist fervor of the Republican period, publishing magazines and questioning their identity in a process that one Hui historian, Ma Shouqian (1989), has termed 'The New Awakening of the Hui at the End of 19th and Beginning of the 20th Centuries'.

years. Chinese linguists identified Muslim groups with supposedly their own language, and who derived their ethnonym from the language family, thus the Uyghur, Kazakh, Tajik, Uzbek, Kyrgyz, and Tartar were identified. In this, the Chinese were heavily influenced by the prior Soviet identification of these peoples in Soviet Central Asia. Bai Shouyi went on to identify the Muslim peoples not identified by language or locality as a catchall residual group known as *Huimin*, not *Huijiao*. Thus the official category of the Hui was legitimated.

More problematic are three other identified Muslim groups, the Dongxiang, Baoan, and Salar, located primarily in the Hexi Corridor of the Gansu–Qinghai Tibetan Plateau, in a region now largely included in the Linxia Hui Autonomous Prefecture. Each of these groups speaks a combination of Turkic, Mongolian, and Han Chinese dialects, and is thus defined mainly by locality; for example, the Dongxiang (East Township) derive their name from the eastern suburb of old Hezhou (Linxia) where they were concentrated. The question remains, however, why these groups received their separate identifications, when other groups such as the Mongolian Hui, Tibetan Hui, Bai Hui, and Hainan Hui, described above, are all identified as Hui. They did not receive separate identities despite their separate localities and languages. Their populations are not insignificant enough to warrant their lack of a distinct identity, since the Baoan numbered 9,027 in 1982 (the Tartar only 4,127), while there were at least 6,000 Hainan Hui (Pang Shiqian 1988), as well as large unnumbered Mongolian, Tibetan, Dai, Yi, and Miao Hui groups (see Ma Weiliang 1986). Chinese minority publications proudly proclaim the recognition of such insignificant groups as the Hezhe, despite their only having a population of 1,476 in 1982, with 300 at the time of the revolution, and 450 reported at the time of their identification in 1953 (Zhongguo 1981:57–68; Banister 1987:322–3).

The present-day Uyghur are concentrated in the oasis cities of the Xinjiang Uyghur Autonomous Region and are known as the settled Muslim Turkic-speaking people of the Tarim Basin. However, the term 'Uyghur' was revived by the Soviets in the 1930s for those oasis peoples who had no name for themselves other than their locality: Kashgarlik (from Kashgar), Turpanlik (from Turpan), Aksulik (from Aksu), as well as Taranchi, Turki, and Sart. The current name was adopted by the Chinese in 1934. However, the term itself had not been used since the 15th century, when it referred to the settled oasis peoples of the Tarim Basin, who were Buddhist and expressly non-Muslim. Once these peoples began to convert to Islam from the 10th to 15th centuries, they rejected the ethnonym Uyghur, which to them meant heathen. It was accepted by the now 6 million Muslims of this area so they could gain recognition by the state and as an autonomous region. The other terms for the Muslim peoples of Xinjiang, such as Kazakh, Tartar, Kirghiz, Uzbek, and Tajik, were taken over by the Chinese from the Soviets, and these ethnonyms are not without their problems.[5]

It is clear that a strict interpretation of Stalin's four identification principles would not have yielded the present ten Muslim groups in China today. Instead, we find a combination of political, strategic, and pragmatic concerns in the early recognition of these groups. This is not surprising given Walker Connor's (1984) thesis that the main concern of the early Bolsheviks in resolving the nationalist question was not ideological or theoretical purity, but strategic survivability: ethnic policy was created on the ground to enlist the support of the nationalities in the building of the new nation-state. For China, this policy was formed most critically on the Long March.

During this long trek from the southwest to the northwest, through the areas most densely populated by minorities, the Communist leadership became acutely aware of the vigorous ethnic identity of the Muslims and other peoples they encountered. Edgar Snow (1938), and the more recent chronicler Harrison Salisbury (1985), graphically described the desperate plight of the Long Marchers, who were persistently harassed by the Japanese and the Nationalists on one flank, and by the 'fierce barbarian tribesmen' on the other.[6] The fathers of the yet-to-be-born Chinese nation

---

5. For a discussion of the problematic nature of these Central Asian identifications in the former Soviet Union, see Wimbush (1985).
6. In *Red Dust*, Nym Wales, the wife of Edgar Snow, reproduces her fascinating Yenan interviews with several of the Long Marchers. Hsu Meng-ch'iu, official historian of the Long March, described how, after narrowly escaping slaughter at the hands of the 'fierce Lolos' and 'wild Tibetans' in Sichuan, the 'Red Army marched on to north Shensi [Shaanxi], pursued by three cavalry elements – those of Ma Hung-k'uei, Ma Hung-p'ing, and Chiang Kai-shek. Because of the speed of the cavalry, many Red troops in the rear were cut off and captured' (Hsu Meng-ch'iu, cited in Wales 1952:74). The first two were (Hui) Muslim warlords who controlled most of Ningxia and Gansu. Hsu also

were faced with extermination or making promises of special
treatment to the minorities, specifically including the Miao, Yi
(Lolo), Tibetan, and Hui. The first Hui autonomous county was
set up in the 1930s in southern Ningxia as a demonstration of the
early Communists' goodwill toward the Hui. In a chapter entitled
'Moslem and Marxist', Snow (1938) records several encounters
with militant conservative Hui Muslims and subsequent strong
lectures to 8th Route Army troops to respect Hui customs lest the
soldiers offend them and provoke conflicts. Mao (1936:1–3) issued
an appeal to the northwest Hui to support the Communists' cause,
even mentioning the renaissance of Turkey under Atatürk as an
example for China's Muslims (see Forbes 1976:77; Lindbeck 1950).
One slogan that Snow (1938:320) observed posted by Hui soldiers
training under the Communist 15th Army Corps was: 'Build our
own anti-Japanese Mohammedan Red Army'. Perhaps Chairman
Mao was more sensitive to the Muslim issue since his brother had
been killed in Xinjiang in the 1930s due to inter-ethnic and intra-
Muslim factionalism. Later Party documents (*Dangshi Wenshi Ziliao*) that have come to light from the Long March reveal that until
1937 Chairman Mao explicitly promised self-determination to the
minorities, offering them not only privileges, but also the right to
secede, as remained the case in the Soviet constitution until the
collapse of the USSR. However, in China this right was withdrawn
by 1940 and limited regional 'autonomy' was offered instead (see
Schwarz 1971). The transition in Chinese terminology from 'self-
determination' (*zi zhu*) to 'autonomy' (*zi zhi*) is slight, but for the
minorities it represented a major shift in policy.

Since the founding of the PRC, international considerations
– particularly the desire for Third World, often Muslim, investment – have encouraged favoritism toward minorities, so that
goals of pluralism and assimilation have constantly shifted, depending on local and international politics. Chinese Marxists were
surprised that these created groups did not fade away with the
land reforms, collectivization, and erosion of class-based loyalties.
Ethnicity is often a vertical phenomenon that cuts across class and

---

records several graphic accounts of 'barbarians' sweeping down out of the
mountains upon the hapless Long Marchers, screaming 'Woo-woo-woo' in
unintelligible dialects – reminiscent of accounts of encounters with Native
Americans in US 'Western' movies.

socioeconomic stratification, and it has maintained its salience despite the land-reform campaigns and other efforts to reduce class-based social differences in China and the former Soviet Union.

That the state employed a Stalinist cultural definition is very important for our understanding of how local ethnic communities responded to policies of incorporation. Walker Connor (1984) has shown that whereas the original creation of ethnic groups was a strategic, temporary recognition of ethnic difference to solicit support in the revolutionary process, it later led to the hardening of ethnic boundaries – the creation of identities that serve as the basis for many of the new nations that have recently grown like snakes out of the head of former Soviet Medusa. After reviewing the resurgence and reinterpretation of so-called traditions, Eric Hobsbawm emphasized their relevance

to that comparatively recent historical innovation, the 'nation', with its associated phenomena: nationalism, the nation-state, national symbols, histories and the rest. All these rest on exercises in social engineering which are often deliberate and always innovative … the national phenomenon cannot be adequately investigated without careful attention to the 'invention of tradition'. (Hobsbawm 1983a:13–14)

Attention to the creation of culture has become a preoccupation since Hobsbawm and Ranger's important volume (1983). In this chapter, I am arguing for the examination of the unique process involved in the creation not only of culture, but also of 'cultures' by authoritarian regimes, as the case of the Hui so clearly reveals.

The social life of labels

The state in China has assigned ethnic labels to the peoples identified by them – labels that I have shown to be quite arbitrary and defined primarily by the state. Nevertheless, it can be argued that over the past fifty years these labels have taken on a life of their own. Like material commodities, which Appadurai (1986a) convincingly argues gain enduring sociopolitical value beyond their original intent, these state designations have contributed to a growing sense of minority nationalism. Bernard Cohn (1971) has recorded the continued use of the rather arbitrarily assigned ethnic labels used by British colonial administrators to sort out the multi-ethnic populations of South India. No matter how anachronistic, these labels often become fixed when designated by those in power to administrate and delineate peoples under their control, taking on a meaningfulness and power of their own.

Hui in China, no matter where one travels, now refer to themselves as Hui. Sometimes, however, less-informed members of the community slip into old habits. I was amused when one of my Hui colleagues who was present at an interview would enter into a dialogue of state-defined discourse with the peasant, correcting his 'politically incorrect' speech. 'No you are not a "Hui religion disciple" [*Huijiao tu*],' he reprimanded. 'You are a "Hui person" [*Huimin*]. Hui believe in Islam [*Yisilan jiao*], not their own Hui religion.'[7] Even on Hainan Island, where Malay–Austronesian speaking Muslims have difficulty communicating in Mandarin Chinese, when I visited them in 1985 they referred to themselves as Hui. In their local language they are known among themselves as Utsat (Pang Shiqian 1988). So also do the various peoples of the Tarim Basin refer to themselves by their locality oasis names, Kashgarlik, Aksulik, Turpanlik – only to outsiders or when visiting the city do they generally call themselves Uyghur. Yet these terms are becoming increasingly accepted by the people as an inclusive ethnonym, stimulating further communication and exchange between them.

This crystallization of ethnic identities based on state-assigned labels was emphasized to me by a Han scholar who went to Xinjiang in the early 1950s as a language student and teacher. After taking a one-month truck ride from Xi'an to Ürümqi, she was assigned to a predominantly Uyghur village that also had Kazakh and Hui residents. At the time she noticed that there was less division among them as Muslims. They worshipped in the same mosque and generally made little reference to their ethnic identities. Following a return trip in 2001, however, she said they no longer prayed together and seemed to have much stronger ideas of their separateness from one another.

With the present benefits attached to ethnic identification in China, such as birth-planning exemption, educational advancement, employment opportunities, tax reductions, and political mobility, this may sound like a return to a situationist view of ethnicity

---

7.   Pang Keng-Fong (1992) and I have both experienced the situation of being referred to as American Hui (*Meiguo Huihui*) when we were mistaken for foreign Muslims during fieldwork.

– the Hui are Hui for utilitarian purposes. However, while I maintain that ethnic identity is an inherently political phenomenon, it is obvious that for the Hui there is an important dialogue involved between the state's preconceived notions of identity and the communities in question, who must respond in dialogical interaction with their own traditions. These traditions are drawn from their reservoir of ideas about ancestry, and are not manufactured in a vacuum – which is what separates an *ethne*, a people, from a mere social convention.

The local expression of Hui identity

The dialogue between Islam and the construction of Hui identity in the Chinese nation-state can be seen in the nature of the response of the communities I described at the beginning of this chapter. For Hui communities in northwest China, Islam is taken to be the fundamental marker of their identity – to be Hui is to be Muslim. An incredible variety of Islamic movements, which I have catalogued elsewhere (Gladney 1987b:518–25), have arisen through internal dialogues and debates in these communities as Hui reformers sought to resolve the tensions created by adapting the ideals of Islam to the changing Chinese social world. Government policy that permits freer expression of Hui ethnic identity has also allowed the resurgence of Islam – since this is the primary marker of Hui identity in these communities, and Islam for them has taken on new, re-created meaning in the changed contexts. With the encouraged and improved relations between China and Muslim Middle Eastern governments, increased travel on the hajj from China (6,000 pilgrims traveled in 2001) and further visits to Islamic holy sites in China by foreign Muslims has led to a heightened sense of Islamic identity – especially for those northwestern Hui who see Islam as the fundamental marker of their identity.

Hui urban communities, such as those in Beijing, tend to express their identity in terms of cultural traditions: the pork taboo, entrepreneurship, and craft specializations. This leads to the growing importance of ethnic economic niches, such as the restaurant, in preserving and expressing Hui identity in the city, which Furnival (1939) so clearly described in the rise of pluralism in Southeast Asia. Hui traditional occupations as small merchants, restaurateurs, butchers, and jewelry craftsmen led to their being depicted as the

'Jews of China' (Pillsbury 1973). Liberalized nationality and economic policies have contributed to the cultural and economic
expansion of those specializations and small businesses that most
reflect urban Hui descent from Hui ancestors – ethnic entrepreneurialism has become 'symbolic capital' (Bourdieu 1977:171–5)
in Oxen Street and other urban Hui centers. This ethnic capital
is being encouraged by the state as a marker of Hui identity. In a
startling recognition of the importance of the business ethic among
the Hui, Fei Xiaotong acknowledged that Hui 'had been blessed
with this talent from their ancestors, who nurtured trading skills
during centuries-long commercial dealings' (Fei 1987:4). Because
the Hui had no common language or locality, or other cultural
markers of identity, Fei argued, Hui capitalism should be encouraged as their ethnic trait in the interests of modernization and development, and not to be criticized as feudal. Fei has perhaps unwittingly given credence to a very Weberian notion of economic
rationality. Incredibly, in China the supposed Protestant work ethic
has been attributed to Muslims.

In southeastern Hui lineages, genealogical descent is the most
important aspect of Hui identity: to be Hui is to be a member of a
lineage that traces its descent to foreign ancestors – who just *happened* to be Muslim. State recognition of these lineages as members
of the Hui nationality has led to ethnic resurgence among previously unrecognized Hui lineages throughout the southeast coast.
In turn, contact with state-sponsored Hui and foreign Muslim
delegations has led to a growing interest for many of these Hui in
their ethnoreligious roots, and even in practicing Islam. Because
the state follows a cultural definition of ethnic identity, the Hui in
Quanzhou who have totally assimilated must manufacture generally Islam-associated cultural traits to insure their continued acceptance by the state and the broader Hui community.

In line with this effort, the state supported the bringing of four
imams from the Ningxia Hui Autonomous Region in 1984 to
Fujian, to train the local Hui in the ways of Islam, which only a few
of them had remembered. Now other Hui who were not recognized by the state in the 1950s as Hui, because they no longer practiced Islam, are seeking to revive those Islamic cultural traditions
thought to legitimate their claims to minority nationality status.
One lineage, for example, sought funds to build a mosque and
establish an autonomous Hui county, and planned to fast during

Ramadan. One delegation of applicants for Hui recognition asked me if their practice, known as *kai jing*, of opening the Quran at the head of largely Buddhist funeral processions qualified them as culturally Hui. The salience of Hui identity and tradition, as it is culturally defined and encouraged by the Chinese state, is gradually being reinculcated in the daily habitus (or practice) of their lives.

The rise of pan-Hui ethnic identity

There were, of course, many traditional contacts among disparate Muslim communities throughout Chinese history. It is significant that Muslim communities in Quanzhou, Hainan, and Yunnan often sent their neophytes to be trained in Islamic madrasahs at mosques in other Muslim centers in Beijing, Hezhou, and Ningxia, despite these novices not speaking the language, or their having a very different cultural background (see Gladney 1987b:139–41). Hui Sufi *tarikat* had extensive hierarchies of membership that included brotherhood communities from Yunnan, to Harbin, to Xinjiang (Yang Huaizhong forthcoming). But these itinerants traveled to such disparate communities as fellow Muslims, believers in the Hui religion (*Huijiao*) of Islam, not as members of an ethnic group. Trade and caravan networks that brought wool from the Qinghai-Tibetan Plateau all the way down the Yellow River to the northern port of Tianjin, in exchange for tea, guns, and luxury items, were often dominated by Hui Muslims (see Lipman 1988; Millward, J.A. 1988). While important economic and socioreligious connections existed, there is little evidence of a transnational pan-Hui identity until the contemporary era.

The shift from Hui religion (*Huijiao*) to Hui people (*Huimin*) is a crucial transition. Its importance is illustrated by reluctance of the Nationalist government in Taiwan to recognize the existence of any Hui people; it recognized only the Hui religion (*Huijiao*), which includes Hui, Uyghur, and Kazakh. There are lineages in Taiwan directly related to the Hui in Quanzhou across the Taiwan Strait, who also do not follow Islamic dietary restrictions and practice local Chinese folk religion, but who no longer maintain any idea of their separate ancestry (see Gladney 1995). It is not salient to them in the Taiwanese sociopolitical world and they have completely lost their identity as Hui, while for members of the same lineage in the China mainland, Hui identity is once again becoming revitalized due to shifts in state policy and the new salience of their traditions.

State definition, minority identity, and Han nationalism

In every modern nation, ethnicity is manipulated and made meaningful according to internal and external dialogues between state policy and interpretations of identity. However, China and other authoritarian regimes differ from pluralistic nations in that ethnicity is not optional: one is born into an ethnic group and is registered as such, or one is not. Leo Despres' (1984) definition of ethnicity as a 'mask of confrontation' is helpful for understanding opposition and ethnicity, but in this case the masks are not easily removed or affixed. No Weberian subjective feeling of commonality or political action will change that. Unauthorized 'associations' of unrecognized groups are still illegal – unlike Irish in Chicago or Jews in New York, who have political power despite not being classified as official underprivileged minorities in the US. Only the officially designated underprivileged minorities and Native Americans find parallel with the minority nationalities of China and the former Soviet Union. Unrecognized groups are not *ethne* for the Chinese state – no matter how much such groups think they are. Under the all-seeing eye of Jeremy Bentham's authoritarian panopticon, as Foucault so vividly portrayed for the modern totalitarian regime, all behavior is monitored.[8] In the multi-ethnic world of China, the state panopticon can better watch people if they are divided into certain cells, or accepted categories of ethnicity and tradition. After delineating the cells, though, the state cannot guarantee the created communities within do not take on a life of their own.

Ethnic identities are not absent outside of the officially recognized nationalities. Unofficial, unrecognized peoples live very ethnic lives. Subei people are stigmatized in Shanghai (see Honig 1992); Danmin (boat people) are ridiculed on the southeast coast;

8. In this powerful metaphor, Foucault describes the central control-tower of a circular prison in which all prisoners can be seen by the watcher, who cannot be seen. This leads, as Bentham points out, to total submission: 'to be incessantly under the eyes of the inspector is to lose in effect the power to do evil and almost the thought of wanting to do it' (Bentham, cited in Fallers 1974). I am grateful to Ann Anagnost (pers. comm.) for first indicating the relevance of this metaphor to the modern Chinese state.

Chinese Jews are becoming a political force, even though they may only number eighty so far (though some estimates put their population between 2,000 and 8,000), due to international attention and the formation of the Society for the Study of Chinese Jewry; and there are differences among Cantonese, Sichuanese, and Hunanese that have until now been discounted as regional because these people are all assumed to be Han. While these groups are well recognized as ethnic outside of China, their failure to be counted among the nationalities within the state's domain has never been challenged.

These extranationality associations cast doubt on the notion of the Han: the assumption that 91 percent of China is one ethnic group is accepted by Chinese and most Western scholars. This should give us pause – perhaps we also have been taken in for very political reasons. Fred Blake's important study, *Ethnic Groups and Social Change in a Chinese Market Town* (1981), identified a profusion of ethnic groups defined by language, place, and occupation, including Hakka, Cantonese, and Hokkien. While all but one of these groups remain unrecognized as minority nationalities in China, no one has objected to Blake's depiction of them as vibrant ethnic groups. This is perhaps because they lived in the New Territories of Hong Kong under British jurisdiction. What will happen to these so-called ethnic groups now that Hong Kong has reverted to China?[9] Will Blake be criticized for confusing subregional identity with ethnicity? Clearly the issue of state hegemony and nationality identification requires further attention.

While research on the rise of Russian nationalism has been popular in Russian studies since the 1970s, by foreigners and by Russians (see Brudny 2000; Conquest 1986; Dunlop 1983; Yanov 1987), as yet no larger studies of the creation of Han nationalism have emerged – mainly because it is assumed, by sinologists, perhaps indoctrinated in the dominant tradition, that 'Han' is generally equal to 'Chinese' – a tradition created and maintained by the current regime. The lack of fit of Russian with Soviet led to much

---

9. It is interesting to note that China has not decided to increase its number of official nationalities, despite the inclusion of thousands of South Asians (mostly Indians, Gurkhas, and Pakistanis) and other ethnic groups in Hong Kong. It has instead grouped them all as 'foreign nationals', although it has included the standard nationalities (for example, the Hui in Hong Kong are counted as part of the total Hui population in China).

discussion regarding Russian nationalism in Soviet studies (All-worth 1980:18). This has not been considered in studies of Chinese nationalism, which address all Chinese as if they are alike. Perhaps the traditional Confucian preoccupation with order and harmony in a society held tenuously together by proper relationships may be one reason why these categories have never been challenged. The very Confucian practice of the 'rectification of names' (*zheng ming*) is of primary concern to the Chinese ethnographers: once the Han and all of the minority nationalities have been identified or named, order is restored, and all is well with the realm. It is not surprising that Engels' *Origin of the Family, Private Property and the State* is so popular in China, because it is clear in this work that the state's primary role is to bring order among conflicting classes.

The Stalinist four 'commons' are already seen to have had a sub-stantial influence on this nascent policy of Han nationalism. The overriding purpose of the rhetoric is clear: a call for the unity of the Chinese nation based on a common charter of descent. Under the KMT nationalist policy the Han and Hui were not considered to be separate *minzu* (peoples, nationalities): the Hui were a reli-gious group with special characteristics, and were to be referred to as *Huijiaoren* or *Huijiaotu*. Hence, in Taiwan the Hui (and other Muslims grouped with them) have never attained a special na-tionality status (Pillsbury 1973). The Han, on the other hand, were subsumed under the greater Chinese 'race' and did not receive any special 'majority' treatment. Interestingly, both the rationale and end-purpose of Sun Yat-sen's and Chiang Kai-shek's nationality discourses are the same: national unity. From Sun Yat-sen's earlier policy of Five Peoples we see the basis of the later Communist minority-nationality platform.

By contrast, I asked a Chinese colleague when it was he first realized he was a Han. No monocultural individual, he had grown up in the cosmopolitan Manchurian city of Harbin, long a center of Sino-Russian trade and northeastern ethnic diversity, populated by Russians, Manchurians, Koreans, Mongols, Olonqen (Oroqen), Daur, Hezhe, and Hui. Yet this intellectual, who conducted post-doctoral research at Harvard, grew up in Harbin without realizing that he was a distinct nationality. 'The first time I knew I was a Han,' he told me, 'was when I was seventeen years old and I regis-tered for work. I filled out the form and the man there told me to write "Han" in the blank category for nationality (*minzu*). I didn't know what to write.' It was when he applied for a job in the state-controlled sector that this Han fully realized his official ethnic status. It had little meaning for him until then. Attention to personal habitus cannot ignore the context of state hegemony and power.

This study has also attempted to emphasize the importance of international relations in ethnic identity. To preserve positive relations with foreign Muslim governments, the Chinese have only been harsh toward their Muslim groups when the most radical politics prevailed. Those extreme leftist radicalisms, as political theorists have shown, often coincided with insecure international borders. When China felt threatened by encroaching rival powers (for example, during the Vietnam War), leftist radicalism prevailed (for example, the Cultural Revolution). Now that no one challenges the legitimacy of the Chinese nation-state – even Tibet has been accepted as part of China by the United Nations – and the Soviet Union has dissolved, China's policy toward its minorities can afford to be more open. If outside threats should arise, minority policies would presumably harden – just as resentment toward Japanese in the USA bears a direct relation to the perceived economic or political international threat of Japan to US interests.

The dialogue and contestation of ethnicity in China

Understanding of the Hui in the past has been hampered by models and policies that could not account for the wide diversity and unity of the Hui. Models that relied on a cultural trait analysis, such as the Stalinist and cultural approaches, foundered on the similarity between Hui and Han, and on the diversity found within the Hui. Although the Hui did not fit the Stalinist model, the government chose to recognize them on the basis of pre-revolutionary ideas for the political goals of incorporation and state-building, in a careful rewriting of history, described by Richard Rubenstein (1978) in his *Cunning of History*. Utilitarian situational approaches had trouble with the continued meaningfulness and power of ethnic identity in the face of hegemonic oppression. Attention to power relations in the ongoing dialogue between the state and local ethnic groups, externally and internally, is critical for our understanding of the current resurgence of ethnic identities, their meaningfulness and salience in the modern world. Foucault reminds us that the state is compelled to address a plethora of non-negotiables:

The state is superstructural in relation to a whole series of power networks that invest the body, sexuality, the family, kinship, knowledge, technology and so forth. True, these networks stand in a conditioning–conditioned relationship to a kind of 'meta-power' which is structured essentially round a certain number of great prohibition functions; but this meta-power, with its prohibitions, can only take hold and secure its footing where it is rooted in a whole series of multiple and indefinite power relations that supply the necessary basis for the great negative forms of power ... (Foucault 1980:24–5)

Ethnicity is but one item of metapower that is constantly negotiated between state and self: the dialogue is ongoing and regularly redefined in changing social contexts. At times it may take the form of protracted negotiation, argument, or one-sided mandate, as in the assignment of the labels of ethnicity. Throughout the history of China's relations with its Muslim and minority peoples, there have been countless moments of resistance to state hegemony and incorporation. In 1989, Hui rose up across China to protest a Chinese book they found as offensive as Salman Rushdie's *Satanic Verses* was to Muslims worldwide (see Gladney 1996a:1–15; 1994). The state responded by meeting all of the Muslims' demands, confiscating the books, arresting the authors, and closing the publishing house. This evidenced a marked change; during the Cultural Revolution the state cracked down on a local Hui uprising in Yunnan and massacred a documented 866 Hui, although other estimates put the total at 1,600 deaths (Gladney 1996a:137–40). Perhaps the 1989 response was more favorable toward the Hui because of the dialogue in which China was now engaging with Middle Eastern Muslim governments that would be reluctant to conduct military and construction trade with a state that repressed its Muslim peoples.

The remarkable ethnogenesis of the Hui and the critical transition from *Huijiao* to *Huimin* is generally absent from modern histories, which attempt to emphasize the long history of the Hui living within the Chinese state.[10] In this dialogical process of

10. Lin Yueh-hwa's discussion of the Yi (formerly Lolo) people in Sichuan also typically depicts a uniform history of a people which 'is an old one in China ... Ever since ancient time, the Yis have been a member of the family of Chinese nationalities' (Lin 1984:90). This masks a wide variety of sociocultural variety among a people now labeled as the 'Yi', which comprise at least three separate ethnolinguistic groups that were for most of their history independent of Chinese rule (Harrell 1989).

ethnogenesis, the Hui are not alone. Field studies of minorities in China have revealed a parallel process of movement from tribe to nation, particularly among the Yi (Harrell 1995), Uyghur (Gladney 1993), Bai (Yokoyama 1988), and Tibetans (Goldstein 1990). In each case a dialogue took place in which local representatives of the Chinese state became convinced of claims to ethnic and cultural legitimacy, thereby leading to their initial recognition. In some cases it has gone the other way, and the state has denied minority recognition. Tibetans have consistently argued that Deng people – currently members of the Tibetan minority, who have applied for separate identification – should not be allowed to be recognized as their own nationality lest the state attempt to divide the Tibetans further, diminish their numbers, and split up their territory. This protracted negotiation has continued to influence both sides over the course of the past fifty years, leading to the crystallization and in some cases revitalization of traditional ethnic identities. The population of the Tujia increased from 2.8 million in 1982 to 5.7 million in 1990. The Manchu population increased 228 percent between 1982 and 1990, from 4.3 to 9.8 million.

The state, holding to a Stalinist-cultural definition of ethnicity, must determine the legitimacy of the cultural claims to ethnic status. Thus, it is the state that decides what constitutes language, economy, locality, and culture itself. The minorities, and applicant groups, must convince the state that their cultural traditions are legitimate enough to warrant political recognition, privilege, and further consideration. Thus the debate continues. For Bakhtin (1981 [1975]:84–6), this vitality is the essence of dialogue. It is also what engenders movement in ethnic change on both sides of the debate. As the dialogue evolves, it is to be hoped that new light will be shed on these emergent identities, the nature of the Han nationality, and the relevance of ethnicity to understanding the modern Chinese nation-state.

9

RELATIONAL ALTERITIES

The re-emergence of the 'tribe'

The notion 'tribe', after lying discarded in the waste bin of anthropological history for nearly two decades, has been frequently
redeployed in popular and more scholarly depictions to account
for the resurgence of ethnic nationalisms and communal identities around the globe. The most notorious example of this is Joel
Kotkin's book *Tribes: How Race, Religion, and Identity Determine
Success in the New Global Economy* (1993), in which he argues that
'tribal identities' (in this case, the Jews, Chinese, Japanese, British, and Indians) are at the basis of transnational business success.
The author, said to be an 'internationally recognized authority on
global, economic, political and social trends', invokes, in the words
of Arjun Appadurai's (1993:423) critique, the 'trope of the tribe' to
explain the coupling of 'race, religion, and identity' in the modern
world order. Although Kotkin's is clearly a popular articulation, it
is mirrored in a growing scholarly literature that seeks to locate
resurgent nationalisms in core, primordial, essentialized identities,
now portrayed as 'tribes with flags' (Glass 1990). By contrast, this
chapter will argue that people *subscribe* to certain identities, under
certain highly contextualized moments of social relations. Not unlike contemporary cable channels, these identities are often regulated by nation-states, and limited to certain lines of stereotypical
representation.

Though anthropologists discarded the notion of 'tribe' more
than two decades ago, since it was felt that the term was often only
applied to less-developed, non-Western societies (in other words,
'they are tribal; we are ethnic'), the idea of tribalism has resurfaced
to explain the recent reassertions of identity politics as distant and
diverse as the former Soviet Union, Eastern Europe, South Asia,

and Africa.[1] Central Asia, given its historic connection to nomadic and pastoralist societies, is most vulnerable to suggestions that it is 'tribalism' that is at the core of the new Central Asian identities (see Garthwaite 1993:142).

By contrast, Benedict Anderson (1991) has led the way for a host of theorists in suggesting that national identity is best understood as historically contextualized, a socially constituted and constitutive process of imbuing 'imagined communities' with the belief that they are somehow naturally linked by common identities. Post-structuralist approaches conceptualize identities as highly contested, multiple, constructed and negotiated within and between the power relations of the nation–state, rather than naturalized and primordial (Gupta and Ferguson 1992; Malkki 1992). Nationalist ideologies become cultural productions (Befu 1993; Fox 1990), legitimized as inventions of tradition and narrated as social histories (Hobsbawm 1983a; Tonkin, McDonald, and Chapman 1989).

It may have become axiomatic that ideas of identity, ethnicity, and nationality are socially constructed, but the problem with suggesting that these identities are generally 'imagined' is that Anderson is often taken too literally (in ways he may have never imagined), as if ethnic and national identities were totally 'invented' (to use Hobsbawm and Ranger's formulation [Hobsbawm 1983a:4], which can be, and just as often as that of Anderson is, utterly misconstrued) out of thin air, a fiction of the collective imagination, or an idea that arose in the smoke-filled drawing rooms of a few nouveau British aristocrats (as Greenfeld [1992] seems to suggest). As a corrective, this chapter was written out of a desire to locate the rise of nationalism (and its contemporary challenges) in particular moments of history, coterminous but not synonymous with the end of empire, the rise of colonialism, the expansion of global capital, and the domination of groups gradually classified and taxonomized as subject

---

1. The debate over the inappropriateness of the term 'tribe' for group identity in anthropology is best summarized in the collections by Gulliver (1969) and Helm (1968). For later references to ethnicity as tribal, see Isaacs' 1976 classic, *Idols of the Tribe: Group Identity*, and the more recent work by Glass, *Tribes with Flags: A Dangerous Passage through the Chaos of the Middle East* (1990). It is interesting that in the current ethnic national conflicts in Eastern Europe, rarely is the term 'tribal' used, but it is frequently employed to describe communal violence in Africa, the Middle East, and Central Asia, perhaps indicating a racist and developmental connotation in the term.

peoples, ethnicities, and eventually nations.[2] A related subtext of this chapter is the attempt to inject social theoretical issues into the current writing on Central and Inner Asia. Long closed to non-Soviet scholars and non-Russian speakers, the region is now open to a wide range of travelers, writers, developers, and investigators who are beginning to have a better idea of what is going on, but have rarely seriously theorized or problematized why we see Central Asia in certain ways, and how Central Asians might see each other.[3]

This is why I take issue with Appadurai's (1993) rather idealistic urging to begin 'thinking beyond the nation' to a time (stardate 3005?) when the nation-state is no longer. In light of recent events in Eastern Europe and the former Soviet Union, this must be called 'wishful thinking beyond the nation'. Similarly, Hobsbawm (1990: 9) has theorized that 'nations exist ... in the context of a particular stage of technological and economic development'. He apparently believes that stage is nearly past. Nations and ethnic or linguistic groups are 'retreating before, resisting, adapting to, and being absorbed or dislocated by, the new supranational restructuring of the globe' to the extent that nationalism 'is no longer a major vector of historical development' (Hobsbawm 1990:182).[4] This idea would

2. Earlier versions of this chapter have benefited from insightful questions and critical comments raised during several prior presentations: the Program for Cultural Studies seminar at the East-West Center in Honolulu (September 1993); a US-government-sponsored symposium, 'The Challenge of Ethnic Conflict to National and International Order in the 1990s: Geographic Perspectives', in Washington, DC (September 1993); the Association for Asian Studies Annual Meetings in Boston (March 1994); the East Asia Symposium, University of Chicago (April 1995); the Institute for Comparative Cultures seminar, Sophia University, Tokyo (May 1995); and the Fifth European Seminar on Central Asian Studies, in Copenhagen (August 1995). Most useful were comments raised by my colleagues in the Sociology Department at Bogaziçi University in Istanbul, Turkey, who were subjected to the earliest notions of the project at the beginning of a Fulbright research year in Istanbul in October 1992.

3. That we see Central Asia as somehow 'central' (to what?) or 'inner' (as opposed to outer?) is theorized in a recent unpublished paper (Gladney forthcoming). The region's centrality is taken for granted and vehemently argued by most Central Asianists (see Frank 1992).

4. See also Julia Kristeva's (1993) rather idealistic, even utopian description of 'nations without nationalisms', in which patriotism and civic pride is to exist in a vacuum of self-discovery abstracted from the *realpolitik* of social oppositions and resource competition.

certainly not account for the struggles for nationhood and cultural survival in Palestine, Chechnya, Tibet, much of contemporary Central Asia, and even Quebec (Handler 1988). These trends indicate that the current constructions of identity politics in the form of ethnic nationalisms represent something more than the re-emergence of tribalism, and that they are not confined to the so-called Third World.

Here I think Greenfeld (1992:491) is correct in suggesting that as long as nationalism is *perceived* as the 'constitutive principle of modernity' (the word 'perceived' being most operative here), postnationalism will only arise with a realized post-modernity, and for that we have a long way to go. Arafat, the new leaders of the fifteen nations of the former USSR, and other would-be national leaders in Chechnya, Aceh, and Somalia are busily making more nations, not thinking beyond them.

This chapter places national identity in a field of contemporary and historical social relations, particularly with regard to certain interacting social groups and newly invented nations in Central Asia, Turkey, and China. Given the long history of interactions with powerful others and colonizing empires on the Eurasian steppe, a purely relativist or, at the other extreme, a dehistoricized, essentialized position with regard to identity formation are particularly questionable. Both extremes ignore issues of power, hegemony, 'internal' colonialism, and cultural economy that have long dominated the region.

It is the articulation of the multiplicities of these identities in exile within the context of where they have been expressed, engaging in the 'borderline work of culture' (Bhabha 1994:7) most often in the modern nation-state, that these identities become salient. Through examining three peoples portrayed as 'nations', and who now speak of themselves using that term (but only one of whom recently acquired a nation-state, and only one other of whom as yet lays claim to such a state), I want to suggest three styles of discourse about ethnic nationalism that, to follow Stallybrass and White's formulation (in their richly written *Poetics and Politics of Transgression* [1986]), pose fundamental transgressions of the contemporary nation-state, and intriguing challenges to it. These are discourses of diaspora, indigeneity, and transhumanity elaborated by the social groups now known as Hui (Dungan), Uyghur, and Kazakh.

I argue that nationalism is not just an imagined idea, but represents certain styles of imagined representation, a mode of representation that contributes to a grammar of action now most often defined by interactions within or resistance to the nation-state. As Hobsbawm (1992:4) argues, 'Nationalism is a political programme … Without this programme, realized or not, "nationalism" is a meaningless term'. Nationalism is not arbitrary, but neither is there any core content to it, any essential essence that is not shifted and redefined in internal and external, often dialogical, opposition, using powerful symbols that John Comaroff (1987) has accurately described as defined by 'totemic' relationality. And, as Duara (1995) has noted, all nationalisms and ethnicities are not necessarily by-products of or contained within the nation-state construction.

Through interviews with many of the people I spent time with in China whom I met again as exiles or (to use the better term) émigrés in Turkey, I began to think much more about the implications of relational alterity for what Rey Chow (1993) calls the diasporic condition, and its destabilizing challenge to the contemporary nation-state. I spent the 1992–93 academic year as a Fulbright Research Scholar in Istanbul, following up on interviews I had in 1988 with refugees who had gone there from China in the 1940s. This was after spending three years in China conducting fieldwork between 1982 and 1986, mainly among the people known as Hui, but with brief trips to Uyghur and Kazakh areas in China during that time. Since then, I have been back to China every year, visited Almaty (Alma-Ata) on several occasions, most recently in May 2000, and attempted in each case to follow up on contacts with Hui, Uyghur, and Kazakh and their relatives I had met during the earlier period. I spent most of my time moving between the boundaries of nation-states among the peoples that cross them, rather than 'squatting' (Geertz 1989:23) in one 'timeless, self-contained' village, neighborhood, town, or state (the preferred hierarchy of structural anthropologists). This attempts to follow Richard Fox's (1991:1) maxim to 'work in the present', or Bhabha's call, among the 'interstices', across the boundaries of multi-sited locations by which the groups I am interested in most define themselves.

The spate of what might be termed 'Soviet nostalgia' in *Foreign Affairs* and other policy manuals that complain of the re-emergence of tribalism in Central Asia and Eastern Europe, now that the 'peacekeeping' hand of the Soviets has been withdrawn, is misplaced, if not dangerously wrong.[5] These peoples were profoundly different than they had been before their domination by the centralizing states of Soviet and Chinese Central Asia, and their multifaceted identities are anything but tribal. Those suggesting pan-Turkism and pan-Islamism as an explanatory panacea for recent events in these regions have equally failed to note that expressions of Turkic or Islamic solidarity are often only one aspect of these complex identities in certain circumstances. In fact, the outcome of the desiccation of post-Soviet Central Asia has been most profoundly disappointing to the pan-Turkists and pan-Islamicists. The welcome translation of Olivier Roy's (1994) *Failure of Political Islam* demonstrates that for Afghanistan, as well as much of Central Asia, the 'perception of Islam and Muslim societies as one, timeless cultural system' does violence to both contemporary social movements sweeping these regions, and to the nature of Islam itself. This chapter attempts to suggest why these pan-ideologies may be even less compelling in the post-Soviet era than in the pre-Soviet period when they arose. The following examples of three families across three nation-states drawn from my field notes will attempt to illustrate some of the issues developed in this chapter.

Three families, three 'nations'

Fatma Wang came to Istanbul via Taiwan with her family fifty years ago. She, with her husband, a high-ranking Kuomintang official, escaped from Xinjiang in 1949, through the mountains to Pakistan, where they lived for more than four years before relocating to Istanbul, where her husband was appointed as a professor. A Muslim Chinese (known as Dungan in Central Asia, or 'Hui' – a term that at one time merely meant Muslim – in China),[6] Fatma has more

5. In an interesting paper, David Prochaska (1995) has suggested that a kind of 'imperialist nostalgia' helps to account for the popularity in France of Algerian orientalist postcards (then and now). The rise of nationalist and essentializing projects today might reflect a 'primordialist nostalgia' for purist communal origins that helps to explain the resurfacing of the term 'tribe'.

6. The problematic and elusive term 'Hui' for the Muslim Chinese of China and Central Asia has its origins in an early Chinese mistranslation of the term for the Uyghur (literally meaning, in Chinese, 'to return'; see Gladney

recent family roots that go back to Sichuan in southwestern China, but she, like many Hui, believes strongly that her earliest ancestors were Persian, and possibly a part of the legendary 'black-robed' Muslim force invited to help the Tang emperor suppress a local rebellion in Sichuan. She is thus descended from the hybrid off-spring of Arab mercenaries or Persian traders who entered China in service to the empire, married Chinese women, and were later implicated in the empire's many hegemonies. To this day, Hui are often seen as somehow between Chinese and non-Chinese, dis-trusted by both sides, the liminal, eternal stranger, inherently useful as mediators, traders, and scapegoats.

Fatma Wang is now the proprietor of the oldest Chinese res-taurant in Istanbul, the Çin Lokantasi, on Lamartin Cadessi. While over the years her food has taken on a decidedly Turkish taste, she can still serve up a zesty, spicy bowl of beef noodles. Her sons, Isa Wan Er Shao and Kurban Wang Er Bang, married Turkish women and, like most Istanbulites, practice a secularized version of Islam that honors Muslim holidays and practices but is not over-religious. The brothers speak Chinese to their Chinese relatives, but Turkish to their siblings and children. 'As long as they are Muslims,' Fatma once told me, 'I don't care who they marry.'[7] The family members tell me that they relate to the Turks not as Turks, but as Muslims: 'We are Muslim first, Chinese last'. They are neither Turk nor Chi-nese, but merely Muslim.

Ibrahim (pseudonym) is the last of his generation living in Zeytinburnu, just south of Istanbul, to call himself a Uyghur. Most of his fellow émigrés now call themselves 'East Turkestanis' or just 'Turks', although many of them came from Xinjiang to Turkey in the early 1960s, following several hard years of exile in Pakistan and

---

1996a:15–21, 324–5). In Central Asia, the Hui are known as Dungan (perhaps related to Muslims from Eastern Gansu, or an old Turkic term meaning 'to return'; see Dyer 1979) due to the improper Russian connotations of the term Hui, even though the Hui rarely use the term Dungan, and some are offended by it.

7.   Ms Rosey Ma, one of Fatma's daughters, who lives in Kuala Lumpur, explained to me (pers. comm.) that her mother did not wish her children to marry non-Muslims or even Chinese, but only Muslims, and the German husband of one of her daughters was required to convert to Islam before the marriage was allowed. For Rosey Ma's insightful history of Muslim Chinese in Malaysia, see Ma, R. (2002).

India, after which they were welcomed into Turkey and provided land and financial assistance by the Turkish government. Ibrahim bey still maintains his Turkish Uyghur language, but his four sons and three daughters have all married Turks and they and their children speak only Turkish. This is curious, since Ibrahim bey is quite active in a political organization to 'liberate the land of Turkestan from the atheist Communist Chinese'.[8]

This transnational organization is supporting Uyghur separatism in Xinjiang, in a deterritorialized identity tied to a former region still regarded as their own, an example of the phenomenon that Arjun Appadurai has described as the 'new transnationalisms', just as the Sikhs in Vancouver are maintaining ties to the Punjab, Armenians in Los Angeles to Armenia, and Irish in Boston to northern Ireland. The organization has claimed responsibility for the bombs that exploded outside the Oasis Hotel on 17 June 1993, as well as the thirty-odd bombings throughout the year in Xinjiang (see Kristof 1993:1; Dillon 1995:17–32). Yet Ibrahim's children know little of or care little about Xinjiang. Although many of them still retain Central Asian facial features, and this formerly made the young men popular with the Turkish girls (because it was thought they had pure 'Turkish Central Asian' blood), few of the second and third generations know of their 'Uyghur' origins: 'We never call each other Uyghur, but only refer to ourselves as East Turkestanis, or Kashgarlik, Turpanlik, or even Turks'. For Ibrahim it is the land of East Turkestan (or, as he sometimes refers to it, Uyghuristan) that is important – the land of his autochthonous ancestors taken by the Chinese invaders. Without that land, or recent memory

8.   Various publications present the views of Uyghur independence movements outside of China. In English, the Eastern Turkestani Union in Europe publishes the monthly *Eastern Turkestan Information Bulletin*, the Australian Turkistan Association publishes the bimonthly ATA News, and in Istanbul, the Eastern Turkestan Refugee Committee (*Dogu Türkistan Göcmenler Dernegi*) publishes *Dogu Türkistan* (*East Turkestan*), the August 1995 issue of which contained a contribution envelope and card with a map of the Xinjiang Uyghur Autonomous Region and the statement, '45 years ago Red China took over the homelands of the Eastern Turkestani Turks ... This holiday, please give generously to their cause'. Many of these publications are translated into Uyghur (written in a modified Arabic script). World Muslim attention to the Uyghur situation in China has become more focused now the Central Asian states are no longer under Soviet rule, and only in China and Albania are Muslims minorities under communist states (see Chapter 11).

of it, his grandchildren lack any strong sense of referentiality. Indigeneity matters rarely to émigrés, only to those who might resist them.

Ramazan Kubilay is the son of the great Tursunbay, a Kazakh who helped lead his people out of China, through Afghanistan and Pakistan to Turkey, about the same time as the Uyghur Ibrahim. Though they came from the same part of Inner Asia (northwest China), the second and third generations of the Kubilay family claim not to have lost their Kazakh language or culture. They continue to reserve one part of their homes to sit on the floor and eat 'Kazakh' style and drink milk tea. To find appropriate spouses for their children, they have searched all over Europe among other Kazakh émigré families. Ramazan Kubilay is one of many extremely successful leather-factory owners, with boutiques throughout Europe, that assist him in maintaining these extended networks of Kazakh in exile, who are now becoming active in advising the leaders of the new state of Kazakhstan.

When I asked why they attempted so hard to preserve what they thought to be a traditional Kazakh identity, they told me: 'We are descended from the great Kazakh nomad leader Genghis Khan (he was Kazakh you know, not Mongol); we know our entire genealogy, and it is the first thing every Kazakh remembers about themselves, besides being Muslim. Whenever we meet another person who looks Kazakh on the street, we don't ask them if they are Kazakh, but what Kazakh lineage, which *jüz* they are from. Then we can see just how closely we are related'.

They are being given more opportunity to do so. The Turkish government gave 10,000 scholarships to invite Central Asians from the Central Asian states to study in Turkey while I was there in 1992–93, and 10,000 more the following year. Many were not prepared for the difficult adjustment that they would have living in Turkey. Not only do they complain about the cramped dormitories and less money than they expected to receive, but also how difficult Turkish is to learn, how horrible the food is (no rice pilaf), and how different the culture is from home. They did not take to Turkish society as quickly as the politicians in Ankara expected. And many Central Asians are returning from Turkey disappointed by what they found there, complaining of its secularism, hedonism, and inferior education, which many of them found far beneath their Russian training. At the same time, Turks in Turkey discovered how different they were from their 'ancestors' and 'distant cousins', leading to increasingly public doubts about Atatürk's dogma regarding the Central Asian origins of the Turks.

The problem is, we do not know much about these 'sub-Turkic' peoples, because they are regarded by the Turkish state as just 'Turks' and are not counted as minorities. Although there have been many studies on the official minorities in Turkey – the Armenians, Greeks, and Jews, and even the Kurds – there has been almost nothing done on the sub-Turkic identities, since most assumed that once these people came to Turkey, they just blended in, becoming Turk, or what is culturally and politically defined as 'white' in the US (see Frankenberg 1993), just as in China, Cantonese, Shanghainese, and Hakka are defined as 'Han' (Zhongguo 1981:2).

One Swedish scholar, Ingvar Svanberg (1989b), noticed the profoundly different acculturation patterns of Uyghur and Kazakh in Turkey. Svanberg estimated that there were 60,000 to 100,000 of these Inner Asian émigrés, but we really do not know, because they are not counted by a state interested in defining a majority through quantifying only certain minorities. Despite the popular Turkish proverb *'Türkyede yetmisbir buçuk millyet var'* ('There are seventy-one and a half nations/ethnoreligious groups in Turkey'),[9] Atatürk's policy was to stress Central Asian Turkish origins, and then limit interaction with Central Asia to keep the Russians from getting nervous about pan-Turkism. Once the borders opened, Turks traveling to 'Turkestan' were surprised to find Kazakh, Uzbek, and Kyrgyz whom they could hardly understand, and who were not interested in acquiring yet another 'elder brother' (*aga bey*) after losing the Soviets.

My study in Turkey was designed to try to understand the construction of this 'whiteness' by looking at sub-Turkic ethnicity, just as I questioned the construction of Han-ness in China by looking at the construction of minority identity among the Hui and other minorities (see Gladney 1996a). This calls into question the nature of majority representation as homogeneous in these regions, and heterogeneous in Europe, as Hobsbawm (1990:66 n.7) seems to suggest (see quote in note 1, page 6, Chapter 2). For Hobsbawm and other Eurocentric nationality theorists (and here I include

---

9.   The 'half' *millyet* ('religious', 'national', or 'ethnoreligious' group) in Turkey refers to the Romany people, or Gypsies.

Greenfeld and Samuel Huntington; for example, his 'West versus the rest' [1993b:4]), Europe and the West is troped as heterogeneous and diverse, while the 'Orient' is broken up into more or less homogeneous national chunks.

The three families discussed above represent three kinds of discourse about identity that diverge widely from each other, although they all came to Turkey at about the same time, and in the case of the Kazakh and Uyghur families, from about the same place. The Hui family now emphasize Islamic identity (masking their diasporic hybridity); the Uyghur emphasize Turkic or national identity (displacing their indigeneity); and the Kazakh family emphasize descent-based transhumant identities (that extend well-beyond the nation-state). All three of these discourses about identity transgress the nation-state in that they make claims against the nation, originally conceived as pure, stationary, and politically circumscribed.

As traced by the Italian scholar Guido Zernatto (cited in Greenfeld 1992:4), the Latin *natio* originally meant foreigners united by place of origin who were not Roman citizens. Like the Greek *ethne*, it meant outsider, less civilized, but without the connotation of the probably Germanic-rooted word 'heathen', or religious minority, which followed the term ethnic into English. 'Nation' took on the meaning of a 'community of opinion' during the 12th-century Church Council of Nicea, where 'nations' represented elite ecclesiastical parties. Greenfeld (1992:5) shows how the term becomes transformed in a 'zigzag pattern of semantic change' over time to mean a 'unique sovereign people', and I shall argue that this is not unlike how groups themselves become transformed from loose associations into what might be called ethnic groups, to nations, and even nation-states.[10] In this chapter I seek to

10. A word about the tyranny of terminology. While I agree with the need to investigate the origins of Western discourses about identity, Greenfeld's lexicographical history and Thomas Eriksen's descriptive taxonomies in the end prove unsatisfactory in that they fail to address the contemporary salience of ethnic nationalist discourse. Thomas Eriksen's *Ethnicity and Nationalism: Anthropological Perspectives* (1993) tells us 'what is ethnicity' and 'what identities do', and in the end moves from the metaphor of the 'melting pot' to that of the 'stir-fry' – the vegetables are all still there, and you add a little power or class-conflict and get a slightly different mix. Greenfeld's helpful definition of the nation as 'a unique sovereign people' captures both the ethnic (ascriptive) and national (descriptive and prescriptive) aspects, but

address this issue with regard to the shifting simultaneity of identity, constructed through relations of alterity, in the context of contemporary nation-states.

The Muslim Chinese: making hybridity

Owen Lattimore, who lived and traveled for many years in northwest China, found that the ambiguity of Hui identity often made them suspect:

In times of political crisis, Moslem Chinese in Sinkiang are invariably caught on one or the other horns of a dilemma. If they stand with their fellow Moslems, sooner or later an attempt is made to reduce them to a secondary position and to treat them as 'untrustworthy' because, in spite of their Moslem religion, they are after all, Chinese. If they stand with their fellow Chinese, there is a similar tendency to suspect them of subversion and disloyalty, because, it is feared, their religion may prove politically more compelling than their patriotism. (Lattimore 1950:119 n.20)

Embedded within the ethnoscape of China and Inner Asia, the Muslim Chinese, known as Dungan in Xinjiang and much of Central Asia, and as Hui in China, are distributed widely. The official nationality census and literature in China list the Hui people as the third most populous (after the Zhuang and Manchu) of China's fifty-five recognized minority nationalities, who altogether comprise around 9 percent of the total population. The Hui are the most widespread minority, inhabiting every region, province, and city, and more than 97 percent of the nation's counties. It is noteworthy that while the Hui may represent a small fragment of the population in most areas (with the exception of Ningxia), they often make up the vast majority of the minority population in Han-dominated areas. This is also true for most of China's cities where the Hui are the main urban ethnic group. It is conventionally thought that

---

does not show us how and why people can transgress these categories, by moving among, within, and against them, or why they should have to in the first place. Neither encyclopedic attempt deals adequately with the power and increasing salience of identity formation depicted as ethnic and national, what Michael Fischer (1986:195) once described as its paradoxical 'id-like' power, its 'ambivalence', its 'multiplicity, contextuality, complexity, power, irony, and resistance' (Kondo 1989:43).

China's Muslim minorities are concentrated in the northwest corner of the country, near post-Soviet Central Asia. Surprisingly, after Ningxia and Gansu, the third-largest population of Hui is found in Henan Province, central China. Their sixth-largest concentration is in Yunnan, and there are more than 200,000 Hui in Beijing, the nation's capital. In her excellent cultural geography of China's frontier urban centers, Piper Gaubatz (1996) has demonstrated the multicultural nature of urban life in which Hui and other ethnic occupations have played an integral role.

There is also extensive economic and occupational diversity found among the Hui, from cadres to clergy, rice farmers to factory workers, schoolteachers to camel drivers, and poets to politicians. In the north, the majority of Hui are wheat and dry-rice agriculturists, while in the south, they are primarily engaged in wet-rice cultivation and aquaculture. After the collectivization campaigns of the 1950s, most Hui were prevented from engaging in the small private businesses that were their traditional specializations. Hui mediation allows them to run successful restaurants throughout China, and across its borders, and I have visited their restaurants in Thailand, Bishkek, Almaty, Istanbul (Çin Lokantasi), and even Los Angeles, where there are four.

From the beginning, the people now known as the Hui have been the diaspora, the immigrant in China. While Robert Young (1995:27) has rightly argued that the current multiculturalist celebration of hybridity 'repeats and reproduces' a racist paradigm of sociobiological evolutionism, we must remember that in China, discourses of identity, ethnicity, and nationalism have been strongly influenced by deeply held Chinese notions of race. In China, 'Race ... would create nationhood', according to Dikötter's (1992:71) cogently argued thesis, and it had much to do with Han Chinese representations of Hui otherness. Even their name, 'Hui', in Chinese can mean 'to return', as if they were never at home in China and were destined to leave.

The Hui are recognized by the state as one nationality, and now use that self-designation in conversations with other Hui and non-Hui. Like their unique Islamic architecture and art, Hui combine often, as they say, 'Chinese characteristics on the outside, and Islamic ones on the inside', with mosques appearing like Buddhist temples on the outside yet embellished internally with Quranic passages. In a painting of the Chinese ideogram for 'longevity' (*shou*), popular with many Hui and mass-produced by the China Islamic Society for public profit, Quranic suras are written to form the character, beautifully illustrating the dual nature of the Muslim Chinese. This hybridity, both Chinese and Muslim, resident and stranger, is critical to their representation of self and other. As Hobsbawm (1990: 70–1) surprisingly predicted: 'No doubt Bosnian and Chinese Muslims will eventually consider themselves a nationality, since their governments treat them as one'.

Relational alterity and oppositional identities

One way to conceptualize contemporary Hui Dungan discourses of identity in China, Central Asia, and even Turkey, is to envision an identity that is relational, relative, and grounded in a historical representation in which the people who have come to be known as the Hui situate themselves. I propose that it might be best understood through the notion of relational alterity, loosely abstracted from anthropological descent theory. Though in an entirely different territorial and economic context, Evans-Pritchard's (1940) classic study of the Nuer first suggested the expansive–contractive character of hierarchical segmentary lineage style among acephalous nomadic societies. When the Nuer (or Dinka) were confronted with an outside power, they unified and organized to a higher degree of political complexity to respond to the *perceived* challenge. When the threat subsided, they diversified and atomized, in an articulated pattern of what Gregory Bateson (1972:96) once described as nested hierarchy. For as Bateson (1972:78) argued, it takes two somethings to make a difference; without an other, you have only 'the sound of one hand clapping'. While Evans-Pritchard's study was mired in the 19th-century colonialist structuralisms that portrayed 'tribal' pastoralists as pre-modern and overdetermined by tradition, his model of alterity is surprisingly relevant to the post-modern, post-Cold War period, where it could be argued the world is becoming increasingly acephalous and breaking down into smaller and smaller relational units. These relations, like Evans-Pritchard's Nuer, are segmentary in principle, taking as their basic components not the face-to-face herding units, but the imagined community of the nation, and its constituent parts.

This approach can be roughly diagrammed for heuristic purposes as an articulating hierarchy of relational alterities, a schematic that segmental kinship theorists have been playing with for some time (Figure 9.1). For example, when A and B encounter a higher level of opposition, D, they form C, moving a node up the scale to form higher-level relations, or conversely, down the scale when the higher-level threat subsides. While this scheme is binary, it is always constructed in a field of social relations, and is inherently ternary in that A and B are always in union or opposition, depending on their interaction with D. As David Maybury-Lewis and Uri Almagor (1989) have argued, it is the attraction (or repulsion) of 'perceived' opposites that is key; there is nothing critical to binarity beyond that perceptual act. Indeed, there is nothing that prevents three groups from becoming a fourth in actual social relations, though it is difficult to portray in two-dimensional diagrams. Also, it is important that these alliances, relations, and oppositions are based on my own observations and reading of social histories; it is not a cognitive map, and the only constraints are those imposed by the specific contexts of alterity.

As I have argued elsewhere, these alterior relations are best perceived as dialogical rather than dialectical (Gladney 1996a:76–8), insofar as strict dialectics (Hegelian versus Maoist) are generally thought to move in a certain direction, always negating a past relation, rather than dialogic interaction that can move back and

Figure 9.1. SEGMENTAL HIERARCHY

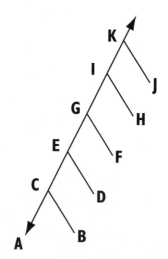

forth, up and down, depending on the nature of the interaction.[11] Here we are merely tracing a 'chain of stereotypical representation' (Bhabha 1994:251), and seeking to outline, in rather static terms, constantly shifting relations and multiplicities of perceived identities that mask many levels of social simultaneity.[12] As Rachel Moore (1994:127) observes, these fluctuating alterities can become so stereotypically fixed and represented that essentializing regimes, elites, and anthropologists often engage in 'marketing alterities' for remarkably different purposes. The hierarchy of alterior opposition emerges within the context of social relations. As Thomas (1994: 171) has argued, these are often 'strategic reformulations' and do not represent 'eternal properties of self-other relations' divorced from particular sociohistorical moments.[13] Nor does this assume a cognitive map, or that there are no other options available depending on shifting social relations.

Bhabha (1994:4) has suggested that, 'This interstitial passage between fixed identifications opens up the possibility of a cultural hybridity that entertains without an assumed or imposed hierarchy'. Essentialized identifications make possible the construction of Hui Muslims as hybrid and, at the same time, threatening to purifying projects. If we examine the case of the Hui Dungan described above, it becomes clear that Hui represent themselves as such

11. As Taussig notes, identity is constantly constructed in imitation of and resistance to an often imagined other, creating samenesses and differences in mimetic interaction: '… mimesis registers both sameness and difference, of being like, and of being other. Creating stability from this instability is no small task, yet all identity formation is engaged in this habitually bracing activity in which the issue is not so much staying the same, but maintaining sameness through alterity' (Taussig 1993:27).

12. In this sense, Eriksen (1993) is correct to stress relationality and relativity. The problem is that he neglects to place stress upon the context of the *perception* of difference, assuming it almost always pertains. For Eriksen, everyone is ethnic, whether they like it or not. 'Virtually every human being belongs to an ethnic group', Eriksen (1993:11) decides for us, 'whether he or she lives in Europe, Melanesia, or Central America'. This ignores the relevance and irrelevance of ethnicity, its historicity, and why, say, majorities (such as the 'whites' in my Introductory Anthropology class, or the 'majority' Han in China, or dominant Turks in Turkey, have a hard time thinking of themselves as 'ethnic').

13. The strategic nature of this scheme is revealed in the rather apt Bedouin proverb: 'I against my brother, my brother and I against our cousin, our cousins and us against the outsider'.

depending on the nature of their interaction with others. Thus, Beijing and Shanghai Hui differ in language, customs, and locality, often leading to disruptive and non-hierarchical competitive business relations, often only until a non-Hui enters the scene. At this moment, the Beijing and Shanghai Hui may unite as 'Hui', and so on up the scale of interactions. When Hui or Dungan move outside of China, their Chineseness may become enhanced in interactions with non-Chinese, or their 'Muslimness' in interactions with non-Muslims. Indeed, the very nature of the Hui as a 'nationality' is based on Chinese nationality policies that recognized them as an official *minzu*, giving them legal status. This initiated a process that I have described elsewhere, in which a Muslim people became transformed into a minority nationality (Gladney 1996a).

It should come as no surprise that outside the confines of the Chinese nation-state the Hui will begin to regard themselves less as a nationality and emphasize other aspects of their identity, such as Islam or their Chinese language. This helps to understand how the Hui at the Çin Lokantasi restaurant in Istanbul often related to others simply as Muslims, hoping to override differences between 'Turk' and 'Chinese'. Here I should note that there is nothing determinative in these relations. They are merely reflections of what I have observed in the field. The hierarchy of segmentation is not fixed; it is determined by the local context of difference, as defined by a specific constellation of stereotypical relations, of hierarchy, power, class, and opposition, that are often shifting and multifaceted, but never arbitrary. Thus, even in China, there have been times where Hui have united with Han Chinese against other Hui, when it was in their interest to do so, often downplaying their Muslim identity in favor of cultural, ethnic, or linguistic similarities to the Han Chinese with whom they sought to share practical interests. The history of Gansu and Xinjiang is filled with these shifting power-alliances (see Forbes 1986), where brother united with brother, and sometimes with the Chinese, against a cousin who was often a rival Hui warlord (Lipman 1997). The relational alterity approach seeks to map out the significant fault lines of relation and opposition, and nodes of hierarchy – a heuristic way of depicting this phenomenon. It does not, of course, pretend to have predictive or universal, dehistoricized explanatory value.

As a group, the Dungan Hui that describe their identity as hybrid, or to follow Lila Abu-Lughod (1991) as 'halfies', transgress the nation-state insofar as it founds itself upon the notion of a unique sovereign group – one nation, one state – despite many examples to the contrary.

The Uyghur: indigeneities of place, space, and state recognition

Chinese histories notwithstanding, every Uyghur firmly believes that his or her ancestors were the indigenous people of the Tarim Basin, now know as Xinjiang. This land was 'their' land. Nevertheless, I have argued elsewhere the constructed ethnogenesis of the Uyghur. In his popular history of Xinjiang, Jack Chen (1977: 100) noted the reintroduction of the term Uyghur to describe the Turkic inhabitants of Chinese Turkestan. While a collection of nomadic steppe peoples known as the Uyghur have existed since before the 8th century, this identity was lost from the 15th to 20th centuries. It is not until the fall of the Turkish Khanate (AD 552–744) to a people reported by the Chinese historians as Hui-he or Hui-hu that we find the beginnings of the Uyghur empire described by Mackerras (1972). At this time the Uyghur were but one collection of nine nomadic tribes who, initially in confederation with the Basmil and Karluk nomads, defeated the second Turkish Khanate and then dominated the federation under the leadership of Koli Beile in 742 (Sinor 1969:113).

The story of the gradual sedentarization of the Uyghur, and their defeat of the Turkish Khanate, which occurred precisely as trade with the unified Tang state became especially lucrative, is spelled out in more detail in the following chapter. Suffice it to note that sedentarization and interaction with the Chinese state was accompanied by socioreligious change: the traditional shamanistic, Turkic-speaking Uyghur came increasingly under the influence of Persian Manichaeism, Buddhism, and, eventually, Nestorian Christianity (Sinor 1969:114–15). Extensive trade and military alliances along the old Silk Road with the Chinese state developed to the extent that the Uyghur gradually adopted cultural, dress, and even agricultural practices from the Chinese (Mackerras 1972:37). Conquest of the Uyghur capital of Karabalghasun in Mongolia by the nomadic Kyrgyz in 840, without rescue from the Tang, who may have become by then intimidated by the wealthy Uyghur empire, led to further sedentarization and crystallization of Uyghur identity.

Indeed, it is the Yugur nationality of Gansu today – not the Uyghur, who fled the Kyrgyz to Central China – who are thought to preserve much of the original Karakoram Uyghur history in their contemporary religious, linguistic, and cultural expression.[14] One branch, which ended up in what is now Turpan, took advantage of the unique socioecology of the glacier-fed oases surrounding the Taklamakan and were able to preserve their merchant and limited agrarian practices, gradually establishing Khocho or Gaochang, the great Uyghur city-state based in Turpan for four centuries (850–1250).

The gradual Islamization of the Uyghur from the 10th to the 16th centuries, while displacing their Buddhism, did little to bridge these oases-based loyalties. From then on, the people of Uyghuristan, centered in the Turpan Depression, who resisted Islamic conversion until the 16th century, were the last to be known as Uyghur. The others were known only by the name of their oasis or by the generic term 'Muslims' (Haneda 1978:7). With the arrival of Islam, the ethnonym Uyghur fades from the historical record. Instead, we find the proliferation of such oasis-based localisms as Yerlik (persons of the land), Sart (caravaneer), and Taranchi (agriculturalists from the Tarim Basin, transplanted to Yili under Qianlong).

During the Republican period, Uyghur identity was again marked by factionalism along locality, religious, and political lines. Forbes (1986), in his detailed analysis of the complex warlord politics of Republican Xinjiang, finds important continuing distinctions between the three macro-regions of Xinjiang: the northwestern Zungaria (Dzungaria, or Junggar Basin), southern Tarim Basin, and eastern Kumul–Turpan ('Uyghuristan') areas. Rudelson's 1997 book confirms this persistent diversity along regional lines, which he insightfully proposes are divided into four macro-regions, segmenting the southern Tarim into two distinct socioecological regions, rather than the three into which most scholars divide Xinjiang (uniting the southern Tarim as one region). The Uyghur were

14. Sabira Ståhlberg (1995), a graduate student who completed extensive fieldwork among the Yugur in Gansu, argued that they are not directly descended from the 9th-century Karakoram Uyghur kingdom, but represent a hybrid group formed after the fall of Western Xia (12th century), combining Tibetan, Mongolian, Turkic, and Chinese influences in the 'ethnic melting pot' of the Gansu corridor.

recognized as a nationality in the 1930s in Xinjiang under a So-
viet-influenced policy of nationality recognition that contributed
to a widespread acceptance today of continuity with the ancient
Uyghur kingdom and their eventual ethnogenesis as a bona fide
nationality (see Chen, J. 1977; Rudelson 1988). This nationality
designation not only masks tremendous regional and linguistic diversity, but also includes groups, such as the Loplik and Dolan, that
had very little to do with the oasis-based Turkic Muslims who became known as the Uyghur (see Svanberg 1989c; Hoppe 1995).

This chapter argues that diversity and factionalism within the
Uyghur reflects a segmentary hierarchy of relationality common
among all social groupings. Uyghur are divided from within by religious conflicts, in this case competing Sufi and non-Sufi factions,
territorial loyalties (whether they be oases or places of origin), linguistic discrepancies, commoner–elite alienation, and competing
political loyalties. It is also important to note that Islam was only
one of several unifying markers for Uyghur identity, depending on
those with whom they were in significant opposition at the time.
For example, to the Dungan (Hui), the Uyghur distinguish themselves as the legitimate autochthonous minority, since both share a
belief in Sunni Islam. In contrast to the nomadic Muslim peoples
(Kazakh or Kyrgyz), Uyghur might stress their attachment to the
land and oasis of origin. In opposition to the Han Chinese, the
Uyghur will generally emphasize their long history in the region.

The indigeneity of the Uyghur poses a fundamental transgression of Chinese historiographies of the region, which is consonant
with colonizing regimes seeking to assert power in a region not
previously their own. By moving the clock back far enough, any
regime can claim the land as unoccupied. Claims of indigeneity
always transgress nation-states that are founded most often under
the conditions of post-coloniality.

The Kazakh: nomadic nostalgia and the power of genealogy

When two Kazakhs who do not know each other meet, they make their
acquaintance by giving the lineage to which they belong and their closest
patrilineal relatives. In East Berlin Kazakhs from Turkey established contact with Kazakh guest students from the Mongolian People's Republic
studying in the German Democratic Republic. As the Xinjiang Kazakhs
the Kazakhs from Mongolia belonged to *Orta Jüz* and generally also to

the same lineages that are found in Turkey. In some cases they have found common kinship relations which even led to organized meetings in East Berlin between relatives coming from Turkey and visitors from Mongolia. (Svanberg 1989b:116)

Ramazan Kubilay of Zeytinburnu, Istanbul, was quoted early in this chapter as stating that he was a direct descendant of Genghis Khan, whom he strongly believed was a Kazakh nomad. Indeed, for most Kazakh nomadism is only a distant memory to which they look in ethnic nostalgia. Robert B. Ekvall concluded his classic ethnography of Tibetan nomadic pastoralism, *Fields on the Hoof*, with the following dire prediction: 'In the framework of communist doctrine and experience … there is no logical and acceptable place for the nomad' (Ekvall 1968:94). He was completely accurate with regard to the former Soviet Union, where among the entire population of more than 7 million Kazakh there are now only a few seminomadic pastoralists remaining in the most remote desert regions. His predictions for China, though not unreasonable at the time, were proven false. Indeed, the past few years have witnessed a resurgence of nomadic pastoralism in some grassland areas, to the extent that the ecological balance of these zones has become threatened through overgrazing. Yang Li and Hsin-i Wu of the Gansu Grassland Ecological Research Institute reported that the privatization of land use and herd stocks in China came at the same time as the 'free-market system was instituted in China and the government decreased the price control measures. Since then, the cost of animal products has soared; this has resulted in the overgrazing of China's grasslands *far beyond carrying-capacity*' (Li and Wu 1990:1; emphasis in original).

While it has yet to be demonstrated that Kazakh pastoralists in the Altai Mountains have posed any threat to the grasslands of the alpine meadows or valley floors, Svanberg and Benson (1988:200–5) have documented a resurgence of traditional nomadic pastoralism with the free-market reforms. As descendants of the Turkish khanate that dominated the Mongolian steppe in the 6th century AD, the Kazakh are pursuing a style of nomadic pastoralism that is derived from these Turkish ancestors, who, according to the late Joseph Fletcher (1979:24), 'developed steppe nomadism in its final form, the form in which the Mongols later adopted it'. Even as Kazakh nomadism disappears from the Central Asian steppe, debate has raged in the former Soviet Union over the role of religion and Turkism in defining Kazakh national identity. While some intellectuals argue for the role of Islam in defining Kazakh identity, others maintain that it is only pan-Turkism that can unite the peoples of the steppe (see Saray 1993:16–17). These endless debates have marred the important role of nomadism for Kazakh national identity, the idea of a nomadic past that unites Kazakh transnationally from China to Central Asia to Turkey, among a people for whom, according to Martha Olcott's study, 'traditional Kazakh culture defined a man through the animals he owned, making private ownership of livestock almost the definition of what it was to be Kazakh' (Olcott 1987:248). While Russian-speaking urban Kazakh in modern Almaty certainly do not wish to become nomads, I argue that a kind of 'nomadic nostalgia' nevertheless characterizes much current discourse regarding the rediscovery of their pastoralist past, a resumed interest in pre-Islamic Kazakh belief systems, an urge to preserve and discover 'pure' Kazakh nomadic traditions in the Altai Mountains of China, and a continued lament over the tragedy of Stalinist sedentarization, and that this discourse impedes to some extent the construction of a contemporary Kazakhstani identity that includes non-Kazakh.

In the Altai Mountains of China, with the pervasiveness of market economies in China and the former Soviet Union, and the increasing contacts of these Kazakh with the large immigrant community in Turkey, the role of animal husbandry and Kazakh identity is resurfacing as an important factor in changes in their socioecological nexus (Kazakh 1987). During interviews with Kazakh immigrants in the Zeytinburnu district of Istanbul (see Svanberg 1989b), I found a population that largely defined itself in terms of its burgeoning leather and tanning industry, with leather fashion boutiques run by extended Kazakh networks in Istanbul, Paris, London, Berlin, Stockholm, and New York. Now that more unrestricted travel has been taking place between Turkey, Kazakhstan, and China (there are direct flights from Istanbul to Ürümqi, Istanbul to Almaty, and Almaty to Ürümqi, which I flew in May and June 1993, as well as the Eurasian rail connection between Ürümqi and Almaty, which I traveled in October 1995), Kazakh once separated by artificial political boundaries are beginning to trade and exchange ideas and products to an unprecedented extent.

The continued salience of nomadic nostalgia to contemporary Kazakh identity in Kazakhstan is clearly demonstrated by their

recently selected national emblem: the flag of Kazakhstan, which
has the famous flying horses beneath the interior dome of the yurt
on a field of blue sky.

In my interviews with Kazakh pastoralists in the Southern Pastures in 1987, 1992, and 1995, I found that whereas a traditional
Kazakh *auyl* had the mutual participation of all members in a wide
range of tasks, each household of the clan in the post-collectiv-
ist period divided up the various tasks of nomadic pastoralism:
herding, marketing, leather processing, and rug making. This was
almost completely abolished during the Chinese collectivization
campaigns of the 1960s and 1970s, in which the deprivatization of
the herds, just as occurred in the USSR under Stalin in the 1920s
and 1930s. There was no inherent incentive to care for the animals
when the state controlled the profits, and traditional shared work-
roles were reassigned to specific collective enterprise tasks. The
traditional household and *auyl* economies were dismantled. Now
that there has been a return to traditional nomadic pastoralism and
the private ownership of animals in China, one would expect a resurgence of traditional household and *auyl* economic organization.
However, unlike the traditional Kazakh social structure as outlined
by Alfred Hudson (1938) and Lawrence Krader (1963), one now
finds that often each yurt will perform specialized tasks for the entire clan or *auyl:* one household will be responsible for herding, another for marketing, and another for production of certain leather
goods, crafts, or rugs. While this may not be the rule for all Kazakh
auyls of the Altai, it represents a new form of household economy
and social organization that is perhaps due to the collectivized
experience of the 1960s and 1970s. These households are also becoming tied into the local and transnational economies through
the marketing of their products. This reorganization of traditional
household economies may be one factor in the increased herd sizes
reported in the Altai, and will be an important aspect in the changing socioecology of the region.

The Kazakh of Kazakhstan and Turkey look to the nomads of
the Altai as their living cultural ancestors. Understanding of this
nomadic way of life will assist in determining the evolving nature
of Kazakh national identity. It is a way of life that is resurgent,
albeit in a somewhat altered form, in China, while passing away
elsewhere. It is clear that in reciting the oft-memorized genealogies among the Kazakh, nomadism and its cultural by-products

loom large as an important factor in their representation of Kazakh identity. For the Kazakh, the tracing of genealogy is a much more powerful force in their identity construction than we have found for either Hui or Uyghur. For Kazakh, their identity is represented as segmentary in principle. For the Hui, a generalized notion of descent from foreign Muslim ancestors is important for contemporary identity. It does not really matter to modern Hui if these ancestors may have been Arab, Persian, or Turk, only that they were Muslim, migrated to China, and maintained their distinctive identities. For the Uyghur, knowledge of genealogy seems to be important only as it relates to the land, as proof of early Uyghur settlement in the Tarim oases, prior to the Chinese or other nomadic Turks. The keeping of detailed genealogies, according to my Uyghur informants in Xinjiang and Turkey, is something the Chinese like to do, not them. Indeed, Kazakh preoccupation with genealogical minutiae not only influences mate selection and nomadic nostalgia, but also may contribute to an increased awareness of identity.

A typical Kazakh genealogy among members of the Saqabay sublineage with whom I interacted in Istanbul is several levels deep. At the highest level, most Kazakh among the Saqabay knew they were descendants of the Orta Jüz (*orta* meaning 'middle', mistranslated 'Horde', or in Turkish '*orda*', which refers to the original tribal military formations). At the level Kazakh refer to as *tayipa* (from the Arabic, *tayifa*), which Svanberg (1989b:115) translates as 'tribe' and Hudson (1938:19) as '*uru*' (Krader 1963 as '*ru*'), they identified with the Kerey. At the next level of *ru*, or lineage (Svanberg 1989b:115), they traced their heredity to the Zantekey. Yet many Kazakh call all of these levels *jüz* or *ru*, and there is no real consistency. At the base is the emphasis upon migration groups known as *auyl* (or *awl*; Hudson 1938:19), which would have comprised different households, related by these complicated descent lines. It was clear, however, that a Saqabay would rarely marry a Barzarkul or Tasbike, and only with great reluctance marry outside of the Zantekey line. As Svanberg notes, beyond the Kerey there was not much knowledge of specific connections to other Orta lineages. This knowledge is increasing, however, with frequent travel to Central Asia, where Kazakh members of the Ulu (or Great) Orda are primarily concentrated. Interactions traditionally would move up the scale from household to *auyl* to lineage. Now there is specific interest only at the lineage level and above, since migration groups have changed dramatically as noted above. It is noteworthy that distinction from Uyghur and Hui only takes place at the sixth and seventh levels of interaction, revealing a much higher range of relations than has been described for those peoples. Kazakh preoccupation with genealogy is reflected in their more detailed scale of relational alterity.[15]

Genealogies travel well. Kazakh notions of transhumance based on the *auyl* that trace to the roots of nomadic descent lines also extend far beyond any contemporary configurations of the nation-state. This allows Kazakh networks that extend throughout Central Asia, China, Turkey, and Europe. It finds its representation on the Kazakh and Kyrgyz flags. As Charles Scott has argued: 'Genealogies are ways of allowing differences, discontinuities, and the priority of exteriority and spatial imagery while one comes to know various ordered regions of human life' (Scott 1990:57).

Unscrambling overstructured identities

Maps of the Central Asian region have begun to clearly delineate the composition of the so-called major ethnic groups and divide them into majorities and minorities (for example, Kazakhstan: 40 percent Kazakh, 38 percent Russian). This contrasts with former maps of Inner Asia that generally blended these groups all together, since former Marxist–Stalinist and modernization paradigms stressed the disappearance of these Central Asian identities, as either Russianized, Sinicized, or secularized. Yet even the ethnic maps show the overlaps among groups of people, and geographic maps indicate that there are no natural boundaries between these regions divided geopolitically during the period known as the Great Game. The game of ethnopolitics is still being

---

15. In an interesting paper, 'Ethnic Composition in Xinjiang', Thomas Hoppe (1995) has presented a strikingly similar hierarchy of opposition among the Kyrgyz pastoralists of southwestern Xinjiang. It is interesting that while Kyrgyz and Kazakh preserve a fascination for lineage and genealogy as former nomadic pastoralists, this is not the case for the Uyghur groupings and Hui groupings discussed in this paper. In a fascinating parallel, Uradyn Erden Bulag (1998:49) demonstrates in his ground-breaking thesis that contemporary Mongols in Mongolia are reviving their genealogy and clan names (*obog*), which had been lost under Soviet influence.

played across the steppes of Inner Asia, though no longer on a scale so 'great'.

This chapter has attempted to provide an approach to relational alterity that seeks to understand different configurations of identity across transnational boundaries among the peoples now known as Hui (Dungan), Uyghur, and Kazakh. Two-dimensional diagrams detract from the emphasis here upon dialogic relationality and run even harder into the dilemma George Marcus (1994:48) aptly describes as the 'problem of simultaneity' in contemporary ethnographic writing. While the specific 'nodes' of relation and alterity might be disputed in reference to the groups discussed above, the argument in general concerns the nature of hierarchy, power, representation, and relationality among these peoples of Inner Asia. It is clear that in some cases the oppositional relations described above may not always pertain – one could find examples, say, of instances where Hui and Uyghur have united against Kazakh interests in Xinjiang or even Almaty – yet the move here is toward a more contextualized, relational approach to identity formation and expression, in which imagination, representation, and subscription play important roles in identity formation, as opposed to essentialized 'tribal' or relativized 'situational' formulations. No matter how often an author doth protest (too much) that this is not the case, two-dimensional line diagrams always freeze and essentialize any portrayal of identity to an inexcusable degree.

Perhaps a different, more subscriptive and relational metaphor than that of structuralist kinship modeling is needed. The analogy of the scrambled cable channel on television tuners, which I proposed in Chapter 2, might be a more heuristic way of looking at the current shifting 'montage' (Marcus 1994:45) of post-Soviet Inner Asian identities. Though 'scrambled' channels often appear blurred and haphazardly jammed together, preventing all but glimpses and snatches of sound from what is 'really' out there, state policies that regulate stereotypical characterizations often help to sort our melange of social identities, making the even the hybrid a pure category ('mixed', 'mestizo', or as they say in Hawai'i, '*hapa*').

It is the modern nation-state, however, with its regulatory powers over not only cable channels, but also citizenship, ethnic national identities, and census categories (see Cohn 1987), which exerts a privileged role in defining the most accessible national channels, and provides the means to unscramble them.

Relational alterities

Like so many blended, scrambled channels, this approach has attempted to describe (to unscramble?) the context of 'both/and' identities: how it is, say, a person who calls himself a 'Turkestani' can be both Kashgari and Uyghur, Muslim and Turk, Chinese and Central Asian. In China, all of these groups are Chinese citizens, and travel on a Chinese passport, whether they like it or not. As this chapter has argued, being Uyghur is not as meaningful for younger émigrés in Istanbul, nor was it between the 15th and early 20th centuries, but it certainly has become relevant for the 8 million to 9 million oasis-dwelling Turkic people who have been labeled Uyghur since 1934 as a result of nation-state incorporation, Great Game rivalries, and Sino-Soviet nationality policies.

These identities are particularly called into question once people move across national borders and become members of the transnational diaspora (see Chow 1994:99–105). The project then becomes not an essentialized attempt at a final definition of the meanings of these representations, but an examination of *when* these meanings come to the fore, and with whom they are asserted. The post-Cold War period has led to a downward movement of opposition: it is no longer a US–USSR–China trilateral configuration, but a much more particularized, multipolar, and multivalent world, where shifting identities may move quickly up and down or even between scales of relation, depending on specific circumstances. Without the Russian and US threat to China's sovereignty, lower-level identities may increasingly come into play, evidenced by increasing 'southern nationalisms' among the Cantonese, Fujianese, Hakka, and others empowered by new-found economic wealth.

This project also calls into question the nature of majority national identities in Turkey, the former Soviet Union, and China. Recent studies of the Marxist influence on national-identity construction in these regions have often ignored the process by which majority groups are constructed: the Turk, the Russian, and the Han Chinese. The Turk in Ottoman history was the tent-dwelling nomad, and not held up as the admirable essence of Turkish nationhood until the rush from empire to nation associated with Atatürk.

A similar transition from empire to nation led the early Chinese nationalists to appropriate a Japanese-derived term for nation (*minzoku*) and label initially five groups under the Nationalists, and later fifty-six under the Communists, as 'nations' (*minzu*). The notion of the Han as a *minzu* (nationality) is a quite recent phenomenon, popularized by Sun Yat-sen in relational opposition to Tibetans, Mongols, Manchu, and Hui, in his Five Peoples policy, and more importantly, to the foreign imperialists, all of whom were perceived as 'nations' (Duara 1995). The category of Han as a people was actually left to China by the Mongols, who included all northern peoples as Han (including the Koreans), as distinguished from southerners (*nan ren*), Central Asians (*semu ren*), and the Mongols. Now that higher-level post-imperial, and then Cold War, oppositions have subsided, China may find itself moving down the scale into serious sub-Han ethnic and national alterities, particularly with the economic rise of the south, contributing to nationalism among the southern Tang instead of the northern Han.

It is clear that we must attend to the nature of shifting national identities in these regions, and to the impact of changing international geopolitics. But geopolitics is not enough, for these processes of identity formation and re-formation cannot be understood without attention to historiography and cultural studies. It is even more apparent that relations between Turkey, Russia, and China will hinge on the shifting identities of the mainly Turkic, mainly Muslim peoples in the region – identities, as this chapter has sought to indicate, not easily united across pan-Turkic or pan-Islamic lines. The styles of national identity among these groups pose fundamental challenges, or transgressions, to the nation-states in which they find themselves: Uyghur indigeneity rejects Chinese claims to 'their' land; Kazakh idealization of nomadic transhumance suggests that no nation-state should be allowed to contain them; and Hui hybridity argues, against the very notion of the nation, that the diasporic condition is part of everyone's modern and post-modern predicament, and that there is no pure nation, ethnicity, or race that can claim state power on that basis alone. Perhaps this belief in hybridity has generally kept the Hui from voicing separatist tendencies.

In China, recognition of official national identities has empowered these groups in their claims against the nation, particularly for the Hui and Uyghur, to a crystallization and ethnogenesis of identities – identities that have now moved above and beyond the bounds of the Chinese nation-state, encouraging other unrecognized groups to push for recognition and political power. And lest one think that these so-called 'marginal' unrecognized peoples are irrelevant to Chinese history and society, we must remember that the Taiping had their origins in the southwestern corner of the country, in Guangxi among the Hakka and Yao, splitting and nearly toppling the Qing empire. The person who helped bring the Qing finally to an end was Dr Sun Yat-sen, a true member of the modern transnational diaspora, a Cantonese raised in Hawai'i, and educated in Japan. Nevertheless, Dr Sun was effective in mobilizing China's internal others against the foreign others, Manchu and Western imperialists, creating a new Chinese national identity that may be just as fragile as the old. Identities shift as individuals move across these many borders, and, as Chuang Tzu reminds us,[16] these identities are formed in relation to others across the field of social and political interactions:

If there is no 'other' then we do not have a 'self', if there is no 'self', then we do not have anything to grasp.

16. I am grateful to Christopher Millward (1994:6) for this translation of one of Chuang Tzu's famous passages regarding losing one's self in Heaven and Earth lectures. See Watson (1968:133).

Part V
INDIGENIZATIONS

10
ETHNOGENESIS OR ETHNOGENOCIDE?

The Uyghur: old and new

Just south of Istanbul, in the Zeytinburnu district along the shore of the Sea of Marmara, a close-knit collection of housing developments, leather factories, and small shops is inhabited primarily by 1940s migrants from what is now the Xinjiang Uyghur Autonomous Region of northwest China.[1] However, one rarely hears any of these terms when ethnic origins are discussed. The general formula is, 'I am a Kashgarlik, from the oasis of Kashgar'. Other ethnonyms include Turpanlik, Khotanlik, Aksulik, or native place-terms indicating the oasis towns surrounding the Tarim Basin and the Taklamakan Desert.[2] One student, when asked her origins while traveling in Turkey, asserted she was from Turkestan, though her home is in Ürümqi, and she is identified by the Chinese state as a member of the Uyghur nationality. This ambiguity recalls the well-known statement by Barthold (cited in Shahrani 1984:27):

When you ask a Turkistani what is his identity, he will answer that he is, first of all, a 'Muslim', then an inhabitant of such or such city or village ... or if he is a nomad, member of such or such tribe.

1. Funding for three years of field research on Muslims in China was provided by the Fulbright–Hayes Foundation, the Committee on Scholarly Communication with the People's Republic of China, and the Wenner-Gren Foundation for Anthropological Research. Field research in Turkey was supported by the Ira J. Kukin Scholars Program of the Harvard Academy for International and Area Studies. In China I was hosted by the Central Institute for Nationalities, the Ningxia Academy of Social Sciences, and the Xinjiang Academy of Social Sciences. I would like to express my appreciation to the agencies and individuals who made this study possible.
2. For a study of immigrants from northwestern China in Istanbul, see Svanberg (1989a).

At the same time, statistics published by population bureaus make explicit reference to a well-defined people referred to as the Uyghur, numbering almost 8.4 million according to the 2000 census (see Statistics Bureau of Xinjiang Uyghur Autonomous Region 2002; Banister 1987:322; Population Census Office 1987: 28; Zhongguo 1981:174). The Uyghur are listed as the second-largest of the ten Muslim peoples in China, and primarily inhabit the Xinjiang Uyghur Autonomous Region.

Uyghur in Xinjiang often make reference to their long-term origins in that place. While I was making my first visit to the Astana tombs in Turpan, in 1985, a local Uyghur official of the Chinese International Travel Service said to me, 'The Uyghur people are the descendants of a high civilization of Central Asian nomadic people who had a kingdom based here in Turpan. The elegant paintings and wrapping in this tomb date to the Han Dynasty [206 BC to AD 220] and are comparable in beauty and sophistication. A mummy in the Xinjiang Provincial Tombs also found in this area dates over 6,000 years old and proves the Uyghur people are even older than the Han Chinese'.

Many Uyghur with whom I have spoken in Turpan and Kashgar argue persuasively that they are the autochthonous people of this region. That more than 90 percent of the Uyghur population are located in Xinjiang, whereas the other Muslim peoples of China have significant populations in other provinces and outside the country, contributes to this important sense of belonging to the land. The Uyghur continue to conceive of their ancestors as originating in Xinjiang, claiming to outsiders that 'it is our land, our territory' (Mann 1985:10), despite the early Uyghur kingdom having been based in what is now Mongolia and the present region of Xinjiang being under the control of the Chinese state. Though Uyghur conceived as themselves as the indigenous people of the Tarim Basin, many Uyghur nationalists claim that mass Han Chinese migration to the region, as well as environmental degradation due to unrestricted development and nuclear testing, is leading not to their ethnogenesis but to their ethnocide (Alptekin, I.Y. 1991).

Historians studying Inner Asia generally trace the origins of the present Uyghur to the formerly nomadic, later settled, oasis-dwelling people who spoke a Turkish dialect and formed the Uyghur kingdom based in Karakoram (AD 745–840) (Mackerras 1972; Sinor 1969:113–22; Schwarz 1984:1–26; Zhongguo 1981:

174). Professor Geng Shimin, the pre-eminent Chinese turkologist, argues that the Uyghur identity did not coalesce until the 15th century (Geng 1984:13). Yet the foremost Japanese historian of Inner Asia, Professor Saguchi Toru, states that the term Uyghur was not used to refer to the present people under discussion until 1935 (Saguchi 1984:62). This leaves a 500-year gap in the use of the term Uyghur to denote a people whom most scholars have assumed to have existed for at least 1,200 years of Inner Asian history. In a provocative discussion of Uyghur identity, Rudelson (1988) argues that the designation Uyghur derives from the influence of Soviet advisors in Xinjiang in the 1930s, fresh from their experience of making official designations of the Soviet Central Asian populations.[3] In his history of Xinjiang, Jack Chen supports this possibility of a re-created Uyghur identity:

At a conference of emigrants from the Tarim Basin held in Tashkent in 1921 after the Russian October Revolution, it was proposed that the name 'Uyghur' be taken to denominate all the groups of these people who had been known hitherto by the names of the localities where they lived – Kashgarlikhs, Aksulikhs, Lobniks, etc. This name was generally adopted in 1934 by the then Sinkiang provincial government. So for the future as we follow their fortunes over the next thousand years we shall refer to them by their new modern name – Uyghurs. (Chen, J. 1977:100)

This approach is typical of modern nationality studies, which subsume a vast amount of ethnohistorical and sociopolitical complexity under the current officially designated ethnonym for a specific people.[4] Rewriting the history of subject peoples is common practice for regimes in power, but it is the re-creation of tradition in response to the official historical interpretation with which this chapter is concerned.[5]

---

3. A.S. Whiting (1957:iv) estimates that during the heyday of the Sino-Soviet axis, more than 10,000 Soviet experts served in the USSR, and up to 7,000 Chinese were trained in the Soviet Union. For a discussion of the debate surrounding the politics of Lenin's defining the Central Asian peoples, see Wimbush (1985:69–78). For a summary of the Soviet influence upon early Chinese nationality policy, see Dreyer (1976:43–62).

4. For example, Lin Yueh-hwa's discussion of the Yi people in Sichuan Province (Lin 1984). For more information, see also Chapter 8, page 174 n.10, this volume.

5. Hobsbawm (1983a) addresses the 'invention of tradition' as the effort of people to come to grips with the changing social present in terms of

In addition to the shifting use of the term Uyghur, and its disappearance and revitalization after 500 years, the people referred
to by that name are now primarily identified as a Muslim people
(see Zhongguo 1981:174–94). Yet a brief look at the history of
the Uyghur will reveal a transition from traditional Central Asian
shamanistic nomads, to Manichaean, then Buddhist and Nestorian
Christian believers. From the 10th to the 15th century, the term
'Muslim' designated all those peoples who were specifically not
Uyghur, for the term Uyghur specifically referred to those Buddhist and Nestorian oasis dwellers of the Tarim Basin who did not
convert to Islam until the mid-15th century.

In this chapter, I argue that Uyghur identity as traditionally
conceived, whether it be cultural, historical, religious, or linguistic,
relies on notions of ethnicity and identity that are inadequate to
account for this shifting identity of the Uyghur. These approaches
to ethnicity generally fail to take into account the most important
development throughout the course of ethnic change in Inner
Asia: the interaction of the state with the nomadic steppe peoples
and the changing oppositions they entail. As we trace the evolution
of Uyghur identity, from steppe-nomad tribal confederation, to
settled seminomadic kingdom, to dispersed oasis traders, and finally, to a minority nationality of the People's Republic of China, we
find a story of ethnogenesis that reveals much about minority–state
relations and ethnic identity in the modern nation-state.

Ethnogenesis and the nation-state
Culture
Ethnogenesis refers to the rise of higher-order ethnic collectivities
where once there were disparate peoples or dispersed populations
(Bentley 1983:7–9). Past discussions of ethnic change and identity
have tended to polarize around positions that argue for a culturally
primordial identity and those advocating a purely circumstantial,
situational or politically motivated basis for ethnic identity.[6] Most
theorists now conclude that ethnicity cannot be reduced to purely

---

their reinterpreted past, which in the case of the Uyghur has much to do
with their incorporation and response to official interpretations of their
ethnohistory.

6.   For an informative summary of this earlier debate, see Bentley (1983); Nagata
     (1981); Despres (1984).

interest-based or primordial action, but must involve a combination or dialectical interaction of the two main aspects of ethnicity: culturally defined notions of descent, and sociopolitical circumstance (see Keyes 1981:28). Generally absent from these discussions of ethnic change is the important role of the state in determining the context and content of modern ethnic identity. For our understanding of the transition from Buddhist steppe empire to minority nationality, the influence of the Chinese and Soviet states in Central Asia on Uyghur identity is most important.

E.K. Francis (1976:114) was among the first to argue that the phenomena of ethnic identities and inter-ethnic conflict were a product of the modern nation-state – before the rise of the nation-state, ethnic identity was not as salient for social interaction and discourse (see also Horowitz 1985:291–3). Other modern ethnicity theorists have elaborated on the important role of the state, which often supersedes local or cultural interests in defining ethnic groups. Charles F. Keyes, in his seminal discussion of ethnic group relations in modern nation-states, provides the following insight:

Traditional states could harbor peoples of diverse ethnic origin in frontier or urban stranger communities without insisting that these communities become part of some 'nation'. In the modern nation-state, peoples of diverse origins, whether migrants or indigenous people, are compelled not only to recognize state authority but also to become part of the nation. Since sovereignty in the modern nation-state is vested in the people, rather than in a monarch legitimated by descent or religious charisma, the subjects of the modern nation-state must needs be integrated into the people. It is the process of national integration carried out not only in the so-called 'new states' but allowed very much so in states like the United States, the Soviet Union and even in 'old states' like the United Kingdom and Spain that has markedly stimulated people to reflect upon their ethnic status (Keyes 1984:15).[7]

The vast majority of examples of the ethnogenesis of undefined and loosely affiliated groups that later became fully fledged ethnic collectivities has occurred in the context of incorporation into and identity within a larger nation-state, often dominated by another ethnic group. These ethnic identities form and re-form according to articulated hierarchies of interaction with the

---

7. From the English version of the original conference paper, which was later published in Russian (Keyes 1984).

particular oppositional power in question. Evans-Pritchard's (1940) study of the Nuer in Africa was the first to point out the unique expansive–contractive nature of hierarchical segmentary lineages among acephalous nomadic societies (see Chapter 9, page 189). While the Uyghur have at times in their history been unified for particular sociopolitical purposes, for the most part the people now known by that name were scattered among disparate oases and tribal confederations. Out of opposition to other tribal confederations, and most notably the Chinese state, the people recognized as the Uyghur emerged.

The ethnogenesis of the Uyghur (ethnic identity)

Although a group of nomadic steppe peoples called the Uyghur have existed from before the 8th century, this identity has evolved through radically changing sociopolitical contexts. The ethnogenesis of the Uyghur is best understood as a gradual evolution through successive stages of interaction with the Chinese nation-state. Like the Xiongnu, who developed perhaps the first nomadic dynasty in reaction to the Qin–Han unification of China, the Uyghur established their kingdom, and migrated from the steppe to the oasis between the 7th and 9th centuries, in reaction to the unification of the Chinese empire under the Sui and Tang dynasties, as Thomas Barfield (1989) has shown. In an informative summary of early Chinese sources, Geng (1984: 1–6) traces the encounters by explorers and pilgrims with settled Central Asian populations from the Han to the Sui dynasties. As detailed in Chapter 9 (page 193), only at the fall of the Turkish Khanate to a people the Chinese historians called Hui-he or Hui-hu do we see the emergence of the Uyghur empire described by Mackerras (1972). As William Samolin, following the Tang histories, observes:

The term Uyghur is usually employed as a political rather than a tribal or territorial designation. Later it was used as a linguistic designation to distinguish one form of Old Turkish. Later the Chinese used Hui-hu, originally Uyghur, for Muslim. This served to add to the confusion. Strictly speaking, the tribal confederation which succeeded the Turkish dynasty of the [Orkhon] Inscriptions in 742 and possessed itself of the Ötükän refugium became generally known as Uyghur after the seizure of power. (Samolin 1964:73)

The gradual sedentarization of the Uyghur, and their defeat of the Turkish Khanate, occurred just as trade with the unified Tang state became especially lucrative (Mackerras 1969:215–18; Rossabi 1969–70). Samolin (1964:74–5) argues that the stability of rule, trade with the Tang, and ties to the imperial court, as well as the growing importance of establishing fixed Manichaean ritual centers, contributed to a settled way of life for the Uyghur tribes. The high Uyghur civilization that became, in the words of Barfield (1989), 'a bridge between the world of the nomads and surrounding civilizations', resulted from their raising the extortion of the Tang state, what the Chinese historians justified as 'tribute', to a fine art. It was in the Uyghur empire's interest to assist the Tang state, to maintain a profitable relationship – the Uyghur were more interested in exploitation than expansion. Sedentarization and interaction with the Chinese state brought socioreligious change, with the traditional shamanistic Turkic-speaking Uyghur being increasingly influenced by Persian Manichaeism (Sinor 1969:114–15). Trade and military alliances with China developed to such an extent that the Uyghur gradually took up Chinese cultural, sartorial, and even agricultural practices (Mackerras 1972:37).[8]

Conquer of the Uyghur capital in Mongolia, Karabalghasun, by the nomadic Kyrgyz in 840 led to further sedentarization and crystallization of Uyghur identity. According to Geng (1984:6), the Uyghur were dispersed across China into three main branches. One collection of thirteen tribes fled southeast from the Mongolian steppe to just beyond the Great Wall, and later disappeared from historical record, presumably assimilating into the northern-Han population (Sinor 1969:116). The rest of the Uyghur, comprising some fifteen tribes, dispersed west and southwest from Mongolia throughout northwest China, forming the basis for the second and third branches. The second branch eventually migrated to what is now Jiuquan, in Gansu Province, and were the ancestors of the people currently identified as the Yugur nationality, concentrated primarily in the Sunan Yugur Autonomous County.[9] The third branch was dispersed in the oases surrounding the Tarim Basin of

8. For a review of the assistance provided by the Uyghur in suppressing the An Lushan and other rebellions in internal China, see Barfield (1989); Sinor (1969:114–15).

9. If one were follow most popular ethnicity theories and take a purely cultural or linguistic approach to analyzing Uyghur identity, the Yugur in Gansu's

the Taklamakan, including Turpan, Karashahr, and Kashgar, where the Uyghur may previously have had dependencies (Mackerras 1972:12). As discussed in the previous chapter (page 194), this group utilized the unique socioecology of the oases around the Taklamakan, and gradually established Khocho, or Gaochang, the great Uyghur city-state based in Turpan from 850 to 1250.[10] It is interesting that while the members of this group are culturally reckoned to be the direct ancestors of the present-day Uyghur, and the region they inhabited became known as Uyghuristan (Elias 1972:72 *ff.*), they added Buddhist and Nestorian Christian beliefs to their Manichaean religious practice, and were the very last of the Uyghur in the Taklamakan oases to convert to Islam.

By the middle of the 9th century, then, we can see that the people now known as the Uyghur had become completely sedentarized. Excavations reveal a wealthy aristocratic civilization that rivaled the Tang and Song courts in its artistic and material sophistication. Sinor (1969:119) recounts the refusal of the Uyghur to be repatriated to Mongolia at the friendly suggestion of the Khitan rulers of the Liao dynasty (907–1125), whose leaders were in close contact with the Turpan Uyghur and even more familiar with a nomadic way of life that was now becoming a distant part of the Uyghurs' past heritage.

Rather than possessing any linguistic uniformity – by this time the Uyghur people maintained their Turkish dialect while their elite had adopted Persian with Sogdian script – the disparate Uyghur peoples took on identities based on their separate oases.[11]

Hexi Corridor should be the likeliest candidates. It is this modern group that most preserves the linguistic, cultural, and religious ties with the Uyghur empire's past. Known as the 'Yellow Uyghur' (*Yugur Shari Yugur*), who fled to Gansu after the Kyrgyz invasion of 840, these people are the only remnants of the original Uyghur kingdom to preserve much of their former Turkish language, written with Old Uyghur script until the 19th century. Manichaean influences in their Lamaist-Buddhist religion are also preserved, and they now are divided into three groups speaking Turkish, Mongolian, and Chinese dialects – all recognized as belonging to one nationality, the Yugur (see Schwarz 1984:57–74; Zhongguo 1981:165–73).

10. For a discussion of this fascinating and rich metropolis, see Allsen (1983); Geng (1984:6–8); Sinor (1969:118–21); and also Le Coq (1985 [1928]), for a description of the four German Turpan expeditions.

11. Citing Mahmud Kashgari's famous 11th-century dictionary, *Divan Lughat it-Turk*, Geng (1984:10–11) argues that while the basis for modern Uyghur

The gradual uptake of Islam by the Uyghur, from the 10th to the 16th centuries, displaced their Buddhist religion, but did little to overcome these oases-based loyalties. When the Kara-Khanid (932–1165) ruler Sadik Boghra Khan converted to Islam in 950, the peoples of the western Taklamakan oases, especially Kashgar, rejected their Buddhist and other Central Asian religious traditions in favor of the more politically and perhaps symbolically advantageous ideology of Islam.[12] The people of Uyghuristan, who resisted conversion to Islam until the 16th century, were thereafter the only people known as Uyghur. The others were known solely by the name of their oasis, or generically as Muslims (Haneda 1978:7). Juten Oda, a Japanese historian of Buddhist Central Asia, depicts this transitional period:

It was Moslims who ceased to be called by the original racial name that were to play the most important part from a political and commercial point of view under the khans or the princes. Nevertheless, the reason why we use the word Uyghuristan is that the Uyghurs who continued to be Buddhists kept their old racial characteristics. In Hami, two groups of the Uyghurs, namely, Buddhist Uyghurs and Moslim Uyghurs, lived together in the same area. (Oda 1978:23)

Once again, ethnoreligious change for the Uyghur was precipitated by sociopolitical incorporation. In this case, the expansion of the Kara-Khanid Islamic rule led to the gradual displacement of the Buddhist, Manichaean, and Nestorian Uyghur by an Islamic identity alien and in opposition to the traditional Uyghur identity to the extent that the name Uyghur was dropped as people became Muslim. Oda (1978:42) records the loss of the use of the term

---

dialect of Turkish was beginning to achieve supremacy as a lingua franca of the Taklamakan region, other separate languages such as Sogdian, Khotanese, and Tibetan continued to be well-entrenched among the local populations. As Islam expanded, Arabic gradually replaced the Uyghur script (Barthold 1956:21; Geng 1984:9).

12. Even in the largely Islamized western oases, Mirza Muhammad Haidar Dughlat, in his 15th-century eyewitness account, complains that the Turkish 'racial' identity of the locals had still not been replaced by Islam: 'The spread of the Musulman religion tends always to the modification of manners and customs, and to the use of the Arabic, Turki or Persian language; but in spite of all, racial characteristics remain, until very gradually expunged by a course of inter-breeding, that must extend over many centuries' (in Elias 1972 [1895]:82).

Uyghur by the people in Hami in 1513 with their annexation by Mansur Khan. Under the Buddhist Kara-Kitai (1137–1210) and Mongol (1209–1368) empires, Buddhist and Nestorian Uyghur scribes and administrators were heavily relied upon (Allsen 1983: 267; De Rachewiltz 1983:288–9). With the arrival of Islam, the ethnonym Uyghur fades from the historical record.

With the fall of the Mongol empire, the decline of the over-land trade routes, and the expansion of trade relationships with the Ming (Rossabi 1969–70), Turpan gradually turned toward the Islamic Moghuls, and, perhaps in opposition to the growing Chinese empire, adopted Islam by the mid-15th century (Hamada 1978:85–8). While this is the first time in the Tarim Basin's history that, according to Geng (1984:12–13), it became 'unified politically, economically, religiously, culturally, and linguistically' and that, therefore, the 'time was ripe for the formation of a new ethnic community, the modern Uyghur nationality', it is remark-able that we find the term Uyghur now completely dropped from the region in reference to the local inhabitants (Elias 1972 [1895]: 100). The Uyghur, who were identified as the non-Muslim, mainly Buddhist rulers of Turpan, converted and the local inhabitants no longer preferred to be known by the non-Islamic term. Instead, as mentioned on page 194, we find the proliferation of such oasis-based localisms as Yerlik, Sart, and Taranchi (Fletcher 1978:69). We do not find a significant unification of the populations of these disparate oases until the late Qing empire conquered the Mongo-lian Zungarians (1653–1754). Until this time, the Tarim Basin was riven by political succession struggles among the Moghul leaders and by religious disputes (Rossabi 1979:171–4).

During the 17th and 18th centuries a brief period of unifica-tion of eastern Xinjiang under the Yarkant khanate was broken up when politico-religious factionalism between two compet-ing Naqshbandiyya Sufi orders, the 'White Mountain' Afaqiyya in Kashgar and the 'Black Mountain' Ishiqiyya in Yarkant, led to intervention by the Mongolian Zungars in the late 17th century. Isenbike Togan-Aricanli argues that throughout this period oases-based local governments prevailed:

The seventeenth–eighteenth century Khwaja rule, in general, showed tendencies of centralization without developing them into a centralized government. At this juncture this seems to be inevitable, as the Khwajagan

played only a centripetal role to counterbalance the centrifugal tendencies of the local begs ... eliminated during the Muslim rebellions of 1864.
(Togan-Aricanli 1988:14)[13]

Joseph Fletcher (1978:90) has argued that despite conquering Xinjiang in 1754 and driving out the Zungar Mongolian overlords of
the Turkish peoples, the Qing did not begin to attempt to incorporate the region into the Han Chinese realm until 1821, when
massive migration of Han Chinese was encouraged. According to
Kim Ho-dong's (1986:5) definitive study of 19th-century Xinjiang, it was only during this early period that the Qing maintained
any secure hold on the region. The Yaqub Beg rebellion that established the thirteen-year Kashgar Emirate (1864–1877) crystallized
Uyghur resistance against what they perceived to be a cultural and
political Chinese threat to their identity. While the Uyghur involved
in this rebellion were divided into the usual local, ideological, and
socioeconomic factions that usually disunited them – which Kim
(1986:74 *ff.*) argues contributed to their downfall – it nevertheless
played an important role in setting all Uyghur apart from the Chinese state, similar to the important events I discussed in Chapter 9,
which are contributing to the rise of pan-ethnic identities in other
nation-states. Although the Uyghur were divided internally during
periods of oppression and revolt, many of them later began to conceive of themselves as united *vis-à-vis* the dominant hegemony. For
the Uyghur of Xinjiang today, no matter what their oasis, social, or
religious orientation, Yaqub Beg is thought of as a folk hero.

The Republican period saw Uyghur identity again marked by
locality-based, religious, and political factionalism. In his comprehensive and fascinating analysis of the complex warlord politics
of Republican Xinjiang, Forbes (1986) makes important ongoing distinctions between the three macro-regions of Xinjiang:
northwestern Zungaria, southern Tarim Basin, and eastern
Kumul–Turpan ('Uyghuristan'). While this provides a much more
profound analysis of local patterns of response to rapid sociopolitical change, the disparate actions of the Uyghur in a weakened
Han Chinese state reflects earlier patterns of disunity during
times of decentralization – a pattern not unique to nomads (see
Barfield 1989).

13. For a further discussion of Kwaja rule, see Schwarz (1976).

Twentieth-century Chinese expansion and Uyghur identity

As we have seen, the incorporation of the oases cities into the Chinese empire with the defeat of the Zungars in the 18th century was limited and short-lived. Until the major migrations of Han Chinese were encouraged in the mid-19th century, the Qing were mainly interested in pacifying the region by setting up military outposts, which supported a vassal-state relationship. Colonization began with the migrations of the Han in the mid-19th century, but this was cut short by the Yaqub Beg rebellion in the second half of the 19th century, the fall of the Qing empire in 1910, and the ensuing warlord era, which dismembered the region until its incorporation as part of the People's Republic in 1949. Competition for the loyalties of the peoples of the oases in the Great Game played between China, Russia and Britain further contributed to divisions among the Uyghur along political, religious, and military lines (Lattimore 1950; Whiting and Sheng 1958). The peoples of the oases, until the challenge of nation-state incorporation, lacked any coherent sense of identity. In his socioeconomic study of Chinese Turkestan, Warikoo (1985:107–8) observed:

National consciousness among the Uyghurs was conspicuously absent. They were isolated amongst numerous oasis-settlements, which were backward and self-sufficient economic units. Each oasis was practically a little state having its own capital, small towns, rural settlements, a central market where all the local produce was exchanged by barter and a separate district administration, thus enabling it to maintain its own individuality. Social segregation of these settlements and their respective populations prevented the formation of a united front against oppressive regimes.

This chapter argues that factionalism within the Uyghur reflects a segmentary hierarchy of loyalties common among ethnic groups. Uyghur are divided from within by religious conflicts, in this case competing Sufi and non-Sufi orders, territorial loyalties (whether they be to oases or places of origin), linguistic discrepancies, commoner–elite alienation, and competing political loyalties. Yet these internal conflicts often became less compelling when confronted by strong, centralized incorporating nation-states.

Sociopolitical incorporation is most critical for Uyghur identity. While hard evidence is lacking for the exact time when the term Uyghur became affixed to the settled Turkish-speaking Muslim oasis peoples, that it became the accepted ethnonym by both the

Soviet Union and the newly established Chinese nation by the 1940s reveals an important shift in the ethnopolitical make-up of the region. Justin Rudelson (1988:23–30), a graduate student at Harvard who has conducted fieldwork in Turpan, is to be credited with suggesting that the Soviet Union may have played a privileged role in helping to define the modern Uyghur identity. Rudelson suggests that the advice given to the Chinese Xinjiang warlord Sheng Shi-tsai by the Soviet diplomat Garegin Apresoff, invited to Xinjiang in 1933, may have included the suggestion that the name Uyghur be used for the settled Tarim Basin peoples, based on the same linguistic–historical formulae that Lenin used to label the Soviet Central Asian peoples in the 1920s (see also Chen, J. 1977:21; Forbes 1986:119–20; Wimbush 1985). Rudelson sites Vaidyanath's (1967:209) use of the term Uyghur (which was not present in the 1917 Soviet Census) in 1924, to denote the oasis peoples of Xinjiang, eventually subsuming the previously distinct Kashgari, Taranchi, Turki, and Sart-Kalmuk, and their being given three 'Uyghur village soviets' within the Uzbek SSR in 1928. The last Republican governor of Xinjiang, the Tartar Burhan Sha-hidi (1984:244), records in his memoirs that at the first Xinjiang Nationalities Congress the term Uyghur was suggested by Han officials and was welcomed by the oasis peoples, who had until that time been only referred to as 'turbaned Muslims' (*Chuantou Hui*), as opposed to the Dungan Hui-hui (see Forbes 1987).[14] In a similar fashion, the Soviet Central Asianist Anatoly Khazanov (pers. comm.) related that a Soviet Nationalities Commission director in Tashkent noted that as late as 1926 few Uzbek recognized that ethnonym for themselves.

As argued above, incorporation of Xinjiang for the first time into a nation-state required unprecedented delineation of the so-called nations involved. The re-emergence of the label Uyghur, though arguably inappropriate because it was last used 500 years previously to describe the largely Buddhist population of the Tur-pan Basin, stuck as the appellation for the settled Turkish-speaking

14. For a description of Burhan's position in Xinjiang and background, see McMillen (1979:23 n.25). While McMillen provides an excellent detailed description of Chinese Communist policy and political incorporation of Xinjiang from 1949 to 1977, he (like many others) generally assumes Uyghur identity, and does not explore its creation by the Chinese state in the early years of Xinjiang's incorporation into the People's Republic.

Muslim oasis–dwellers. It has never been disputed by the people themselves or the states involved. There is too much at stake for the people labeled as such to wish to challenge that identification.

That Islam became an important, though not exclusive, cultural marker of Uyghur identity is not surprising given the sociopolitical oppositions with which the Uyghur were confronted.[15] Omer Kanat (1986:113–19) disputes Denise Helly's (1985:99–101) hypothesis that the political mobilization of East Turkestanis along religious lines was the reaction of a feudal society to the socialist modes of production being introduced by the Chinese on the grounds that the Uyghur had been undergoing agrarian and industrial reforms over the past four decades. The Chinese certainly were faced with a complex sociopolitical situation in Xinjiang, while in the throes of industrial, agrarian, and political change, but Helly's (1985:107) argument that Islam played an important role as a unifying ideology of resistance, rather than a pure resurgence of Islamic orthodoxy, is well founded and important for an understanding of changing Uyghur identity.[16]

However, it is also important to note that Islam was only one of several unifying markers for Uyghur identity, depending on those with whom they were in significant opposition at the time. For example, to the Dungan (Hui), the Uyghur distinguish themselves as the legitimate autochthonous minority, since both share a belief in Sunni Islam.[17] In contrast to the nomadic Muslim peoples, the Uyghur stress their attachment to the land and their oasis of origin. In opposition to the Han Chinese, the Uyghur will generally emphasize their Central Asian Turkish features and language. Shahrani (1984:29) insightfully notes that the response given to Barthold, quoted at the beginning of this chapter, that Central Asians were Muslim first, might very well have been a reflection

---

15. For a case study of the influence of nationality policy and its relation to the growing importance of Islam among southeast-coast Hui lineages descended from foreign Muslim ancestors but who no longer practice Islam, see Gladney (1995).

16. For an excellent collection of articles addressing the complex issue of the shifting meaning of Islam and its reinterpretation in the context of changing political economy, see Roff (1987).

17. Forbes (1987) describes the innumerable conflicts between Han, Uyghur, and Hui (Dungan) during the warlord politics of the Republican period, as each sought to form alliances and survive the tumultuous period.

of their perception of opposition to him as a European Christian. Each aspect of Uyghur identity gains importance depending on the hierarchy of oppositions with which the Uyghur are faced.

Islam is a fundamental aspect of Uyghur identity, but so is their attachment to land and language. Each marker of identity takes on salience and enhanced meaningfulness in the context of significant oppositions. The importance of sociopolitical opposition for defining ethnic identity in multi-ethnic contexts was first fully analyzed by Sir Edmund Leach (1954), in his discussion of competing ethnic groups in highland Burma.[18] It is certainly the articulated hierarchy of ethnic expression in the competition for scarce resources and local power that is most critical for our understanding of current Uyghur identity.

The incorporation of Xinjiang and modern Uyghur identity

Unheralded sociopolitical integration of Xinjiang into the Chinese nation-state has taken place since 1949. While Xinjiang has been under Chinese political domination since the defeat of the Zungars in 1754, until the middle of the 20th century it was but loosely incorporated into China proper. The extent of the incorporation of the Xinjiang Region into China is indicated by Han migration, communication, education, and occupational shifts since the 1940s.

Han migration into Xinjiang has swelled their local population to an incredible twenty-six times more than the 1940 level, with an annual growth of 8.1 percent. The increase of the Han population has been accompanied by the growth and delineation of Muslim groups other than the Uyghur.[19] Accompanying the remarkable rise of the Han population, a dramatic increase in the Hui (Dungan) population can also be seen. While the Hui population grew in Xinjiang between 1940 and 1982 by more than six times (averaging an annual growth of 4.5 percent), Uyghur population

18. For the use of shifting cultural symbols as markers of identity, see Nagata (1981); Trottier (1981).
19. For a study of Chinese minority identification policy, the identification of the fifty-four minority nationalities in the 1950s, with special attention to Muslim minorities, and its reliance on a Soviet Marxist cultural model of ethnicity, see Gladney (1987b:36–43); see also Walker Connor's (1984) description of Marxist–Leninist ethnicity theory and policy.

has followed a more natural biological growth of 1.7 percent.[20] By the 2000 census, the Hui population in Xinjiang had grown to 844,211 and the Uyghur population to 8.6 million (Statistics Bureau of Xinjiang Uyghur Autonomous Region 2002). The Han population, previously estimated at 6.9 million, was revealed to be 7.5 million, and the census showed that the Han population grew at 31.6 percent (double the rate of the local minorities) (Human Rights Watch 2001). The dramatic rise of Han migration and increasing competition for scarce resources was the impetus for several Uyghur uprisings in the late 1990s (see also Naby 1986; Rudelson 1988:31–3).

The 2000 census shed some light on the steady influx of Han settlers into Xinjiang in the past years – a trend that had always been underplayed by the local authorities and attributed to 'seasonal migrants'. The census revealed figures distinctly higher than those published beforehand: the Han population, previously estimated at 6,870,000, was in fact 7,490,000. Most remarkably, the census showed that during the 1990s, the Han population grew by 31.6 percent, twice the rate of the local ethnic minorities (up 15.9 percent), who supposedly benefit from more lax family-planning policies compared to the rest of China.

Chinese incorporation of Xinjiang led to a further development of ethnic socioeconomic niches. While earlier travelers reported little distinction in labor and education among Muslims, other than that between settled and nomadic (Lattimore 1950), the 1982 census has revealed vast differences in socioeconomic structure.

It is noteworthy that 84 percent of the Uyghur are involved in the production of agriculture and husbandry, the same as the average for all ethnic groups. The Hui, however, have only 60.7 percent involved in farming and husbandry, with trade and commerce taking up many more of their numbers. The Uyghur rank far below the Uzbek and Tartar in the scientific and technical occupations, primarily due to the larger proportion of the urbanized intellectuals

20. The slow population-growth of Uyghur between 1953 and 1982 may be due to emigration to the then Soviet Central Asia. Banister (1987:324), based on published Soviet population studies, suggests that the Uyghur excess population growth in Central Asia was from 33,000 to 41,000 during that period. The Soviet Uyghur newspaper, *Kommunizm Tugi*, on 12 October 1987 reported that the Uyghur population in Soviet Central Asia was 250,000 (Alptekin, E. 1988:2).

among Uzbek and Tartar. This is also reflected in reports on education among Muslim minorities in China (see Chapter 12).

The Uyghur are about average in terms of university graduates and illiteracy in China, as compared with other ethnic groups (0.2 and 45 percent respectively). The Tartar achieve the highest representation of university graduates among Muslims (39 percent) and the lowest percentage of illiteracy (9 percent), far below the average of all China (32 percent). The main drawback of these figures is that they reflect only what is regarded by the state as education, namely training in Chinese language and the sciences. However, as Eden Naby (1986) confirmed, there continues to be among elderly Uyghur intellectuals a high standard of traditional expertise in Persian, Arabic, Chagatay, and the Islamic sciences, which is not considered part of Chinese 'culture' and education. Although elementary and secondary education is offered in Uyghur, Mandarin has become the language of upward mobility in Xinjiang, as well as the rest of China.[21] Many Uyghur have been trained in the thirteen nationalities colleges scattered throughout China since they were established in the 1950s. It is these secular intellectuals trained in Chinese schools who are asserting political leadership in Xinjiang, as opposed to traditional religious elites. Many Uyghur in Ürümqi point to the establishment of the Uyghur Traditional Medicine Hospital and madrasah complex in 1987 as an initial counterbalance to this emphasis on Han education.[22] However, most Uyghur I have spoken with feel that their history and traditional culture continues to be downplayed in the state schools and must be privately re-emphasized to their children. It is through the elementary schools that Uyghur children first participate formally in the Chinese nation-state, dominated by Han history and language, and most fully enter into the Chinese world. As such, the predominant educational practice of teaching a centralized, mainly Han subject content, despite the widespread use of minority languages, continues to drive a wedge between the Uyghur and their traditions, inducting them further into the Han Chinese milieu.

21. For a discussion of commoner–elite conflict among other minorities as a result of education in the Han Chinese system, see also Dreyer 1970.
22. See Ibrahim Muti'i (1989) for an excellent historical synopsis of the role of the Central Asian Islamic madrasah in traditional Uyghur education. Professor Muti'i argues that it was the madrasah, more than religious or cultural continuities, that most tied the Uyghur into Central Asian traditions.

Xinjiang has been further incorporated into the Chinese state through the extensive expansion of rail and telecommunications.[23] While it took Zuo Zongtang six months to bring an imperial Qing army from Lanzhou to Ürümqi to suppress the Uyghur uprising led by Yaqub Beg at the end of the 19th century, today Ürümqi is only five hours by airplane and seventy-two hours by train from Beijing.[24] Roads now link all the major towns in the region, and while traveling overland to Kashgar from Ürümqi may take more than four days, the buses are filled with Uyghur engaging in trade and visiting relatives. Although travel is arduous and expensive for the locals, it is at least possible, and contributes to pan-Uyghur identity through increased inter-oasis communication.

Uyghur not only travel widely throughout Xinjiang, but are found in every city in internal China. The increased incorporation of Xinjiang into the political sphere of China has not only led to the further migration of Han and Hui into the region, but also opened China to an unprecedented extent for the Uyghur. Uyghur men are heavily involved in long-distance trade throughout China. They go to Tianjin and Shanghai for manufactured clothes and textiles, Hangzhou and Suzhou for silk, and Guangzhou and Hainan for electronic goods and motorcycles brought in from Hong Kong. In every place, and especially Beijing, due to the large foreign population, they trade local currency (renminbi) for foreign exchange certificates (*waihuijuan*). Appearing more like foreigners than the local Han, they are often less suspect. 'We use the hard currency to go on the hajj,' one young Uyghur in the central market square of Kunming, Yunnan Province, told me in 1985. 'Allah will protect you if you exchange money with me.'

23. Uyghur continue to resent the influx of Han that expanded rail and road networks have facilitated. It was one of their main complaints during the December 1986 and June 1988 student protests (see FBIS 1988d). A popular story is told that the first train into Ürümqi in the 1960s made the sound '*chi chi chi*' ('eat, eat, eat'), and upon its departure sounded like '*chibaole, chibaole, chibaole*' ('I'm full, I'm full, I'm full'). Short-term rotations of Han workers for three to five years, rather than permanent residence, has satisfied both Uyghur and disgruntled Han who want to go home – the cause of a 1979 hunger strike in Aksu involving more than 70,000 Uyghur.

24. This point was made by the Russian explorer Valikhanov, who, dressed as a Muslim, visited Kashgaria in the late 1850s, and claimed that it would take six months for China to send a reinforcement army from Lanzhou in the event of an uprising (Kim 1986:9).

While some may save for the hajj, most purchase import or luxury goods with their hard currency and take them back to Xinjiang, selling or trading them for a profit – a practice that keeps them away from home six months out of the year. As Uyghur continue to travel throughout China, they return to Xinjiang with a firmer sense of their own pan-Uyghur identity *vis-à-vis* the Han and the other minorities they encounter on their travels.

International travel has also resumed for the Uyghur. An important development in recent years has been the resumption of the construction of a rail line between China and Russia through the Ili corridor to Almaty – a link opened to international travel in 1992 that was disrupted with the breakdown in Sino-Soviet relations thirty years earlier (FBIS 1988a). This was the shortest rail connection of East and Southeast Asia with Europe, and trade was expected to blossom, according to the plans envisioned in the protocol signed on 24 October 1988 (FBIS 1988c). With the resumption of normal Sino-Soviet relations in 1983, trade and personal contacts expanded enormously. The Chinese press reported a fivefold increase over the previous year, with trade worth 100 million Swiss francs in 1988, up from 21 million Swiss Francs in 1987. Contracts worth 200 million Swiss francs were signed for the future by 1988 (FBIS 1988f) and were quickly met. This expansion led many Uyghur to see themselves as important players in the improved Sino-Soviet (now Sino-Russian) exchanges. On a trip from Moscow to Beijing through the Ili corridor, I was surprised to find that many of the imported Hong Kong-made electronic goods purchased by Uyghur with hard currency in Canton and Shenzhen found their way into the marketplace and the hands of relatives across the border in Almaty – relatives who were also identified by the Soviet state as Uyghur.

To an unprecedented extent, the continued incorporation of Xinjiang into China has become inexorable, and perhaps irreversible. To be sure, the Uyghur are still oriented culturally and historically toward Central Asia in terms of religion, language, and ethnic customs, and interaction has increased in recent years due to the opening of the roads to Pakistan and Almaty. Certainly, pan-Turkism was appealing to some but not all Uyghur during the early part of the 20th century (see Forbes 1986:112–16). Historical ties to Central Asia are strong. Turkey's Prime Minister Turgut Ozal espoused a popular Turkish belief when, on a 1985 visit to

Beijing that sought to open a consulate there, he commented that the Turkish nation originated in what is now China.[25] Yet separatist notions, given the current political incorporation of Xinjiang into China, while perhaps present, are not practicable. To a question regarding political separation, one prominent Uyghur, in an interview with the *Los Angeles Times*, responded: 'Some people would like to, but there is no hope' (Mann 1985:10).

The opening of China to the outside world has meant much to the Uyghur, who may easily travel beyond China's borders through Pakistan along the Karakoram Highway, through the Ili valley into Kazakhstan, or by direct CAAC flight to Istanbul from Ürümqi (opened in 1987). The Chinese press reported that Uyghur pilgrims traveling on the hajj to Mecca increased to 500 in 1988, with a total of more than 6,500 hajji between 1980 and 1987 from Xinjiang (FBIS 1988b). These contacts have allowed the Uyghur to see themselves as participants in the broader Islamic *umma*, while at the same time being Muslim citizens of the Chinese nation-state (see Gladney 1987a:497–500). As they return from the hajj, many Uyghur, who generally travel together as a group, have told me that they gained a greater sense of affinity with their own as one people than with the other multi-ethnic members of the international Islamic community.

State-promoted tourism of foreign Muslims and travelers to Muslim areas in China in hopes of stimulating economic investment is also an important trend related to this opening of Xinjiang and its borders. Ürümqi, a largely Han city constructed over the past fifty years, is undergoing an Islamic facelift with officially endorsed Central Asian and Islamic architecture that serves to impress many visiting foreign Muslim dignitaries. The Chinese press reported that in 1987 there were 73,800 domestic and foreign tourists in Xinjiang, an increase of 52 percent over 1986 (FBIS 1988e). After the opening of the Karakoram Highway across the border with Pakistan to individual foreign tourists in May 1986, one Chinese researcher reported that there were 2,400 foreign visitors in two months, not including Pakistanis (pers. interview). While passing

25. Several Uyghur men in Istanbul commented that Turkish women are often interested in marrying them because they believed they possessed 'pure Turkish blood'. However, most Uyghur and Kazakh I interviewed continued to seek wives from within their own peoples, no matter how difficult (see also Svanberg 1989b).

from Kazakhstan into Xinjiang through the Sino-Soviet border near Panfilov in October 1988, I was told by the local Soviet customs official that more than fifty groups had crossed that year. A few days later in Kashgar, I was surprised to note that Pakistanis staying in the Qinibake Hotel, formerly Chini Bagh, the old British consulate, had so increased since my last visit in 1987 that there was almost no room for other foreigners, most of whom stayed in the Seman Hotel, the former Russian consulate, or the newer Kashgar Guest House.

Most of these foreigners come to see the colorful minorities and the traditional dances and costumes by which their ethnicity is portrayed in Chinese and foreign travel brochures.[26] One Japanese tourist with whom I spoke in Kashgar who had just arrived by bicycle from Pakistan across the Karakoram Highway said that a tourist brochure told him that the real Uyghur could only be found in Kashgar, whereas most Uyghur believe that Turpan is the center of their cultural universe. Yet many of these Kashgari will in the same breath argue that much of traditional Uyghur culture has been lost to Han influence in Turpan, and that because the Kashgari are the repositories of the more unspoiled 'Uyghur' traditions, tourists should spend their time, and money, in Kashgar. This search for the so-called 'real Uyghur' confirms that the nationality statistics and tourism agencies have succeeded. The re-creation of Uyghur ethnicity has come full circle: the Chinese nation-state has identified a people who have in the past fifty years taken on that assigned identity as their own, and in the process, those who have accepted that identity have sought to define it and exploit it on their own terms.

Uyghur identity and the Chinese nation-state

Past studies of the peoples of Xinjiang have generally been marred by overattention to geopolitical machinations on the Inner Asian frontiers, to the neglect of the complex identities of the multi-

26. Kathleen Adams (1984:469) has demonstrated the important role travel agencies play in creating expectations among foreign tourists for certain 'cultural experiences' based on packaged preconceived notions of identity and ethnicity in Tana Toraja, Indonesia. These cultural performances often mask a host of complex expressions of identity that may bear little resemblance to the performers.

ethnic players in that game, often accepting the labels ascribed to them by the dominant powers. Minority nationality studies have generally examined ethnic change in terms of Han cultural assimilation, or Sinicization, as it has been often termed (Dreyer 1976:264–5; Lal 1970).[27] Yet despite more than 100 years of varying degrees of political incorporation, not only have these people retained much of their ethnoreligious identity, but new expressions of identity have evolved in interaction with nationality policy and socioeconomic change. The peoples of Inner Asia have been particularly resistant to Han cultural assimilation, while Xinjiang has been brought fully into the Chinese nation-state.[28] I would argue that it is not 'Hanification' (*Han hua*) that is at issue for ethnic identity, but 'Chinese nationalization' (*Zhongguo hua*). To be sure, when Han culture and the Chinese state become merged as one and the same (known as *da Han zhuyi*, 'great Han chauvinism'), especially during periods of a weakened central state, such as the Cultural Revolution, then ethnic and religious differences are challenged.[29] 'Local nationalism' (*difang minzu zhuyi*), the resurgent expression of local ethnic identities, is then portrayed as feudalistic, and education is seen as assimilation into the 'higher' Han culture. While there have been periods when this has dominated the nationality program in China, it was officially rejected by the Deng Xiaoping regime.[30] Ethnic pluralism under the Chinese nation is the official

27. This idea derives from Ch'en Yüan's (1966) classic work, which argued all minority peoples that came into long-term contact with the Chinese empire gradually Sinicized to Han customs.

28. Lucien Pye (1975:497) makes the astute observation that administrative integration of Xinjiang was the goal of the early Communists; assimilation was regarded as unrealizable.

29. Though Islam was regarded with other religions as feudal superstition during the Cultural Revolution, it is protected under the constitution. While Islam is officially regarded as extraneous to the cultural and linguistic heritage of the Muslim peoples, who in the census were not registered by religion but by 'nationality' (see Gladney 1987a:36–43), John Voll (1985:143) makes the important point that recognition of the 'special character of their national life' gives tacit recognition to the importance of Islam.

30. Ma Weiliang (1980:78, cited in Banister 1987:315–16) summarized this landmark policy reversal: 'In our struggle against local nationalism in 1957, we magnified class struggle, accused some minority national cadres of attacking the party because they explained the true conditions in their regions and expressed the complaints and wishes of their people, and labeled them as local nationalists. We criticized proper national feelings, national desires, and

goal of the present government – whether or not it will be fully achieved is yet to be seen. An important shift is revealed in the following statement by the former president of the Kashgar Teacher's College, Abdul Karim Baodin: 'Now, there is recognition by the Party and the government that cultural diversity does not conflict with political loyalty. This has brought tremendous changes for us' (Parks 1983:1).

Ethnicity models that seek to define Uyghur identity according to purely cultural markers, such as religion or language, do not take into account the wide diversity within the Uyghur, or their complex ethnohistory. Instrumentalist approaches to ethnicity that might portray the Uyghur as interest-motivated actors seeking benefits under the present favorable policies fail to account for the resilient continuity of Uyghur identity in the face of periods of oppression and political instability. We have seen that any adequate understanding of modern Uyghur identity must take into account not only ethnohistory and political motivation, but also incorporation into and interaction with the Chinese nation-state. To a certain extent, the Uyghur are who they are because the Chinese state has labeled them as such. In response to that ascription, the present Uyghur identity has evolved and interacted in dialectical fashion.

It is no surprise that the émigrés from Xinjiang living in the Zeytinburnu district of Istanbul do not regard themselves as

---

demands as bourgeois nationalism. In 1958, we again departed from the reality of minority nationality regions, ran counter to objective laws, advocated the so-called "reaching the sky in a single bound," ... undermined the economy of the minority nationality regions, and created tension among the minority nationality regions. In 1962, the national conference on the work among the minority nationalities correctly summed up our experience and lessons drawn, and pointed out profoundly that [we must understand fully] the protracted nature of the existing national differences ... But later in 1964, under the domination of "left" deviation, we again vigorously criticized the so-called "Right capitulationism" and "revisionism" in the national united front work, and refuted many of our good experiences ... During the Great Cultural Revolution, Lin Biao and the "gang of four" ... artificially created large numbers of horrible, unjust, false, and wrong cases, and used the big stick of class struggle to attack and persecute many minority national cadres and the masses. They slandered minority national customs and habits and spoken and written languages as "four old things," ... undermined very seriously the party's policy towards the minority nationalities and the economic cultural reconstruction in their regions, and caused serious calamities. This is an extremely bitter experience from which we learned a lesson'.

Uyghur; the Turkish state does not regard them as such either. This does not suggest that ethnic identity is merely a product of state creation or dissolution. Rather it is a combination of dialectical interaction on both sides of the agreed-upon ethnonym, and in the centralized nation-states of Inner Asia, throughout history, the state has played a privileged role in directing the expression and ethnogenesis of Uyghur identity.

11
CYBER-SEPARATISM

Reconstructing Uyghur identity

National identities never arise in a vacuum. Rather than being purely cultural or primordial bases for identity, national identities are constructed in relation to the interpretation of one's own myths of nostalgic descent from a common ancestry. This imagined identity, to use Benedict Anderson's (1991) phrase, is formed in the context of changing socioeconomic circumstances – situations most often defined in the modern world by the nation-state, which has regularly abrogated to itself the task of identifying, labeling, and colonizing ethnic identities. I argued in Chapter 10 that the Uyghur provide an excellent illustration of this process in which a group of oasis-dwelling Turkic-speaking people shared a general historical experience but did not begin to think of themselves as a single national identity until the early part of the 20th century, when Soviet and Chinese states identified them as one of several Turkic nationalities. Accounts of Xinjiang by foreign travelers from the mid-16th century to the early 20th century, by famous explorers such as Muhammad Haidar, Sven Hedin, and Owen Lattimore, contained no references to any collective group referred to as Uyghur, but instead found people identifying themselves as Turki (from their language family), Sart (meaning 'caravaneer' in old Persian), and other oasis-based ethnonyms, such as Kashgarlik, Turpanlik, and Khotanlik.

I have described elsewhere the process of ethnogenesis in which these separate identities crystallized into the people now known as the Uyghur, with a population of 7.2 million according to the reasonably accurate 1990 census (representing a growth of 20.9 percent over their 1982 population, while the Han only experienced a 10.8 percent growth [*Renmin Ribao* 14 November

1990:3]).The total Uyghur population according to the 2000 census was 8.4 million, a 17 percent increase since 1990 (Statistics Bureau of Xinjiang Uyghur Autonomous Region 2002). While this process of ethnogenesis is not unique to the Uyghur, and indeed has been documented by other case studies of ethnogenesis in China, such as the Hui (Gladney 1987a), the Yi (Harrell 1995), the Naxi (McKhann 1995), and the Miao (Diamond 1988), it is also a natural process of identity formation experienced by many groups of peoples who are often registered and incorporated into the modern nation-state (see Bentley 1989; Cohn 1987; Keyes 1984). For the Uyghur it has meant both their subjection to Chinese rule and their rise as a transnational ethnic group, their coalescence as an entity of 8.4 million that is recognized across China, and now the world – the not entirely unwilling subjects of tourist brochures, religious and political tracts, and academic investigations. I have written about the objectification of this identity and the rise of Uyghur identity. In this chapter I explore the consequences, expected and unexpected, of this essentialized identity for Chinese foreign policy and national identity, which I suggest is tied to three processes: the transnationalization, the Islamization, and the exoticized representation of the Uyghur by the state. Finally, I suggest that in the light of the 'war on terrorism' launched in relation to the events of 11 September 2001, a widespread movement largely among the Uyghur diaspora through the use of the Internet has contributed to a 'cyber-separatism' campaign that is anything but virtual. I argue that through processes of transnationalization and Islamization, which can be illustrated by such events as the so-called Salman Rushdie protest, the trans-Eurasian railway, and the Sino-Saudi missile deal, the Uyghur have been appropriated by the Chinese state in order to promote its foreign-policy objectives, particularly in the Muslim Middle East, while the representation in art and the media of the Uyghur, and other minorities, as exotic and even erotic has contributed to the construction of a monolithic Chinese national (Han) identity and the justification of the continued state hegemony over the Chinese people.

   In this chapter I shall be arguing, therefore, that the nationalization and transnationalization of a Turkic-speaking, oasis–dwelling people in the Tarim Basin of northwestern China, now known as the Uyghur, has contributed to the contemporary construction of Chinese national identity in general, and served the specific interests of the Chinese state in its Middle Eastern relations, as well as engendering a diasporic Uyghur response, which can best be described as cyber-separatism.

The transnationalization of the Uyghur: Salman Rushdie and trans-Eurasian railways

Except for a few self-justifying statements by former Premier Li Peng, the Chinese government has attempted to put the events of the 1989 Tiananmen massacre behind it. It has not been completely successful. While the world has largely forgotten the uneventful Asian Games of late summer 1989, it still vividly remembers Tiananmen. Nevertheless, a slogan posted throughout China ties the two together strikingly: 'Unity, Friendship, Progress' (*tuanjie, youyi, jinbu*). This slogan was posted during the Asian Games and still remains on walls and banners throughout China, urging the population to pull together after the tragic crisis, and unite with each other out of friendship for the sake of national progress. It will probably also be widely used during the upcoming 2008 Olympics in Beijing, for which the city is busily making preparations. The fact that it is posted and translated in such minority languages as Uyghur underscores the government's concern to keep the various peoples of the People's Republic united. 'United nationalities' (*minzu tuanjie*) is a slogan that the state has used since the 1950s to urge the country's fifty-six nationalities to come together for the good of the country. Yet, as I have more fully analyzed elsewhere (Gladney 1996a), the phrase is often turned around to mean the unity and ethnic solidarity of the individual nationality *against* the Han majority and state apparatus – a far cry from its Leninist origins in the slogan 'Workers of the world unite!'

The Uyghur in Xinjiang are not friendly, united, or making progress. One unresolved conflict that disgruntles the Uyghur, and that stems from the time of Tiananmen, was the 'Salman Rushdie' protest that took place in Beijing on 12 May 1989, the day the students, led at that time by the Uyghur student Wu'er Kaixi (Uerkesh Daolet),[1] declared their hunger strike, which galvanized the nation in support of them. At the very time the government was preparing its tanks and armed mobile units to move against

---

1.　For a discussion of his role in Tiananmen, see Gladney (1990:64–5).

the students, it allowed – indeed, strongly supported – a Muslim protest that paraded across Tiananmen Square, calling for the banning of a book, *Sexual Customs* (*Xing Fengsu*), that Muslims found offensive. (Condemned as 'the *Satanic Verses* of China', it compared minarets to phalli, tombs to vulva, and the pilgrimage to Mecca as an excuse for orgies and sodomy, with camels, no less). To demonstrate Muslim solidarity, representatives of four of the ten Muslim nationalities in China led the protest, including a Uyghur, a Hui, a Kirghiz, and a Kazakh, who held aloft their letter of permission from the state and the list of their demands.[2] The state not only met all the demands of the Muslim protesters – banning the book (and allowing its burning in the main square of Lanzhou city), arresting the authors (for their own safety; a collection of 100,000 renminbi had been taken up by Muslims for their execution, in much the same way as the US$2.5 million *fatwa* was taken up against Salman Rushdie in 1989), and closing the Shanghai Cultural publishing house – but also actively encouraged the protest by providing a police escort and transportation from the square back to the Central Nationalities Institute, where it had originated.

This event is still unresolved for the Uyghur, in that there are several Uyghur in Ürümqi who continue to sit in jail for taking part in the protest. While the state forgave the violent protests of the Hui against the book throughout the country, which included trashing the government building in Lanzhou and overturning and burning a car carrying copies of the book, as well as other violent clashes in Xi'an, Xining, and Kunming, it has not yet released several Uyghur who were arrested for taking part in the 19 May 1989 Ürümqi protest, a protest the Uyghur claim was instigated by Hui from Gansu who brought the book, written in Chinese, to the attention of the Uyghur. While several reasons may be given for this seeming inconsistency, here I might only suggest that it underlines the continued uneasiness that the Chinese government feels about unrest and political involvement in the northwest border area of Xinjiang. While the government has promoted Hui exchange with the Middle East, and has been more tolerant of Hui protests (such as an incident in November 1990 in Yunnan Province, when the state moved quickly to ameliorate a conflict between Hui and

2.   Pictures of the leaders of the protest, as well as the march across Tiananmen Square, are reproduced in Gladney (1996a).

Han over an automobile accident), it has been quick to crack down on any Uyghur political or ethnic strife, such as the Qurban uprising in June 1988 (FBIS 1988a:61), which led to several arrests of student leaders, and the March 1990 incident in Artux, near Aksu, which caused the deaths of at least twenty-four Uyghur and Kirghiz. The state is much more nervous about Turkic unrest on its northwest border with post-Soviet Central Asia than among its more domestic, internal Hui Muslims.

Then why promote a Sino-Eurasian railway that runs right through former Soviet and Chinese Central Asia? Tracks were laid for this railway during the heyday of Sino-Soviet rapprochement in the late 1950s, but were torn out in 1962 after the breakdown in those relations and the exodus of nearly 60,000 Kazakh and Uyghur from the Ili area. In 1987 the state began renegotiating the re-establishment of the railroad – a time of relative peacefulness in Chinese and Soviet Central Asia. One Chinese railroad engineer with whom I spoke in Samarkand in September 1987, who was part of a joint investigative team to lay the grounds for the project, argued that the railway would do little to benefit Central Asia; it was seen more as a southern link between Eastern Europe, Moscow, and Beijing. Central Asia did not gain much from the railway, and it was not to be easily disrupted by tensions in the area, much as the Trans-Siberian Railway has had little impact on Inner and Outer Mongolian economies and national identity, although it has been open continually for the past three decades and has benefited Sino-Russian trade tremendously. The trans-Eurasian railway was completed in the fall of 1990, far ahead of the 1992 schedule (FBIS 1988a:9), and led to a jump in Sino-Russian trade (see Chapter 10, page 223). While state planners in China may have worried what the fallout from *glasnost* and national movements in the USSR might have been on this project, their going ahead with it signals Chinese determination to maintain control of the Central Asian rail link, no matter what the economic and political costs.

There have been several unintended consequences for Uyghur transnational identity from both the Salman Rushdie protest and trans-Eurasian railway events. Uyghur are now increasingly convinced that the state is making a clear distinction between its promotion of the Hui and the Uyghur on a national level. The prosecution of Uyghur in Xinjiang, and the release of Hui in Gansu and Qinghai for the same protest, has demonstrated countrywide that the state treats these Muslim minorities differently. In Xinjiang, the Hui have long felt disgruntled that they find themselves in an autonomous region that nominally belongs to the Uyghur, and whose People's Government is largely staffed by Turkic Muslims, whereas most Hui in Xinjiang are post-1950 immigrants who speak not Turkic languages, but mainly Chinese dialects.[3] On a national scale, though, the Hui have enjoyed greater official government support, perhaps due to their cultural proximity to the Han, dispersal throughout all of China, and status as the most populous Muslim minority. Government-sponsored exchanges with the Middle East have featured more Hui interests and involvement, and while there is a Ningxia Branch of the state-sponsored Middle Eastern Construction Corporation, there is as yet no Xinjiang branch. Nevertheless, on a private level, the Uyghur may be taking better advantage of the situation.

Individual Uyghur travel abroad has been enormously facilitated by the opening of the Karakoram Highway into Pakistan in May 1986, the border with Kazakhstan in 1987 and with Kyrgyzstan in 1991, and the trans-Eurasian railway in 1990. Unlike the Hui, the Uyghur have many relatives abroad in Central Asia, the Middle East, and Turkey (many of whom fled there in the 1940s), who assist them with obtaining the invitations, visas, and hard currency necessary for foreign travel (see Alptekin, E. 1988). Out of thirty-four students from China at the prestigious Al-Azhar University in Cairo, only six were Hui, while the rest were Uyghur, studying on private scholarships provided by relatives, Saudi Arabia, and the university. The trans-Eurasian railway may assist them to get there. One Uyghur with whom I spoke at Al-Azhar University said he traveled to Egypt via the Trans-Siberian Railway from Beijing to Moscow, and from there to Europe, Turkey, and finally Cairo, all through the support of his relatives. 'If I could have taken the Xinjiang train to Tashkent,' he stated, 'and then gone on to Turkey, I could have saved a lot of money.' The Karakoram road to Pakistan is still a tortuous journey of at least six days, with frequent closures and hazards. The rail link should prove much more convenient for building transnational links. One Uyghur whom I met in Kashgar during the 2001 spring festival was one of three Uyghur who were part of a Sino-Russian educational exchange of 200 students in fall

3.	For Hui–Uyghur relations in Xinjiang, see Forbes (1987).

1999. This Uyghur came to China via the railroad and stated that it is being actively pursued by other Uyghur and Central Asians for private travel, although the trade is still primarily oriented to Moscow and Beijing. Pilgrimage to Mecca has increased from the first state-sponsored group since 1964, of nineteen in 1979, to more than 6,000 in 2001, most of them privately financed (Shichor 1989:7; Gladney 1996a:400–1).

Islamization and Chinese geopolitics

Only in the past few years has China once again attempted to play its Islamic card – a strategy begun in the 1950s of promoting its Muslims, and positive policies toward its Muslim minorities, to gain favor with mainly Muslim Middle Eastern countries. I regard this as a case of the 'Islamization' of a geopolitical issue and the minorities involved, not the conversion of most Uyghur to Islam, a process that began in the early 15th century (see Haneda 1978), in that in this case Islam is used by the state as a means of promoting international relations, rather than as a religious ideology to be followed. On the surface the state exploits its favorable policies toward Muslims, but in reality as a communist state it actively discourages Islamic practice.

James Piscatori (1987:247), in his essay on the nature of international relations among Asian Muslim countries, writes:

China, without the burden of Afghanistan, is more effective [than the Soviet Union] in the use of Islam in its relations with the Arab states … [T]he regime in Beijing believes that the use of Islam can help to legitimate it in the eyes of the Arab regimes, and the record shows that it has had some success at it.

It was not always successful, however. Members of the first delegation of Muslim pilgrims to Mecca in 1953 were denied visas in Pakistan, and the impasse was not resolved until Zhou Enlai, during the Bandung Conference in April 1955, approached Prince Faysal ibn Sa'ud about the problem, signaling the importance the Chinese government placed on resolving the issue (Shichor 1989: 3). As a result of Zhou Enlai's Islamic diplomacy, the pilgrimages were allowed to begin with a maximum of twenty Muslims from China every year, led by two Hui, Da Pusheng and Ma Yuhuai, in July 1955.

The then President of China, Yang Shangkun, in his visit to six Middle Eastern countries after the Tiananmen massacre, underscored the new importance that China placed on its Middle Eastern relations by affirming its continued commitment to trade with the Middle East, political stability, and fair treatment of Muslims. In a surprising move that demonstrated how important China saw its relationship with Egypt to be, he unexpectedly announced that China would donate the multimillion-dollar International Conference Center in the suburb of Heliopolis, Cairo, which Chinese construction firms had been engaged in building for the previous three years. Along with the large Cairo Stadium, which was also built by the Chinese, as well as the Cornish Highway along the Nile, the International Conference Center stands as yet another monument to improving Sino-Egyptian relations.

As one of five members of the United Nations Security Council, and despite a long-term friendship with Iraq, China went along with most of the UN resolutions in the 1991 war against Iraq. Although it abstained from Resolution 678, making it unlikely that Chinese workers will be welcomed back into Kuwait (Harris 1991a:7), it enjoys a relatively untarnished reputation in the Middle East as a valuable source of low-grade weaponry and cheap labor.

But what does this have to do with the Uyghur? The enormous exchange of workers, pilgrims, and students to the Middle East has allowed the Uyghur many more opportunities to travel abroad, re-establish connections with relatives, and become exposed to the Turkish and Muslim world outside of China. Joseph Fletcher long argued that China was very much in tune with socioreligious movements in the Middle East, and that each 'tide' of Islamic influence in China resulted from the opening of China to the movement of Muslims, mostly on the hajj, between China and the pilgrimage cities (Fletcher 1988). While speaking with a Uyghur factory worker in Istanbul's Zeytinburnu district in 1988, where most of the Turkic immigrants from China are concentrated, I was surprised to learn that although he referred to Xinjiang as *Dogu Turkestan* (East Turkestan), he still regarded himself as a Uyghur, and hoped to return someday to promote Islam among his people. In the late 19th and early 20th centuries, most of the Muslims who were to exert substantial influence on Islam in China studied at Al-Azhar University, the oldest university in the world and the foremost Sunni Islamic training institution.[4]

I have already noted that in 1993 twenty-eight of thirty-four students from China at Al-Azhar University were Uyghur, most of whom were financed by loans from relatives and by scholarships from the Mecca-based Muslim World League. Muslims from China complained that while the Egyptian government provided ten scholarships a year to Al-Azhar University, the Chinese government had not taken advantage of them since the first group of ten students (including two visiting scholars) was sent in 1981. The Chinese government claimed that the terms of the scholarships, which included room and board, free tuition, and 50 Egyptian pounds (US$16) a month, were not adequate for the students to live on, though it was the same amount as given to the majority of other Third World students. By contrast, the Chinese government at that time allowed ten students a year to take advantage of scholarships at Cairo University, and supported Egyptian students studying Chinese at Ain Shams University. This led one Hui student at Al-Azhar to complain to me that, 'The Chinese government only wants its students to come to Egypt to study science, not religion, even though it claims to support open study abroad'. According to an official Chinese government website, since 1996 China and Egypt have been officially exchanging twenty students a year, and there are about 350 Chinese students presently in Egypt. This includes approximately 200 'self-financed' students, who are mostly studying Arabic and Islam-related subjects.[5]

Indeed, the example of one Uyghur student at Al-Azhar University supports this view. He was one of three Uyghur (six Hui and one Kazakh) who was among the first group that came to Al-Azhar on a state-sponsored exchange in 1981. He explained that although he grew up in a fairly average, not especially religious Uyghur household in Ürümqi, in 1980 he was one of ten Uyghur high school students selected to take an exam to test their general knowledge and Arabic. Although he claimed not to know

4. For an interesting Chinese summary of this earlier period, see Pang Shiqian (1988 [1951]). For a discussion of the role of the Al-Azhar University in educating China's Muslims, see Ma and Yang (1988).

5. Report entitled 'Educational Exchanges between China and Egypt' at http://www.chinaembassy.org.eg/eng0100/eng0104/edbk.htm (visited by author on 15 May 2003).

any Arabic, and very little about Islam, he was selected to travel to the China Islamic Society in Beijing, where he studied Arabic for six months before being sent to Al-Azhar. Because his Arabic was poor, he studied for another two years, then was required to repeat high school, because Al-Azhar did not recognize his Chinese diploma. After a year and a half, he tested into the university, where he studied for four more years, completing his bachelor's degree in arts in 1990. He now works as a translator for a Chinese construction team in Cairo, and is waiting to return to China, where he says he will probably be assigned to teach Arabic at the China Islamic Association.

It is clear that while there are many more conservative, even fundamentalist, Muslims in China desiring to study abroad at Al-Azhar University and elsewhere, the Chinese government is supporting those who are less religiously inclined. It is so concerned about promoting Islam through these academic exchanges that it now only supports study at Cairo University, not Al-Azhar. All the other students from China at Al-Azhar are on private scholarships from relatives and Saudi Arabia. Because Hui Muslims have few relatives abroad, the majority of these students are Uyghur, and the vast majority of Muslims from China residing in Saudi Arabia and Turkey are Uyghur as a result. If and when these Uyghur do return to their homes in Xinjiang, one can expect that they will exert tremendous influence, as has been found historically among returned Muslim hajji and Islamic scholars to China (see Fletcher 1988; Gladney 1987a).

While the Chinese government publicly asserts that it is allowing the free religious expression of Islam in China, and allowing its Muslims to travel abroad, it is clear that it is only tolerating a minimum of Islam to maximize its formal relations with the Middle East. While the Uyghur and the Hui are willing to be used as players in China's use of the Islamic card, it is clear that they are exploiting the opportunities as much as possible for their own benefit – moves that may lead to unexpected consequences for the Chinese government, despite its efforts to control the situation.

Cyber-separatism: virtual voices in the Uyghur opposition

Although silenced within China, Uyghur voices can still be heard virtually, on the Internet. Perhaps due to Chinese restrictions on public protest and a state-controlled media, or the deleterious effect of a war on domestic terrorism that, as this chapter says, began in the late 1990s, very few Uyghur voices (at least not public ones) critical of Chinese policies can be heard in the region today. Addressing primarily an audience of perhaps more than 500,000 expatriate Uyghur (few Uyghur in Central Asia and China have access to these Internet sites), there are at least twenty-five international organizations and websites working for the independence of 'East Turkestan', and based in Amsterdam, Munich, Istanbul, Melbourne, New York, and Washington, DC. Estimates of the number of Uyghur living outside China in the diaspora differ widely. Uyghur in Central Asia are not always well-represented in the state censuses, particularly since 1991. Shichor (2002) estimates approximately 500,000 living abroad, about 5 to 6 percent of the total world Uyghur population. Uyghur websites differ dramatically on the official population numbers, from up to 25 million Uyghur inside Xinjiang, to up to 10 million in the diaspora.[6]

Although the UN and the US government have agreed with China that at least one international organization, the East Turkestan Islamic Movement (ETIM), is a Uyghur-sponsored terrorist group, the vast majority of the East Turkestan independence and information organizations disclaim violence. Supported largely by Uyghur émigrés who left China prior to the Communist takeover in 1949, these organizations maintain a multitude of websites and activities that take a primarily negative view of Chinese policies in the region. Although not all organizations advocate independence or separatism, the vast majority of them do press for radical change, reporting not only human-rights violations, but also environmental degradation, economic imbalances, and alternative histories of the region. In general, these websites can be divided roughly into

6.   See, for example, http://www.uyghur.org, the site supported by Anwar Yusuf, President of the Eastern Turkestan National Freedom Center in Washington, DC, who has suggested there are up to 25 million Uyghur worldwide. Shichor (2002), based on information from Enver Can in Munich, estimates there are about 500 Uyghur in Germany (mostly in Munich), 500 in Belgium (mostly from Central Asia), 200 in Sweden (mostly from Kazakhstan), 40 in England, 35 in Switzerland, 30 in the Netherlands and 10 in Norway. In addition, there are an estimated 10,000 Uyghur in Turkey, 1,000 in the United States, 500 in Canada, and 200 in Australia (mostly in Melbourne).

those that are mainly information-based and others that are politically active advocacy sites. Nevertheless, whether informational or advocatory, nearly all of them are critical of Chinese policies in Xinjiang. The main distinction is that the vast majority of informational sites can be accessed from China.[7]

Key informational websites that mainly provide Uyghur and Xinjiang related news and analyses, include the Turkestan Newsletter (Turkistan-N) maintained by Mehmet Tütüncü of SOTA[8] (http://www.turkiye.net/sota/sota.html), the Open Society Institute's http://www.eurasianet.org, the Uyghur Information Agency's http://www.uyghurinfo.com, and the virtual library Eastern Turkestan WWW VL (http://www.ccs.uky.edu/~rakhim/et.html), based at the Australian National University. The last-mentioned of these sites, maintained by Abdulrakhim Aitbayev, contains reports of Chinese police actions in various parts of Xinjiang Region, as well as links to other sites and articles that are generally critical of China.

An increasing number of scholars are building websites that feature their work on Xinjiang, and provide links to other sites and organizations engaged in research and educational activities related to the region. One of the best sites in this genre is that by Nathan Light of the University of Toledo (http://www.utoledo.edu/~nlight), which not only includes most of his dissertation and useful articles on Uyghur history, music, and culture, but also directs readers to other links to the region. While there is a multitude of Internet sites and Web links to sites on Xinjiang and Uyghur human-rights issues, there is as yet no central site that is regularly updated. Information on Uyghur organizations and Internet sites can be found at http://www.uyghuramerican.org. An interactive question-and-answer site with an updated special report entitled

---

7.	The availability of a website in China can be checked by using Real-Time Testing of Internet Filtering in China, a free service provided by the Harvard Law School's Jonathon Zittrain and Benjamin Edelman (http://www.cyber.law.harvard.edu/filtering/china/test). Constantinos Vrakas directed me to this site, and provided important information for the revision of this chapter in his paper 'Uyghur Dot-Com: The Role of the Internet in the Uyghur Virtual Diaspora' (2003).

8.	The acronym SOTA is derived from the initials of the Dutch abbreviation of 'Foundation for Research into Turkestan, Azerbaijan, Crimea, Caucasus and Siberia'.

'China: Uighur Muslim Separatists' can be found at the Virtual Information Center (http://www.vic-info.org), an open-source organization funded by the US Commander-in-Chief Pacific Command (CINCPAC).

A growing number of sites related to Central Asia contain information and discussion of events in Xinjiang, even though the region is often normally not considered a part of Central Asian studies, and, due to its rule by China, often falls under Chinese studies or Inner Asian studies. See, for example, the Harvard Program on Central Asia and the Caucasus (http://centasia.fas.harvard.edu), which is run by Dr John Schoeberlein, and maintains the Central Eurasian Studies World Wide site (http://cesww.fas.harvard.edu), and the email distribution list Central-Asia-Harvard-List, which frequently reports on Xinjiang-related issues. 'For Democracy, Human Rights, Peace and Freedom for Uzbekistan and Central Asia' (http://www.uzbekistanerk.org) is an informational website with links to Uyghur and East Turkestan sites. In addition, Silk Road sites increasingly focus on the Uyghur issue. For example, the Silk Road Foundation has a general information site for Central Asia (http://silk-road.com/toc/index.html), with sections on Xinjiang and a page containing links to other Uyghur-related sites. Interestingly, a NOVA/PBS website reports on the Taklamakan Mummies, an issue often used to establish claims of territorial history by China and the Uyghur, with one page providing a research report concerning the tracing of the mummies' ethnicity (http://www.pbs.org/wgbh/nova/chinamum/taklamakan.html).

While most of these sites do not claim to take a position on the Uyghur independence issues related to Xinjiang, most of them tend to report information that is more supportive of Uyghur claims against the Chinese state. An example is the GeoNative 'informational site' (http://www.geocities.com/athens/9479/uighur.html) maintained by the Basque activist, Luistxo Fernandez, who seeks to report 'objectively' on minority peoples less represented in the world press. Yet his site, which does provide a useful chart on English/Uyghur/Chinese transliterated place names, after providing a basic summary of the region, contains the statement: 'Chinese colonization by Han people is a threat to native peoples'.[9]

9. The entire paragraph reads: 'Area: 1.6 million sq. km. Population: 14 million (1990 census), Uyghur: 7.2 million (official), 14–30 million (estimates by

An important addition to 'informational' websites is the site maintained by the Uyghur service of Radio Free Asia (RFA), as part of its regular broadcast to Xinjiang and surrounding regions, reportedly beamed from transmitters in Tajikistan and Kyrgyzstan (see http://www.rfa.org/service/index.html?service=uyg). According to its site, RFA broadcasts news and information to Asian listeners who lack regular access to 'full and balanced reporting' in their domestic media. Through its broadcasts and call-in programs, RFA aims to fill what is regarded as a 'critical gap' in the news reporting for people in certain regions of Asia. Created by the US Congress in 1994 and incorporated in 1996, RFA broadcasts in Burmese, Cantonese, Khmer, Korean, Lao, Mandarin, Vietnamese, Tibetan (Uke, Amdo, and Kham), and Uyghur. Although the service claims to adhere to the highest standards of journalism and aims to exemplify accuracy, balance, and fairness in its editorial content, local governments have often complained of bias in favor of groups critical to the regimes in power. The Uyghur service has been regularly blocked and criticized by the Chinese government, and has been cited in the past for carrying stories supportive of so-called separatists, especially the case of Rebiya Kadeer, but despite the new cooperation between the US and China in the war on terrorism, the site has continued its regular broadcasting. When I asked the Uyghur director of the service, Dr Dolkun Kamberi, if the increased Sino-US cooperation on terrorism and the labeling of ETIM as an international Uyghur terrorist group had led to any restriction on their funding or broadcast content, he said that there had been no changes in funding level or content. Frequent Uyghur listeners to the program, however, have complained to me that the site no longer criticizes China as strongly or frequently for its treatment of Uyghur in Xinjiang.

Funding for the informational sites is generally traceable to academic organizations, advertising, and subscription. It is much harder to establish funding sources for the advocacy sites. While

-----

the Uyghur organizations abroad). Capital: Urumchi. The Sinkiang-Uyghur Autonomous Region in China (Xinjiang Uyghur Zizhiqu in Chinese) is also known under the names Eastern Turkestan or Chinese Turkestan. Uyghur people prefer Uyghuristan. It is inhabited by the Uyghur, also known under names Uighur, Uigur, Uyghur, Weiwuer, Sart, Taranchi, Kashgarlik. The other native peoples are Kazakh, Uzbek, Kyrghyz, Tajik, Tatar. Chinese colonization by Han people is a threat for the native peoples'.

most sites are supported primarily by subscribers, advertising, and small donations from Uyghur and other Muslims outside of China and sympathetic to the Uyghur cause, there is no evidence that the organizations and the sites they sponsor have ever received official government sponsorship. Other than the RFA Uyghur service, which is supported by the US government, there is no other official government-supported site that disseminates information related to Uyghur human-rights issues. However, many Uyghur organizations in the past have claimed sympathy and tacit support from Turkey, Saudi Arabia, Iran, Australia, Germany, France, the Netherlands, and Canada.

Advocacy sites that openly promote international support for Uyghur- and Xinjiang-related causes, and the organizations they often represent, take a strong and critical stance against Chinese rule in Xinjiang, giving voice, they say, to a silent majority of Uyghur in Xinjiang and abroad who advocate radical political reform, if not outright independence, in the region. These sites include those of the International Taklamakan Human Rights Association (http:// www.taklamakan.org), which contains links to several articles and websites concerning East Turkestan, Uyghur, and Uyghuristan; the Uyghur American Association (http://www.uyghuramerican.org), which contains links to articles and websites concerning issues of human rights and territorial freedom among Uyghur in Xinjiang, and lists twenty-two other organizations around the world that do not have websites; and the East Turkistan National Congress (http://www.eastturkistan.com), led by Enver Can in Munich.

An interesting US-based site is that of the Citizens against Communist Chinese Propaganda (http://www.caccp.org – with one page entitled 'Free East Turkistan!'), which bills itself as a counterpropaganda site (using the 'fight fire with fire' approach). It is based in Florida and led by Jack Churchward, who started the organization Free Eastern Turkestan, which originally made its name for itself through a series of protests against a Chinese owned and operated theme park, Splendid China, located in Kissimmee, Florida. The organization found the park denigrating to Uyghur and Tibetans especially (with its miniature replicas of mosques and the Potala Palace). The Uyghur Human Rights Coalition has a website (http://www.uyghurs.org) reporting human-rights abuses of Uyghur in China, and containing links to articles and other sites. KIVILCIM runs an East Turkistan information website advocating independence, but in Uyghur language (http://www.kivilcim.org along with http://www.doguturkistan.net). Other popular advocacy sites include: http://www.uygur.net; http://www.turpan.com; http://www.afn.org; and http://www.eastturkestan.com. Because most of these sites are cross-linked, they often repeat and pass along information contained on other sites.

Biz Uyghur (http://www.bizuyghur.com) is perhaps the most useful of the advocacy sites, although it claims to be informational. Nevertheless, it presents information that tends to be pro-independence and, probably for that reason, is unable to be viewed in China. It is mainly in Uyghur, Turkish and Chinese, and by 15 May 2003 had had only 8,116 visitors, according to a counter on the site. The site features a history page (*tarix*) that is strong on post-1940s Xinjiang, with many photographs from that era, as well as more contemporary photographs of the 2003 Baren County earthquake. It also maintains a large store of accessible Uyghur music pages, videos, and traditional *muqam* folk performances, and a bulletin board for on-line Uyghur discussions, some of which are quite anti-Chinese on policies in Xinjiang. Of the twenty-five postings on the bulletin board between 20 March and 15 May 2003, only nine writers gave their specific locations, with five from Xinjiang (Kashgar, Ürümqi, Khotan, and Ghulja), two from Turkey, one from Central Asia (Kazakhstan), and one from Europe (Belgium).

There are a number of publicly known Uyghur advocacy organizations, which grew to nearly twenty in the late 1990s, but seemed to have declined in membership and activities since September 2001.[10] In the US, one of the most active information and advocacy groups in the Washington, DC, area is the Uyghur American Association, the chairmen of which have been Alim Seytoff and Turdi Hajji.[11] Like many advocacy groups, it was founded in the late 1990s. It supports various public lectures

10. A list of some of the international Uyghur and East Turkestan organizations can be found on http://uyghuramerican.org.
11. See their website introduction (at the link 'About Us'), http://uyghuramerican.org: 'The Uyghur American Association was established on 23 May 1998 in Washington, DC, at the First Uyghur American Congress. The growing Uyghur community in the United States created a need for a unified Uyghur organization to serve the needs of the community here and to represent the collective voice of the Uyghur in East Turkistan'.

and demonstrations to further raise public awareness of Uyghur and Xinjiang issues. The Uyghur Human Rights Coalition (http://www.uyghurs.org), directed by Kathy Polias, and located near the Georgetown University campus, tracks human rights issues and has organized several demonstrations and conferences in the Washington, DC, metropolitan area, especially pushing for the release of Rebiya Kadeer.[12] The Eastern Turkistan National Freedom Center (http://www.uyghur.org), whose leader is Anwar Yusuf, made a clear stand for an independent East Turkestan in his meeting with President Bill Clinton on 4 June 1999, on the tenth anniversary of the 1989 Tiananmen Square massacre. Yusuf stated that there is no fear of launching a civil war in the region.[13] One of the earliest Uyghur advocacy organizations, established in the US in 1996, is the International Taklamakan Human Rights Association (ITHRA, http://www.taklamakan.org), whose president is Ablajan Layli Namen Baret, maintains the active list-server, UIGHUR-L, as well as list-server covering events in Inner (Southern) Mongolia, SMONGOL-L.

In Europe, most of the Uyghur organizations are concentrated in Munich, where there is the largest number of Uyghur émigrés,

12. See their organizational statement ('About Us', http://www.uyghurs.org): 'The Uyghur Human Rights Coalition (UHRC) is a 501(c)(3) nonprofit dedicated to educating Americans, particularly university students, about the Chinese government's human rights violations against the Uyghur people of the Xinjiang Uyghur Autonomous Region of China (known to the Uyghur as East Turkestan). Through its educational efforts, the UHRC strives to build a broad base of support for the Uyghur people's struggle to obtain democratic freedoms and self-determination and to protect their culture and environment'.
13. Email communication from Anwar Yusuf to the author, dated 14 March 2002: 'I also said to you that China is afraid of civil war with the people of Xinjiang, and which is why China always brutally crush [*sic*] the every effort of the Uyghur Muslims which advocates independence for Xinjiang. In short, I said that it would be the most joyful event for the people of Xinjiang if China would disintegrate as his Communist neighbor Soviet Union did. I said that the people of Xinjiang did not have fear of widespread civil disorder. The people of Xinjiang have fought against the Chinese for over two hundred years without any fear. Why are they supposed to fear a civil war? As a representative for those brave Uyghur Muslims, I and my organization Eastern Turkistan National Freedom Center do support a free and independent Xinjiang, and that is exactly what I told President Clinton when I met with him on June 4, 1999'.

including the Eastern Turkistan (Uyghuristan) National Congress (http://www.eastturkistan.com), whose president is Enver Can; the East Turkestan Union in Europe, led by Asgar Can; the Eastern Turkestan Information Center (http://www.uyghur.org), led by Abduljelil Karakash, which publishes the on-line journal *World Uyghur Network News*; and the World Uyghur Youth Congress (http://www.uyghurinfo.com), chaired by Dolqun Isa. In the Netherlands, there is the Uyghur Netherlands Democratic Union (UNDU), led by Bahtiyar Semsiddin, and the Uyghur House, chaired by Shahelil. The Uyghur Youth Union in Belgium is chaired by Sedullam, and the Belgium Uyghur Association by Sultan Ehmet. In Stockholm, Sweden, the East Turkestan Association is chaired by Faruk Sadikov. The Uyghur Youth Union UK, in London, is chaired by Enver Bugda. In Moscow, the Uyghur Association is chaired by Serip Haje. In Turkey, organizations include the East Turkestan Foundation, led by Mehmet Riza Bekin in Istanbul; the East Turkestan Solidarity Foundation, led by Sayit Taranci in Istanbul; and the East Turkestan Culture and Solidarity Association, led by Abubekir Turksoy in Kayseri. The Canadian Uyghur Association is based in Toronto and chaired by Mehmetjan Tohti. The Australian Turkestan Association, in Melbourne, is chaired by Ahmet Igamberdi. In Kazakhstan there are several organizations based in Almaty listed on the Internet, but they are difficult to contact in the region, having met with recent government sanctions. They include the Nozugum Foundation; the Kazakhstan Regional Uyghur (*Ittipak*) Organization, chaired by Khahriman Gojamberdie; the Uyghuristan Freedom Association, chaired by Sabit Abdurahman; the Kazakhstan Uyghur Unity (*Ittipak*) Association, chaired by Sheripjan Nadirov; and the Uyghur Youth Union in Kazakhstan, chaired by Abdurexit Turdeyev. In Kyrgyzstan one finds in Bishkek the Kyrgyzstan Uyghur Unity (*Ittipak*) Association, chaired by Rozimehmet Abdulnbakiev, and the Bishkek Human Rights Committee, chaired by Tursun Islam. While these are the main organizations listed on the Internet, many of them are no longer accessible, and there are several other smaller organizations that are not listed.

It is difficult to assess who the audience is for these websites and organizations, for they are all blocked in China, and mostly inaccessible in Central Asia due to either the inadequacy of the high cost of Internet access. Almost none of the sites has been deliberately created with the purpose of reaching the Uyghur in China, since few are in Chinese and Uyghur. Many Uyghur I have talked with in China and in Central Asia have never heard of most of these sites. Interestingly, government officials in Xinjiang who are interested in the information provided on the sites also have said they do not have access. I was quite surprised, therefore, when on 26 March 2003, while in Kashgar, I went to the Fatima Wangba Internet café, across the street from the Seman Hotel, and was able to access the discussion list UIGHUR-L (at http://www.taklaman.org/uighur-l). At that website, I was able to read a history of the Uyghur in Xinjiang that was quite contrary to the officially approved Chinese government position.[14] Nevertheless, this site is probably rarely accessed by local Uyghur (I asked a few of my Kashgari friends and they were as surprised as I was

14. The site contained, as 'Human Rights Situation in Eastern Turkistan' (http://www.taklamakan.org/uighur-l/archive/5_12_1.html), the following history of the Uyghur by Ablajan Layli Naman (Barat): 'The Uighurs are the longest continually settled people in Central Asia. Archaeological and historical materials have proved that Uighurs lived in Eastern Turkistan since the beginning of time. In 1884, the Manchu Qing Dynasty conquered and formally annexed the territory of Eastern Turkistan and named it "Xinjiang" meaning "New Dominion" or "New Frontier." After the Manchu empire was overthrown by the Chinese Nationalist [*sic*] in 1911, Eastern Turkistan was also transferred to the new Chinese government. The Chinese presence was essentially colonial in profile: Chinese troops and Chinese administrators. Even as late as 1944 at the time of the short-lived independent Eastern Turkistan Republic the Chinese constituted a small fraction of the population. The Peoples' Liberation Army entered Xinjiang Province in 1950 and power was bloodlessly transferred. While there are aspects of intrigue involved with this in regard to the fate of the independent Eastern Turkistan Republic – both on the side of the Soviet Union and Mao's China – one aspect of this power transference continues to impact strongly today in the region: the special role of the Chinese Army. Initially, this included elements of both the remnant Kuomintang (which had been long separated from Nanking rule) and the Peoples' Liberation Army which formed the nexus of a colonial revolution in Xinjiang: the Bin Tuan. This organization has maintained a special colonial role in Xinjiang and has institutionalized a leading role for Han Chinese in the region, usually at the expense of the local inhabitants. Much of the Uighur struggle to achieve human rights in Xinjiang is related to the experience this institution has inflicted upon the region. Bin Tuan is the Xinjiang Production and Construction Corps. This is a somewhat twisted translation of Chinese words: "Bin" means "soldier" and "Tuan" means "group." Put together they mean "an organization or group of soldiers"'.

to find the site available), and it may no longer be accessible.[15] The Chinese government, in its Order 195, stated specifically it would be in complete control of the Internet under the Ministry of Information Industries (MII), created in 1988. The MII generally carefully monitors what goes in and out of the eight international gateways, with the power to arrest and imprison those engaged in distributing 'harmful' material, including pornography, gambling, and the publication of anything deemed 'counterrevolutionary' (see Franda 2002; see also Harwit and Clark 2001). It is clear that Uyghur in the Western diaspora, particularly in Europe, Turkey, the US, Canada, and Australia, are frequent readers and contributors to these sites. In addition, events in the region since 11 September 2001 have led an increasing number of journalists and interested observers of the region to begin visiting the sites more regularly. In terms of content, it is interesting to note that a cursory monitoring of these sites reveals very little that can be associated with militant or radical Islam, and almost no calls for an Islamic jihad against the Chinese state. Most of the issues, as noted above, involve documenting the plight and history of the Uyghur under Chinese rule in Xinjiang, as opposed to their glorious, independent past and long history in the region. It is also important to note that few Chinese inside or outside of China have visited these sites, so they are quite unaware of these alternative histories. Although there are several sites available in Turkish and Uyghur, there is not one in Chinese. As such, like all Internet-based groups, the audience is self-selected and rarely reaches beyond those who already support and are interested in the agenda supported by the site.

Financial support for these organizations and websites comes mostly from private individuals, foundations, and subscriptions (although these are rare). While it has been reported that wealthy Uyghur patrons in Saudi Arabia and Turkey, who became successful running businesses after migrating to these countries in the 1940s, have strongly supported such organizations financially in the past, there is no publicly available information on these sources. Many Uyghur who migrated to Saudi Arabia and Turkey in the 1930s and 1940s became successful in construction and restaurant businesses, and were thus in a much better position to support

---

15. For a critical discussion of China's 'digital divide' and the often surprising accessibility of many Internet sites, see Harwit 2003.

Uyghur causes than the more recent Uyghur émigrés. Uyghur in Central Asia and in the West who have been able to migrate from Xinjiang in increasing numbers in the past twenty years or so have generally been much poorer than the earlier émigrés in the Middle East. This is starting to change, however, as they and their children become better-established in the US, Canada, Europe, and Australia. Yusuf, president of the Eastern Turkestan National Freedom Center (based in Washington, DC), once claimed that he had received substantial support from patrons in Saudi Arabia, but by the late 1990s funding had begun to dry up due to a surplus of organizations and waning interest in the Uyghur cause (pers. interview, 14 April 1999).

Although most of these websites have limited funding and circulation, they should not be dismissed as forming only a 'virtual' community without any substantial impact on events within Xinjiang. The websites have not served only as important sources of information unavailable in the official Chinese media; some scholars have begun to argue that Internet sites often help to sway public opinion by virtue of their widespread availability and alternative reporting of important events.[16] While analysts are divided about the potency of the Internet for swaying public opinion or influencing domestic events, there is an emerging consensus that it has clearly altered the way information is circulated and opinions are formed. Perhaps more importantly, scholars have concluded that the 'virtual communities' formed by Internet websites establish links and connections that can lead to broad social interactions and coalitions, which have had an impact on political and socioeconomic events. For example, it has been shown that social movements in East Timor, Aceh, Chechnya, and Bosnia have been given strong support through these Internet communities, which have not only increased information but also generated large financial transfers.[17] While cyber-separatism would never be able on its own to unseat a local government, it is clear that it does link

16. For studies of the influence of the Internet in influencing wider public opinion in Asia, see a recent collection of essays in a 2002 special issue of *Asian Journal of Social Science*, 'The Internet and Social Change in Asia and Beyond', 30(2), edited by Zaheer Baber.
17. For studies related to the Internet's role in building community and mobilizing support for specific causes, see Foster (1997); Jones (1997); Jordan (1999); Rushkoff (1994); Smith and Kollock (1999).

like-minded individuals and raise consciousness on issues about which information was often inaccessible to the general public. For an isolated region such as Xinjiang, and the widely dispersed Uyghur diaspora, the Internet has dramatically altered the way the world sees the region and the Chinese state must respond to issues within it. While the Uyghur within China have not had the same level of organization as the Falun Gong, the use of the Internet by the latter group can serve as an example of how an externally based activist organization with a local following could organize in 1999 a protest with 10,000 participants. Stephen O'Leary (2000) of the *Online Journalism Review* traced the savvy use of the Internet by the Falun Gong.

It is clear that it is not only Internet-based organizations that are involved in separatist activities in and around Xinjiang. As noted above, the East Turkestan Islamic Movement (ETIM) was recognized by the United Nations in October 2002 as an international terrorist organization responsible for domestic and international terrorist acts, which China claimed included a bombing of the Chinese consulate in Istanbul, and assassinations of Chinese officials in Bishkek, and of Uyghur officials in Kashgar thought to be collaborating with Chinese officialdom.[18] The designation 'terrorist', however, created a controversy in that China and the US presented little public evidence to positively link ETIM with the specific incidents described ('China Also Harmed by Separatist-Minded Eastern Turkestan Terrorists', *People's Daily* 10 October 2001; Eckholm 2002; Hutzler 2002). In 2001, the US State Department released a report that documented several separatist and terrorist groups operating inside the region and abroad, militating for an independent Xinjiang (McNeal 2001; see also the excellent thesis Fogden 2002). The list included: the United Revolutionary Front of Eastern Turkestan, whose leader, Yusupbek Mukhlisi, claims to have thirty armed units with '20 million' Uyghur primed for an uprising; the Home of East Turkestan Youth, said to be linked to Hamas, and with a reported 2,000 members; the Free Turkestan

18. The East Turkestan Islamic Movement (ETIM) is a shadowy group known only to be previously active in Afghanistan and founded in the mid-1990s by Hassan Mahsum. Mahsum had served three years in a labor camp in Xinjiang, and recruited other Uyghur, including his number-three leader Rashid, who was captured with the Taliban and returned to China in spring 2001 (see Hutzler 2001).

Movement, whose leader, Abdul Kasim, is said to have led the 1990 Baren uprising (discussed in Chapter 14); the Organization for the Liberation of Uighuristan, whose leader, Ashir Vakhidi, is said to be committed to the fighting Chinese 'occupation' of the 'Uighur homeland'; and the so-called Wolves of Lop Nor, who have claimed responsibility for various bombings and uprisings. The State Department report claims that all of these groups have tenuous links with al-Qaeda, the Taliban, Hizb ut-Tahrir (Islamic Revival), and Tableeghi Jamaat. Many of these groups were listed in the Chinese report that came out in early 2002, but failed to mention ETIM. It came as some surprise, therefore, when, at the conclusion of his August 2001 visit to Beijing, Deputy Secretary of State Richard Armitage identified ETIM as the leading Uyghur group to be targeted as an international terrorist group.[19] At the time, very few people, including activists deeply engaged in working for an independent East Turkestan, had ever heard of ETIM.[20] Even the US military did not seem to be aware of the group, for the 28 September 2001 'Special Report: Uighur Muslim Separatists' issued by the Virtual Information Center in Honolulu not only did not mention ETIM, but also concluded regarding separatist violence in Xinjiang that there is 'no single identifiable group but there is violent opposition coordinated and possibly conducted by exiled groups and organizations within Xinjiang'.[21]

The main criticism raised by those skeptical of this designation of ETIM as terrorists is that, with so many groups identified, it

19. Conclusion of China-visit press conference in Beijing by Deputy Secretary of State Richard L. Armitage, US Department of State, 26 August 2002.
20. For example, Mehmet Hazret, in a recent interview, claimed he had never heard of ETIM: 'I hadn't even heard of ETIM until the Chinese government mentioned its name in a report in January 2002', he said. 'But I knew the leaders of this group whom the report mentioned. For many years, they were in Chinese prisons for political reasons, and they escaped from China. We don't have any organizational relations with them because politically we don't share the same goals. But I cannot believe they carried out any terrorist attacks as the Chinese authorities say they did, because they themselves are victims of Chinese state terrorism'. Radio Free Asia, Uyghur service, 'Separatist Leader Vows to Target Chinese Government (RFA)', 24 January 2003. http://www.rfa.org/service/index.html?service=uyg
21. 'Special Report: Uighur Muslim Separatists' at the Virtual Information Center, 28 September 2001, p. 6 (http://www.vic-info.org). This statement is no longer found on the website, however, because this report was replaced by an updated one, 'China: Uighur Muslim Separatists', on 23 March 2003.

has not been made clear why ETIM in particular was singled out, unless it was for the political purpose of strengthening US–China relations. Calling ETIM 'scapegoat terrorists' the *Oxford Analytica* report on the issue ('China Increases Suppression in Xinjiang', 20 December 2002) says that ETIM and other groups are only a 'dubious threat' and have been used as an excuse for increased repression. It is important to note here that despite many months of pressure from the Chinese government upon the US to list ETIM as an international terrorist group, the US was not convinced of the group's significance until two Uyghur were arrested while reportedly reconnoitering the US embassy in Bishkek, Kyrgyzstan. When interrogated by US and Kyrgyz security personnel, the men were found to be in possession of plans of the embassy and information regarding US staff, which led the US to believe these Uyghur were targeting US interests in Central Asia. This more than anything convinced the US that these men, whom they believed to be part of ETIM, were an international threat, and therefore that ETIM should be listed as a terrorist group under Executive Order 13224. Interestingly, Yusupbek Mukhlisi's United Revolutionary Front was not listed along with ETIM, despite its frequent claims of responsibility for violent acts in Xinjiang, such as the 1997 train derailment and police-station bombings,[22] and since listing ETIM the US has resisted continued Chinese efforts to list other known Uyghur groups, including the East Turkestan Liberation Organization (ETLO). At the same time, many Uyghur have complained to me that although there have been many reported terrorist bombings in Tibet, and frequent organized protests against Chinese rule that have led to violence outside of that region, given the sympathy shown to Tibetans in the West, they do not see the US ever siding with China in condemning a Tibetan independence organization as terrorist.[23] And, despite widespread international protests,

---

22. 'Exile Group Claims Bomb Blast in Xinjiang', Agence France Presse (Hong Kong), 1 March 1997.

23. Bombings in Tibet and other 'terrorist acts' have been frequently reported in the press: 'Explosion Hits Tibet's Capital After China Announces New Regional Leader', Agence France Presse (Hong Kong), 9 November 2000, FBIS, CPP20001109000079; 'London Organization – Migrants' Shops Bombed in Tibet', Agence France Presse (Hong Kong), 27 December 1996, FBIS, FTS19970409001372; 'Tibet Blames Dalai Lama for Bombing in Lhasa', Tibet People's Radio Network (Lhasa), 27 December 1996,

on 27 January 2002 China executed a Tibetan monk found guilty of lethal bombings in Tibet (Pomfret 2003).[24] Many feel that is it is only because they are Muslims that one Uyghur group has been singled out as being terrorist. The real issue for this chapter, however, is that despite this designation of ETIM, there are active Uyghur-related militant groups that can be said to be supportive of terrorism, but have never been proved to be directly implicated in any specific incident.

Following Armitage's announcement and the State Department's report, the Chinese State Council issued its own report on 21 January 2002, charging that from 1990 to 2001 various Uyghur separatist groups 'were responsible for over 200 terrorist incidents in Xinjiang' that resulted in the deaths of 162 people and injuries to 440 others. The report, 'East Turkestan Terrorist Forces Cannot Get Away with Impunity', also dismissed allegations that Beijing had used the US-led war on terror as a pretext to crack down on Uyghur. The report condemned numerous Uyghur groups, including Hazret's ETLO, ETIM, the Islamic Reformist Party 'Shock Brigade', the East Turkestan Islamic Party, the East Turkestan Opposition Party, the East Turkestan Islamic Party of Allah, the Uyghur Liberation Organization, the Islamic Holy Warriors, and the East Turkestan International Committee.

It is important to note that an Internet search for many of these organizations and their backgrounds reveals little, if any, information. In addition, these organizations and many of the Internet news and information organizations discussed above have rarely, if ever, claimed responsibility for any specific action, although many are sympathetic to isolated incidents regarded as challenging

---

FBIS, FTS19970409001370; Che, Kang, 'Bomb Explodes in Lhasa, Local Authorities Offer Reward for Capture of Criminals', *Ta Kung Pao* (Hong Kong), 30 December 1996, FBIS, FTS19970409001371; 'Suspect Detained for Bomb Attack on Tibetan Clinic', Agence France Presse (Hong Kong), 14 January 1999, FBIS, FTS19990114000015; 'Explosion Hits Tibet's Capital after China Announces New Regional Leader', Agence France Presse (Hong Kong), 9 November 2000, FBIS, CPP20001109000079.

24. Radio Free Asia reported that the government is silencing any reporting on the execution: http://www.rfa.org/service/article.html?service=can& encoding=2&id=98250. The Chinese government released its first White Paper on Xinjiang on 26 May 2003, which summed up its policies consistent with what has been described above (see http://english.peopledaily.com.cn/ 200305/26/eng20030526_117240.shtml).

Chinese rule in the region. Interestingly, there seems to be very little support for radical Islam, and a search for the term 'jihad' (holy war) among the various websites and news postings related to these groups turns up almost no use of the term or call for a religious war against the Chinese. Many of the Uyghur nationalists are quite secular in their orientation, and overthrow of Chinese rule is related to issues of sovereignty and human rights, rather than those of religion. By contrast, Uyghur expatriates with whom I have spent time in the US, Canada, Turkey, and Europe tend to be quite religious, yet I have rarely heard them call for a holy war against the Chinese. Again, their concerns are more related to historic claims upon their ancestral lands, Chinese mistreatment of the Uyghur population, and a desire to return home to a 'free East Turkestan'. A Uyghur family with whom in 2000 I spent the Ramadan feast in Toronto, Canada, maintained a deeply religious life that they claimed was not possible in China. Although they disavowed violence, their daily prayer was for an independent 'Uyghuristan', where their relatives could be free to practice religion. In Istanbul, the Uyghur community is quite active in the mosques in Zeytin-burnu and Tuzla, and strongly advocate a 'liberated East Turkestan', but on several visits to these communities since 1993 I have never once heard them call for a jihad against the Chinese government, even in its mildest sense, which John Esposito (2002) has described as 'defensive jihad', or protecting Islam from persecution.[25]

Since 11 September 2001, very few groups have publicly advocated terror against the Chinese state, and most have denied any involvement in terrorist activities, though they may express sympathy for such activities. A case in point is ETLO, led by the secretive Mehmet Emin Hazret. In a 24 January 2003 telephone interview with the Uyghur service of Radio Free Asia, Hazret admitted that there may be a need to establish a military wing of his organization that would target Chinese interests. He nevertheless denied any prior terrorist activity or any association with ETIM. 'We have not been and will not be involved in any kind of terrorist action inside or outside China,' Hazret said. 'We have been trying to solve the East Turkestan problem through peaceful means. But the Chinese

---

25. For a discussion of the various meanings of *jihad* in Islam, see Esposito (2002:26–35). For studies among Uyghur and other Turkic communities in Istanbul, see Gladney (1996b); Svanberg, (1989b).

government's brutality in East Turkestan may have forced some individuals to resort to violence' ('Separatist Leader Vows to Target Chinese Government', Radio Free Asia, Uyghur service, 24 January 2003). Hazret, a former screenwriter from Xinjiang who migrated to Turkey in his forties, denied any connection between his organization and al-Qaeda or Osama bin Laden. Nevertheless, he did see the increasing need for military action against Chinese rule in the region: 'Our principal goal is to achieve independence for East Turkestan by peaceful means. But to show our enemies and friends our determination on the East Turkestan issue, we view a military wing as inevitable … The Chinese people are not our enemy. Our problem is with the Chinese government, which violates the human rights of the Uyghur people' ('Separatist Leader Vows to Target Chinese Government', Radio Free Asia, Uyghur service, 24 January 2003). Once again, a common pattern to his response regarding Chinese rule in the region was not to stress Islamic jihad or religious nationalism, but to emphasize human-rights violations and Uyghur claims on East Turkestan.

Chinese authorities are clearly concerned that increasing international attention on the treatment of its minority and dissident peoples has put pressure on the region, with the US and many Western governments continuing to criticize China for not adhering to its commitments to signed international agreements and human rights. In 2001 China ratified the International Covenant on Economic, Social, and Cultural Rights, Article 1 of which says: 'All peoples have the right of self-determination. By virtue of that right they freely determine their political status and freely pursue their economic, social and cultural development'. Article 2 reads: 'All peoples may, for their own ends, freely dispose of their natural wealth and resources without prejudice to any obligations arising out of international economic cooperation, based upon the principle of mutual benefit, and international law. In no case may a people be deprived of its own means of subsistence'. Although China continues to quibble with the definition of 'people', it is clear the agreements are pressuring China to answer criticisms by Mary Robinson and other high-ranking human-rights advocates about its treatment of minorities. Clearly, with Xinjiang representing the last Muslim region under communism, large trade contracts with Middle Eastern Muslim nations, and five Muslim nations on China's western borders, Chinese authorities have more to be concerned about than international support for human rights. It is important to note that many Uyghur leaders, including Erkin Alptekin (pers. comm.) continue to argue that many of these Uyghur organizations (including ETIM) are non-existent or at most 'one-man' entities with no followers, set up to bolster asylum chances for Uyghur exiles who must demonstrate a real fear of persecution to avoid repatriation to China.

China's Uyghur separatists are small in number, poorly equipped, loosely linked, and vastly outgunned by the People's Liberation Army and People's Police. Note also that although sometimes disgruntled about other rights and mistreatment issues, China's nine other official Muslim minorities do not in general support Uyghur separatism. There is, for example, some enmity between Uyghur and Hui (Dungan) in the region. Few Hui support an independent Xinjiang, and 1.3 million Kazakh in Xinjiang would have very little say in an independent 'Uyghuristan'. Local support for separatist activities, particularly in Xinjiang and other border regions, is ambivalent and ambiguous at best, given the economic disparity between these regions and their foreign neighbors, including Tajikistan, Kyrgyzstan, Pakistan, and especially Afghanistan. Memories in the region are strong of mass starvation and widespread destruction during the Sino-Japanese and civil wars in the first half of the 20th century, including bloody intra-Muslim and Muslim–Chinese conflicts, not to mention the chaotic horrors of the Cultural Revolution.

Many local activists are not calling for complete separatism or real independence, but generally express concerns over environmental degradation, nuclear testing, religious freedom, overtaxation, and recently imposed limits on childbearing. Many ethnic leaders are simply calling for 'real' autonomy according to Chinese law for the five autonomous regions that are each led by first party secretaries, who are all Han Chinese controlled by Beijing. Freedom of religion, protected by China's constitution, does not seem to be a key issue; mosques are full in the region and pilgrimages to Mecca are often allowed for Uyghur and other Muslims (although recent visitors to the region have reported an increase in restrictions against youths, students, and government officials on attending mosques). In addition, Islamic extremism does not as yet appear to have widespread appeal, especially among urban, educated Uyghur. However, the government has consistently rounded up any Uyghur suspected of being 'too' religious, especially those identified as Sufis or the so-called Wahhabi (a euphemism in the region for strict Muslims, not an organized Islamic school). These periodic roundups, detentions, and public condemnations of terrorism and separatism have not erased the problem, but have forced it underground, or at least out of the public's eye, and increased the possibility of alienating Uyghur Muslims even further from mainstream Chinese society. During the 2001 APEC meetings in Beijing, it was widely reported that Uyghur travelers were not allowed to stay in hotels in the city, and were often prevented from boarding public buses due to fear of terrorism.

The history of Chinese–Muslim relations in Xinjiang has been one of relative peace and quiet, broken by enormous social and political disruptions, fostered by internal and external crises. The relative quiet of the past two to three years does not indicate that the ongoing problems of the region have been resolved or the opposition dissolved. The opposition to Chinese rule in Xinjiang has not reached the level of the Chechnyan rebellion against Russia or the Palestinian intifada against Israel, but is similar to the that of Basque separatists of the ETA in Spain, or former IRA in Ireland and England; it is opposition that may erupt in limited, violent moments of terror and resistance. And just as these oppositional movements have not been resolved in Europe, the Uyghur problem in Xinjiang does not appear to be one that will readily go away. The admitted problem of Uyghur terrorism and dissent, even in the diaspora, is thus problematic for a government that wants to encourage integration and development in a region where the majority population are not only ethnically different, but also devoutly Muslim. How does a government integrate a strongly religious minority (be it Muslim, Tibetan, Christian, or Buddhist) into a Marxist–capitalist system? China's policy of intolerance toward dissent and economic stimulus does not seem to have resolved this issue.

Contesting otherness

Uyghur and other minorities in China are fully aware of the use the state is making of their identities in international relations and in the construction of national identity, which allows for the justification of internal control over not only individual sexuality, but also cultural and political difference. Through several protests – at

the Overseas Hotel in Ürümqi in the fall of 1987, I witnessed a
Uyghur march against a Han exhibition of 'minority art' that the
Uyghur found denigrating and degrading – Uyghur have often
attempted to object to their *National Geographic*-like portrayals as
'happy, sensual natives'. But in China there is more to it than the
National Geographic romanticization of the primitive. I would argue
that it is because the construction of Han identity is so tenuous, so
questionable, and the position of Han superiority so insecure, that
the portrayal of the other as sensual, immoral, and even barbarous
becomes so important. This is also why the erotic portrayal of minorities is still permitted in a society that strictly controls any other
even slightly pornographic material, not only that of the Han, but
also of foreign publications and video media. While every society
tends to allow the exoticization and eroticization of the other and
the stranger, in China is an active project of the state. It is the internal other that is appropriated for nation-building and reinforcing
the prurient moral code of the totalitarian state. By allowing this
continued portrayal of the minorities in state-sponsored media, at
the same time as it restricts such portrayals of Han and foreigners, the state reinforces its hegemonic control over its peoples, as
well as promoting its notion of civilization and moral authority.
For domestic consumption, minorities – Muslims included – are
portrayed as exotic and erotic, but for international purposes, the
nationalities – Muslims especially – are represented as traditional
and content.

At the same time, Uyghur and other minorities are taking
advantage of their official minority status, and objectified identities, ill-fitting or not, to promote their own religious, political,
and personal interests. Opportunities to study and travel abroad
are hard to come by, even for Han, and the Uyghur are eager to
take advantage of every little crack in the Chinese system. When
the state allows those cracks to appear, albeit for very specific
foreign-policy and economic reasons, they may not be able to
anticipate the many unintended results – results that might include a strengthened transnational Uyghur identity, both Turkish
and Muslim.

Although the Internet may provide a virtual space of dissent and
contrary views, it has had only limited success in mobilizing such
subaltern groups as the Uyghur and Falun Gong. Nevertheless, it
indicates that there is increasing space for subaltern voices to be

expressed and the inability of the state to stamp out alternative movements and visions of Chinese rule. Unfortunately, the space for the expression of subaltern voices remains for the most part outside of China, in the diaspora or on the Internet. This displacement continues to add pressure on subalterns within China either to suppress their own voices or to emigrate, a choice many do not wish to make. China certainly has come a long way since the repressive years of the Cultural Revolution, and many subalterns are taking advantage of various openings in the 'cracks of capitalism' now appearing. Despite these openings, one should not forget the ominous words contained in the Chinese national anthem: 'The Chinese race is at a most crucial moment; we should stand up and build up a new Great Wall with our blood and flesh'. If this becomes a project of the current government under Hu Juntao, just as establishing proof of China's 'uninterrupted 5,000-year civilization' was one of the key goals of the former Jiang Zemin administration, it is clear that China's subalterns will remain in that position for some time to come.

Part VI
SOCIALIZATIONS

12
EDUCATING CHINA'S OTHERS

Making Muslims

We have made Italy, now we have to make Italians. (Massimo d'Azeglio, at
the first meeting of the parliament of the newly united Italian Kingdom
[cited in Hobsbawm 1991:144])

How are Muslims 'made' in China? This chapter suggests that while
they are born at home (or in hospitals), they may very well be *made*
in the school. There are least two types of schools for Muslims in
China: state-sponsored and mosque-sponsored (which sometimes
receive state funding). As yet, there are few if any non-Muslim
private schools in China to which Muslims have access. Although
I and others have written extensively about Muslim minority
identity and identification in China, few have specially addressed
the role of education and the transmission of Islamic knowledge in
the 'making' of Muslims there. While there are at least ten official
Muslim nationalities in China, with extremely divergent histories
and diverse identities, this chapter suggests that through centralized, state-sponsored education, and a tradition of fairly regularized
Islamic education in China, the education of Muslims, both public
and private, or state-sponsored and Islamic-inspired, are fairly systematized. The systematization of the transmission of knowledge
to Muslims in China, I would argue, has played a privileged role in
influencing Muslim identities.

This chapter examines two sides of this transmission of knowledge about and among Muslims in China. This involves the state
education of Muslims as members of China's fifty-five minority
nationalities, as well as Muslim education of their own populations.
In this way, the chapter seeks to some extent to answer John R.
Bowen's (1995:1061) question: 'How do people negotiate among
competing and conflicting sets of norms and ideals?' With respect

to the Muslims in China, they do it through public and private systems of education.

As has been noted, given that there are ten official Muslim nationalities in China, Muslim identities range widely, from Turkic to Indo-European, 'Central Asian' to 'East Asian', 'northerner' to 'southerner', rural to urban, religious to secular, and educated to illiterate. In addition to a shared Islamic heritage (much of which is forgotten by some, and denied to others), there are at least two main streams of educational training that to a remarkable extent bring these divergent Muslim nationalities together through a systematized fulcrum of socialization: state-sponsored education and traditionally maintained Islamic education. While both aspects of this educational socialization will vary for each of the ten Muslim nationalities, I would argue that the similarities at least bind them closer together than the Han Chinese majority and the other forty-five minority nationalities. One aspect of this is the representation of Muslims as members of minority nationalities and specifically as Muslims. This representation of other and self is perhaps the most public of the widespread transmissions of knowledge about Islam in China and will be dealt with first. Corrections and confirmations of these representations will then be addressed in sections on China's education of minorities and then Muslims. I shall only then turn my attention to traditional and contemporary Islamic educational trends in China. Finally, I shall conclude with a discussion of public and private discourse regarding Islam in China.

Education and China's civilizing mission

Since the late 20th century, the focus of much writing on China's minorities and national identification program has been on the 'civilizing mission' of China's policy toward its 'backward minorities' (see Anagnost 1994; Borchigud 1995; Gladney 1987b; Harrell 1995). In state-sponsored media and publications, and public representations, the Han majority are represented as the most 'modern' and, by implication, the most educated.

Minorities, generally less educated in the Chinese school system than the Han majority, are thought to be somewhere behind the Han culturally. Education plays a privileged role in executing China's national integration project (see Hawkins 1983; Postiglione, Teng and Ai 1995). This is reflected in popular discussion about education and 'culture' in China. One of the most difficult questions I had to ask in China was one regarding education. The way to pose the question in Chinese is, literally: 'What is your cultural level?' (*Nide wenhua chengdu duoshao?*) 'Culture' here refers only to learning in state-sponsored schools and literacy in Chinese characters. In the volume of 'nationality statistics' published by the Department of Population Statistics of State Statistical Bureau and Economic Department of the State Commission for Ethnic Affairs, the educational sections are all listed under the category of 'cultural levels' of the various minority nationalities as compared to the Han (Department of Population Statistics 1994:38–70). I still remember asking this question to an elderly Hui hajji in Hezhou, who answered that he 'had no culture'. This Islamic scholar had spent twelve years living in the Middle East, and was fluent in Persian and Arabic, and a master of the Islamic natural sciences. Efforts to integrate 'nationality general history' (*minzu changshi*) into the state-school curriculum do not even begin to address this issue of pervasive Han chauvinism. It may be a strong factor that keeps Hui children from wanting to go to mainly Han schools.

Muslims, as minorities, are generally thought to be less educated than the majority and are portrayed are exoticized and even eroticized in the public media in similar fashion to other minorities, even though the Muslims are generally much more conservative socially and morally (see Chapter 4). This is quite remarkable given the long tradition of learning idealized by Muslims (the desire, as the Prophet said, to 'Seek Knowledge, even unto China'), the proliferation of Muslim centers of learning in China, and that at least two Muslim groups, the Tartar and Uzbek, are considerably better-educated than the general populace, including the Han Chinese. This is not unusual, however, given that the Korean minority in China is also popularly perceived as a backward minority, even though the Koreans in China possess the highest literacy and educational rates, far surpassing the Han and other groups (with three times more college students, proportionally, than any other nationality; see Yeo 1996:25; Lee 1986). The Koreans, like all Muslims, are members of the minorities of China, and they are thus in need of education.

This may reflect also the view in China that education was the means to acculturation into Chinese civilization, which depended on the learning of Chinese. Minorities and foreigners perforce had less possibility of attaining such in-depth knowledge of Chinese and would therefore always be on the periphery. Yet this knowledge was not limited to elites. Myron Cohen argues that interaction between elites and common people in China's educational system led not just to 'a common culture in the sense of shared behavior, institutions and beliefs', but also to 'a unified culture in that it provided standards according to which people identified themselves as Chinese' (Cohen, M. 1991:114). As long as one maintained these standards, one was Chinese. Yet knowledge of those standards was communicated in Chinese, in state schools. In imperial China, exhortations and rituals articulating the standards set by those in power helped to extend beyond establishing a 'tiny literate reef' amid 'illiterate oceans' of the general populace (see Woodside and Elman 1994:3). As David Johnson (1985:47) notes, 'The values and beliefs of a dominant class take on the radiance of truth in the eyes of ordinary people'. Yet this top-down view often excludes those it fails to inspire, particularly groups like Muslims, Tibetans, and Mongols, who follow different moralities according to different religious texts. Charles Stafford (1992:371–2) has argued that in Taiwan, schoolchildren are given strong moral instruction as early as the fourth grade, including being taught such virtues as 'filial to relatives, repaying the nation' (*xiao qin bao guo*) and 'sacrifice the body, repaying the nation' (*xian shen bao guo*). The link here between nation, morality, and education is altogether clear. In mainland China, morality, culture, and education are also linked to the state's nationalization program.

This is perhaps why 'culture' (*wenhua*) in China is so tied to literacy, and literacy in Chinese. The Chinese term *wen*, translated as literature, writing, inscription, is a central part of the idea of culture. Strassberg's (1994:5–6) work on 'inscribed landscapes' emphasizes the transformative power of writing in traditional China that helps to incorporate the landscapes into the realm. By the same token, literacy inculcates not only Chinese language, but Chinese culture, *wenhua*, into those minorities who are to become Chinese. Literacy and education are thus central to China's nationalist project of integration. As Pamela Crossley (1990:4) has argued, belief in the tenets of Chinese classicism, including 'a reverence for the imputedly inherent transformative power of civilization, a distaste for displays of military power, [and] a contempt for commerce and semiliterate or illiterate cultural values' contributed in the West to notions of the inevitability of Sinicization and assimilation of minorities and other marginals. In other words, to learn Chinese meant one became Chinese. This notion has been shared by Chinese and Western scholars alike, who adhere to a Sinicization paradigm that links literacy and education with assimilation, the primary method of China's 'civilizing project'. As LaBelle and Verhine (1975) have theorized, access to education contributes to the nature of social stratification in many societies. In China, Muslim minorities have increasing access, but as will be seen below, there seems to have been little progress in their educational development.

Representation of Muslims as minority nationalities

Muslims are grouped and displayed in all of China's many nationality publications, including the state-sponsored magazines *Nationality Pictorial* (*Minzu Huabao*) and *United Nationalities* (*Minzu Tuanjie*), as well as various collections, such as *Chinese Nationalities* (1989), *China's Minorities* (1994), *A Picture Album of Turpan Landscape and Custom* (1985), and *Nationality Style and Figures* (1985). A cursory examination of photographs and paintings of Muslims in these state-sponsored publications reveals no real difference from the usual portrayal of minorities in China as 'exotic' and 'erotic'. Rarely have Muslims been distinguished from this corpus, since they are generally treated in similar fashion to other minority subjects.

Those who were recognized by the state as minority nationalities are always portrayed in the state-sponsored media as happily accepting that objectivized identity. The caption for a photograph of several minorities in traditional costume pictured in a brochure introducing the Nationalities Cultural Palace (*Minzu Wenhua Gong*) in Beijing reads: 'The Happy People of Various Nationalities' (*Minzu Gong* 1990:12). In one survey of Han Chinese college students, southern minorities, which are often represented as happy and colorful, were ranked as 'positive primitives' whose qualities included 'beauty, friendliness, singing and dancing, industry, primitivity, and ignorance' (Fong and Spickard 1994:26).

In a published painting of several minorities on the Great Wall, discussed in Chapter 4 (page 57), the Muslims fit right into this scheme of minority representation, a representation that generally focuses on the naturalness, primitivity, backwardness, sensuality, and even sexuality of the minority subjects. A popular art school now known as the Yunnan School, which I have also described in Chapter 4, frequently uses Muslim subjects in its extraordinarily eroticized paintings.

Even allowing that the sexual practices of the southwestern minorities may be more 'open' than those of the Han, they are not the only minorities portrayed as sensual and erotic (see Chapter 4, page 78). Such representations continue, despite the protestations of the minorities, which serves to highlight the remarkable contrast between the Han and minority spectacle. Muslims also protest publications about Islam that they find denigrating, as evidenced by the Chinese 'Salman Rushdie' protest against an encyclopedic portrayal of Islam, in a book entitled *Sexual Customs* (see Gladney 1994),[1] as sensual and eroticized, a representation that has a long history in China. Despite the government's crackdown on such publications, these kinds of representations of Islam and Muslims continue. For most Han Chinese, who have never even entered a mosque and learn little about Islam in public schools, this representation in the public sphere is their only exposure to knowledge about Islam or Muslim identities in China.

Muslim self-representation

Because China does not yet have a free press, it is still impossible for Muslims to represent themselves in the public sphere entirely without state mediation. Even relatively recent popular novels such as Zhang Chengzhi's *A History of the Soul* (1991) and Huo Da's *Jade King* (1993) (or in Chinese, *Muslim Funeral*, 1992), which were written by Muslims about Muslim lives and conflicts, have passed through state bodies of literary approval. Both of these works, though controversial in their own right, are remarkable in their serious and upright portrayal of Muslim society in general, and are modern attempts to reveal a Muslim morality in a way similar to earlier Muslim efforts to portray Islam as 'Confucian'.

A 1985 pictorial published by the China Islamic Association, *A Collection of Painting and Calligraphy Solicited for Charity in Aid of the Disabled*, presents an entirely different view of Muslims than that found in *Nationality Pictorial* and the Yunnan School of painting. Here, Muslims are represented as studious, hard-working, devout,

1.   For a more detailed explanation, see pages 352–3, Chapter 15, this volume.

and dedicated to the family and society. There is even a presentation of Chinese calligraphy by Muslim artists (and at least one Han artist who wrote calligraphy in praise of Islam!), reminiscent again of Muslim attempts to establish their literary and artistic credentials in the classic Chinese arts of painting and calligraphy. The various editions of a publication by the China Islamic Association, *The Religious Life of Chinese Moslems* (1957, 1978, 1985), feature not only various mosques and prominent Muslims, but also a great deal of emphasis on education. The Muslim-sponsored pictorial *Islamic in Beijing* (Hadi Su Junhui 1990) contains fine examples of Islamic architecture, art, and scholarship in Beijing, and also has photographs of famous Muslim scholars and teachers. Similarly, the Xinjiang publication by the Uyghurs Jori Kadir and Halik Dawut, *Examples of Uyghur Architectural Art* (1983), has fine examples of mosques and tombs dedicated to religious figures, as well as tombs to Muslim scholars such as the poet Yusup Has Hajip and the lexicographer al-Kashgari. Indeed, many of the Muslim tombs being quickly restored across China are dedicated to Muslim scholars and religious personages, only some of whom were Sufis (Gladney 1987a).

These few examples reveal that Muslims have a very different view of themselves than that found in most state-sponsored public media. They are members not only of a minority nationality, but also of a long religious and scholarly tradition that has contributed to Chinese culture and society. The transmission of this image of Islam and Islamic knowledge in China is a difficult task for a population that occupies only 2 percent of the total, and one that has generally been stigmatized throughout much of Chinese history. Although the Muslim minorities are generally thought to be lower in 'cultural level' than most Han Chinese, and less educated, their pride in their own tradition of Islamic learning is now beginning to be communicated to non-Muslims. And, as will be seen below, for most Muslim nationalities in China, including the Hui, Uyghur, Uzbek, and Tartar, their general Chinese education equals or exceeds that of the Han, although this is not the general perception, and is one that is only gradually changing in China.

Chinese education of Muslims

International travel and exposure for China's Muslims in the 20th and 21st centuries has meant a rush to attain both Chinese and Islamic education in hopes of 'modernizing' China's Muslim communities. In the early decades of the 20th century, China was exposed to many new foreign ideas and in the face of Japanese and Western imperialist encroachment sought a Chinese approach to governance. Intellectual and organizational activity by Chinese Muslims during this period was also intense. Increased contact with the Middle East led Chinese Muslims to re-evaluate their traditional notions of Islam. Pickens (1942:231–5) records that from 1923 to 1934 there were 834 known Hui Muslims who made the hajj, or pilgrimage, to Mecca. In 1937, according to one observer, more than 170 Hui pilgrims boarded a steamer in Shanghai bound for Mecca (Office of Strategic Services 1944:127). By 1939, at least thirty-three Hui Muslims had studied at Cairo's prestigious Al-Azhar University. While these numbers are not significant when compared with pilgrims on the hajj from other Southeast Asian Muslim areas, the influence and prestige attached to these returning Hui hajji was profound, particularly in isolated communities. Fletcher (n.d.) observed, 'In this respect, the more secluded and remote a Muslim community was from the main centers of Islamic cultural life in the Middle East, the more susceptible it was to those centers' most recent trends'.

As a result of political events and the influence of foreign Muslim ideas, numerous new Hui organizations emerged. In 1912, one year after Sun Yat-sen was inaugurated provisional president of the Chinese Republic in Nanjing, the Chinese Muslim Federation was also formed in that city. This was followed by the establishment of other Hui Muslim associations: the Chinese Muslim Mutual Progress Association (Beijing, 1912), the Chinese Muslim Educational Association (Shanghai, 1925), the Chinese Muslim Association (Beijing, 1925), the Chinese Muslim Young Students Association (Nanjing, 1931), the Society for the Promotion of Education among Muslims (Nanjing, 1931), and the Chinese Muslim General Association (Jinan, 1934).

The Muslim periodical press flourished as never before. Although, as Löwenthal (1940:211–50) reports, circulation was low, there were more than 100 known Muslim periodicals produced before the outbreak of the Sino-Japanese War in 1937. Thirty journals were published between 1911 and 1937 in Beijing alone, prompting one author to suggest that while Chinese Islam's traditional religious center was still Linxia (Hezhou), its cultural center had shifted to Beijing (Office of Strategic Services 1944:27). This took place when many Hui intellectuals traveled to Japan, the Middle East and the West. Caught up in the nationalist fervor of the first half of the 20th century, they published magazines and founded organizations, questioning their identity as never before in a process that one Hui historian, Ma Shouqian (1989), termed 'The New Awakening of the Hui at the End of 19th Century and Beginning of the 20th Century'. As many of these Hui hajji returned from their pilgrimages to the Middle East, they initiated several reforms, engaging themselves once again in the contested space between Islamic ideals and Chinese culture. This zeal for 'modern' education led to the establishment of more modernist Islamic movements in China, including the Ikhwan (known in China as the Yihewani) and the Salafiyya. The Yihewani differ from the traditionalist and Sufi Muslim groups in China primarily in ritual matters and their stress upon reform through Chinese education and modernism. Because of its emphasis on nationalist concerns, education, modernization, and decentralized leadership, the order has attracted more urban intellectual Muslims. The Yihewani are also especially numerous in areas like Qinghai and Gansu provinces, where they proliferated during the Republican period under the patronage of Hui warlords. Many of the large mosques and Islamic schools rebuilt with government funds throughout China in the late 1970s and early 1980s tend to be staffed by Yihewani imams.

The spread of Islamic reform movements in China during the late 19th century saw Beijing's establishment as the 'cultural center of Chinese Islam'. These movements in many ways displaced central and western China (in places such as Hezhou, Yunnan, Kashgar, and Zhengzhou) as the main sites for Muslim learning, shifting many of China's Muslims from traditionalist and Sufi Islamic associations to that of the modernist Yihewani. While Muslims in the northwest saw religious conservatism and revival as the answer to their social and cultural problems, the Muslims in many urban centers, and especially in Beijing, decided that education was the solution:

[The decline of the Hui in Beijing] is associated with the following four things: 1) the degeneration of Islam among all religions, 2) the degeneration of China among the nations, 3) the degeneration of Beiping [Beijing] among the capitals, 4) the degeneration of Niujie where the Hui people are crowded together. In fact, it isn't the degeneration of the people but the backwardness of their education … The relationship between education and living standard is one of cause and effect. Obviously, without education there would not be people of talent, without talented personnel there would be no better means of livelihood. (Wang Shoujie 1930:18–19)

The question of what kind of education would be appropriate was debated throughout the Republican period, with various private Hui schools attempting different combinations of secular and religious education. In the early days of the People's Republic, these private schools became secularized and nationalized. Religious education was now the responsibility of the mosque and home, whereas secular education was the responsibility of the state. Shortly after the establishment of the PRC, the Beijing city government combined the Hui middle schools Cheng Da Normal School, Northwest Middle School, and Yanshan Middle School into the Hui Institute (*Huimin Xueyuan*). In 1963 the Hui Institute was changed to the Hui Middle School. In 1979 it was reopened under that name after having been divided during the Cultural Revolution into the Capital Middle School and the Number 135 Middle School.

Post-1949 Chinese education of Muslims

In 1949 there were nineteen Hui primary schools created out of former private 'Muslim' (*Mu zi*) schools. By 1953 there were twenty-eight Hui elementary schools, all of which were renamed during the Cultural Revolution. Children were required to attend the schools in the neighborhoods where they lived. While this is still mainly the case for Hui primary schools, there are now thirteen Hui primary schools and six Hui nursery schools in Beijing, all in neighborhoods with concentrated Hui populations. Primary education, now universally required throughout Beijing, is the area of real gain. In 1949 there were only about 2,700 Hui in primary school in Beijing. Now there are no Hui primary-school-aged children out of school.

The curriculum in all of these state-run institutions is set by the Ministry of Education and is exactly the same as that of other schools, with the main differences being that no pork is served at the schools and no tuition charged to Hui students. In 1985 the State Commission for Ethnic Affairs published 'nationality general knowledge' (*minzu changshi*) curriculum for the Hui middle schools. The state's goal to strengthen education among minorities reflects a call made in the 1930s: 'This research explains that whenever nationality education work is seized upon [*zhua haole*], then nationality relations and nationality unity will be greatly strengthened' (Beijing City Sociology Committee *et al.* 1984:19).

Despite a great deal of emphasis on minority education since the 'golden period' of the 1950s, the Hui still lag behind the Han in Beijing, especially in post-primary education. Out of 364 Han who graduated from Beijing's Number One Middle School in 1982, forty-seven (13 percent) went on either to college or to higher technical schools. Out of the seven Hui who graduated, not one went on (Beijing City Sociology Committee *et al.* 1984:20).

From 1979 to 1981 there was a slight decline among Han and Hui in high school entrance. Although the Hui occupy about one-fourth of the Oxen Street population, they represent only 5 to 14 percent of those entering high school. Fewer than 6 percent of Hui in the Oxen Street area had attended middle school prior to 1955. A 1983 education survey of the Xuanwu District (where Oxen Street is located) revealed that out of every 1,000 Hui, 5.1 percent are college graduates, 22.6 percent are high school graduates, 30.6 percent are middle school graduates, and 41.7 percent are primary school graduates. The same survey among Han in the Xuanwu District revealed that 23.34 percent are college graduates, 21.54 percent are high school graduates, 25 percent are middle school graduates, and 17.58 percent received an elementary education. Over four times more Han than Hui graduate from college in this area, and there are almost two and a half times as many Hui with only an elementary school education as there are Han. In 1982, 1.2 percent of the Han students who took the high school exam were admitted, whereas only 0.67 percent of the minority examinees were admitted (Beijing City Sociology Committee *et al.* 1984:21).

This brief examination of the educational situation of the Hui in Beijing is indicative of national trends for most Muslims in urban areas in China. It is clear, however, that there are large gaps between rural and urban Muslim education, which has a direct impact on the national statistics. While it is generally true that the educational level of the Hui is lower than that of the Han majority among whom they live, at the national level Hui educational attainment has apparently been reasonably good. In 1982 the Hui had kept pace with the national average, and were substantially better-educated than the other Muslim minorities, with the exception of the Tartar and Uzbek.[2] The main advantage the Hui have is language; other Muslim minorities have to contend with learning the Han language as a second language to enter middle school and university.[3] The Hui speak the Han dialects wherever they live.

Since 1982, Muslims have made some gains in public education in China compared to the rest of the population, according to the 1990 census. Comparison with figures from the 1990 census reveal that for the Hui, educational rates have remained basically the same. Significantly, college graduation rates for all Muslims except the Tartar and Uzbek are similar to the rest of China (about 0.5 percent). The primary distinction for Tartar and Uzbek is that their numbers are small and that they are primarily concentrated in urban areas. Although their college educational rates are extraordinarily high compared to the rest of the population (2.7 and 3.7 percent respectively in 1990), there at least ten other minority groups with higher educational rates in China than the Han (including the Koreans, Manchu, Russians, Daur, Xibe, Hezhe, Ewenke, and Oroqen). It is clear that the most rural Muslim groups (the Dongxiang, Baoan, and Salar in Gansu), and the still seminomadic or pastoralist (Kazakh and Kyrgyz) suffer from the least access to public schools, although there do seem to be some gains in primary school education among the Uyghur, Kazakh and Dongxiang. The gap between rural and urban, nomadic and sedentary, is most dramatic in illiteracy and semiliteracy rates. While Hui made some gains between 1982 and 1990 (with illiteracy reduced from 41 to 33.1 percent), the two groups with the highest illiteracy rates in 1982, the Dongxiang (87 percent) and the Baoan (78 percent), showed only marginal gains in literacy by 1990 (illiteracy reduced to 82.6 percent and 68.8 percent, respectively). This compares to an overall reduction in illiteracy in China between 1982 and 1990 from 32 percent to 22 percent, a dramatic drop that apparently has not reached the Muslim communities in rural Gansu.

2.   The Uzbek and Tartar minorities have fared very well in education, since they are almost exclusively living in urban areas in Xinjiang.
3.   The Dongxiang have the highest illiteracy rate in China, at 87 percent.

At the other extreme, when college educational levels among Muslims are compared with the rest of China, not only have they done comparatively well, but there were some gains between 1982 and 1990, particularly for the most-educated Muslims, the Tartar and Uzbek. The most remarkable gains have been in undergraduate education for the Uyghur, Kazakh, Kyrgyz, Salar, and Tajik. Whereas the Han undergraduate college population grew from 0.2 to 2.4 percent during that time, these groups experienced even greater gains (Uyghur 0.1 to 2.1 percent; Kazakh 0.2 to 3.3 percent; Kyrgyz 0.1 to 2.9 percent; and Tajik 0.1 to 2.5 percent).[4]

For the most part, however, there was not much change between 1982 and 1990 in Muslim education in China, despite significant state efforts to promote education in minority and Muslim areas. Not only are primary and secondary education provide in several primarily Muslim languages (especially Uyghur, Kazakh, Kyrgyz, and Tajik), but the state provides the normal minority nationality incentives for preferred college entrance. The state in China has made strong efforts to provide equal educational access for minorities and Han in rural and urban areas (Kwong and Hong 1989). It is noteworthy, however, that second-language education is not widely available among the least-educated Muslim populations concentrated in the Hexi Corridor of Gansu, the Dongxiang, Baoan, and Salar, because these groups speak a mixed combination of Chinese, Turkish, and Mongolian, and the state for the most part provides primarily Chinese-language education. In all Muslim areas, however, the state has sought to adapt to Muslim needs by providing *qing zhen*, or halal food that does not contain pork, with special 'Hui' schools in urban areas. Yet even these efforts do not seem enough to raise Muslim minority education in China. This may have to do with the content of education that is set by the central education bureau, rather than its medium of adapting to local languages and Muslim customs.

For example, in my Beijing city research, many Hui parents in the Oxen Street district told me that while they were glad for the Hui schools and the priority Hui are now receiving in education,

4. The 1982 census included a category for college education, whereas the 1990 census broke that category into undergraduate and technical-school figures. For 1982 and 1990 comparisons, these figures have been combined. Official figures based on the 2000 census are not yet available.

they felt their children would be more motivated to study if there was more ethnic content. Many of them remember that Hui schools in the early 1950s often invited famous Hui scholars such as Bai Shouyi and Ma Songting to give lectures on Hui history and historic Chinese Muslim personages. The Hui Middle School in Oxen Street also offered Arabic as a second language, so students did not have to go to the mosque to learn it. Unlike many northwestern Hui parents, those in Beijing are not tempted to withdraw their children from school and send them to the mosque for religious education. Instead, they argue that there is more of a need to integrate secular and religious education to motivate their children. They also point out that the Islamic schools, even with the course for training imams at the Chinese Islamic Association in the Oxen Street district, cannot supply enough imams for the number of mosques that need them. One of the reasons is that many young men upon graduation use their Arabic or Persian to become interpreters or translators overseas, where they can travel and earn more money, instead of becoming imams. The distinction between ethnicity and Islam in the city is still too strong for most Hui parents, and they think it might help the country if the two were brought closer together.

Like other minorities, the Hui in Niujie receive special consideration on their exams for entrance to middle school, high school, and college. In general, they receive two 'levels' of ten points each for college entrance preference. For example, if the threshold for college entrance on the state exams is 300 points, a Hui who scores 280 points will be accepted. This may make a difference. I knew a Hui who scored 281 on the exam and was admitted to Beijing Normal University (*Beijing Shifan Daxue*). His Han neighbor complained bitterly of this to me, since he scored 295 and was not admitted to the college of his choice, but had to go to a 'television university' (*dianshi daxue*), where most courses are taught on videocassette. Athletes who place among the top six (*qian liu ming*) in provincial competitions are also given two stage preferences. Hence, it is conceivable that a Hui athlete could score 260 on the exam and still be admitted to college with a total score of 300, because he receives four stage preferences. Preference for high school and college minority education is just beginning to show long-term effects, and more recent records should reveal a significant improvement over the 1979 to 1981 figures cited above.

From the government's perspective, the greatest stress has been placed upon raising the educational level of rural Hui villagers. In 1958, more than 90 percent of the Hui in Changying, a suburban village on the outskirts of Beijing, were found to be illiterate. By contrast, almost all of the children above the age of ten in the neighboring Han villages could read. The commune had to send in outside accountants to handle the brigade paperwork for the Hui. By 1980, there were eight Hui college students from the village, 650 high school students, 3,000 middle school students, and 3,000 primary school students. The municipality and district government donated 300,000 yuan to build a nationality primary school (*minzu xiaoxue*) in Changying, with the plan of making it into a cultural center for all the Beijing suburban villages to emulate. The faculty are paid a higher wage than those of other primary schools and there is twice the budget for the children's meals and snacks. Out of 647 students, 85 percent are Hui, a proportion higher than any other nationality school in Beijing. The faculty are 30 percent Hui. Of the first class, 95 percent entered middle school, and 50 percent tested into high school.

There are still problems to overcome, however. The Hui principal said that Hui parents do not value education as much as do the Han. They would rather have their children help out with the family sideline enterprise. The brigade government has developed special training programs to help families realize the importance of a public education. One of the issues that the local officials have yet to address, however, is the nature of education for these Hui. The imam mentioned that while desire for 'Han' learning was low, many of the younger Hui were quite motivated to study Islamic history and Quranic languages. The Party Secretary countered that this was not regarded as education by the state and therefore could not be encouraged by state schools. It was part of religion, he said.

For other Muslim minorities, efforts have been made to bring state education to the minority areas, including the pastoral areas, through the novel program of setting up schools in the pastures, or more commonly, requiring Kazakh and Kyrgyz herders to leave their children in school until they can join them in the herding areas during vacation. Despite these efforts, Muslim illiteracy rates (with the exception of the Tartar and Uzbek) remain high, and there has been little overall change in Muslim minority education in the past several years. The reason, again, may have more to do with *what* is taught, rather than *how* it is taught. The lack of nationality content and Muslim world history may be forcing Muslims interested in their people's history to go to the mosque rather than public schools and libraries for such 'religious' knowledge. This is odd, because other world religions are frequently mentioned in the public schools, including Buddhism and Christianity, although often in a critical fashion.

The gender gap: male /female education discrepancies among Muslim nationalities

It is clear that China's policy of coeducation runs directly against traditional Muslim sensitivities. While it could be argued that China's Muslim women are more 'liberated' than their Middle Eastern counterparts, in that they are not subject to the strict rules of purdah, the 1990 data on education suggest a significant male/ female discrepancy in access to state-sponsored education, at both ends of the spectrum. China, as a society dominated by male influence related to the East Asian tradition of patrilineal descent and patrilocal residence, is characterized by male preference in terms of birth, education, and social mobility (Shi 1995). For Muslims, this is even more significant in terms of public education. The rates of illiteracy and semiliteracy among Muslim females are nearly twice as high as those of Muslim males. While China's overall rate of illiteracy is about 22.2 percent, the Muslim average (excluding the Tajik and Uzbek) is about 45 percent. The rates diverge even more across gender boundaries. Hui females average 42.7 percent illiteracy and semiliteracy, compared to 23.7 percent among Hui males and 12.3 percent among Han males (Han females average 31.1 percent). For the three least-educated Muslim groups, the Dongxiang, Baoan, and Salar, the rates are even worse: Dongxiang males 73.8 percent, females 92 percent; Baoan males 53.3 percent, females 85.3 percent; and Salar males 49.2 percent, females 88.9 percent. Earlier, Hawkins (1973) argued the importance of minority education for intergroup relations in China. These data reveal that high rates of illiteracy among females and males for at least three Muslim nationalities bode ill for intergroup relations with Han Chinese and the Chinese state.

At the other extreme, college education among Muslim males and females reveals a similar gender gap. Whereas 0.4 percent of

Han males have received university education, this is true for only 0.1 percent of females. Among the least-educated Muslim groups, this gap is negligible, since so few have attended college. But it is interesting to note that three times more Kazakh males than females attend college (0.35 to 0.1 percent, respectively), and two times more Uyghur males than females (0.16 to 0.08 percent, respectively). Among the more educated Muslim minorities, the Uzbek male/female college ratio is equal (1.3 percent for both) and for the Tartar it is only slightly different (2 percent for males and 1.5 percent for females). This indicates that more-educated Muslims tend to send males and females to school together. This is not true, however, for the more rural and less-educated Muslim populations.

China's Muslim males and females never pray together; it is no wonder they do not want their children to study together. Although China is distinguished in the Muslim world by having many women's mosques, which are often attached to or even independent of men's mosques, it is clear that men and women rarely mix together for ritual or religious education. However, on one holiday – that of Fatima's birthday, celebrated widely among Muslims in China – I have witnessed men and women praying together. In general, however, women pray at home, in the back or side of the mosque, separated by a curtain, or in an adjacent or separate 'women's mosque' (*nu si*).[5] While it is not clear how well-educated China's Muslim women are in Islam, they are active in studying the Quran and in establishing mosques. This is not true for their participation in public education. It is clear that if China wants to improve the education of its Muslim population, it not only needs to consider a more inclusive curriculum of Muslim history, but it also may need to end coeducation in Muslim areas. An examination of traditional Islamic education in China suggests that although it is generally equally exclusive toward women, it is also highly developed and permeates all of China's Muslim communities, male and female. This cannot be said for public school education.

5. For more on Muslim women in China, see the 'Women in China's Islam Project' in Zhengzhou, initiated by Ms Xie Jiejing and Maria Jaschok (of the University of Hong Kong); see also Allès (1994); Cherif (1994); Pang Keng-Fong (1992); Pillsbury (1978). For highly informative recent studies on gender, women's mosques, and food culture among the Hui, see Allès (2000), Gillette (2002), Jaschok and Shui (2001)

The rise of Islamic education and its influence on Chinese education

Muslim education in China varies dramatically between groups and between male and females. Not only were the Baoan and Dongxiang among the most illiterate groups in China in 1982 and 1990, but the Tartar and Uzbek continue to be among the best educated. These trends are continuing in the 1990s, but with rising Islamic conservatism there is some concern that gains in Chinese education may be lost. As I noted in my earlier study in Ningxia in the mid-1980s, rising Islamic conservatism led to the decline in interest in government-sponsored education. A decrease in public school enrollment, and an increase in children studying the Quran in private madrasahs attached to local mosques, is another phenomenon that had local Ningxia cadres concerned. This growing interest in pursuing religious education has not yet reached large proportions among the Hui in Na Homestead; only ten school-age children were not attending public school in 1985. Instead, they were studying the Quran at home privately. There are four officially permitted *manla* (young Quranic students) in the village. In more heavily populated Hui areas, however, this is becoming a more noticeable trend. In Guyuan County, Jiefangxiang (Liberation Township), only twelve out of 104 school-age children in the village are attending school, and twenty-seven of those not in school are studying the Quran in the mosque.

This trend has become even more pronounced in conservative Muslim areas, such as Linxia Hui Autonomous Prefecture, Gansu Province, where Muslim minorities are 52.7 percent of the population.[6] School enrollment has regularly decreased since 1978, from 77.2 percent at that time to 66.6 percent in 1979, to 60 percent in 1980, to 57.3 percent in 1981, and to 50 percent in 1982. In Hanfeng Commune, a completely Han area, enrollment of children reaches as high as 93.9 percent, and among girls it is 79 percent. In the neighboring mountainous Badan Commune, an all-Muslim area, enrollment was 23.9 percent in 1982, with only 9.1 percent of girls enrolled. By the end of the school year, only 2.9 percent of the girls remained in school. This reflects the common practice

6.   Of a population of 1.3 million in 1981, the Hui were 37.7 percent (489,571), the Dongxiang 17.2 percent (223,240), the Baonan 0.6 percent (7,683), and the Salar 0.3 percent (4,364).

of children attending school for the first few weeks of registration, but returning full-time to the farm before completing the term.[7]

In a *China Daily* (1987c:1) front-page article entitled 'Keep rural girls in school', Liu Su,[8] the Vice-Governor of Gansu Province, reported that out of 157,300 school-age children not in school in Gansu, 85 percent of them were girls. Children leave school for a variety of reasons, including the farm's need for income-producing labor under the newly introduced responsibility system. Yet many Hui point to traditional Islamic views that have made them reluctant to send their children, especially daughters, to public schools.

When asked about their reluctance to send their children to school, Na Homestead parents expressed doubts about 'the value of learning Chinese and mathematics'. 'It would be much more useful,' I was told by one mother, 'for our children to learn the Quran, Arabic and Persian.' If a child excelled, he or she might become a *manla*, and eventually perhaps an *ahong*. Their status in the village would be much higher than the average middle school or even high school graduate, as would their income (estimated at 100 to 500 yuan a month for a well-known teaching *ahong*). Children who are in poor health are often kept at home to study the Quran. In large families with more than one son, generally one child is encouraged to study to become an *ahong*. Although the government officially allows each mosque to support from two to four full-time *manla* — who should be at least eighteen years old and junior middle school graduates — many younger children study at home without official approval.

Ningxia, as the only autonomous region for China's Hui Muslims, tends to monitor *ahong* training and religious practice more closely than other areas where Hui are concentrated. In Yunnan's

---

7.   For further information on the economic situation in Linxia, see Linxia Hui Autonomous Prefectural Basic Situation Committee (1986). Other helpful introductions to Hui autonomous counties that I have been able to collect, include: Dachang Huizu Zizhixian Gaikuang (1985); Minhe Hui and Tu Autonomous County Basic Situation Committee (1986); Mengcun Huizu Zizhixian Gaikuang (1983); Menyuan Hui Autonomous County Basic Situation Committee (1985); Hualong Hui Autonomous County Basic Situation Committee (1984); and Changji Autonomous Prefectural Situation Committee (1985). For the Hui in Gansu, see Ma Tong (1983).

8.   All names used in this study are real unless indicated as pseudonyms.

Weishan Yi and Hui Autonomous County, several mosques had more than twenty resident *manla* studying under well-known *ahong*. In Gansu's Linxia Hui Autonomous Prefecture, at the South Great Mosque there were more than 130 full-time students. In Linxia city's Bafang district, where most of the Hui are concentrated, there were at least sixty full-time *manla* in each mosque. Mirroring the spiritual importance of Mecca and the centrality of theological learning of the Iranian city of Qum for China's Hui Muslims (*cf.* Fischer 1980), Linxia's famous mosques and scholars attract students from all over China.[9]

Renowned mosques in Yunnan's Shadian and Weishan counties tend to attract students from throughout the southwest, including Hainan Island. At an ordination (*chuanyi*) service I attended at the Xiao Weigeng Mosque in Weishan County in February 1985, the ten graduates included one Hainan Island student and six students from outside the county who had studied there for five years. The Hainan student had a brother studying the Quran in Beijing. The next class admitted thirty students, ten from the local village, ten from other villages, and ten from outside the county, including one from outside Yunnan. That these *manla* travel long distances to study under celebrated *ahong* demonstrates that national ties continue to link disparate Hui communities. It also reveals the growing importance of religious education in the countryside.

In the northwest, in addition to allowing from two to four students (*halifat*) to train privately in each mosque, the government has approved and funded two Islamic schools (*yixueyuan*) in Yinchuan and Tongxin. In 1988 the state provided funding to establish a large Islamic seminary and mosque complex outside the West Gate of Yinchuan, near Luo village. Similarly, in Ürümqi the Islamic college was established in 1985, and other regional and provincial government's have followed suit. This indicates a

9. A rather new development is the sending of Hui *manla* to mosques in Xinjiang, where Arabic-language study is much more advanced due to the influence of the Arabic script in Uyghur and to the proximity to Pakistan, with its Karakoram Highway. In September 1987, while visiting a mosque in Kashgar, I met a Hui *manla* from Hezhou who was studying there for six years for precisely those reasons. He mentioned his desire to travel to Mecca through Pakistan, and how much more inexpensive and convenient the hajj had become since the opening of the highway. He served at the only Hui mosque among the 160 Uyghur mosques in the city.

'regionalization' of state-sponsored Islamic education, which until the 1980s had been officially concentrated at the China Islamic Affairs Commission in Beijing, established in 1956.

The increased promotion of exchange with foreign Muslim countries is exposing more urban Hui to international aspects of their religious heritage. Among urban Hui, Islamic knowledge tends to be higher than in rural areas, perhaps because of increased educational levels and more media exposure. The majority knew of Khomeini and the location of Mecca. Unlike the vast majority of Hui in rural areas, many urban Hui interviewed knew of and often read the magazine *Zhongguo Musilin* (*China's Muslims*), published by the Chinese Islamic Association. Few were aware of and interested in the sectarian disputes in the Iran–Iraq conflict, but most knew of Shi'ism.

Public and private discourse on Islamic knowledge in China

This chapter has examined the nature of the transmission of Islamic knowledge from two perspectives: first, that of the public state-sponsored representation and education of China's Muslims; and second, that of the Muslims themselves, their self-representation and methods of Islamic education. It is clear that neither of these streams of Islamic knowledge transmission is separate from the other; both have intermingled, but they have never really merged. It is surprising that although those these two streams have at times flooded over into each other, they have never fully blended, and as a result many Muslim communities continue to live in very different worlds than those of their neighbors of Han and other nationalities. The rise of private schools in China today may see the return of private Muslim schools (*muzi xuexiao*), which arose in Beijing at the beginning of the 20th century. While much of the data for this chapter is drawn from the Hui, shared Islamic concerns make quite similar many of the traditions and debates among Muslims in China regarding education, modernization, and the state. At the same time, all Muslims in China, no matter what their language or nationality, have been subjected to the same government educational policy and centralized curricula.

Until state education in China begins to incorporate more Muslim information about Islam, these streams will continue to run parallel, leading to continued misunderstandings and misrepresentations. In addition, until Chinese educational policy recognizes 'cultural levels' that are based on other knowledge traditions and languages, many more-conservative Muslims might continue to resist sending their children – especially their daughters – to state schools. Given the money to be made in the free-market economy, at which many Muslims are quite adept, there may be even less incentive to attract and keep those Muslim children in state schools. The mosque might become an even more practical source of an alternative education, a source of knowledge that has persisted throughout China's Muslim regions since the Prophet Muhammad enjoined the new Muslim community of the world to seek knowledge even unto China.

13
SUBALTERN PERSPECTIVES
ON PROSPERITY

Cell phones and beepers: capitalism comes to the Hui

Last Spring, in a solemn ceremony at Beijing's ancient Temple of Heaven, Li Xiaohua the one-time peasant became the first Chinese to own a Ferrari. ('China is Taking a Great Leap into the Auto Age', *Toronto Globe and Mail* 18 August 1994)[1]

Ding Yongwei beeped me. On a February 1994 visit to Quanzhou city in southern Fujian Province, Mr Ding called me on his cellular phone from his private car.[2] I received the call on the beeper (in Chinese, known as a '*bi pi ji*'), which he had lent me (and had to show me how to use, since I had never used one before).[3] When I first met Mr Ding in 1984, I had just begun to study the collection of villages where the people surnamed Ding resided, officially recognized as members of the Hui minority nationality in 1979 (see Gladney 1996a:290–5). The villagers at that time still depended

1. For further discussion, see footnote 10, page 304.
2. The visit was due to participation in a UNESCO-sponsored conference 'Contributions of Islamic Culture on China's Maritime Silk Route', Quanzhou, Fujian, 21 to 26 February 1994. The conference was hosted by the Fujian Academy of Social Sciences and the Fujian Maritime Museum.
3. A United Press International article, 'Chinese Mobile Phone Industry Booms' (17 April 1994), reported that the number of cellular-phone users in China increased by 20 percent in the first quarter of 1994 to 784,000, while that of pager owners increased 13 percent to more than 6 million. 'Rapidly growing sales have catapulted China into the third largest mobile telecommunications market in the world after the United States and Japan. The 1993 sales of mobile phones reached 461,000, 2.7 times higher than all previous years combined … Pagers, called "beeper machines" in vernacular Chinese, and, more recently, cellular phones, known as "big brothers," have become something of a status symbol to China's nouveau rich. Many businessmen adorn themselves as a way of showing off their new wealth'.

primarily on agriculture and aquaculture for their living, and had only just begun to experience the rapid rise in income that would lead to Mr Ding lending me his beeper just ten years later.

In a formal interview, Mr Liu Zhengqing, the Vice-Mayor of Chendai township, told me that the Ding villagers were so wealthy that in one village of 600 households, there were 700 telephones, most of them cellular. When I asked my old friend Ding Yongwei if he was doing well, he held out his cellular phone and declared: 'If I wasn't wealthy, could I be holding this?' (*'Bu fu de hua, zheige nade qi ma?'*) He later explained that the government's decision to recognize the Ding community as members of the Hui minority in 1979 was primarily responsible not only for their new-found economic prosperity, but also for a tremendous subsequent fascination with their ethnic and religious roots. In this case, the Ding claim to be descended from foreign Muslim traders who settled in Quanzhou in the 9th century. When I first began to learn about this area in the early 1980s, these Hui were known to be among not only the least-developed people in southern Fujian, but also the most-assimilated into the local Han Chinese culture (Zhuang 1993). Now, just ten years later, the members of the Hui nationality in this township have prospered far more quickly than the Han Fujianese, accounting for one-third of the township's income, even though their population amounts to only one-seventh of the total.

This chapter will consider the economic success of the Hui in two communities in China, contrasting 'Muslim' entrepreneurialism with recent changes in capitalistic practice among the Han, with whom these Muslims have lived and interacted for nearly 1,200 years. I shall argue that while the Muslim Chinese may not be more 'predisposed' toward business than any other Chinese, there has been a less ambivalent view toward the market among Muslims than the Han. This has to do not only with role of the market in promoting Islam among the Hui, but also with the role of the state in encouraging Muslim participation in the market, while formally restricting Han entrepreneurialism as antisocialist. Changes in PRC policy toward private business under Deng's maxim 'To get rich is glorious' stimulated a profound debate about the market among the Han Chinese in general, as well as a tangible ambivalence, as evidenced by widely publicized corruption cases, growing income discrepancies, and active debates in the public media. This ambivalence does not exist among the Hui. Indeed, it is quite the opposite. Entrepreneurial ability has been promoted as their main 'national characteristic'.

I have noted elsewhere that while I was conducting my field-work in northwestern China, where Muslims are more populous and lived in more isolated rural enclaves, it was often the case that Hui came in contact with Han only in the marketplace, in the trad-ing arena where they maintained distinct competitive exchange and exploitative relationships (see Gladney 1996a:315–28). We can also see in more recent market-related debates among the Han a similar point of divergence, where Han often debate the merits of prosperity (and its concomitant social problems), while Hui regard market success as an opportunity for ethnic and religious advance-ment. Indeed, in his extensive discussion of Hui economic history in China, Lai Cunli (1988:310) has argued that 'the commercial capital of the Hui nationality played an active role in the sprouts of Chinese capitalism'.

The flourishing of traditional economic practice among the Hui flies in the face of a centrally planned Stalinist policy that, as Stark and Nee have argued (1989), originally sought to limit pri-vate enterprise and to encourage national integration. I argue that one of the reasons ethnic nationality has become such an impor-tant aspect of one's identity in the People's Republic (and indeed, in the former and emergent nations of the Soviet Union and East-ern Europe) is the legitimation that Stalinist–Leninist legalization provides for such categories of national identity, endowing it with a legality to an extent that it promised power for those who could claim it, one that could be used by them for their own benefit, as well as by others, often to their detriment in times of national chauvinism. Rather than any inherent predisposition for trade, I suggest that it was state policy that encouraged and stimulated en-trepreneurialism among the Hui, while at the same time restricting it as still 'antisocialist' among the Han. I have sought in the past to argue that the rise of ethnic consciousness was an unintended consequence of departures from centralized economic planning in China, as well as in the former Soviet Union (see Gladney 1995). In this chapter I shall argue that economic success in two Hui communities reflects a very different discourse with respect to the market among Hui than takes place among the Han, an approach that shifts in the state's policy have helped to stimulate among the Hui, while at the same time having led to profound ambivalences among the Han, even as many become enriched through participation in the market.

Muslim nationality, Chinese state

Having one foot in the Muslim world and another well-planted in Chinese civilization, the Hui Muslim nationality (which numbered 8.6 million according to the 2000 census) were traditionally well-situated to serve as cultural and economic mediators within Chinese society, as well as between the Han Chinese majority and other non-Han minorities in Chinese society. This traditional role was severely limited during the collectivization and religious reform campaigns in the late 1950s and early 1960s. With the relaxation of restrictions on private enterprise, and on ethnic and religious expression in the early 1980s, not only did traditional Muslim trading roles re-emerge, but Muslim communities prospered as well. In this chapter I shall specifically examine economic and social changes in two Hui communities, including a recently recognized Hui lineage community on the southeast coast and a Sufi community in the rural northwest, arguing that although the state allowed, and indeed encouraged economic privatization and ethnic expression, it neither was prepared for nor envisioned the speed and vitality with which Muslims returned to their ethnoreligious roots and exploited opportunities for self and community advancement.

This material is drawn from my larger study (Gladney 1996a), but here I shall focus more directly upon entrepreneurialism and economic activity, and also update some material in the Hui communities of Quanzhou and Ningxia. The cases are drawn from two communities, one on the southeast coast of China, where the nation has recently prospered at a dramatic rate, as well as another in the northwest, an area that has generally lagged behind coastal China in economic development. Nevertheless, similar issues with respect to the market pertain to both communities and are worth considering here.

Hui Muslims were known throughout Chinese history as specialized tradesmen in such areas as transport, wool trade, jewelry working, and operating small food stands. Specializations ranged widely in scale and varied regionally according to the socioeconomic position of the Hui in urban or rural settings. Before 1949, the term 'Hui' referred to any person claiming to be Muslim or of

Muslim descent. At Yenan, and later during the first Chinese census in 1953, Hui came to designate one nationality (*minzu*), which distinguished it from the nine other identified Muslim nationalities in China (Uyghur, Kazakh, Kyrgyz, and so on), as well as from the Han majority nationality and fifty-four other minority nationalities. As Walker Connor (1984:25) noted, this policy of nationality recognition in China was in keeping with a *temporary* Stalinist–Leninist policy that sought to enlist minority support for the new nation, and that national consciousness, once awakened, like class-consciousness would gradually fade with national unification and the erosion of class difference. In keeping with this policy (perhaps even more faithfully than the Soviets), Chairman Mao and the early Yenan Communists eventually only promised autonomy, and not the possibility of secession, for the minority regions who submitted to state authority (see Gladney 1996a:87–93).

Traditional Hui Muslim specializations were virtually lost after the 1955 collectivization reforms, but have rapidly returned since the 1978 economic liberalization policy. Not only in the ancient Silk Road maritime port Quanzhou, where this chapter begins, but also throughout the villages and towns where Muslims now live, Hui have prospered at an incredible rate through strong participation in small private businesses and industry – in many places far surpassing their Han neighbors. Local Hui say they are gifted as small businessmen and new economic policies have allowed them to express that aspect of their ethnic identity. Yet these policies were originally intended only to raise their standard of living, as well as their consciousness, to that of the Han, never to surpass them.

Many of these policies were originally intended to encourage economic development and the Four Modernizations. In the process, they have allowed freer religious expression of Hui identity. With this resurgence of ethnoreligious identity, socioeconomic development has also improved. Once criticized as 'capitalist tails' who thrived on business ventures, the Hui were constantly accused of maintaining feudalist, antisocialist, and exploitative practices. By contrast, in a 1987 interview, Fei Xiaotong suggested that socioeconomic development of minority areas would be enhanced if the minorities themselves played a greater role. Minority participation in economic development should be encouraged, rather than a continuance of the former policies of providing government assistance to minority areas and promoting minority customs, such as traditional songs and dances. Professor Fei specifically suggested that Hui entrepreneurial talents should be given more freedom in order to assist the expansion of local market economies:

In July and August last year, I visited Linxia Hui Autonomous Prefecture, Gansu Province, during which I was deeply impressed by the fact that the Hui people there are very smart traders. They have been blessed with this talent from their ancestors, who nurtured trading skills during centuries-long commercial dealings between farmers and herdsmen. This tradition has been developed mainly due to their geographical locations, which are inserted between the Qinghai-Tibet Plateau inhabited by nomadic groups and the country's farming areas ... I think that the Hui people might play a significant role in the development of these two regions. (Fei Xiaotong, quoted in 'Minorities Hold Key to Own Prosperity', *China Daily* 28 April 1987, 4)

This statement is significant in that it identifies 'entrepreneurialism' as one of the main 'nationality traits' (*minzu tedian*) that distinguishes the Hui and binds them together as a nationality. According to the Stalinist definition of nationality, which has served as the cornerstone of Chinese nationality policy, to be recognized as a nationality a group must possess one or more of the 'four commons': a common economy, locality, language, or 'culture'. The Hui have been traditionally difficult to identify according to this scheme because of their vast diversity: they share no common area, practice, language, or identity, and the state has been reluctant to allow Islam as the one trait binding them together, because not all Hui believe in Islam (some are Party members or secularists) and the Chinese Communist state does not wish to encourage them to do so (see Gladney 1996a:21–36). Nevertheless, it is Islam, or the memory of it, that is the only thing that all Hui have in common, and they are the sole minority in China to share only a religious identity. Clearly, not all Hui are entrepreneurs, even though it is something to which they might aspire.

By identifying the Hui as sharing 'entrepreneurialism' as their common 'culture', instead of Islam, a Stalinist secularist rationale for their recognition is now provided. Hui entrepreneurialism can therefore no longer be criticized as feudal or exploitative, since it is part of their minority culture and identity. This recognition of the unique contribution Hui entrepreneurial abilities might make to economic development represents a dramatic shift from past criticisms of these characteristics as capitalistic and feudal. Perhaps to seek historical support for this state policy, Lai Cunli, in his 312-page survey *Hui Economic History*, which was commissioned by the China Minority Nationality Research office of the State Commission for Ethnic Affairs, provides a detailed historical recitation of the entrepreneurial role Hui have played throughout Chinese history. He then argues that their 'minority culture' was uniquely entrepreneurial compared to other nationalities in China, and that this 'business culture' was responsible for making major contributions to the development of China's economy (Lai 1988:3, 283). Lai (1988:276) concludes, 'One can see that business activity of the early Hui ancestors was an extremely great influence on the formation of the formation of the Hui nationality'. The well-known Hui historian Ma Tong argues that the early Hui ancestors being primarily traders, businessmen, and soldiers had a profound influence on their later formation as a nationality:

Based on the analysis of historical records, Arab, Persian, Central Asian and other foreigner businessmen, soldiers, officials, and missionaries who believed in Islam and came to China are the ancestors of the Hui nationality, since they resided in China and even married Han women, they gradually formed into the Huihui nationality, and became an important member of our country's great multi-national family ... From the very earliest period, the vast majority of Islamic disciples in China were engaged in trade and business activity. (Ma Tong 1983:86–7)

Perhaps as a result of this revisionist cultural history and open state support for Hui traditions of entrepreneurialism, a new Islamic college was recently set up in Xi'an, advertising courses in small business and 'Muslim entrepreneurialism', as well as improved opportunities for foreign travel that training in Arabic and Persian would provide.

Ethnoreligious revitalization in a northwestern Sufi community

The following text was inscribed on the entrance to a well-known mosque in Ningxia, northwestern China. It reveals much about local Muslim sentiment toward the new-found prosperity in the region.

Suggestions for Muslims
We suggest that Muslims practice the five tenets regularly;
do not put off today until tomorrow, tomorrow to the next day.

When natural and national disasters come, it is too late to regret;
days and months pass, and the truth is lost.

In a glance, children become adults, and adults become elderly;
very many people do not consider death.

Every day you clean and order your house to establish its future,
but abandon prayer, neglect to give alms, and are very stingy.

You have one hundred, but want a thousand; you get it and desire ten
thousand;
your desire is uncontrollable, without satisfaction; the more you have the
more you desire.

Today you go east, tomorrow west, mind and body are never at peace;
anxiety becomes happiness, happiness becomes anxiety; anxiety is great,
happiness is limited.

You don't practice the prayers on time; they are postponed until
tomorrow;
because of laziness, you waste the future (for 10,000 years); what a pity!

You are a created person; why not consider the results more carefully?
Maintaining the prayers will not interfere with your daily life.

Because of contentment you disregard the lessons, committing myriad
errors;
if you were very wealthy, but you died suddenly, your wealth would be
gone forever.

Hoarding money amounts to nothing; in the end even a little bit can't be
taken with you.
You build many houses, but in daily life you have need of only one.

Stocking up on food, you can only eat to the full one *jin* and a half *liang*.
Your trunks stuffed with clothes; they amount to nothing; you can only
wear one outfit.

Abounding in grace, extremely wealthy, it looks good for a little while.
You enjoy it for this life, but in the afterlife, you certainly will owe a great
deal.

Prosperity has come to Na Homestead with Hui involvement in
free enterprise in the village since the early 1980s.[4] With prosperity,

4. Based on 1984 statistics, Na Homestead comprised 767 households, with a
    total population of 3,871. There were 745 Hui households, amounting to
    more than 95 percent of the population. More than 60 percent of the Hui in
    the village were surnamed Na. Although Najiahu is located in the Ningxia

Hui villagers have had to be reminded of the purpose of wealth: not for personal gain, but to serve the community and the faith, both vulnerable for Muslims ensconced in a society dominated by Chinese Communists. Located near a bend of the Yellow River just south of Yinchuan city, Na Homestead is a rather isolated Hui village in a majority Han area of Ningxia Hui Autonomous Region. It is noteworthy that 'religious enterprise' has become so profitable in the village that several of the highest-ranking Communist Party cadres have left the Party to become imams (religious elders) in the mosque.

As an economic indicator, mosque income (*sifei*) derived from offerings (*nietie*) rose dramatically. According to the mosque's own careful accounting records, in 1985–86 it averaged more than 20,000 yuan (US$6,700) annual income from offerings. Based on an outside study, over a four-month period during 1984–85, offerings of grain produce, goods, or money totaled 8,997.23 yuan (about US$3,000). An economic survey of expenditures of 113 Hui households in Na Homestead revealed that average giving to the mosque was 47 yuan per household, or 8.40 yuan per person, in 1984 (Wang Yiping 1985:7; Gong 1987:38). If this average is applied to the entire Hui community of the village, then the mosque's total income in 1986 was well over 32,500 yuan (US$10,833). The money supports the staff of seven *ahongs*, including one 'teaching' or head *ahong* (*kaixue ahong* or *jiaozhang*) and four student *ahongs* (*halifat*, from *khalî fa*, 'successor', or *manla*, from *mullah*), and the daily upkeep of the mosque. Offerings are given during the three main religious holidays, and to individual *ahongs* when they read the Quran at weddings, funerals, and naming ceremonies. Giving at funerals by the family to guests and to the mosque ranges from 100 to 1,000 yuan. Reportedly, as much as 2,500 yuan has been paid when the status of the deceased was extremely high.

On one holiday celebrated in Na Homestead, the Prophet's Day or Muhammad's Birthday (*Shengji*), on 7 December 1984, I witnessed offerings brought by children and adults: bags of flour or rice and fistfuls of money. A group of mosque officials dutifully

---

Hui Autonomous Region, only 32.1 percent of the total population of the region in 1982 was Hui (Ningxia Hui Autonomous Region Population Census Office 1983:6), and the majority of Hui lived in the southern end of the region. Little has changed since these statistics were published.

registered each offering according to amount, name, and team number. Gifts totaled 3,000 kilograms of wheat, 2,500 kilograms of rice and 300 yuan (US$100), equal to approximately 3,313 yuan (US$1,100). None of the donated money is required for the restoration of the mosque building (*qianliang*). The mosque has received more than 90,000 yuan (US$30,000) from the State Commission for Ethnic Affairs between 1981, when it was identified as a national monument, and 1991.

Donations to the mosque came from a village considered fairly poor by neighboring village standards, with an average annual income of 300 yuan (about US$100) per household. Average per capita annual income in Yongning County in 1982 was substantially higher, 539 yuan according to the Population Census Office (1987:206). Poor households (*pinkun hu*) occupied 2 percent of the village. Mosque income, however, does not necessarily reflect total giving per household. A study of seventeen households from three different villages belonging to different Islamic orders found that of an annual average income of 96.67 yuan, 8.96 yuan (9.26 percent) were given to religious concerns in 1980.

Na Homestead has 5,036 *mu* (326 hectares) of land under cultivation, planting mainly rice, winter wheat, sorghum, and some fruit from a few orchards. Average land per person is 1.37 *mu* (0.08 hectares), and 6.95 *mu* (0.45 hectares) per household, somewhat less than in neighboring Han villages. Average grain yield per *mu* in Na Homestead is about 200 kilograms, less than the regional average of 238 kilograms. Important shifts in the involvement of the local labor force since the private responsibility system was introduced in 1979, however, reveal significant socioeconomic change. These changes in the labor force reveal a significant decline in collective activity and power since the dismantling of the commune, as documented elsewhere in China (see Diamond 1985; Lardy 1986:99–102; Shue 1984). In 1978, 27.8 percent of the village population was involved in the labor force. However, by 1984 that figure had grown to 49.6 percent of the village, reflecting similar pre-1950 levels. In the entire Ningxia region, 83.5 percent of the total Hui population were engaged in agriculture and husbandry, according to the 1982 census (Ningxia 1983:74). In terms of the entire country, the 1982 census reported that 60.7 percent of all Hui and 84 percent of all ethnic groups were engaged in agriculture and husbandry (Population Census Office 1987:xx, 28).

Agriculture and husbandry, industry and construction, and small sideline enterprises (such as cottage industries, private shops and food stands, and transportation and service industries) are the three main industries. A significant change in sideline industries has absorbed much of the increased labor. While only 1.6 percent of the labor force was involved in these small enterprises in 1978, involvement increased to 16 percent by 1984, slightly less than the 1950 levels of 17.6 percent. In a study of 113 households, sixty people were engaged in sideline businesses, representing 19 percent of the labor force. In 1978, only one person was involved in food-related small business, and no one from the village was involved in service or transportation. By 1984, however, eighty-five people were in the food trade, twenty-six in service industry, and twenty-four in transport (Zhu 1985:4). In terms of the small food industry, eight households opened small restaurants in Yanghe township, with several others selling *yang zasui* – a traditional Hui spicy stew made from the internal organs of sheep.

Participation in the free market and the private responsibility system has also encouraged Hui in Na Homestead to increase their planting of vegetables and cash crops, significantly higher than 1978 levels. While agricultural income derived from cash crops in 1984 was only half as much as 1957, it was more than three times that of 1978, before the responsibility system was instituted in Na Homestead. Before 1949, Hui proclivity for growing cash crops in this area was noted by Fan Changjiang. He observed that the opium produced by Han and Hui peasants in the Yanghe area was of a very high quality, but the Han could not make much of a profit from it. The Han smoked too much of the opium themselves and were too weak to gain financially from it. However, the Hui did not smoke opium and their fields produced 120 *liang* (6 kilograms) per *mu* whereas Han fields yielded only 70 *liang* (3.5 kilograms) per *mu* (Fan 1937:312).

Some Hui complain that they have no alternative than to engage in small business, because the land they have been allotted is too small in area or unproductive. After the 19th-century Hui rebellions, the Hui in Shaanxi, Gansu, and Ningxia were often forced to live in areas with steep mountains and saline flatlands, which the Han avoided. While attempts to redress many of these inequities were made during the land-reform campaigns of the early 1950s, some Hui feel that they still have poorer land than Han and are thus compelled to be more interested in business. On his 1980 tour of southern Ningxia's Guyuan District (six counties), where the Hui are most concentrated (occupying 45.7 percent of the total population in Guyuan, 49.1 percent of Ningxia Region's total Hui population), Hu Yaobang remarked that this area was China's most impoverished region. In 1983, the State Council set up a special committee to encourage economic development in Guyuan District, Ningxia, and Longxi and Dingxi counties, Gansu.

The Hui from Na Homestead also played an important role in the local free-market economy. The Hui operated 70 percent of the new restaurants, food stands, and private sales stalls in the nearby Yongning County Seat market area, even though they constituted only 12.6 percent of the population. They also participated in the central free market in Wuzhong city, 30 kilometers south. There, Hui merchants comprised more than 90 percent of those doing business, in a city that was 95 percent Han. Most of the Hui came into the city to do business from outlying Hui villages like Dongfeng township, which was 95 percent Hui. This active entrepreneurial participation is an important aspect of Hui ethnoreligious identity. As one Han peasant from Na Homestead remarked, 'The Hui are good at doing business; the Han are too honest and can't turn a profit. Han are good at planting, Hui at trade'.

Only 2 percent of households in Na Homestead were *wanyuan hu* (thousand-yuan households) at the time of my study, reporting an annual income of more than 10,000 yuan. While this is not a large percentage compared to some areas in China, it is unusual in a fairly poor northwestern region. The prestige and influence of these *wanyuan hu* was significant. Na Jingling, the most successful of Na Homestead's new entrepreneurs, made his original fortune through setting up an ice cream (*binggun*) factory in 1982. A former mechanic for the commune, he has since moved into the transportation and construction business with his brother. They entered into a contract with two other investors and built an 'Islamic' hotel (the Pure and True Islamic Hotel, *qingzhen Musilin fandian*) in Yinchuan city at a cost of 1.4 million yuan. The hotel features a restaurant and shopping facilities with 'Arabic' architecture.

Economic prosperity among rural Hui as a result of favorable government policy and Hui entrepreneurial abilities has led to an unintended and unexpected increase in support for religious affairs. Na Jingling, for example, wants to use his profits to help the

Hui in Ningxia, support the mosque, and build a 'really *qing zhen* (pure and true)' Islamic hotel. Other Hui *wanyuan hu* told me that because Allah was responsible for their new-found wealth under the new government policies, they should devote some of their profits to promoting Islam and constructing mosques. Red posters on the walls in every mosque clearly list by name and amount who has given to the construction projects, with names of these *wanyuan hu* and their donations writ large. Wealthier Hui sometimes complained to me of the pressures brought to bear on them to contribute to the mosque. Local cadres complained that they could not stop religious donations without angering local Hui and interrupting economic development. Yet no one complained about the benefits of prosperity for contributing to the well-being of the community and to Islam.

Hui economic prosperity and ethnic reinvention in Fujian

The Fujianese lineage community surnamed Ding has lived in Chendai township on the southern Fujian coast since the Wanli period of the Ming dynasty (1573–1620), where they supposedly fled from Quanzhou city to avoid persecution for being associated with the former Muslim mayor under the defeated Mongols. Since that time they have been known for their specialized aquacultural economy. Before 1949 they not only were engaged in this industry, but also produced opium and had many small factories that made woven bags and sundry goods. These goods were exported extensively, which led to the migration of many Ding Hui to Southeast Asia, Taiwan, and Hong Kong in their business endeavors. After 1955, when private industries were collectivized in China, these small factories were either curtailed or transferred to the larger commune, of which the Ding lineage comprised seven brigades.

I have discussed elsewhere the revitalized Hui national identity among the Ding in Quanzhou, and the unintended consequences of departures from centralized state planning in the region (see Gladney 1995; 1996:260–91). Here I shall summarize the recent tremendous economic growth in the region for the purposes of this chapter's focus on Muslim prosperity in China. Since 1979 and the implementation of the economic reform policies in the countryside, the members of the Ding lineage community have been recognized as being of the Hui nationality, and have once again become engaged in private small factories producing athletic shoes and plastic goods, like the brightly colored plastic sandals, rugs, and other sundries found in most Chinese department stores. Of the 3,350 households in the seven villages (former brigades) in Chendai (in which 92 percent are Hui), more than sixty ran small factories in 1991. By 1994, most households derived their primary incomes from these 'sideline' enterprises. By the late 1990s, all households had become engaged in running small factories, or derived their primary income from them. In the larger factories there are more than 100 workers, and in smaller ones only ten or more.

Average annual income in the predominately Hui Chendai township in 1983 was 611 yuan per person, whereas in the larger, Han-dominated Jinjiang County it was only 402 yuan in 1982 (Population Census Office 1987:175). By 1984 Chendai income reached 837 yuan per person for the town, while the Hui within Chendai averaged 1,100 yuan. Their income increased 33 percent in 1985. By 1989, the entire township's income had jumped to an average annual income of 1,000 yuan per person (Ding 1990:3). This indicates a substantial increase of local Hui income over Han income, in the county as well as the township. It is clear that economic success was not limited to the Hui, since Han in Fujian also prospered during this period.[5]

Finally, income from sideline enterprises in agriculture and small industry has also grown at an incredibly rapid rate. In 1984, Chendai was the first town in Fujian Province to become a *yiyuan zhen* (100 million *yuan* town). More than half of the Hui in the town have their own two- to four-level homes paid for with cash from their savings. Many of the multilevel homes that I visited had small piecework factories in the first level (making a tennis shoe sole here, the lining there, laces elsewhere, and so on), while the various stem family branches lived in the other levels. For example, Ding Yongwei, mentioned at the beginning of this chapter, has two sons. On the first level of his four-storey stone-block home, he has a small factory that produces the stretch fabric that is used to line the inside of athletic shoes. He obtains the materials from a distant relative in the Philippines. His youngest son and wife live on the second floor. His oldest son, wife, and two children live on the

5. Note that 1989 figures are based on Ding (1991), whereas records for 1979 to 1993 are derived from my field notes and the township records.

third floor (as a Hui, Ding's son is allowed to have two children). Ding Yongwei and his wife occupy the top floor.

Income from sideline enterprises multiplied by a factor of eight during 1979. Prior to 1978 most of the labor force (69.9 percent) in Chendai was engaged in agriculture and only 30 percent in industry. By 1992 this had shifted dramatically, with 93 percent of the labor force engaged in industry and sideline enterprises.

The Ding believe that this was due to their recognition as Hui. When they were recognized as part of the Hui nationality in 1979, they became eligible for assistance as members of an underprivileged minority. They received several government subsidies that spurred their economy. From 1980 until 1984, the government gave more than 200,000 yuan to the seven Hui teams. With the funds, they built a running-water system, ponds for raising fish, and the means to expand their razor-clam industry. The Ministry of Education gave 40,000 yuan to build a middle school, and 33,000 yuan for a primary school. They also receive benefits as a minority nationality in preference for high school and college entrance. Under special birth-planning policies for minorities, each couple is allowed to have one more child than a Han couple. Hui representation in the local government is also higher than their proportion in the population. Two of the ten Party committee representatives (*changwei*) were surnamed Ding in 1985, as was the town's Party Secretary.

Over 50 percent of the Ding lineage members have overseas relatives – mainly in the Philippines, Indonesia, and Singapore – a higher proportion than among their Han neighbors (see Li 1991: 337–46). They have re-established communication with these relatives and have been assisted by frequent remittances. This outside income is an important factor in the rapid economic development of the seven Ding villages. All seven Hui villages have elementary schools, thanks to donations from overseas relatives, averaging 20,000 yuan each. Neighboring Han villages have one elementary school for every three or four villages. The Ding say their close and frequent contact with overseas relatives is a result of their strong feelings of ethnic solidarity, which they say surpasses that of neighboring Han lineages with their overseas relations. It is remarkable, however, that a conversation with one wealthy village family that maintained extensive overseas relations revealed that overseas relatives are often reluctant to admit their Islamic heritage.

PRC policy that accords special economic and political privileges to these recently recognized Hui along the southeast coast and encourages their interaction with foreign Muslim governments has had a significant impact on their ethnic identity. Fujian provincial and local municipal publications proudly proclaim Quanzhou as the site of the third most important Islamic holy grave and the fifth most important mosque in the world.[6] Religious and government representatives from more than thirty Muslim nations were escorted to Muslim sites in Quanzhou as part of a state-sponsored delegation in spring 1986. Foreign Muslim guests are frequently hosted by the local Quanzhou City Islamic Association. The UNESCO-sponsored Silk Roads Expedition arrived in Quanzhou in February 1991 as its main port of entry on China's maritime Silk Road, virtually bypassing the traditional stopping-place of Canton. During the four-day conference and Silk Road festivities, in which I participated, the foreign guests and Muslim dignitaries were brought to the Chendai Ding village as part of their orientation, to highlight the recent economic prosperity and government support for the modern descendants of the ancient Muslim maritime traders.

It is also important to note that the reforms and prosperity that have come to Ding villagers have not been restricted to the Muslim Hui Ding; they have benefited the entire township. Chendai township has not only a 10 percent Han population, but also many among the Ding who do not believe in Islam, including folk religionists and even about eighty households of Christians, who were nevertheless registered as members of the Hui 'Muslim' nationality. These Ding converted in the 1930s under the influence of a Western Lutheran missionary, and they too have recently rebuilt their church, possibly because the local government allowed the construction of the Islamic prayer hall. As noted above, although the Ding lineage only occupies one-seventh of the town's population, it accounts for more than one-third of the area's total annual income. Economic prosperity has been accompanied by ethnic and even religious revival. These lineages have always maintained a Hui identity that, in conjunction with recent events, only now is

6. See the pamphlet compiled by the Committee for Protecting Islamic Historical Relics in Quanzhou and the Research Centre for the Historical Relics of Chinese Culture, Yang Hongxun (1985:1–15).

beginning to take on a decidedly Islamic commitment, something quite unforeseen when the state chose to recognize the Ding as Hui in 1979.

Reflections on Hui prosperity, north and south

It is clear that Hui in Quanzhou and Ningxia regard their new-found prosperity in entirely positive terms, as an indication of their ethnic solidarity in Quanzhou and as a reward for their religious perseverance in Ningxia. In Quanzhou, material success is attributed to ethnic entrepreneurialism among a lineage that maintains only a distant memory of Islam, but a memory that is now being revived. In Ningxia's Na Homestead, Allah's blessing and the necessity of tithing is frequently invoked. It is important to note that in both cases, government policy has played a key role in restricting ethnic entrepreneurialism prior to the 1980s, and encouraging it in the Deng era and subsequently.

The rationalization for material wealth was appropriately summarized in a 1994 article in a Muslim Chinese newspaper about a prosperous Hui business in Chang Zhou, just south of Quanzhou. The article was published in a then-new local Muslim-run newspaper, *Qiming Xing*, based in Nanjing, which reports on Hui Muslim and other minority activities throughout China. Similar to the state-sponsored magazine *Zhongguo Musilin* (*China's Muslims*), and the journal *Ahlabo Shijie* (*Arab World*), this state-approved daily newspaper reports positively on Muslim affairs inside and outside of China. In an article published on 15 June 1994, entitled 'The Concept of Economic Development and Qualified Personnel', the newspaper juxtaposed a photograph of a Muslim imam, Zhao Huayu, in his new car, next to a recently refurbished mosque. The article reported on his successful company, the Muslim Technique Economy Trade Company in Chang Zhou city in the following manner:

Since the China Islamic Association in Chang Zhou City has invested in this company and it is located in the mosque, the profits it gains should naturally be used to develop the local nationalities' religious affairs ... Imam Zhao Huayu automatically became the president of the company ... [and he is also] head of the Chang Zhou City Islamic Association and the Standing Committee of the city's People's Political Consultative Committee [*zhengxie*]. All the leaders of the city know about this good-looking, bearded religious leader [*qingzhen jiaozhang*], so they are willing to give the green light to approve things easier … After the company was in business for one year, they bought a car. In the old way of thinking [*cong jiu guandian lai kan*], this was regarded as 'extravagant' or 'seeking personal pleasure'. But according to the new perspective, having a car is beneficial; it saves a great deal of time and allows for more good deeds to be done.

Here, interestingly enough, the imam became the head of the business. As noted in Na Homestead above, the Party cadres became imams. Perhaps under current government policy, they too have founded their own businesses. In each case, their success is lauded because it allows their people to prosper and the mosque to benefit, as the picture in the newspaper demonstrated. In a controversial and widely circulated 1993 novel about Muslims in Beijing, *Muslim Funeral* (*Musilin de Zangli*), a Hui woman writer, Huo Da, suggests that the reason Han in Beijing do not negatively stereotype the Manchu as they do the Hui is that the Hui were poor and uneducated. The novel's protagonist suggests that this kind of stigmatized identity should be a thing of the past and that Muslims should overcome this negative characterization through working hard in business and doing well in school (Huo 1993:162).[7] In the 750-page novel, which describes three generations of a traditional jade-carving Hui family in Beijing, economic prosperity and entrepreneurialism are never questioned – only unsuccessful entrepreneurialism. Indeed, the pivotal point of the novel is the decision of the Hui jade-carver to give alms and sustenance to an elderly Hui Muslim pilgrim *en route* to Mecca, an act of kindness that significantly alters the entire course of the succeeding generations.

Han capitalism in socialist China

While Hui have been 'officially' portrayed as a mercantile nationality in China, and the preceding discussion has demonstrated that they have sought to capitalize on this stereotype, this has clearly not been the case among the Han Chinese. Indeed, Deng's program of transforming China from a socialist centrally planned economy,

---

7. The Chinese novel by the Hui woman writer Huo Da, entitled *Muslim Funeral* (*Musilin de Zangli*), was first published in 1988 and reprinted in 1993. It was translated into English in 1992 and published as *The Jade King: History of a Chinese Muslim Family* (Beijing: Panda Press).

to a capitalist market economy that is politically controlled at the top but economically liberal in the marketplace faced three main obstacles, which I shall briefly describe here as essentializations of agriculturalism, communism, and Confucianism, legacies in China that are anticommercial in nature. These legacies have led to clear ambivalences toward the market and economic prosperity at a popular and policy level among the so-called Han.

While it is difficult, if not somewhat ludicrous, to generalize about the 1 billion or so Han Chinese, I shall only point out here how the Chinese themselves have attempted to essentialize and explain the fundamental nature of Han identity. Just as Fei Xiaotong theorized that entrepreneurialism is the national characteristic of the Hui, he posited that agriculturalism best defines the essence of Han identity. In a 1988 Tanner Lecture in Hong Kong, 'Plurality and Unity in the Configuration of the Chinese Nationality', later published in the *Beijing University Journal*, Fei traced the rise of the Han people from multi-ethnic origins prior to the Qin dynasty (3rd century BC), and their almost unilineal descent to the present day, despite absorbing and being conquered by various foreign tribes and nations:

The first step of this gigantic process was the coming into being of the Hua Xia group; the second the formation of the nation of the Han, which meant that the nucleus evolved and became enlarged. The unification of Central China by the Qin Empire was the last step which completed the development of the Han community into a nationality entity [*minzu*] ... Its people radiated in all directions into the areas around it and, centripetally, absorbed them into their own groups and made them a part of themselves ... As the non-Han rulers' regimes were mostly short-lived, one minority conqueror was soon replaced by another, and eventually all were assimilated into the Han ... Such densely intermingled habitation makes it possible for some Han to be melted into the local ethnic groups; but it is mainly for Han groups, who have infiltrated into non-Han communities, to work as the centripetal force around which to build a unified entity participated in by various groups. (Fei 1989:47)

The vast technical superiority of the Han, Fei argues, led to the almost automatic assimilation of the various non-Han peoples, and supports the continued policy of national unification (*minzu tuanjie*, or *ronghe*) promoted by the Chinese state today:

What, then, has made the Han a nucleus with such centripetal force? The main factor, in my view, has been their agricultural economy. Once a nomad tribe made its entrance into the plain and found itself in the midst of the careful, orderly society of the farmers, it would eventually throw itself all too voluntarily into the embrace of the Han ... But as the national minorities generally are inferior to the Han in the level of culture and technology indispensable for the development of modern industry, they would find it difficult to undertake industrial projects in their own regions, their advantage of natural resources notwithstanding ... Therefore, our principle is for the better developed groups to help the underdeveloped ones by furnishing economic and cultural aids. (Fei 1989:47, 54)

Fei Xiaotong's understanding of ethnic change and national identity is informed by a strong commitment to Stalinist–Leninist nationality policy, based on Morgan's theory of stage development evolutionism, and Engel's prediction of the withering away of class and national identity with the removal of private property. While there are many nationalities in China, the Han are defined as the cultural and technical vanguard, the manifest destiny of all the minorities. Fei suggests that pastoralists (such as the Mongols, Tibetans, and Turks) and mercantile peoples (such as the Hui) were fundamentally different from the Han agriculturalists, much the same as some Japanese scholars have argued that Japanese identity is based on rice-growing, as opposed to the Ainu and foreigners with whom the Japanese interacted (see Ohnuki-Tierney 1994). If the essence of Han identity is defined in terms of agriculturalism, where is the place for capitalist development?

A second official essentialization that is fundamentally anticommercial is that of the Communist legacy in China. From the idealized representations of the early suffering by the Communist Party in Shanghai and Jiangxi, to the depredations and epic struggles of the Long March, to the struggle sessions against landlords and capitalists during the 1950s land-reform campaigns, to the disastrous collectivist extravaganzas of the 1960s, to the antifeudalist, antirevisionist attacks of the 1960s and 1970s Cultural Revolution, and to the early opposition even Deng Xiaoping faced at the beginning of his reign, the Communist legacy has been one of anticommercialism. While private entrepreneurs have been the scourge of the Communists, selfless service on behalf of the masses, as immortalized in the figure of Lei Feng, has been their essentialized ideal. Whether it be the inability of the state to control the activities of petty entrepreneurs (*getihu*), as Thomas Gold (1989) has suggested, or the powerful destabilizing nature of the marketplace, as Ann

Anagnost (1997) has argued, it is clear that private business has been suspect under the Chinese panopticon. Indeed, the recent capitalistic fervor in China to get rich quick by any means can easily be seen as evidence of resistance toward and rejection of this long-held anticommercial Communist dogma, at the official and the popular levels.

Finally, essentialized interpretations of Confucianism in China have consistently supported the devalorization of the merchant. While Confucianism in general has been criticized as feudalistically supporting a patriarchal hierarchy, the socialist legacy in China has never taken issue with the Confucian subjugation of the merchant. It is also clear that central to the debate is 'which Confucianism', in that a 1993 edited volume on the subject of Confucianism, produced by economists, anthropologists, political scientists, historians, and philosophers, presented a cacophony of views about Confucius and Confucianism (Tu, Hejtmanek and Wacman 1993). Suffice it to say that regardless of the capitalistic success of neo-Confucianism in the Chinese diaspora in Taiwan, Hong Kong, and Southeast Asia, in China itself anti-Confucian Communist policy has also involved anticommercialism. Neither communism nor Confucianism have ever come to terms with the nature of profit, and both have consistently viewed it, and those associated with making it, negatively.

I would like to suggest that these essentialized interpretations of Han identity, communism, and Confucianism have contributed to a strong ambivalence toward private market success in contemporary China. This ambivalence is evidenced in debates in the public media over prosperity, as well as highly publicized trials and executions in capitalistic corruption cases.[8] These debates are similar, but in an entirely different context, to US evangelical Protestant debates about capitalistic success, as outlined by Craig M. Gay (1991). As among evangelicals, Chinese have become either '*very* critical or *very* defensive of capitalism and bourgeois culture' (Gay 1991:207; emphasis in the original). This should not be surprising, in that for both communities there is something much more at stake than the

8.   Agence France Presse reported on 19 August 1994 that three Chinese working in state enterprises were executed for corruption. Jin Zhilin, Wu Weidong, and Xie Peng, employed in three different companies, were accused of having embezzled funds or received bribes of 753,000 yuan (US$87,700), 500,000 yuan (US$58,275), and 131,000 yuan (US$15,260) respectively.

nature of the market: social and national identity itself is at issue. As Gay (1991:161) notes: 'Indeed, it seems clear that capitalism as such is not the only thing at issue in the debate but that the various evangelical factions are contending for entirely different socio-cultural visions of American society for which capitalism serves only as a kind of symbol either positively or negatively'. This is why, in China, ambivalences about capitalism and economic prosperity reflect fundamental essentialized notions of Han identity, communism, and Confucianism.[9]

A central preoccupation in the Chinese press with economic liberalization is the debate about 'moral decay' and 'corruption' that inevitably follows. One source that reveals many of these debates is a series of frank discussions aired and reported in a column entitled 'What They Are Saying', in the English-language newspaper *China Daily*, containing material selected from various local Chinese newspapers around the nation. Because it is a newspaper published for the benefit of China's mainly foreign English-language readership, it is possible that the reporting on local debates over the merits of state policy is a bit more open than that found in *Renmin Ribao* (*People's Daily*), the official government newspaper intended for national consumption. One article cited a poll published in the Chinese newspaper *Legal Daily* (12 May 1994) by Li Gaungru, Cao Jian, and Li Feng, which said that although the general public was in support of market reforms, 'in market competition, some people seek high profits at the expense of honesty … people should make money on the basis of fair and legal competition … it is essential to regulate market performance with coercive legal measures' ('Danger to Economy Lies in Moral Decay', *China Daily* 18 May 1994:3). In one section, 'Feudal Remnants', the authors complained, 'Remnants of feudal economic relations bring about political and professional privileges and lead to economic monopoly … Graft, malfeasance and bribery are not the by-products of a market economy. Instead, they are unavoidable results of remaining feudal economic relations' ('A Call for Quality, Not Quantity', *China Daily* 26 May 1994:3). Another report, by Yan Kalin, in the Chinese newspaper *Economic Daily*, revealed that businesses were in the habit of hiring people only on condition of

---

9. For an excellent discussion of the role of ambivalence in shaping social and moral discourse, see Peletz (1993); Weigert (1991).

receiving 'warranty funds' or pay-offs, and demanded other forms of contributions as illegal means to raise cash. The article concludes: 'Illegal fund-raising should be eliminated through strengthening financial control and extending financial reforms' (cited in 'Proper Financing May Quash Dodgy Levies', *China Daily*, 29 April 1994: 3). Finally, in a full-page editorial, Fan Hengshan, an official with the State Commission for Economic Restructuring, complained that the 'Market economy is misunderstood by too many folk'. Revealing again a concern about correct notions of 'profit', Fan stated: 'A healthy market economy is backed by manufacturing industries, not profiteering ... Some people in their thirst for profits, provide false information to mislead the futures and stock markets, produce inferior products, or break contracts' ('Market Economy is Misunderstood by Too Many Folk', *China Daily* 6 May 1994:4).

Even a cursory examination of the local press reveals that ambivalences about the market economy are to be resolved through education about the 'correct' use of profit and the heavy hand of the state in controlling prices, catching criminals, and curbing excesses. 'China's Gilded Age', chronicled in a two-part story by Yin Xiaohuang in the *Atlantic Monthly* of April 1994, indicates that underneath the silver lining there was much turmoil in Deng's China. A 1994 story by Sheilla Tefft in the *Christian Science Monitor* revealed these ambivalences in an article 'Family Time in Wealthy China'. Wang Guopin (a pseudonym) was a successful Shanghainese with a living room well-stocked with a CD player, VCR, color television, refrigerators, and the other accouterments of financial success in capitalist China.[10] Yet Wang saw uncanny parallels in his recent

10. In addition to telephones and CD players, automobiles became the newest status symbol in Deng's China, as reported in the *Toronto Globe and Mail* Beijing article 'China is Taking a Great Leap into the Auto Age' on 18 August 1994. The most recent report of registered private cars in China in 1992 revealed 700,000 registrations, but the article reported that one dealership in Beijing sold 200 cars a month in 1993. A certain Li Xiaohua purchased his first Toyota in 1981 from a Libyan diplomat and now boasts a large collection of vehicles: 'Last spring, in a solemn ceremony at Beijing's ancient Temple of Heaven, the one-time peasant became the first Chinese to own a Ferrari. China is taking a great leap into the auto age. Not so long ago, workers, peasants and soldiers lusted after clunky Flying Pigeon bicycles. They came in black, black or black, cost several months' pay and required scarce ration coupons. Today, a car is the ultimate status symbol in the world's fastest growing economy. "Private cars are a measure of the standard of living

situation with the days of his youth in Shanghai under the corrupt Nationalists: 'Although paramount leader Deng Xiaoping and other ruling Communists admonish Party members for widespread greed, corruption is as rampant as under the Nationalists … "The next generation always has money on its mind, and that is a crisis" ' ('Family Time in Wealthy China', *Christian Science Monitor* 25 August 1994). One 1994 article reported that embezzlement and bribery cases in China surged 81 percent in the first half of the year compared to 1993, with the Supreme People's Procurator investigating 20,000 cases involving 3,000 officials from Party, state, judicial, law-enforcement, and economic-management departments over six months ('Surge in Corruption Threatening China's Reforms', Agence France Presse English Wire, 30 August 1994).[11]

While most observers laud China's booming economy, some of the most critical concerns of officialdom in China are not only rampant corruption, but also the grossly imbalanced rates of economic growth of the interior and coastal regions, and the urban and rural regions.[12] Delegates to the March 1994 meeting of the National People's Congress warned Beijing authorities of serious

---

of a country," says Li, whose $175,000 acquisition put him on the cover of *Car Fan*, a new Chinese magazine. The millionaire real-estate developer owns seven cars, including two Mercedes-Benz 600 sedans – one white and one black – and a red Mazda sports car driven by his wife, Zhang Jifang. To lure status-conscious customers, He Guang parks his two-tone Rolls-Royce more or less permanently on a platform next to the plate-glass windows of his Beijing seafood restaurant. "He hardly ever drives the Rolls," explains a manager. "He usually uses his Mercedes …" Chairman Mao's grandson, Wang Xiaozhi, 21, recently confided to the official newspaper *China Daily* that his "biggest wish" is to own a car. Wang, a former hotel worker who is now in college, contents himself by drawing pictures of cars, studying mechanics and collecting auto parts.'

11. A former Vice-Minister of the State Science and Technology Commission was the highest official to be prosecuted to that time, receiving a sentence of twenty years.

12. In 'Economy Continues Growth in July' (Agence France Presse, 16 August 1994), it was reported that exports rose 35.7 percent to US$10.4 billion in July of that year, and the consumer price index also rose to 24 percent more than the same month one year previously. An AFP report of 18 July 1994 estimated the overall growth in the first half 1994 to be 11.9 percent. On 30 August 1994, another AFP report estimated inflation at 24.2 percent in July in China's major cities, with food prices up 31.9 percent, and grain and vegetable prices up 57.8 percent and 29.7 percent, respectively.

dissatisfaction over runaway prices, corruption, and the growing gap between rich and poor. Xing Fengsi, vice-president of the Central Communist Party School, attacked the sharp disparity between rich and poor, warning that: 'If not dealt with properly, this will cause social unrest and political instability' ('NPC Delegates Warn of Unrest over Corruption, Prices', United Press International, 21 March 1994). One report noted that even the Chinese press predicted social instability if the economic reforms were not handled correctly during the transitional period following Deng's death. One writer, in a letter published on the front page of the *China Business Daily*, complained of the get-rich-quick atmosphere that was exacerbating the social and economic disparities Chairman Mao tried to eliminate. Citing a huge gap between farmers and city-dwellers, the haves and the have-nots, and the officials and the people, the writer warned in Maoist discourse: 'Where there are disparities there are contradictions. Where there are contradictions there are conflicts' (cited in Schlesinger 1994).

Uneven economic growth has led to huge migrations of people in search of work and better lives, from the interior and northern regions to the southern coastal areas, and from the villages to the cities.[13] One 1994 article reported that these 'floating populations', which were officially estimated at 100 million, would grow to 200 million by the end of the 20th century ('China's Rural Exodus is Threatening Stability of Coastal Regions', Agence France Press English Wire, 24 August 1994). Some estimates say that figure has been surpassed. Investment in the central and western provinces was urged in order to avert 'chaos'.[14] Yet a fundamental problem was that the southern and urban economic boom was fueled by

13. Uneven economic growth between the coastal regions and hinterlands has also meant growing disparities between the minorities, who are generally concentrated in the interior southwestern and northwestern border regions. See 'China's Minorities Fight Poverty Trap', Agence France Presse English Wire, 22 June 1994; also Mackerras' (1994:198–233) helpful discussion of economic trends among the minorities. While Hui have generally sought to take advantage of business opportunities, in general the income levels of Hui and other Muslim minorities lag far behind those of the rest of the country (see Gladney 1995).

14. On 19 August 1994, the *Financial Times* reported that in an effort to close the economic gap between the coastal regions and the interior, China planned to provide US$1.16 billion in soft loans over the next six years to rural enterprises in remote areas.

cheap migrant labor that came from the interior. These migrant laborers contributed to China's dramatically increasing unemployment rate ('268 Million without a Job in 2000', Agence France Presse, 16 August 1994).[15] In one Fujianese tennis-shoe factory I visited in Quanzhou in February 1994, of the eighty-nine workers employed, only five were local, and they were primarily in managerial positions. The rest worked on piecemeal wages that ranged from 25 to 75 yuan per day (US$3 to US$7), and were often hired by the day. The village population had swelled to three times its normal size, with two-thirds of the population non-local. As in Guangdong, the locals controlled the enterprises; poorer non-locals were the workers. Since the factory was owned by a member of the Hui minority, I asked the owner if there were problems with anti-Hui sentiment among the poorer workers. He was somewhat surprised by my question: 'These people are glad to take the money from anybody; they don't even know I'm Hui. What they don't like is the fact that we Fujianese have so much more money than they do'. In this region, then, ethnic tension has shifted from Hui versus Han to local versus non-local. In this case most of the workers came from Zhejiang, and so there were Fujianese–Zhejiangese tensions in evidence.[16]

Even prior to his death in 1997, Deng's legacy was being critically evaluated by the dispossessed in China's runaway economy. The unusually somber passing of Deng's ninetieth birthday was

15. Agence France Presse reported that the Chinese Labor Ministry expected the number of unemployed to reach 200 million in rural areas and 68 million in the cities. At the time the article was written, there were 100 million 'surplus workers' in the countryside, with registered unemployed expected to be 5 million by the end of 1994.

16. By the same token, urbanites and wealthy locals generally attribute all the crimes and social problems to the *mangliu* (migrants), who frequently lack permanent housing, local registrations, and work permits, and often live in temporary residences on the outskirts of the cities. Yin Xiao-huang, on his return to China, was surprised to find growing prejudice among urban residents toward peasants: 'A Shanghai taxi driver insisted that migrant peasant workers were all potential "criminals". In my home town peasant beggars from Anhui slept right on the sidewalks, but no one paid any attention to them. When I mentioned this to my friends, they shrugged and replied, "So what?" Some of them even argued that peasants in inland areas live in poverty because they waste money and because the lack of efficiency there turns diligent workers into layabouts' (Yin Xiao-huang, 'China's Gilded Age: Part 2', *Atlantic Monthly* April 1994).

due not to concern over his health, according to one reporter, but to ambivalence about his record. Uli Schmetzer ('Deng Turns 90, Strong Leader Needed for Reforms', *Chicago Tribune* 21 August 1994) reported from Beijing that Deng's reforms were as precarious as his health:

As China continues to shift toward capitalism, millions of Chinese have been marginalized in the race for riches or laid off by profit-oriented state enterprises. These workers no longer see Deng as the idol who led China from the madness of Mao Tse-tung's Cultural Revolution into an era of peace and prosperity, and from isolation into the brotherhood of nations. 'Deng gave us private plots, but greedy party officials last year took the land away to build a computer factory,' said Wang Bao, a peasant from a village north of Beijing. 'Deng is too old to stop this nonsense.' One seasonal laborer added: 'I used to wake up certain I had a job. Now life is much harder. Deng cannot do anything. He started it; now it's everyone for himself.' Leftists looking for a role in the succession have criticized the feverish pace of reforms. A recent internal party campaign accused Deng of ordering the use of live bullets against demonstrators in Tiananmen Square on June 4, 1989. The report also paved the way for the ailing leader to become the scapegoat for a massacre that still haunts China's relations with the West.

While this report was somewhat typical of Western reporters looking for the 'cracks' in Chinese capitalism, ignoring the tremendous support that the market reforms had among much of China's citizenry, it nevertheless evidenced a growing ambivalence over the benefits of the market liberalization for everyone, and the growing inequities between rich and poor. When in Beijing in March 1994, I met with one official at the Beijing Foreign Affairs Bureau who noted that the word on the street was what most Chinese leaders feared was not another Wu'er Kaixi, or student leader, rising up to challenge their authority, but another Mao Zedong. This indicates that while, at the time, Deng's supporters felt the market reforms had not gone far enough, his detractors later suggested they may have gone too far.

Another popular issue under discussion in China has been the rise in stress and obesity due to the market reforms. A 1994 news article reported on a survey showing a marked rise in cardiovascular disease caused by stress and obesity ('Obesity and Stress Becoming the Downside of Economic Boom', Agence France Presse English Wire, 5 August 1994). More than 80 million people were undergoing treatment for hypertension, a 25 percent increase over 1984. The article attributed the stress and obesity problems to the economic boom. The *Los Angeles Times* (30 August 1994) reported that the government was so worried that China's new wealth would produce 'a nation of couch potatoes' that it was instituting a campaign encouraging exercise and promoting fitness, with at least two new sports to be taken up by each person and twenty minutes of exercise a day.

Finally, the rise in new-found wealth led to a search for a new role model. Giles Hewitt (1994) of Agence France Presse reported that 'as China's economic boom sees the gods of mammon and profit replacing the virtuous, self-sacrificing paragons of the old Communist pantheon, many are mourning the demise of the latter-day hero'. In what is described as a moral crisis facing its people, the *Guangming Daily* asked 'Where are the heroes?' Fueled by stories of people demanding money for assistance, even in life-threatening situations, nostalgia for the days of the altruistic Communist hero Lei Feng has begun to surface.[17] A 'bravery fund' in Jiangsu, established to reward modern-day heroes, has now collected 2.1 million yuan in donations. The article quoted Zi Zhongjun, a professor of the Chinese Academy of Social Sciences, who compared China to the USA in the 1950s and 1960s: 'At that time, materialism was rampant and young Americans became disaffected with the pervasive social mood and morality'.

Han and Hui market perspectives: contrasting moralities

The debate in China over the social ills concomitant with Deng's market reforms, as carried on by Jiang Zemin and his successor, Hu Juntao, reflects a fundamental ambivalence about prosperity, profit, and the capitalist road that China has embarked upon. While there were those who fully supported the new-found freedoms of

---

17. Another article revealed that in Deng's China, as exemplified by his successors, the image of the selfless Party member Lei Feng, whom Chairman Mao designated as the ideal role model for Communist self-sacrifice and compassion, was not yet moribund, but had been transformed. At Yuantian, a Japanese-funded company in Dalian, managers began to hand out 'Lei Feng cards' to model workers. Yet rather than being certificates of praise for altruistic acts, these cards were awarded to the most productive workers. The cards could be cashed in for salary bonuses and foreign travel opportunities.

the market, the growing reports of concerns about runaway inflation, increasing income disparities, and rampant corruption and
crime, with a widespread fear of social upheaval accompanied by
growing nostalgia for the 'good old days' of Maoist egalitarianism,
revealed many unresolved opinions about Deng's reforms, opinions
easily manipulated by those factions on both sides of Deng politically, and who may have wished to succeed him. The essentialized
legacies of Han agrarianism, with its influence on rural simplicity
and dependency on the land, Confucianism, with its hierarchically
maintained and well-ordered social world that placed merchants at
the low end of society, and communism, with its emphasis upon
egalitarianism and the common good over personal profit, will not
easily be dislodged after more than fifty years of Party rule. Deng-
ists and their successors can only hope there is not another Chairman Mao unsuccessfully seeking his way into university.

By contrast, Hui, Uyghur, and other Muslim communities bring
to their economic engagements an interest in taking part in trade
and desire for maximizing their opportunities of advancement.
Whether their motivations be personal enrichment, religious en-
hancement, or strengthening community solidarity, their margin-
alization in Chinese society has put them in a position where trade
and mediation are important skills needed for survival and self-
strengthening, developed over years of relative isolation within the
Chinese majority or in opposition to a non-Muslim state – their
profit-making skills are highly prized and unproblematized.

What the state has not been able to control or foresee, however,
is the important influence Hui ethnoreligious tradition has had on
Hui entrepreneurialism and religious practice. While it is clear the
early Chinese Stalinist nationality policy sought to separate nationality and religion, and encourage economic development to speed
assimilation with the more advanced, namely Han, nationalities
(see Connor 1984:67–71; Dreyer 1976:43–50), it has not worked
out that way. With economic development have come ethnoreligious revitalization and a growing awareness of Muslim links
to the outside Islamic world. Just as the state has encouraged and
courted investment from foreign Muslim governments in China,
only to find that foreign Muslims have generally preferred to build
mosques instead of factories, so among the Hui the state has not
been able to divorce national from religious interests, economic
development from Islamic awareness.

While sharing differing rationalizations about their participation in the capitalist economies, Hui Muslims have much in common with their Han neighbors. Quanzhou Hui who comfortably worship their Muslim ancestors, raise pigs, and fully participate in southern Min Fujianese political culture, would object to the facile dichotomies of East/West, Muslim/Confucian, and secular/sacred. Instead, their daily interactions with Islam, Confucian traditions, local southern Min popular religion, and Southeast Asian business connections have produced a vibrant cultural identity that cannot easily be placed in any category, although they continue to be labeled as Hui by the state. In the northwest, Na villagers share views of family solidarity, patriarchy, hierarchy, thrift, hard work, perseverance, and honesty that could easily be considered Confucian. Yet their explicit motivations for economic prosperity are often described in terms of religious and ethnic goals. In each case, one finds not predisposition for market success, but adaptation to government policy and the harsh realities of socioeconomic contexts for personal survival. Neither prosperity, nor even the social ills that may come with it, are problematic for these Hui; prosperity is generally seen as good for their people, and often for their religion.

This is not the case for the Han, where moral ambivalence characterizes many aspects of market practice. In addition, studies have suggested that Han identity, broadly represented as homogeneous and unified, is rapidly breaking apart along cultural and regional lines of local expression (see Friedman 1994). It is now popular to be Cantonese and Shanghainese in China, and there has been a resurgence of local power bases, often drawn along cultural fault lines.

By comparing Muslim and Han economic practice and views toward economic success in China under Deng and his successors, this chapter has sought to suggest the need for more contextualized, community-based studies, rather than broad generalizations about Confucianism and Islam. Debates about certain practices within the Han and Muslim communities reveal more than generalizations about them. The Hui, standing somewhere between China and the Middle East, provide an important counterpoint to those who wish to draw broad distinctions between Muslim and Confucian, or East and West.

Part VII
POLITICIZATIONS

14
GULF WARS AND DISPLACED PERSONS

China and the Middle East

Thanks to the events of 11 September 2001 and the subsequent war on terrorism, China has become widely recognized as a nation with a significant Muslim population. With nearly 18 million Muslims (the 2000 census reported 18.6 million, with many Muslims still unaccounted for or refusing to register as members of the primarily Muslim nationalities), China ranks as one of the most populous Muslim nations. And although its Muslim population is miniscule when compared with its total population (Muslims account for less than 2 percent of China's 1.3 billion), or insignificant when one looks at the vast Muslim populations in other Asian nations, such as Indonesia, Bangladesh, and Pakistan (although it is more than those of Malaysia, Thailand, the Philippines, or any other East Asian nation), this chapter argues that the Muslims of China play an important role, disproportionate to their numbers, in influencing China's domestic and international politics. The varied reactions of China's Muslims to the events of the past twelve years in the Gulf tell us much about the changing position of this subaltern subject.

The People's Republic of China, as one of five permanent voting members of the UN Security Council, and as a significant exporter of military hardware to the Middle East, has become a recognized player in Middle Eastern affairs. After a temporary but precipitous decline in trade with many Western nations after the Tiananmen massacre in June 1989, the importance of China's Middle Eastern trading partners (most of them Muslim, since China did not recognize Israel until 1992) rose considerably. This may account for the fact that China established diplomatic relations with Saudi Arabia in August 1990, with the first direct Sino-Saudi exchanges taking place since 1949 (Saudi Arabia canceled its long-standing diplomatic relationship with Taiwan and withdrew its ambassador, despite a lucrative trade history).[1] In the face of a long-term friendship with Iraq, China went along with most of the UN resolutions in the 1991 war against Iraq. Although it abstained from Resolution 678 on supporting the ground war (Harris 1991a), and did not endorse the US-led coalition war against Saddam Hussein in 2003, China continues to enjoy a fairly 'Teflon' reputation in the Middle East as an untarnished source of low-grade weaponry and cheap reliable labor.[2] In the words of the late Imam Shi Kunbing, former leader of the famous Oxen Street Mosque in Beijing: 'With so much now at stake in the Middle East, the government cannot risk antagonizing its Muslim minorities'.

1. For an excellent discussion of the rise in military trade between China and Saudi Arabia, culminating in the recognition of the PRC by Saudi Arabia in 1990, see Shichor (1989). At the same time, the Saudis severed relations with Taiwan, despite Taiwan's prosperous economy and long-term friendship with Saudi Arabia, indicating the importance of China's arms exports in its Middle Eastern relations. Arms have always played a prominent role in Sino-Middle Eastern relations. The recognition of China by Egypt in May 1956 was extremely important to China, in that Egypt was the first country to recognize the PRC since 1950, causing the first crack in the diplomatic blockade, and was regarded as quite a coup for a Muslim hajj delegation, led by a Uyghur from Xinjiang, that helped to establish the initial contacts (see Shichor 1979:40–5; see also Behbehani 1981; Calabrese 1991). From the very beginning, the recognition of China by Egypt was linked to the arms trade: by recognizing the PRC, which was not at that time representing China at the UN, Nasser had managed to obtain a back channel for Soviet arms (which were barred from being exported to Egypt due to the UN blockade). For the role of China's Muslims in Sino-Middle Eastern affairs, see Christofferson (1993).
2. Dr Lillian Harris (1991a), a political historian of China, argued that China forfeited its chances of working in the rebuilding of Kuwait by abstaining in the vote over Resolution 678, and missed an opportunity to extend its influence in the Middle East, though in her later book (Harris 1993b:3–6) somewhat revised her calculation of China's post-war role in the Gulf. China somehow continued throughout the 1990s to work hard not only to keep channels open to Iraq for future trade opportunities, but also to preserve its position in the region as a cheap source of low-grade conventional arms and reliable labor. Former President Yang Shangkun made a six-country trip in fall 1990 to the Middle East, to explain China's position on the conflict, dispense cheap arms, and unexpectedly to donate the expensively furbished Egyptian International Conference Center in the Heliopolis district of Cairo, which had been built at considerable expense over the previous three years by Chinese construction companies.

Interestingly, although China's government did not endorse the war against Iraq in 2003, and only voiced 'strong concern' about the possible collateral injury of civilians, urging a peaceful resolution, its Muslim population was ahead of the government in publicly condemning the war. In a statement issued on 23 March 2003, Chen Guangyan, vice-president of the China Islamic Association, said: 'We strongly condemn the United States and its allies for attacking Iraq and not turning to diplomacy to resolve this conflict … We side with the war protesters in the US and elsewhere around the world. We strongly urge the US to stop its campaign and to return to the negotiating tables to resolve this issue. War is wrong' (Cheng 2003). The next day, Hajji Muhammad Nusr Ma Liangji, lead imam of the Great Mosque in Xi'an, which boasts 70,000 members, made the following statement:

Though we don't go to the Middle East that often, we are all part of the same brotherhood … Mr Bush's invasion of Iraq is an incursion on Iraq's sovereignty. Islam is a religion of peace and the US shouldn't do this. No one in the world agrees with this and we in the Muslim community in China absolutely object to this. (Cheng 2003)

I was able to visit the headquarters of the China Islamic Association in the Niujie district of Beijing shortly after these statements were made, and Hajji Yu Zhengui, president of the association, confirmed that Muslims across China were deeply angered by the US-led war, and had been asking the government for permission to engage in public street protest. As of late March 2003, permission had not been granted, though there were rumors of small Muslim protests in Changzhi (Shanxi), Tianjin, Nanjing, Beijing, and Shandong. The Chinese did give permission for some limited protests by foreigners and students in late March and early April, but perhaps out of fear that a Muslim protest might get out of hand, possibly disturbing social stability, or even worse, disrupting improving Sino-US relations, the Muslims were never allowed to protest the war on Iraq.

China's Muslim subalterns have clearly grown into a more prominent position in China's domestic and international relations. Even so, studies have tended to describe the 'Muslims of China' as speaking with one voice, as if there was one 'Islam in China' and a unified Muslim identity, despite there being officially ten nationalities comprising mainly Muslims, and there being tremendous differences of Islamic and political opinion *within* each of those nationalities. By examining responses of certain Muslim communities to the Gulf wars and their aftermath in China, this chapter will seek to demonstrate not only the growing importance that Beijing places on its Muslim population, but also the difficulty in trying to generalize about a single Muslim position on recent Middle Eastern events.

Transnational Islam and Muslim national identity in China

Domestically, China can ill afford to ignore its many Muslim voices, which have grown more vocal in recent years. Although Muslims are proportionally small in population, the majority of them are concentrated in the northwestern regions bordering Mongolia, Russia, Kazakhstan, Kyrgyzstan, Tajikistan, Afghanistan, and Pakistan. Although fewer than 10 percent of China's population resides in these areas, more than 60 percent of the country's land mass is distributed in minority regions, with Muslim populations concentrated in the north and northwest. Han Chinese migration in the past few years has begun to shrink Muslim dominance in these areas (the Han made up 49 percent of the population of the Xinjiang Uyghur Autonomous Region, according to the 1990 census), but the Muslim presence is still clearly felt in all of these border regions. In addition, many of China's oil, mineral, and nuclear power resources are concentrated in the northwest. The opening of the Pakistan–China Karakoram Highway in May 1986, the establishment of the direct air route between Ürümqi and Istanbul in 1988, and the completion of the trans-Eurasian railway through Central Asia in October 1990 have led to dramatic increases in the trade of peoples, goods, and hard currencies.

Muslim unrest in these areas (of which there have been several notable but short-lived instances in December 1986, 15 June 1988, 12 to 19 May 1989, 5 to 6 April 1990, August 1993, and several episodes in the late 1990s) is of significant concern to the Chinese state. The protest of many of China's Muslims in May 1989 over a Chinese book that they claimed was as offensive to them as Salman Rushdie's *Satanic Verses* indicated new levels of nationally coordinated Islamic activism. Muslims from Beijing, to Xi'an, to Ürümqi organized marches, met with government leaders, and achieved their goals of banning the book, closing the publishing house, and having the authors arrested.[3]

The killing of twenty-two mainly Uyghur Muslims (according to the state press, with unofficial accounts of between fifty and sixty fatalities)[4] in Baren, a small township of Akto County, Kizilsu Kirghiz Autonomous Prefecture, southwestern Xinjiang, on 5 to 6 April 1990 over an apparent land-rights dispute led to the closing of the entire Xinjiang Autonomous Region to foreign journalists and, most importantly for the local economy, to foreign tourism for more than six months.[5] Uyghur separatists militating for an 'independent Turkestan' destroyed a government building with two bombs in August 1993, and there have since been at least thirty separate bombing incidents in the Xinjiang region. Support for the Uyghur separatists comes from sympathizers in Central Asian and Uyghur émigré communities in the Middle East, especially Turkey. Kazakh, Tajik, Uzbek, Tartar, and Kyrgyz all have a majority of their populations *outside* China, and they have had increasing contact with them as international trade has been encouraged under Deng Xiaoping and subsequent governments. As China's most important *transnational* minorities (with the exception of the Tibetans who continue to be a particularly painful public-relations thorn – but little else – in the soft underbelly of China's human-rights record), the Muslims are an important player in the geopolitics and international economics of China's trade with Central Asia, the Middle East, and Muslim ASEAN nations.

Internationally, Muslims are playing an increasingly important role in China's consideration of its foreign affairs. Not only are the numbers of pilgrims on the hajj growing at a phenomenal rate, but the flow of Middle Eastern visitors to China has also increased dramatically. Pilgrimage to Mecca has increased from nineteen

3. For more information on the 'Salman Rushdie' scandal in China among the Hui and the Uyghur, see Gladney (1994).
4. See Xinjiang Television Network, 21 and 22 April 1990 (FBIS-CHI-90-078, 23 April 1990:60, 62); Istanbul's *Gunaydin*, 24 May 1990:11 (FBIS-CHI-90-104, 30 May 1990:72); *Christian Science Monitor* 18 April 1990:4; *Far Eastern Economic Review* 19 April 1990:10–11; *New York Times* 23 April 1990:A3; Amnesty International 1992:2–5.
5. For an informative analysis of local Uyghur leadership response to this and earlier uprisings, see Toops (1991). See also the analysis of Xinjiang's position in Sino-Middle East relations by Harris (1993a).

pilgrims in 1979 to more than 6,000 in 2001, most of them privately financed (yet there is no way to know just how many pilgrims exited China via Pakistan or the Xinjiang–Saudi Arabia–Turkey air route; see also Shichor 1989:7; Gladney 1996a:332–6). There has been such an increase in private and state-sponsored foreign Muslim tourists and businessmen coming to Beijing that in 1990 the city opened a special four-star 'Muslim Hotel' on Wang-fujing Avenue, its main shopping arcade, as well as declaring the Oxen Street Muslim neighborhood a 'Muslim United Nationality Cultural District' to attract Muslim tourists.

Several state-sponsored Chinese construction companies that provide low-level and inexpensive development projects to Third World Muslim nations – and that built such well-known projects as the sports stadium outside Cairo, the Corniche roadway along the Nile, the Kenya–Tanzania highway, and numerous other road, bridge, and dam projects – include Muslims from China as transla-tors and 'cultural consultants'. These Muslims know how to deal with their coreligionists abroad, and they can often speak to them in fluent Arabic. In the 1990s, several joint state and private-collec-tive 'Muslim construction corporations' were established in China, with Hui Muslims at the head of their organizations in order to foster increased numbers of development contracts. Between 1991 and 1993, direct foreign Muslim investment in China led to the building of the Xiamen International Airport and the Minjiang Hydroelectric power plant in Fujian Province, as well as several major development projects throughout the northwest. Most un-expectedly, as a result of foreign Muslims being courted to invest in China, several large donations have gone to building mosques and madrasahs in Xinjiang, Gansu, Qinghai, and Ningxia – the Chinese government wants to build factories, while foreign Muslims may often want to build edifices to Allah.

While exact trade figures are hard to come by, and rarely include military transfers, the International Monetary Fund recorded that between 1982 and 1988 China exported a total of US$2,089 mil-lion and imported only US$577 million in trade with fourteen Arab states and Iran (International Monetary Fund 1990). Shichor (1989:14) estimates that before the 1991 Gulf War there were nearly seventy special Chinese construction corporations working in the Middle East, many of them led by Muslims, with an average of 50,000 Chinese workers every year in the Middle East, and a total turnover of US$8 billion. After the war began, there were supposedly more than 4,000 Chinese workers stuck in Iraq, whom the Iraqis initially refused permission to leave (Harris 1991a), and up to 10,000 Chinese workers in Egypt at the height of their trade from 1985 to 1987. Egypt, surprisingly enough, is the proud owner of Chinese-made submarines.

Many of these projects are coordinated through the China Islamic Association, a state-sponsored administrative agency founded in 1957 to oversee all Muslim affairs, coordinate Islamic publications, train future Islamic scholars and imams, and liaison with local mosque communities. The explosion of exchanges with foreign Muslims in recent years has meant both the increased influence of this agency in China's international affairs and its decentralized authority at the local level. Throughout China, Muslims are now building mosques and madrasahs on their own initiative, and sending increasing numbers of Muslims on the hajj with private, community-based funding. Despite the widespread closures and destruction of mosques in China during the Cultural Revolution, there are now many more mosques in China than there were before 1949. Many of these religious orders do not recognize the China Islamic Association's authority in their internal affairs, citing the freedom-of-religion clause in China's constitution. More importantly, local Party leaders are loath to interfere with Muslim activities lest they be accused of discriminating against minorities and of harsh treatment of Muslims. Most local cadres would rather ignore minor infractions and wait for the central government to step in. But Beijing is a long way from Xinjiang and Ningxia.

These developments underscore the importance the state places upon its Muslim minorities. It also reveals the diversity within the Muslim communities that are distributed throughout the entire country (the 1990 census revealed that there are Muslims in 97 percent of all counties in China). In the 1950s, China embarked upon a Soviet-inspired nationalities identification program and recognized ten nationalities as being primarily Muslim. These included the Turkic-speaking Uzbek, Tartar, Kazakh, Kirghiz, and Uyghur, and the Persian-speaking Tajik, all of whom had been identified by the Soviets, as well as four groups unique to China, the Dongxiang, Salar, and Baoan, who speak Turkic-Altaic dialects, and the Hui people, who speak mainly Chinese languages, and with whom this chapter is primarily concerned.

Islamic movements and revivalism in China

This chapter addresses itself to issues raised by views of the Hui and Uyghur toward the events in the Gulf. It does not address the views of the other Muslim nationalities because I did not have the opportunity to interview many of them regarding their views on the Middle East problems and the war on terrorism. Muslim opinion, unless it agrees with the government's position, is also not well-represented in the press, because the media are state-controlled and monitored by Beijing. While in Beijing and on the southeast coast of China for three weeks in February 1991, during the height of the first Gulf War, I held meetings with Hui representing several points of view and from various parts of the country. I also conducted interviews with officials in the China Islamic Association, the Chinese Academy of Social Sciences, and the Central Institute of Nationalities, as well as a wide range of unofficial contacts that were established during an earlier study (Gladney 1996a). During the 2003 war on Iraq, I conducted similar follow-up interviews with local Muslims and government officials in Guangzhou, Ürümqi, Kashgar, and Beijing. Their views, although anything but unified and exhaustive, reveal much about the prevailing contours of Muslim opinion in China.

As noted above, while the 8.4 million Uyghur are primarily concentrated in Xinjiang, the Hui are the most widely dispersed of the ten Muslim nationalities in China, and account for nearly half of all Muslims in the country (8.6 million, according to the 2000 census). The Hui are the one Muslim nationality whose members do not have their own language, speaking the mainly Han Chinese and minority dialectics in the areas where they live. Although all of the Muslims in China are Sunni (with the exception of a few Shi'ites among the Persian-speaking Tajik of Xinjiang and some Uyghur in the Khotan region), the Hui are split among a wide variety of religious factions, including Sufi brotherhoods (primarily Central Asian Naqshbandiyya, Qadariyya, and Kubrawiyya), Wahhabi-inspired Ikhwan and Salafiyya movements, and the traditionalist Hui Muslims, who call themselves the Gedimu.[6] Joseph

---

6. These factions dividing Muslims in China, described as *jiao pai* (literally 'teaching factions'), have been erroneously translated as 'sects' in English, such as the 'new sects' that criticized earlier traditional expressions of Islam in China, which were referred to as 'old sects' (see Israeli 1978). While the

Fletcher (1988) was the first to identify in China several 'tides' of Islamic movements, which swept across China's frontier areas during moments of openness between China and the outside world. While Islam expanded gradually across the maritime and inland silk routes from the 7th to 10th centuries, through trade and diplomatic exchanges, it was under the Mongol's Yuan dynasty in the 13th to 14th centuries that large populations of Central Asian Muslims found their way into the Chinese heartlands. This led to the establishment of fairly self-contained Muslim village enclaves and urban core-communities across China, with the largest concentrations of Muslims in towns across the northwestern plains and oases-linked trade routes (Xinjiang, Qinghai, Gansu, and Ningxia), throughout the villages and cities of the North China plain (Hebei, Shanxi, Henan, Shandong, and Anhui), in the southwest border areas along the ancient Burma Road (Yunnan and Sichuan), and along the maritime Silk Route in the port cities along the southeast coast (Guangdong, Quanzhou, Hangzhou, Yangzhou, and Suzhou).

The widespread dispersal of Muslims due to internal migrations, trade opportunities (particularly the wool, horse, tea, jewelry, and opium trades that Muslims tended to dominate), and periodic persecutions and rebellions led to what is now an incredibly diverse and widely distributed Muslim population. The 1982 census revealed that there were Hui Muslims living in 2,308 of 2,372 counties and cities across China (Population Census 1987:xvi). It was not until the advent of several Sufi movements in the 17th to 19th centuries that these communities began to be linked into more tightly organized, hierarchical orders. Largely influenced by Central Asian Sufism, Naqshbandiyya, Qadiriyya, and Kubrawiyya

---

Chinese terms were inexact and often meant only 'teachings' in general, subsequent scholarship has revealed a wide variety of Islamic expression and organization in China, which can only be roughly rendered in English by such terms as factions, orders, solidarities, brotherhoods, and so on (see Gladney 1987a, 1996:36–62; Lipman 1981, 1984; Ma Tong 1983). Where possible, I prefer to refer to the organized movements by the names they call themselves (Qadariyya, Naqshbandiyya Banqiao, Salafiyya, Yihewani, and so on), rather than force them into any sociological categories of organization.

7. For a more extended discussion of the proliferation of Sufi orders in China and the contemporary prominence of Sufi tombs in community rituals, see Gladney (1987a:499–510). See also Ma Tong (1989).

Sufi brotherhoods proliferated across northwestern China.[7] By the late 19th and early 20th centuries, Muslim Chinese returning from the pilgrimage cities influenced by Wahhabi ideals began to contest and criticize what they saw as Islamic inaccuracies and Chinese cultural accretions among the Sufi brotherhoods and the traditional, non-aligned Muslim Chinese communities (who began at that time to be referred to as the Gedimu).

Ma Wanfu, the most influential of the early Wahhabi-inspired Hui Islamic reformers, introduced to China in the 1890s the Ikhwan al-Muslimin (or Muslim Brotherhood; known in Chinese as the Yihewani) – a religious movement highly influenced by China's nationalist concerns in the early 20th century, and divided by warlord politics. While the Muslim Brotherhood elsewhere in the Islamic world at times has been regarded as antimodernist and recidivist, this is not true of the movement in China. Perhaps due to the unstable political climate of Western and Japanese imperialist aggressions, internal civil war, and the earlier collapse of the Manchu empire in which these Muslim reformers found themselves embroiled, they quickly became involved in Islamic renewal movements *and* local warlord politics.[8] Another Wahhabi group that arose at the time, but was quickly suppressed, was more committed to an apolitical Islamic reform movement that stressed moral purity and scriptural authority. This movement became known as the Salafiyya (from the Arabic *salaf*, 'veneration' of the early founders of Islam), and has only reappeared since the end of the oppressive antireligious policies of the Cultural Revolution in 1976 (see Gladney 1999).

Following the Ikhwan, the Salafiyya promote a scripturalist Islam that is rationalist and antiexperiential. Like the late Rashid Rida (1865–1935), their fellow Salafi leader in Syria, they emphasize opposition to Sufism and cultural syncretism, rather than modernism (Lapidus 1988:666–7). Perhaps as a result of the drift of the Ikhwan toward secularism and nationalism, the Salafiyya in China put more stress on scripturalism and orthodox practice. Emphasizing divine unity, they criticize the Sufis and Gedimu alike for their patronage of tombs, saints, and the miraculous. Just as the discrediting of the Sufis and urban Muslim intellectuals by the

8.   For the best history in English of the Yihewani (Ikhwan) in China, see Lipman (1994), and the comprehensive Chinese study by Ma Tong (1983:127–54).

French in Morocco helped to promote the cause of the Salafiyya (Eickelman 1976:227–8; Lapidus 1988:707), so the domination of the Ikhwan and other Islamic orders by the Communist Party in China might have contributed to the Salafiyya movement's call for a purified, non-accommodationist, and largely non-political Islam. The further disintegration of Communist-Party-led states in most of the world, if not eventually China, may also give credence to the Salafiyya's cause. The Salafiyya is one of the few Islamic movements in China that can claim a resistance to Chinese cultural assimilation *and* collaboration with the state. This may have accounted for its dramatic rise in popularity since 1980, and may augur for its place at the forefront of a new tide of Islamic revivalism in China, particularly since it is a movement strengthened by recent interactions with the Middle East by China's Muslims. In the past these different movements held widely divergent theological, ideological, and political views, leading to major splits and violent confrontations. The case of the 1991 Gulf War provided an excellent example of the diversity of opinion among China's Muslims and their changing perceptions of the Middle East. The Gulf crisis thus serves as an excellent illustration of the vast differences dividing Muslims in China, and some of the significant concerns still uniting them, which has continued to influence domestic subaltern affairs during yet another Gulf War in 2003.

The first Gulf War and China's Muslims: dividing lines

The following statement is excerpted from a letter dated 10 February 1991, written by a Muslim Chinese who has a master's degree in ethnology from one of China's most prestigious universities in Beijing.[9] After receiving his three-year postgraduate degree, he

9. The letter was collected while I was carrying out research in China from 11 to 26 February 1991 among Muslims in Beijing and Quanzhou, Fujian. I also conducted interviews with Muslims from China who are residing and studying in Cairo, between 20 and 31 March 1991. I would like to thank the American Academy of Arts and Sciences and UNESCO for sponsoring the research trips. Conclusions of this study are also based on three years of prior research among Muslims in China, from 1982 to 1986 (see Gladney 1996a:98–111). Revisions to the original chapter were carried out while I was a Fulbright Research Scholar affiliated with the Sociology Department of Bogaziçi University, Istanbul, in 1992–93.

returned to work as a Communist Party bureaucrat in his native Lanzhou city, in the heart of the northwestern region, where many of China's 18 million Muslims live. He is thus an articulate representative of the view from the conservative Muslim northwest, although he is a Party member.

At first I was fully against Saddam Hussein. Though my heart was with his call for all Muslims to support him, my mind cried out against the atrocities he committed against other fellow Muslims. No leader, especially a Muslim, has the right to invade another country, no matter what the reason. I supported the United Nations' condemnation of Iraq and prayed that Saddam would recognize his mistake and withdraw. I believe that eventually this is exactly what would have happened, if the US had only waited longer and applied the United Nations' sanctions. But then the US invaded Iraq. In the name of rescuing Kuwait, the US went much too far: it bombed thousands of innocent civilians, destroyed countless holy mosques and shrines, not to mention other non-military targets such as schools, hospitals, and residential areas, and, most offensive to me as a Muslim, the US sent hundreds of thousands of troops to the holy Islamic lands in the Arabian peninsula. This stirred up so many memories of the crusades that I realized the war in the Gulf had much less to do with rescuing Kuwait than it had to do with colonialism, the reassertion of Western geopolitical power, and, of course, oil. If it had to do with applying the United Nations sanctions, as the Americans claim, then why have they not enforced them before? The US did not send troops to Afghanistan, despite the UN sanctions, and it, of course, has always ignored repeated UN condemnations of Israel's treatment of the Palestinians and occupation of the West Bank. It is clear that the US only intervenes when its own interests are at stake (such as Grenada, Panama, and Libya). In this case it is oil that really is at stake (since Kuwait previously sold 70 percent of its oil to the US). It is because Saddam Hussein has stood up to this kind of self-interested militarism that I now have reversed my opinion of him: I now believe that Saddam is a hero, not only for all Muslims, but for all peoples oppressed by foreign imperialism, be it political or economic. When my fellow Muslims are being bombed mercilessly by a foreign infidel power, despite their attempts to sue for peace, I can only support them with my heart and pray that Allah will rescue Saddam Hussein so that he can lead all Muslims, one-fifth the world's population, in forging a united Muslim coalition that will enforce the justice of Allah's glorious Quran throughout the entire world.

But this is not the only voice representing Islam in China. In addition to this pro-Saddam position, I identified at least two other radically divergent views held by Muslims in China. Some were primarily pro-Chinese, in that they supported the state's position where the interests of China took precedence over Islamic concerns, and others held a third position in which more local interests prevailed. These Muslims were primarily concerned about the fallout the 1991 Gulf War would have on their relations with the non-Muslim Han majority in China and their rather fragile economic position within the nation.

With regard to Saddam Hussein, I could find few major differences of opinion that followed these traditional Islamic cleavages. Instead, I located differences of opinion along a continuum that is less geographical or ideological, but is positioned more according to one's relation with the Chinese state. On one end, those who opposed Saddam Hussein were more in line with the state's position, while those who supported him contested the official Chinese government stance, and those who were in the middle were primarily concerned with the effect of the conflict on their own local affairs. These divergent positions among Muslim communities in China illustrate the influence that increased Sino-Middle Eastern relations has had on China's domestic Muslim populations.

Mutual withdrawal and a 'peaceful resolution'

At one extreme were those who fully supported the position of China's government toward the Middle East situation: Saddam was wrong to have invaded Kuwait, the UN sanctions should be enforced, but China should not be involved directly in the conflict. These included Hui Muslims, some of them Party members and some of them devout Muslims, who opposed Saddam Hussein on nationalistic, patriotic grounds, and others were simply playing it safe.[10] Believing that China should steer its own course in foreign

---

10. Party membership does not exclude participation in the Hui nationality. Hui argue that there is no contradiction here: as members of a minority nationality that is descended from Muslim ancestors, Islam for them is something they are free to believe in and free not to believe in; disbelief and Party membership do not mean they are not Hui, nor is it impossible in China to find Party members who are practicing Muslims. In Stalinist fashion, the Chinese state seeks to encourage a growing distinction between ethnicity and religious heritage, so that Islam may no longer be closely associated with being a member of the Hui nationality, although many conservative Hui Muslims, especially in the northwest, resist this distinction.

relations, uninfluenced by US and Middle Eastern geopolitical positions, these Hui argued for a measured, conciliatory approach. A 'peaceful resolution' (*heping jiejue*) of the conflict was the slogan of the state's official press, and it was the most repeated phrase I heard when interviewing these individuals.

The most renowned Muslim I spoke with representing this view was Ma Zhaoqun, vice-president in 1991 of the China Islamic Association, a hajji several times over, and fluent in English, Arabic, and, of course, Mandarin. The venerable seventy-two-year-old scholar is no longer able continue his studies because of his diminished eyesight, but he keeps completely abreast of Muslim affairs internally and externally. In an interview in his home on 22 February 1991, he stated: 'Saddam Hussein is a brilliant tactician. He knew that Kuwait was vulnerable militarily and ideologically. Most Arabs never accepted the boundaries separating Kuwait from Iraq, anyway, which were drawn by the British and French colonial powers. Nevertheless, as a Muslim he should never have invaded another person's territory by force. The Quran justifies violence in defense of one's life and property, as was the case whenever Muhammad the Prophet, Bless-His-Name, went to war. I support China's position and the UN sanctions.'

A popular Chinese biography of Saddam Hussein (*Sadamu juanji*, which was not credited to an individual author), which I found circulating in several Hui households in Beijing, was the source of many Hui Muslim intellectuals' views on the Iraqi leader. I did not obtain a copy of the volume, which was published in the early 1980s and did not cover recent events in the Gulf, but its officially sanctioned publication by a state-sponsored press reflected China's early policy of strong support for the rise of the Baath Party. Two days after the Baathist revolution in 1958, China immediately established relations with Iraq to show its solidarity with what it regarded as the first 'real revolution' in the Middle East (Shichor 1979:87). Iraq was one of China's closest trading partners in the Middle East until the invasion of Kuwait. The Iraqis fired two Chinese-made Silkworm missiles at US ships during the war, and exchanged countless more with Iran during the Iran–Iraq war (1980–1988); these weapons were part of more than US$12 billion worth of arms deals with China (Shichor 1988:320–1).

Most urban Muslim intellectuals I spoke with seemed to share Hajji Ma Zhaoqun's view. Professor Ma Qicheng, retired

vice-director of the Department of Ethnology at the Central Institute of Nationalities, said that China was right to condemn Hussein but also to stay clear of the conflict: 'We should continue the
embargo, not sell any more arms to Saddam, but not get further
involved. Iraq has been a long-time friend of China and I am sad-
dened that the US is relentlessly bombing the Iraqi people. They
are the ones who will really suffer in this conflict, not Saddam
Hussein'. Hajji Muhammad Zhang Zhihua, a teacher of Arabic at
the Arab and African Studies Institute at Beijing's Number Two
Foreign Languages College (which mainly trains foreign interpreters and tour guides), served several years in Egypt and the Middle
East as an interpreter for state-sponsored construction projects. He
was one of the first Hui Muslim students trained by the state in
Arabic and Quranic studies at the China Islamic Association in
Beijing, and his first teachers were both from the Al-Azhar University in Cairo, so he speaks fluent Egyptian Fusa Arabic.

Recent political events in China and abroad have dramatically
affected the value of studying Arabic in China. Hajji Muhammad
Zhang's Arabic classes were so popular that two-thirds of his 100
students were privately paying their tuition (unlike the officially
matriculated state-supported students at the university, who attend
virtually for free) in order to become interpreters in the Middle
East. Most of the students who pay to learn Arabic privately
are Hui and Uyghur Muslims from the conservative northwest
(Ningxia, Gansu, Qinghai, and Xinjiang), who have had some exposure to Quranic Arabic in the mosque, but lack high-school di-
plomas or other credentials to gain them entry into the four official
state-sponsored Quranic madrasahs (in Beijing, Ningxia, Xi'an, and
Ürümqi) or regular foreign-language Arabic programs (at Beijing
University, Beijing Foreign Languages University, or Shanghai's
Foreign Language Institute).

In a surprising development, for the first time many of the students interested in learning Arabic now include non-Muslim Han
students. By studying Arabic, many hope to increase their chances
of receiving scholarships to attend Middle Eastern universities,
because it is now much more difficult to get into Chinese universities or to go to Western countries. Opportunities have declined
dramatically for students to study abroad in the United States,
England, Australia, Canada, France, and other Western countries
that lent support and safe harbor to many dissident intellectu-

als who did not return to China after the Tiananmen protests. The Chinese government now strictly limits opportunities for its students to study in these countries because they are seen as responsible for China's brain drain (according to the most conservative estimates released by the state, fewer than 30 percent of Chinese students traveling to Western countries since 1978 have returned to China),[11] and for ideologically 'pollution', for many of the democratic ideals of the 1989 democratic movement in China are thought to have been derived from the West.[12] Whereas English and French were once almost exclusively the foreign languages of choice for Chinese students, and Japanese and German continue to be popular, Arabic is an increasingly prominent foreign language for Muslims and non-Muslims, signaling a subtle shift in China's foreign relations and language policy.

With regard to the first Gulf War, Hajji Muhammad Zhang, the Hui Arabic teacher who has traveled frequently in Egypt, Iraq, Pakistan, and the pilgrimage cities, said: 'The state is correct not to get too involved in this crisis. We have too much at stake to risk anything more than silent approval of the UN resolutions. In no way should we be associated with the US invasion of Iraq, or send troops to liberate Kuwait. We have our own interests to worry about'. Imam Shi Kunbing of the Oxen Street mosque, during his Friday sermon on 22 February 1991, confirmed this position

11. The state-sponsored *Beijing Review* (28 January 1991) reported that only 29.8 percent (12,500) of the students sent abroad since 1978 had returned. These figures are very difficult to judge, since the vast majority of students were privately sponsored (*zi fei*), not state-sponsored (*gong fei*), and the official figures primarily report on state-sponsored students, who are much more likely to return, because their study is initially funded by the government. Leo A. Orleans (1988) reported that between 1978 and 1988, only 19,500 students had returned to China, most of them belonging to the state-sponsored group, despite a rough estimate that 40,000 to 64,000 students had gone abroad during that time. Government statements have reflected an even greater drop in returned students since the Tiananmen incident in 1989. Premier Li Peng reported that 700 students had returned since June 1989, out of a reported total of 40,000 Chinese students in the United States alone in 1989; one Hong Kong source stated that only 520 of 8,000 (6.6 percent) state-sponsored students had returned (see Rosen 1992).

12. For an analysis of the role of China's minorities in the Tiananmen protests, with particular attention to the leadership of the Uyghur Muslim student leader Wu'er Kaixi (whose name in Turkic-Uyghur is Uerkesh Daolet), see Gladney (1990).

when he said: 'We support our government's position. Let us hope for a "peaceful resolution" of this conflict'.

Colonialism under different masters

'Saddam Hussein was right to take back Kuwait; it was a creation of the imperialists anyway,' Professor Feng Jinyuan vehemently declared. 'The US is "liberating Kuwait" only to return it to its monarchical overlords. Where is the US's concern with democracy and human rights now? All they care about is oil and the preservation of continued colonial interests in the Gulf. They have no right to interfere in Muslim affairs.'

Such is the position of an academic at the Institute of World Religions of the prestigious Chinese Academy of Social Sciences, who has written several books in Chinese on the history of Islam, as well as an Arabic-only publication of his book *Islam in China*.[13] His position is similar to that quoted in the letter on page 323: he rejects the role of the United State in the conflict and supports Saddam, specifically *in reaction to US involvement*.

I spoke by telephone with a Hui former classmate of mine in Lanzhou, a member of the prominent Salafiyya Islamic order (described on pages 321–2). He had similar views but for very different reasons. My friend argued that all true Muslims should support Saddam Hussein, no matter what errors he has committed in the past: 'By raising the issue of the plight of the Palestinians and by standing up to the US and attacking Israel, Saddam has shown the world that Muslims have a new strong leader that can unite them'. He said that all conservative Muslims in the northwest supported Saddam 'because they were Muslims'. When I asked him how he could support a man who attacked his fellow Muslims in Kuwait and Saudi Arabia, he replied that these people were merely tools of the Western imperialist powers and were only concerned with oil revenues, not Quranic justice: 'We Muslims in China are twice as devout as the Saudi and Kuwaiti shaykhs who spend their wealth in the brothels of Southeast Asia and Bahrain. We don't smoke, drink, or waste our money. Why should we support these people? They are getting what they deserve for their profligate lifestyles'.

13. See Feng Jinyuan's impressive collection of articles on Islam in China, Feng and Li (1985).

Imam Zhang Huatang, the Hui spiritual leader at the Xiamen mosque in Fujian Province, whose home mosque was the great Southgate Mosque in Qinghai, renowned as the center of the conservative Ikhwan brotherhood when it flourished in the 1930s in northwest China under the patronage of a Muslim warlord, put it most succinctly: 'We needn't worry about our brothers in Kuwait. Allah will protect the righteous. Saddam is our new Arab Muslim hero, and all Muslims should support him'. Imam Zhang spent twelve years in prison for his strong religious views during the Cultural Revolution, and he does not fear what the state might do to him now if he speaks his mind. 'China is a free country when it comes to religion,' he reminded me. 'We Muslims are free to believe, and those atheist Party members are free not to believe. Time will tell who is right.'

But what about the cost of lamb?

On the streets of Beijing and Xiamen, where I was able to talk with Muslims coming out of prayer or frequenting local Muslim restaurants, I was surprised by the lack of concern over the 1991 crisis.[14] The Muslim intellectuals, conservatives, and clerics had their strong views, but the 'man on the street' seemed to be more concerned with a recent increase in the price of lamb. When there were any noticeable emotions expressed, they seemed to be in step with the many Han Chinese I talked with. People were glad the United States and coalition forces had sent troops and were bombing Iraq because, they said, 'it was exciting'. Chinese are known throughout Asia as a people who like to watch *renao* (literally 'hot and noisy', or excitement), and this may very well be another case of a spark of activity in an otherwise boring and uneventful Spring Festival (Chinese New Year was on 15 February 1991).

It might also reflect much deeper concerns, however. Some political analysts suggested that many Chinese supported the bomb-

14. Hui Muslims are China's most urban minority. According to the 2000 census, in Beijing city alone there were more than 250,000 Muslims. In Xiamen the resident community of Muslims is small, but so many domestic and foreign Muslims pass through that important port city that there are two Muslim restaurants and the local mosque has received an Islamic facelift, now graced with three large domes above the entrance to its southern Chinese-style mosque with a traditionally sloping red-tile roof over its prayer hall.

ing of Iraq because it was a long-time friend of China, and it thus represented a roundabout way of causing the unpopular Chinese government to lose face, a view similar to the widespread euphoria at the fall of Romania's Ceausescu (also an old friend of the Chinese regime) in December 1989. This politicized view was supported by one Hui student, who told me: 'All these slogans about "peaceful resolution", "peaceful resolution!" Who are Li Peng and Jiang Zemin to talk about that, when they "peacefully resolved" our Tiananmen June 4th protest by resorting to tanks and bullets.' The continued anger over the crushing of the student protest was still palpable in Beijing, and it often expressed itself obliquely – the only possible avenue for political dissent in post-Tiananmen China. One Hui who made the connection between the protest and Muslim disgruntlement happened to be a taxi driver: 'The government killed hundreds of students in Tiananmen and at least twenty of our fellow Muslims in Xinjiang last year. I'm sure glad somebody is pounding one of Li Peng's friends in the Middle East'.

It is difficult to measure whether this political dissatisfaction was widespread beyond Beijing. Certainly, more Islamic concerns prevailed in the northwest. In Beijing, even more common was the view that Muslims were not concerned about this conflict because it had not yet affected them. They were still too concerned about the rising price of lamb to worry about Saddam Hussein.

In general, many of these Hui Muslims were members of the Ikhwan and Gedimu, who traditionally supported the Chinese state in its foreign and domestic affairs. They opposed radical Islam, at home and abroad, because it could never succeed in a country that was only 2 percent Muslim. Muslims outside of the northwest are subsumed in a sea of Han Chinese and cannot afford to appear too 'radical' – they are ostracized enough merely for not eating pork. For them, it was more important to survive, economically, politically, and ideologically. As a result, people were often guarded about their views on the subject and especially reluctant to speak to a foreigner about them. Indeed, it is risky for anyone to talk politics in China these days, even if it is about a war very far away.

At one luncheon for a conference that I attended in 1991, there was a table of mainly Chinese military men, which I managed to join. After about one hour of small talk, toasts to Sino-American friendship, and mutual polite introductions, I asked them if they would share with me their views on the Gulf crisis, since I rarely had the opportunity to speak with Chinese officers. The conversation immediately died, people looked nervously at their plates, and the most senior officer, a lieutenant colonel, finally said: 'We favor "peaceful resolution" of the conflict.' Everyone smiled (recognizing the well-worn and very safe slogan), and somebody mentioned that a new course of food was on its way. While military officers in any country would be reluctant to discuss government policy with an outsider, their response indicated clearly the official line circulating in China at that time.

Clearly China's Hui Muslims during the first Gulf War were not very supportive of Saddam Hussein, but neither were they strongly concerned about the fate of Kuwait or angered by a US-led multi-lateral invasion of Iraq. They certainly did not feel that the first Gulf War was directed against Muslims. More informed than ever before, they were divided in opinion, interested in the outcome, and generally satisfied with the government's position on the conflict. This view changed dramatically during the most recent Gulf conflict.

The war on Iraq: a war on Islam?

One week after Operation Freedom was launched during the 2003 war on Iraq, I was walking down the street on my way to the Old Hui Noodle House (*Lao Hui Mianguan*), when a young Uyghur man noticed me coming from the opposite direction, and said 'Hello' in English. I replied '*Yaximusiz*' (Are you well?) in Uyghur. He then asked me in Uyghur if I spoke that language, and I said I did, but poorly, and that my Turkish was somewhat better. He asked me if I was Russian, and I told him that I was an American. For the next thirty minutes he loudly cursed and harangued me for personally contributing to the war on Muslims in Iraq. I tried to explain in Uyghur, Turkish, and Chinese that I opposed the war (though I certainly shared no love for Saddam Hussein). This did not satisfy him in any way. His voice grew so loud and his cursing so animated that we drew a small crowd. I eventually had to walk away, with him continuing to shout at me and blame me for killing 'many Muslim babies' in Iraq. I was not only concerned that he, as well as some of the other Uyghur in the small crowd who seemed to be agreeing with him (I noticed the Han Chinese who gathered just watched stoically), might grow violent, but that if the police were called he might be questioned or worse.

What struck me about this encounter was not his heated opinion on the matter – I had encountered other Muslims, Uyghur
and Hui, in Guangzhou and Ürümqi over the previous two days
who were also quite critical – but that he would attack me personally not only for being American, but also for not doing more
to stop the war. He told me that he was happy I spoke Uyghur so
that I could understand how deeply he hated President Bush and
the US people. He believed the US was trying to rid the world of
Muslims. When I raised examples of US support for Muslims in
Bosnia and Albania, he just laughed and said that was all because of
oil. Later I realized I was taken aback by his attitude not only because the first Gulf War did not provoke such emotion among any
Muslims in China that I encountered, but also because whenever
I had met with the Uyghur people, having interacted with them
since 1982, they had always been extraordinarily happy to meet
someone, especially a non-Muslim American who took an interest
in their lives and history. That I had made efforts to learn Chinese
and then Uyghur only increased the level of warmth and hospital-
ity. This had clearly begun to change. I began to wonder if, after my
having worked in China for twenty-one years, Muslims there were
beginning to share other, generally Middle Eastern Muslim views
that were often critical of US policy in the Middle East, and regard
US individuals as anti-Muslim and responsible for those policies
that they found offensive to Islam or Muslim identity.

Shortly after this encounter, Hajji Ma Liangji, imam of the
Great Mosque in Xi'an, who was quoted at the beginning of this
chapter, made the following public statement:

> Osama bin Laden is a terrorist, but you see he really has nothing to do with
> Islam, which preaches peace and love … But it is Mr Bush who is forcing
> those of us who otherwise didn't have a strong feeling about Osama one
> way or another to side resolutely against the US. September 11 was wrong,
> but Mr Bush's use of violence … is absolutely wrong. (Cheng 2003)

This echoed a growing anti-US sentiment among Muslims in
China that I did not feel was present at all during the first Gulf War;
nor did I ever detect it in my twenty-one years of conducting research among Muslims in China.[15] Although I never encountered
such a strong and angry opinion among Uyghur in Kashgar as I did

15. For reflections on more than twenty years of conducting multi-sited fieldwork
     in China, see my paper 'Lessons (un)Learned: 10 Reflections on 20 years of

from the young man on the street in Ürümqi, I did detect a strong feeling of disapproval for the war and Westerners in general. One evening I tried to visit the Great Idgah Mosque in central Kashgar and the doorman would not let me in. Despite efforts in Uyghur and Chinese to explain that I had visited the mosque several times before, had worked in China, and was not a tourist, he would not let me enter. Even after I offered to pay a ticket price usually charged to tourists, he would not even allow me into the court-yard, despite the fact that it was after the sunset prayer and there was almost no one in the mosque. As I left he said to a Uyghur standing next to him, 'We do not want *kafir* [non-Muslims] in our *masjid* [mosque]'.

Ms A Yi Sha Cui Rui Chun (Chinese surname Cui, Muslim name Aisha) is the proprietor of a small Muslim dress and gift shop near the China Islamic Society headquarters in the Xuanwu Dis-trict of Beijing. When I visited her Moslem Dress and Personal Adornment Factory on 29 March 2003, she showed me several intricate 'hajj gowns' made in her factory to help identify Muslims from China while on the hajj (with Chinese and Arabic embroi-dered on the front of the garment) as well as an extraordinary collection of Chinese Islamic paintings by the renowned Hui artist Hajji Abdul Hakim Liu Jingy Abdul. When I told her the story of my encounter with the young Uyghur man in Ürümqi, she said that while Hui in Beijing were not as worked up about the war, they too were unified in their opinion against it: 'We Hui feel that it is a not just a war against Iraq, but it could be against Islam'. Over lunch at the China Islamic Society, I met with the new president, Hajji Yu Zhengui, and the deputy dean of the China Islamic In-stitute at the association, Mr Gao Zhanfu. Both Hui scholars who recently moved to Beijing from northwest China, and whom I had known since 1983, they confirmed what Aisha had told me. Muslims in China were not only unified in their opinion against the war, but that there had been numerous requests from around the country for permission to protest. They explained that the role of the China Islamic Association was to relay these feelings to the Chinese government and that Muslim opinion was of great

Fieldwork in the Peoples Republic of China', presented at the symposium 'Anthropology in and of China: A Cross-Generation Conversation', Center for Chinese Studies, University of California, Berkeley, 8-9 March 2002.

interest to China's leaders. Interestingly, there seemed to be similar US interest in Muslim opinion in China. The US Ambassador to China, Mr Clark T. Randt Jr, had visited the Islamic Association twice since becoming ambassador in July 2001, the first time a US ambassador had ever visited the Islamic Association.

Growing anti-US and anti-Israeli policy in the Middle East was first brought to my attention by an article in a Muslim gazette that reported a Hui protest against the Palestine conflict ('Appealing Call', *Tianmu Musilin jianxun* (*Tianmu Muslim Bulletin*) 14, 20 May 2002:3).[16] The paper reported that the imam of a mosque in Tianjin was seeking to raise an army of martyrs to fight against Israel and help liberate Palestine. When I first learned of this activity, I was amazed to think that just a decade ago Muslims in China were not only not very interested in the first Gulf War, and almost completely uninformed about the preceding Iran–Iraq war, but few were deeply concerned about Arab–Israeli tensions. While Hui (and for the most part other Muslim minorities in China) are not at all supportive of some Uyghur separatist activities, and Muslims in China are generally quite divided over many other issues, the increasing unity of opinion about the war in Iraq and the importance of the Middle East for Muslims in China indicates dramatic changes over the past two decades for China's Muslims.

Open doors, guarded expressions

The views of China's Muslims about the Gulf crises of 1991 and 2003 are impossible to summarize or categorize neatly, particularly when in the past many felt reluctant to express them, the media in China are restricted, and there is strict government control over any public protests by Muslims. Nevertheless, the preceding discussion indicates an important development in China over the past twelve years: Muslims in China are now increasingly well-informed about events in the Middle East, even if they are uncomfortable about openly discussing them. When I began my research on Muslims in China in 1982, the Iran–Iraq war was well under way. Not only was there very little news coverage of the event in the Chinese press,

16. *Tianmu Musilin jianxun* is a periodical produced by the Northern Mosque of Tianmu Community, Beichen District of Tianjin. I would like to thank Dr Wang Jianping for directing me to this source.

but the Muslims I spoke with were completely uninformed about the conflict. Few knew that there was a difference between Sunni and Shi'ite, because almost all of China's Muslims are Sunni, and although most had heard of Khomeini, few except for a handful of Islamic scholars acknowledged that he represented an entirely different Islamic school of thought. The most political view I could get anyone to express was, 'Muslims should not fight Muslims'.

Clearly, the views expressed here, though quite divergent, are very well-informed. It is their variety that illustrates the tremendous exposure to global Muslim events that the members of China's Muslim population are now experiencing. They travel to the Middle East, read foreign Islamic publications in Arabic and Chinese translation, listen to foreign Muslim sermons on audio-cassettes, entertain foreign Muslim guests (as well as the occasional Western scholar interested in Islam), and even have access to broadcasts of the Al-Jazeerah Channel via Chinese television news summaries.[17] While there was no unified position regarding the first Gulf War, and no single 'subaltern voice' that spoke on behalf of the others, there certainly are numerous Muslim voices that both praised and condemned Saddam, for very articulate and divergent reasons. Yet I could not find one Muslim voice that praised the war against Iraq. Increasingly, many Muslim voices in China are turning against the US, or any policy that they feel hurts Muslims around the world.

The rising prominence of China in Middle Eastern affairs and the increasingly important role its Muslims play in China's response to those events are evidence of a new period of transnational interaction with the Islamic world for China's Muslims. The winds of Islamic opinion now increasingly blow across China. If radical Islamist and/or nationalist flags unfurl in one corner of the Muslim world, they cannot but be saluted or contested by some in another, more eastern corner.

17. An Al-Jazeerah Channel bureau was opened in Beijing in November 2002. The bureau chief, Mr Ezzat Shahrour, a former Palestinian diplomat, told me during an interview on 30 March 2003 that the Chinese authorities were so eager to have the station broadcasting from Beijing that they sped up their permits and the setting up their new office on the top floor of one of the Jianguomenwai diplomatic-compound buildings.

15
BODILY POSITIONS, SOCIAL
DISPOSITIONS

Images of Tiananmen

Do you know under Heaven
– How many twists and turns there are in the Yellow River?
– How many boats there are
On each of the twists and turns?
– How many poles there are
On each of the boats?
– How many oarsmen there are
On each of the twists and turns
To pole the boats along?
(Traditional Chinese folk song and refrain from *River Elegy*)

As we approach the fourteenth anniversary of the Tiananmen Square massacre of 4 June 1989, I am still unable to merely re-evaluate the bodily symbols of the carnage in pure isolation from the events themselves. These events were mediated to us, or most of us, through a montage of television, newspaper, magazine, and theater images, engaging the entire country, if not the whole world, for one brief moment, in the *spectacle* of a new catastrophic *China Syndrome* (Baudrillard 1981:83). The events turned us all into 'China watchers', as the Chinese feminist literary critic Rey Chow (1990:2) has noted in a provocative essay, 'Violence in the Other Country: China as Crisis, Spectacle, and Woman'.[1]

---

1. This chapter was originally presented with various media images, including slides from 'Beijing Spring', a photo-essay collection by the Pulitzer prize winning photographers David and Peter Turnley (1989); footage from the film *River Elegy* (Xia 1988), discussed later in this chapter; and various clips from news coverage of the events in June 1989 and shortly thereafter, primarily from CNN, ABC, NBC, and CBS. None of the images presented is of my own creation, and thus the images are of second-order mediation.

Hence, in this chapter, once again we will become China watchers, as well as readers, for it is my argument that far from any fixed meaning inherent to the individual symbols themselves, it is their confusing mixture, their pastiche, their intertextuality and interreferentiality, that gives the symbols their compellingness and power, a power that is ongoing, transfixed in our minds through the media. This is how most of us were confronted with the incidents associated with the 'Beijing Spring'. I, and many others who have studied and lived in China, were forced to watch the events unfold on television sets in living room, and then re-read about them, in various documentary publications concerning the event, far from the events themselves. Yet these images are all too familiar – therein lies the danger of mediated symbols: as with photographs, overexposure makes the extraordinary commonplace, the bizarre blasé, the transmitted images historicized, detemporalized, and thus powerless. My innovation is that I do not provide the narrative supplied with the videotapes and chronicles, as is common with most slide shows, for the images on our television sets and in the documentaries already came to us narrated, by informed observers and even 'China experts', many flown in like academic SWAT teams at the very height of the movement to give us the final hermeneutic, by which to understand the confused and conflicting images, even as they unfolded before our eyes. As if sports announcers at an athletic event, these 'sinologists' and 'journalists' literally called the shots on Tiananmen Square.

It is noteworthy that in the reporting of the original event, there was a kind of kaleidoscopic confusion reported by those who were in the square. It was only much later that order was imposed on the chaotic, interpretation on the miasmic social phenomena. The only point that most of the 'eyewitnesses' could agree on was that it happened. They each reported only small chunks, unmitigated moments within the events themselves, an incredible simultaneity of overly layered symbols and actions that were entirely confusing even to those who produced them. I interviewed a number of Chinese who had fled shortly after 4 June, and most still had little idea of what happened where, when, and with whom. Some even

I would like to thank Gail Herschatter, Lisa Rofel, and Chris Kruegler for earlier critical comments, as well as Carol Breckenridge and Arjun Appadurai for their initial encouragement to undertake this project.

spent hours at my home watching my taped CNN news broadcasts and Ted Koppel overviews. As the events unfolded, from the
pro-democracy parades, to the hunger strike, to the crackdown, no
one present had an overall view, something that we still seem in
desperate need of (as the ongoing debates about where, when and
how many were killed reveal; even the student leader, Chai Ling,
upon her escape, was asked if she had 'really' seen anyone killed in
the square [*New York Times* 14 October 1989:A3]). Among the eyewitnesses in Beijing, those who could do so often sought this overall view from the media, and found such sources only by retreating
to Western hotels. Craig Calhoun, at that time a sociologist from
the University of North Carolina who was teaching at the Beijing
Foreign Studies University, reported his own frustration at being
cut off from the events and the news of the happenings in Beijing,
even though he was just such an eyewitness:

> Finally two expatriate friends and I recognized the solution. We rented
> a room in the Shangri-La Hotel, a fancy Hong Kong/PRC joint ven-
> ture a mile down the Xisanhuan road. There we enjoyed the benefits
> of Cable News Network reports every half-hour around the clock.
> There we found the CBS crew ensconced on the fifth floor, though
> Dan Rather had already departed. Fang Lizhi and his American friend,
> Perry Link, passed through as the former struggled with whether to seek
> asylum in the US embassy. My Chinese students came and watched the
> television reports. They used the phone to call friends around town and
> nearby, checking and cross-checking various reports. We sent and received
> FAXes. We cabled in reports to London newspapers and held interviews
> with American television stations by long-distances.
>   We were, according to these reports, 'eyewitnesses', voices from the
> center of things. Our words became the stuff of television reports. Yet,
> in order to gain some perspective beyond what our own immediate ob-
> servations gave us, we were dependent on those same television reports,
> especially CNN, beamed to Beijing by satellite ... No one could really
> know the whole story, of course, but the only possible approach to a
> 'complete' view depended on the role of telephones and mass media (as
> well as a face-to-face network of gossip and discussion) in synthesizing
> the reports of many witnesses. We lived crucially in both the physical
> space of Beijing and the placeless (or 'metatopical') space of the interna-
> tional information flow. (Calhoun 1989:54–5)

From the above account, one is left with the incredible image
of the 'eyewitness' eyeing CNN newscasts from a foreign hotel
room in Beijing, while at the same time talking to CNN reporters

by telephone about what was going on in the city – the mediated image has come the full hermeneutic circle, literally feeding off itself. Many local Chinese had to depend on the rumor mill, or the state press (each with their own circularities). Exposure to and manipulation of the media by all sides in the events in June 1989. is well known: students produced banners in Western languages that often quoted and courted Western ideas, such as citations from Patrick Henry ('Give Me Liberty or Give Me Death') and Lord Acton ('Absolute Power Corrupts Absolutely'). At the same time, and shortly thereafter, the state-controlled media fought back: over the following summer, a four-hour and then a nine-hour documentary were shown on state television, purporting to give the 'True Story of Tiananmen', and the state media also produced a Chinese and English glossy pictorial by that title, with claims that the soldiers showed considerable restraint. These claims were supported, for example, by the well-known image of the tanks being stopped by a single man with an upraised hand. They *could* have run him over, according to the state media, but they held back. The same televised image; two radically different interpretations.

Just as events came to us through our television screens and the clips from those reports are still carried in our memories and imaginations, I argue that there were also certain mediated 'texts' in the minds of Chinese that made these symbols and the interpretations attached to them all the more powerful. In attempting to conduct what Arjun Appadurai (1990) terms an 'ethnography of the imagination', I do not claim to have the whole story, but through image and narrative wish to illustrate that many of the dramas enacted, or perhaps re-enacted, on Tiananmen Square may have been prefigured in the minds of the Chinese population, assisted tremendously by the television series *River Elegy* (*He Shang*).

Tiananmen requiem

River Elegy was perhaps the most watched, and certainly the most hotly debated, television series in Chinese history. Six segments comprising a total of four hours aired twice in China, beginning on 15 June 1988, before being banned shortly after a scheduled third showing in May 1989. Reflecting an enormous project by

the central government to reach all of China with a single mediated message, Chinese Central Television (CCTV) is beamed
throughout China, including Taiwan and Hong Kong. It is estimated that more than 90 percent of China's population have access
to public television sets, all of which were able to receive the two
showings of *River Elegy*. In addition, the subsequent discussion in
all of China's major news media and the culmination of the debate
in the volume *Discussions of River Elegy* (*He Shanglun*; Cui 1988)
reached a wide literary audience. Likened to the significance of
the Apollo moonwalk or the Olympics to the international exposure of the event by the media, the national impact of the series
River Elegy was tremendous in terms of almost total saturation of
Chinese society.

River Elegy opens with a short scene showing various peoples in
China, including Tibetans, Buddhists, and Muslims, as well as Han
Chinese, prostrating their bodies in prayer and supplication, and
then swiftly cuts to several vistas of the Yellow River, in a heavy-
handed underscoring of its main theme: the Yellow River is the
very stuff of Chinese civilization, its source, its object in traditional
worship, its impetus for development, and its scourge. Taming the
Yellow River and channeling it for productive rather than destruc-
tive purposes has been at the intersection of history and legend in
China, for it was one of the central projects of Chairman Mao and
the legendary first emperor of China.

The metaphor of the Yellow River strikes at the heart of the
crisis of Chinese national identity: just as the state has attempted to
contain and tame the Yellow River, it has circumscribed the freedom of the Chinese people. Like the Yellow River's inexorable flow
beyond its boundedness, the people will burst forth if not allowed
creative expression, a flowing out into the world, to the 'azure blue
sea of the international realm'. Likewise, by damming the Yellow
River, preventing its flow to the sea, something about Chinese
culture is also hemmed in, damned to a repressive, backward existence. The series takes the other great figures and accomplishments
of Chinese civilization – the Great Wall; the archetypal dragon;
the excavated terracotta warrior-guardians of the entombed Qin
emperor; the inventions of compass, paper, and gunpowder; and
the architectural wonders of temple, city, and pagoda – as symbols
not of China's greatness, but of its truncated potentiality. This native possibleness has been dammed by a repressive state in the past

(and present), which now, like the Yellow River, threatens to burst forth. While these symbols have been generally portrayed in the state-run media as demonstrating China's greatness, they are now antiquated, revealing how China has failed to live up to its glorious heritage and keep pace with the modern world, conquered by foreigners in the past militarily, and in the present economically, who have humiliated China using the very technologies that Chinese invented. The television series equates the poverty of China to the most destitute of African nations.

Significantly, the series regards the problems of China's past and present as internal to China, not due to outside foreign imperialist aggression or past feudal oppression, as China's backwardness has been traditionally accounted for. Instead, China's underdevelopment results from a central flaw in Chinese culture, and following Wittfogel (1957), the narrator suggests it is due to 'oriental despotism' – the ecopolitical control over China's resources in the hands of a few. The Chinese people alone are responsible for allowing their government to repress and restrain their potentiality. Insecure over their identity as a nation, they have been too timid to engage in real reforms, as the narrator suggests:

History chose the Chinese, but the Chinese have failed to choose history … To save our civilization, we must open our door and welcome *science* and *democracy* … Why is it so difficult for social change to occur in China? Perhaps it is because we always worry: if we change our ways, will we still be Chinese? It never occurs to us that as the countries of the West underwent their many social changes during the past 300 years, no one there worried if after these changes they would still be Italian or German. *Only in China do we worry about our identity so much.* (*River Elegy*, Segment 2; emphasis added)

In search of the origins of Chinese identity and nationhood, the series looks back to the Yellow River as the cradle of Chinese civilization, and as the source of that civilization's disappointment. The environmental origins of the Chinese 'species' becomes a sociobiological, even racial, determinant:

Where are the roots of the Chinese found? Probably every yellow-skinned Chinese knows that the Chinese nation was nurtured by the Yellow River. Yellow water, yellow earth, and yellow people; a mystic, natural connection. It is almost as if we were trying to convince the world that the yellow skin of the yellow people was dyed yellow by the Yellow River. (*River Elegy*, Segment 1)

Echoing these sentiments, Ian Buruma (1990:45) found, during a visit to post–Tiananmen Hong Kong, that 'to be Chinese was no longer a simple matter':

To be Chinese, then, is not the same as to be a citizen of China, but the relationship with the motherland is complicated, vague, and wide-open to political manipulation. 'China,' wrote a Chinese-American in a Hong Kong magazine, 'is a cultural entity which flows incessantly, like the Yellow River, from its source all the way to the present time, and from there to the boundless future. This is the basic and unshakable belief in the mind of every Chinese. It is also the strongest basis for Chinese nationalism.' (Buruma 1990:45)

Lest anyone doubt the direction of the full force of *River Elegy*'s critique (for example, Geremie Barmé [1988:40] of the *Far Eastern Economic Review* suggested that the television series continued to support the status quo), the last few scenes of the series are blatantly inscribed with the following declarations in bold Chinese characters (on a background of yellowed feudal architecture, including the government buildings of the Forbidden City): 'The characteristics of despotism are secrecy, autocracy, and arbitrary rule'. In stark contrast, on a background of a deep-blue sea being crossed by a white (possibly exploration) ship and surrounded by glistening snowcapped peaks, the following proclamation is written: 'The characteristics of democracy *should be* transparency, popular will, and scientism' (*River Elegy*, Segment 6; emphasis added).

These bold statements, all of which became slogans on banners and posters throughout Tiananmen Square, are followed in the segment by a brief picture of Zhao Ziyang reading a pro-reform statement at the 13th Party Congress. Then the viewer is shown the brilliant image of the Yellow River emptying into the deep-blue sea. The contrast is stunning. And lest anyone lose the intended meaning behind the juxtaposition, the narrator voices-over the following interpretation:

The Yellow River is destined to cut across the loess plateau. The Yellow River will ultimately enter the azure ocean … The Yellow River has arrived at the mouth of the ocean – a magnificent but painful juncture. It is here that the mud and silt carried turbulently along for thousands of *li* will be deposited to form a new mainland. It is here that the surging waves of the Yellow River will collide together. The Yellow River must cleanse itself of its terror of the ocean. The Yellow River must keep the indomitable will and vigor that came with it from the high plateau. The life-giving water comes from the ocean and returns to the ocean. After a thousand years of solitude the Yellow River finally catches sight of the azure sea. (*River Elegy*, Segment 6)

Yet to fix the interpretation of the metaphor even more firmly in the imaginations of the viewers, the narrator makes the following conclusion about reform:

Reform on a deeper level means a major transformation of the civilization – a painful, dangerous, and arduous process that *may require the sacrifice of this generation* or of several generations to come. We are standing at the crossroads: either we let our ancient civilization fall never to rise again, or we help it to acquire the mechanisms for a new life. Whatever we do, there is no way that any of us can shirk our historical responsibility. (*River Elegy*, Segment 6; emphasis added)

This position shocked many in China, and not only the hardliners, who felt China itself was being deconstructed, and not just its traditions. Those who criticized *River Elegy* shortly after it was released as being 'nihilist' and 'reactionary' (see Morrison 1989:258) questioned not only its historical accuracy, but, more importantly, its refusal to blame the problems of the Chinese past and present on anyone but the Chinese people themselves: not the foreign aggressors, the feudal society, or even the Gang of Four. China alone is held to blame, and this leads to a requestioning of what it means to be Chinese in the new introspective light. Even the ultra-left politician Wang Zhen, at the thirtieth anniversary of the establishment of the Ningxia Hui Autonomous Region, considered attacks by the filmmakers on China's traditional symbols, such as the Yellow River, the Great Wall, and the dragon, as attacks on the Chinese people and what it means to be Chinese. To support this position, the government banned *River Elegy* and sought to arrest several of the scholars who were interviewed in and advised on the making of the series, including the filmmaker, Su Xiaokang, who escaped to France. While the state may be able to arrest, ban, and purge the program and its makers, it can never remove the texts from China's history or from the imaginations of those who watched it. Nor can it purge the world of the post-Tiananmen image of China, now fixed in the media and the consciousness of those of us who observed the event in its mediated form.

The threat spoken of in *River Elegy* is ominous and specific: unless something is done soon, there will be another disastrous upsurge of enormous significance. Zha Jianying, a Chinese writer present in Beijing in the spring of 1989, noted that the series was made in an atmosphere pervaded by a palpable sense of fear for the future, as China's intellectuals debated the merits of neo-authoritarianism over democracy, and the dangers of bourgeois liberalism. In one segment, Chinese scientists are shown predicting that in the near future there will be a flood of the Yellow River of the proportion of 1 in 10,000 years. As the waters surge, so does popular unrest: footage of student marches in the May 4th and other nationalist movements, protesting crowds in the Sino-Japanese War, and mobilized masses in the Cultural Revolution are all flashed past the viewer in a rapid, almost random pastiche, a staccato reminder that Chinese society itself regularly erupts in such chaos.

Without the always explicit interpretation and heavily narrated images, *River Elegy* could qualify as China's first post-modern television series. Yet its objective is always before its viewers, and its makers. In a conversation that I had with Yuan Zhiming, one of the filmmakers who also fled the country, he stated: '*River Elegy* was made with a purpose: by sifting through China's film archives for episodes of social protest and mass movements, we wanted to stir up the people and the government to support the reform programs which we thought were going too slow and in danger of being turned back' (pers. interview). This is the major contribution of *River Elegy*: it sets the stage for the Beijing Spring by accumulating these former texts of revolutionary nationalism, and juxtaposing them against present social crises. Unless *certain* people are willing to sacrifice their bodies for the welfare of the country, the series argues, another social disaster is bound to take place. It can only be averted by opening, in the case of the Yellow River, to the sea or, in the case of the Chinese people, to the outside (mainly Western) world. Despite the short-term problems, such 'spiritual pollution' from the West, corruption, and economic fluctuation, the long-term consequences of restricting the flow of society outward are even more disastrous. China must continue to flow toward reform, despite the twists and turns.

Bodily efficacy and River Elegy

There are always periods when the State as organism has problems with its own collective bodies, when these bodies, claiming certain privileges, are forced in spite of themselves to open onto something that exceeds them, a short revolutionary instant, an experimental surge. A confused situation: each time it occurs, it is necessary to analyze tendencies and poles, the nature of the movements. All of a sudden, it is as if the collective body of the notary publics were advancing like Arabs or Indians, then regrouping and reorganizing: a comic opera where you never know what is going to happen next (even the cry 'The police are with us!' is sometimes heard). (Deleuze and Guattari 1987:366–7)

It has been suggested that most of the symbols of the pro-democracy protest in Beijing were derivative, borrowed from Japan (headbands), Korea (occupation of the square), the Philippines (two-fingered victory sign), Gandhi (hunger strike), the US (sit-down strikes, the Statue of Liberty), and the former Soviet Union (banners and *glasnost*), or other 'foreign influences'. Other semiotic historians, primarily China scholars, have argued that there was almost nothing new to Tiananmen, except perhaps the tanks. The history of student protests in China since 4 May 1919 has been infused with symbols of protest easily available to most Chinese educated in the state-controlled centralized school curriculum, which is heavy on revolutionary history: banners parodying leaders and representing various schools, student speeches, parades through Tiananmen Square, and the content of the various slogans themselves, even the singing of the 1919 equivalent of 'Down with Li Peng' to the tune of 'Frere Jacques', was present in 1919 (see Wasserstrom 1990). By contrast, more post-modern analyses have argued that it was a potpourri of all of these texts: the students randomly, even playfully, chose whatever was available from a vast repertoire of non-violent symbolic options – the salad-bar approach to social protest.

All of these arguments have merit, but they do not address a central question: Why was it that the students selected these particular texts, and deselected others?[2] It is more interesting in some ways to examine what was missing from the protests than what was present. The students did not occupy buildings (as at Kent State University, USA), they did not organize economic boycotts or strikes (as in South Africa), they did not boycott political organizations (in fact they sought access to them), and, most importantly,

2. For an exhaustive list of possible methods of non-violent protest, many effectively employed by the students in Beijing, see the summary by Gene Sharp (1973), who was in Tiananmen Square during the last two weeks of the 1989 movement.

they did not endorse any violent alternatives (as in South Korea, Japan, and South Africa). The last-minute violent defenses improvised on the square were just that; they had little to do with the movement or its intent.

The lack of a strategy, which is what many commentators now say led to the failure of the student movement, was precisely its genius. The students drew upon scripts, consciously or unconsciously, that were immediately obvious in their meaning to everyone in China. This became apparent to me when I visited Beijing in January 1990: my colleagues, classmates and friends were still privately talking about the major influence of *River Elegy* on the spring 1989 movement and enduring controversy. Witnesses present also commented on the many discussions provoked by *River Elegy* in the square (see Calhoun 1989:64–5). Partly as a result of the television series (portraying in several vignettes such important texts as the Statue of Liberty, students lecturing the masses, parades of university students under school banners, and pictures of French enlightenment figures juxtaposed against those of Chinese revolutionary heroes), partly as a result of the active collective memory of those who had engaged in mass movements before (remember that most of the twenty-year-old college students were not even born during the height of the Cultural Revolution, 1966–1969), and especially as re-enactments of the many Chinese revolutionary history scripts known to all in China, these symbols were selected over others and reinvested with meanings, all of which had their own genealogies and velocities. *River Elegy* may have served as a kind of tunnel of superconductivity in which some of a range of symbols was selected, reinvested with contemporary significance, and shot, ricochet-fashion, into the minds of the nearly 1 billion people. As Baudrillard (1981:16) reminds us, it is these simulacra, these simulations of reality, that often become more powerful than the historical memory of the event itself.

By participating in the theater of the revolutionary real, Chinese citizens reclaimed an alternative reality, their enshrined past, much as Carol Breckenridge has discussed with regard to video-coach tourism in India, popular because, among other things, it offers many tourists the opportunity to embody, as Guy Debord suggests, 'the image of a possible role' (Debord 1983:60, cited in Breckenridge 1990:27). By participating in the protestations of the Beijing Spring, the students could attempt to become patriotic revolu-

tionaries through their imaginations and bodily re-enactments
– 'possible lives' made impossible for those born in 'post-revolu-
tionary' China, yet something even Mao sought to instill in the
younger generations during the fateful Cultural Revolution to
prove their love of and loyalty to the country. These tensions between
patriotism, dissidence, and revolution have never been resolved
in China.

Following Mayfair Yang's (1989:42–3) helpful discussion of
Michel de Certeau's (1984:35–9) distinction between strategy and
tactics, I would argue that the embodiment of past revolutionary
activities in the Tiananmen protest was not due to long-term planning and overdetermined intentionality. As tactical reactions and
immediate responses to unpredictable unfolding events, student
practices were not well-thought-out devices or strategies. Exiled
participants I have talked with, including Wu'er Kaixi, Shen Tong,
Liu Yan, and Cai Jinqing, have noted that there was no overall plan
or strategic organization to the protest. Even the hunger strike, the
most effective tactic employed by the students, which galvanized
the sympathies of China's citizenry, according to Wu'er Kaixi was
suggested at an impromptu meeting of a few student leaders at his
dormitory room on the evening of 12 May 1989; there was almost
no prior planning involved (pers. interview, 20 January 1990).
Though much time and energy were often devoted to organization by the students, in the end it was response to the state's movements that mattered. It was action and reaction: Hu Yaobang's funeral – a memorial protest; the 26 April condemnatory editorial by
Deng Xiaoping – an outpouring of controlled anger and a peaceful, disciplined protest; the imposition of martial law (20 May) – a
blockade of the military; the visit of Gorbachev and the Western
press – the opportunity to press home demands for substantial dialogue and representation; the crackdown – the futile response with
'weapons of the weak'; and the arrests – the new alternative movement in exile. All of these moves and countermoves were not so
much political maneuvers by astute street activists as they were gut
reactions geared to keeping one purpose alive: the delegitimation
of the current regime.

This is perhaps why the Chinese students in the square attained
such a brief but irreversible moral victory over the state, and
why their tactics gained such incisive efficacy: each was specifically geared to delegitimize, to de-face, the state. Like well-honed

weapons, these symbolic tactics had proved morally efficacious in the past, as the movie *River Elegy* had so eloquently demonstrated, and they were likely to work again. I disagree with those who feel the students may have failed through lack of organization, not withdrawing from the square soon enough, or not having enough specific demands, and that the Communist leadership won by finally showing their true identity (Leys 1989). In the semiotic battle over legitimacy and face, victory cannot be measured in terms of the temporal appropriation of physical space and the destruction of bodies: it can only be measured by time and morality, of which the Chinese leadership at this point seem to be in great need. While the students have temporarily suffered a defeat in China, the events there may have had a tremendous symbolic influence on Eastern Europe. Just as Honecker considered calling in the tanks to East Berlin, and was dissuaded from using the 'Chinese solution', Gorbachev reportedly attempted to prevent other Eastern European leaders from following the 'Chinese model' – a mechanized deployment of maximum deadly force that bore striking resemblance to the Prague Spring of 1968, which also was resisted by the placing of protesters' bodies in front and on top of armored vehicles and tanks, and admitted as a tragic mistake by the newly installed Czech government.[3]

Bodily dispositions and Tiananmen

Three of the most important overarching symbols of the moral campaign by the students against the state include, I argue, the hunger strike, the 'Goddess of Democracy', and the occupation of Tiananmen Square. Each of these meta-symbols revolved around bodies: bodies of students, figures of representation, and zones of physical displacement.

Student bodies and Confucian hierarchies of the self. The 'hunger strike' gained momentum because it devolved upon the primary symbol

---

3. Startling original footage of the blockage of Soviet tanks and armored troop carriers in the Prague Spring by Czech bodies, many of whom stood in front and crawled on top of the vehicles, much like the individual in the streets of Beijing, can be seen in the film *The Unbearable Lightness of Being*, which was popular among Chinese students abroad, but I believe was prevented from being shown in China, due to its supposed 'sexual', not political, content.

of the Tiananmen protest: the bodies of the students themselves. As Jean Comaroff (1985:6–7) has argued:

Indeed, it is a truism that the body is the tangible frame of selfhood in individual and collective experience, providing a constellation of physical signs with the potential for signifying the relations of persons to their contexts. The body mediates all action upon the world and simultaneously constitutes both the self and the universe of social and natural relations of which it is a part. Although the process is not reflected upon, the logic of that universe is itself written into the 'natural' symbols that the body affords.

In the traditional Confucian hierarchy, it is the body/position of the scholar-official who, under the emperor, ranks highest in value, above farmers, workers, and merchants. By extension, those training to become scholar-officials, the students, occupy a special place in the social and ontological hierarchy. Little old ladies, mothers with children, and the populace in general ventured forth in front of the invading trucks of armies, to 'save our students'. The bodies of the students, it was generally agreed, were more sacrosanct than their own. To students of Eastern philosophy, this valorization of intellectuals in Chinese society has a familiar ring.

Tu Weiming, the Harvard philosopher and 'living Confucianist', in a provocative article on embodiment in Confucianism, noted that Mengzi (Mencius) defined the sage as 'the person who has brought the bodily form to fruition', because he, as one who has attained the highest moral excellence within humanity, 'assumes that the body is where the deepest human spirituality dwells' (Tu 1989:476). This results from the lack of a Cartesian dichotomization between the mind and body in Eastern thought, which locates the self in the 'heart-mind' (*xin*) that is expressed through the vital energy and raw material of the body (Yasuo 1987). While there is 'self and body' imaging, as Emily Martin (1987:77) has found in the West, in Confucianism it is not 'separation' that is stressed, so much as the transformative power of the enlightened self through the body. The person who has learned to control the body through the education of the heart-mind has attained true self-realization:

The body, as our physical nature, must be transformed and perfected so that it can serve as a vehicle for realizing that aspect of our nature known as the nature of *i-li* (rightness and principle), the moral nature, or simply the heart-mind (*hsin*). Even though the body is a constitutive part of our nature, it is the heart-mind that is truly human. (Tu 1989:477)

In Confucian thought, the body is at its most 'docile'. 'A body is docile', according to Foucault (1979:136), when it 'may be subjected, used, transformed and improved'. Both the Chinese state and the Chinese students believed this: their bodies therefore became the sites of intense contestation. In Confucianism, the 'authentic purpose of education' is the transformation of the self; it is the role of the educated in the political process to seek the humanization of society:

The Confucian faith in the transformability and perfectibility of the human condition through communal self-effort implies that personal growth has not only ethical value but political significance. The ritualization of the body is relevant to political leadership as well as to social harmony in the family, neighborhood, and clan. Since Confucians believed that exemplary teaching is an integral part of political leadership, the personal morality of those involved is a precondition for good politics. (Tu 1989:481)

The students, through learning and exemplary moral behavior, had every right to condemn the governmental leaders for their many personal corruptions and, more importantly, their gradual disengagement from the transformation of self and society. Dismayed at finding the avenues to power in China still blocked by nepotism and favoritism, instead of based on Confucian paths of moral integrity and educational attainment, the students were repeating complaints voiced in the Democracy Wall Movement, which took place a decade earlier in Beijing. Wang Yifei, one of the leaders of the short-lived 1979 protest, and influential in the thinking of Chen Erjin, the greatest intellectual the movement produced, and still widely read in China, revealed this frustration when he wrote: 'If we call Western capitalism "money capitalism," then we should call Eastern socialism – "power capitalism"' (cited in Munroe 1984:19). The corruption of Party officials and their tight control over the disbursement of power in China was the complaint most often voiced among students and citizens. In this project, the students were completely in line with the central message of *River Elegy*: the instructing of the Chinese people and government as to the correct functioning of society by China's designated contemporary scholars and intellectual elites. In both, they are unabashedly elitist: elevated and refined language pervades *River Elegy* (as well as condescending asides about uneducated peasants), just as long pinky-nails, Western dress, and university insignia decorated the bodies of those in the square. It was outrage over Deng Xiaoping's refusal to recognize the protests as 'patriotic' and led by students and intellectuals – instead he labeled them 'hooligans' and 'instigators of social turmoil' in his 26 April editorial – that brought many students into the square. A high (but self-serving) item on the agendas of intellectuals and students was better working and living conditions for both these groups, which most thought inadequate and demeaning to their status and role in society ('Taxi-drivers, small salesmen, and workers in factories make more than we do,' was a common complaint voiced by those on the square).

This also suggests why the students were reluctant to allow the workers into the movement: their bodies did not possess the same symbolic power *vis-à-vis* the state. At one point on the Hu Yaobang memorial march of 16 April, students linked arms to prevent non-students from joining in; at another point, student leaders on the square, who at first were reluctant to allow workers in at all, gave them a small corner on the northern end. The cordons of student guards around the square were there as much to keep workers and common people out as to protect the students within.

While the state feared the economic power of the workers – and worker involvement is what may have led to the eventual decision to crack down on the movement – from the students' and greater public's point of view, the workers might divest them of the only weapon they had: the symbolic power of the student's bodies. It was not until significant worker involvement took place that the state cracked down, using it as an excuse. The state media later portrayed the 'hooligans' primarily as workers or unemployed youths, not as students, rationalizing the arrests and executions as not directed at students, who were misled 'by a few conspirators'. It was an important media point that the 'hooligans' who defaced the picture of Mao over the Gate of Heavenly Peace were not students, though one was a teacher. What is surprising is that the Western media seemed to buy into this rationalization, attributing the burning of trucks and limited violence that did occur primarily to non-students, with little outward evidence to support such an assertion. Afterwards, it was disconcerting to hear people somewhat mollified to learn that although the state had executed hundreds, perhaps thousands, there were no students among them. Upon hearing reports from released intellectuals, like Wang Luxiang and

Xie Xuanjun, two of the makers of *River Elegy*, who were arrested shortly after the crackdown, that they were treated better than the 'common' protesters and workers, and even put up in hotels, several scholars here expressed great 'relief' (even though it is clear from the state broadcasts that the vast majority of prisoners were brutally handled). That the state treated the intellectuals' bodies differently, even under arrest, supports the idea of this valorized hierarchy.

Sexuality and the student body politic. The rediscovery of individualism, sensuality, and selfhood by the students as expressed in their slogans, the Woodstock atmosphere on the square, and the Bakhtinian carnivalesque that characterized almost the entire movement, is revealed in the Wu'er Kaixi story about the student who stripped himself naked, stood on top of the one of the university buildings and declared, 'I am what I am!' (reported in Bernstein 1989:11). Assertion of self and sensuality can be a rebellious act in China, where the state monitors women's menstruation, domestic life, career, and family planning. Orville Schell's (1989:73–84) portrayal of the relatively recent preoccupation with body-building magazines in China as a legal venue for soft-porn eroticism, and the popularity of cosmetic surgery – the reconstruction of Western-style noses, breasts and buttocks on primarily Chinese women – represents an attempt to contest the state by wresting control of one's body from it. By recovering, and at times reconfiguring, their own faces, the students took face away from the state (see Yang, M. 1989:37).

The resurgence of interest in the body and sexuality in China, which led to the proliferation of slightly risqué magazines and even private 'pornography video studios', also offended some sensibilities. A demonstration by Muslims throughout China at the very same time as the student protests involved the former taking offense at an innocuous book, *Sexual Customs* (Ke and Sang 1989), a bestseller on the soft-porn market (see Chapter 11, page 232). Protests broke out in Beijing on 12 May, followed by violent uprisings in Ningxia, Gansu, Qinghai, and Xinjiang involving more than 100,000 outraged Muslims. The state met all of the Muslim demands (unlike those of the students), approving the protests, banning the books, and arresting the authors (who were later released and then rearrested for their own safety; Muslims in Gansu had taken up a collection of more than US$200,000 for the execution of the authors, in a manner similar to the *fatwa* against Salman

Rushdie). Prominent slogans held aloft by the Muslims in Chinese and Arabic included 'Ban China's *Satanic Verses*' and 'Kill China's Salman Rushdie' (see Gladney 1994, 1996:1–14).

Sexual practice in the square was apparently much more casual than elsewhere. At least one marriage was performed there (that of Li Lu, later a Columbia University graduate), and one Chinese student leader related to me that though he was assigned a tent to himself in the square, he could never sleep there because it was in frequent use by various couples. This recalls the 'free love' practices in Yenan among the early Chinese Party leaders that was apparently quite common until things 'went too far' (a local peasant girl became pregnant by one of the well-known Long Marchers) and Chairman Mao called a halt to it (after he had divorced his former wife for Jiang Qing) – an aspect of life from the *Yenan Way in Revolutionary China*, popularly known but not discussed in Mark Selden's (1971) otherwise exhaustive account. In this case, students were engaged in making not only revolution, but also love.

In his fascinating discussion of nationalism and sexuality, George Mosse (1985) argues that it is when the state is at its most authoritarian, even fascist, that it is most often tempted to appropriate the human body into itself and define the very nature of respectability, or as Claude Leforte (1986:279) would say, to think of itself as actually 'embodying the will of the people'. Under these circumstances, the state engages in what Foucault termed 'the policing of the sex':

Sex was not something one simply judged; it was a thing one administered. It was in the nature of public potential; it called for management procedures; it had to be taken charge of by analytic discourses. In the eighteenth century, sex became a 'police' matter ... (Foucault 1980:24–5)

Sex, in China, and the administration of sexuality, is well within the prerogative of the state. The alliance of nationalism with bourgeois morality, Mosse (1985:9) argues, 'forged an engine difficult to stop'. The students in Tiananmen Square may have sought to derail this traditional body-engineering in China through the reappropriation of their own bodies away from the state in their bodily positions of sexuality, protest, and fasting.

By instituting the hunger strike (a replay of the 1980 Hunan Teacher's College strike), the students adopted a very traditional role: that of seeking to 'die for the affairs of the nation'. This well-known Chinese phrase comes from the tale of Qu Yuan, a loyal minister of the 3rd-century-BC who committed suicide when the emperor failed to take his advice. The very meaning of the word 'elegy' (*shang*) in *River Elegy* connotes 'the premature death of one who has not reached adulthood' (as quoted in the excellent review of the series by Wakeman 1989:19). The premature death of the river is a metaphor for the demise of China itself, and of those willing to sacrifice themselves for the country, in the face of a recalcitrant despotic state. *River Elegy* is replete with this theme: from the coverage of the 'sacrifice', at the very beginning of the program's first segment, of two young athletes who died trying to be the first to raft the Yellow River for the competitive glory of China, ahead of better trained and equipped Americans; to the story of Qiu Jin, a female nationalist executed in 1907, a victim of her patriotism; to the final call at the end of last segment for reform, 'a painful, dangerous, and arduous process that may require the sacrifice of this generation or of several generations to come' (*River Elegy*, Segment 6). As the students in Tiananmen Square literally laid on the line their bodies, the most potent symbol they had in opposition to the state, Beijing students were also well aware of the death of Hai Zi, a Beijing University student poet who committed suicide in March 1989, apparently in part due to his frustration with the affairs of the nation. Although some students went so far as to douse themselves with kerosene, the threat to immolate themselves never materialized, yet this underscores the lengths to which some students were willing to go to 'sacrifice themselves for the nation'. The following statement from an interview with Wen Xie, a student leader at Columbia University, indicates that this belief in the need for self-sacrifice of primarily *student bodies* for the nation is still quite alive:

If you are talking about a complete democratic system, I think it is going to be a long march. But in the short run, I think Chinese intellectuals and the students will be the pioneers, or soldiers, to sacrifice themselves for the beginning of the democratic process. So many students died for democracy ... (Burras 1989:102)

Reflecting an awareness that by taking part in the movement the students were literally risking their lives, so much so that many of them publicly wrote their wills before going into the square, journalist Melinda Liu reported the following story that was passed around Beijing. It suggests an ominous and uncanny premonition on the part of the students in their concerns over the results of the anticorruption campaigns:

One joke that made the rounds in May had Deng discussing the mettle-some student protests with Zhao. 'All we need to do is kill a few young people, and this unrest will be finished,' Deng announces.
  Aghast, Zhao asks, 'How many? Twenty?'
  Deng shakes his head.
  'Two hundred?' Deng says no again.
  'Two thousand?' asks the agitated Zhao.
  Deng replies: 'No, only two.'
  Relieved, Zhao responds, 'Which two?'
  Deng answers: 'Your son and my son.' (Turnley and Turnley 1989:30)

Democracy got a goddess. Darling of the Western press, the so-called Goddess of Democracy (I say so-called because in Chinese the Statue of Liberty is also deified: *Ziyou Nushen*, means 'Goddess of Liberty/Freedom', but this was not picked up in the media) also involved the construction and display of an alternative body – one that delegitimized the state in a very critical way. Erected in front of the picture of Mao, it created a potent juxtaposition: a female mother figure, a 'goddess' of foreign origin with Chinese features, and one occupying the heart of Tiananmen Square, versus Chairman Mao, a male father figure, deified during the Cultural Revolution, advocating Marxist ideologies of foreign origin 'with Chinese characteristics', whose statue was displayed throughout China and even, on one occasion during the Cultural Revolution, paraded down the square. *River Elegy* captures this moment – an incredible enactment of the theater becoming the real, and the real as theater – in one particularly long clip of a large statue of Mao, dragged down Changan Avenue in front of the Imperial Palace, just as the Goddess of Democracy was to be paraded in mimetic fashion two decades later on 30 May. Few in China could miss the obvious parallel and parody.

At a public lecture, Marsha Wagner, East Asian Librarian at Columbia University and a witness to the events in Beijing, argued that the hunger strike was effective precisely because most of the populace felt the government would be concerned over the health of the students as its children. The similarities and distinctions are significant: no longer accepting of the family metaphor of the country, with the father figure of the state, the students wished to be thought of as the children of no one but the idea, whatever it means, of democracy. This was in marked contrast to the speech by Li Peng (at the hastily called 19 May audience with student representatives, where he was confronted, and humiliated, by Wu'er Kaixi in hospital garb, and which was broadcast throughout China and the world via its own state television), who said that because the Party thought of the students as children it wished they would end the fast and not harm themselves. It was not surprising that toppling the Goddess was the first symbolic action of conquest once the PLA forces reoccupied the square at 5.30 a.m. on 4 June, Beijing's bloodiest Sunday in recent memory.

Here I note that while many claim 'democracy' was an abstract, almost meaningless term to the students, I would agree with Ben Schwartz's (1989) assessment that this is overblown: a bit of parochial orientalism that suggests somehow Chinese do not understand or, worse, are not suited for democracy. Perhaps in response to this notion, Ye Yang, a former professor of comparative literature at Bates College, Maine, and a leader of the Independent Federation of Chinese Students and Scholars in the US, in a public talk stated: 'We Chinese are not like ET [the cuddly "extraterrestrial"]: we want the same things you do'. Many people in China yearn for change, and that is often labeled as the *-ism* of the day; Melinda Liu (in Turnley and Turnley 1989:32) reported an elderly Chinese woman as saying, 'I don't know what democracy is, but we sure need more of it'. This impending sense of dissatisfaction, of despair, and of intolerance for the failures of the current regime, and even of Chinese culture itself, is reflected in the yearning for a new social order and is the basis for *River Elegy*.

The students clearly possessed the 'minimalist' definition of democracy, what Andrew Nathan (1985:226) argues is central to current democratic theory in the West: the notion that democracy is a technique, an attempt to make the government accountable to and representative of the people. At this level, the students' call for 'real' dialogue, an open press, and the re-embodiment of their goals in the figure of the Goddess of Democracy, most of which was prefigured in the montage of texts that flashed past in *River Elegy*, posed an alternative construction of society, a more 'democratic' one, perceived as life-threatening to the current leadership. The student's version of democracy was perhaps more modeled on the goals of *perestroika* than on anything in the West. Upon Gorbachev's arrival, he was greeted with an outpouring of welcome by the Chinese populace (so much so that he could not make it into the square to place a wreath at the Memorial to Revolutionary Martyrs, as originally planned). One banner read '*Demokratizatsiya – Nasha Obshchaya Mechta*' (Democracy – Our Common Dream) (Morrison 1989:173). More than anything, the Sino-Soviet rapprochement and de-escalation of tensions in East Asia may have led the students to take the Gorbachev visit as an opportunity to press home the argument that the state has no further rationale for its continued domination of public life. (Note that Gorbachev's visit in May was much more symbolically significant to the students than that of George Bush Sr three months earlier.) Now that there is no longer any perceived external threat to China's national security, internal repression is difficult to justify.

To demonstrate that their movement was not chaotic, or a threat to state security, the students effectively maintained peaceful control of the square, and even the Chinese media at one point revealed a desire to distance itself from state control by contesting the state's claim that the students were engaging in 'social turmoil' (the news broadcast showed open streets and regular bus runs despite the student occupation of the square). Chaos (*luan*) – feared by many Chinese above any personal calamity – was avoided through the extraordinary discipline of the students, despite their disorganization. At one level, however, the state was right: it had lost control, temporarily at least, of its own society. The heart of the city, Tiananmen Square, was being effectively run by the populace, under the eyes of a goddess not of the state's choosing. Loss of control was more threatening to the state than chaos.

Bodily occupation of the public sphere

The student encampment in Tiananmen Square, the political center of post-imperial China, which replaced the Temple of Heaven as ritual center, was the most effective means of de-facing the state. By occupying the square with their bodies, the students also appropriated the symbols of the Chinese state. The Monument to the People's Heroes, with the inscriptions of former 'people's revolutions' around its base, the surrounding buildings of the Great Hall of the People and the Museum of Revolutionary History, and

even *the entombed body of Mao himself* in his mausoleum, all effectively belonged to the students. Again, the students could have occupied a building, such as the Great Hall of the People, or even the
Forbidden City, where they could have stayed more comfortably
and perhaps held out longer, but they chose the square instead.

In a fascinating paper, James Hevia (1989) chronicled how,
after the Boxer Rebellion, the allied British and French troops on
28 August 1900 sought to humiliate the Chinese government by a
triumphal march that moved down what is now Changan Avenue,
across Tiananmen Square and up to the Forbidden City – just as
the Chinese emperors were traditionally carried in their palan-
quins from the Temple of Heaven back to the Forbidden City after
performing the yearly offering rites to Heaven. Perhaps as mimesis
of these rituals of royal installment (Bryant 1989:414–15), this procession was re-enacted by the students for us hundreds of times on
our television screens as they cruised down Changan Boulevard
past Tiananmen Square, with banners trailing and slogans shouting. It was also re-enacted for the Chinese on their television sets
in *River Elegy*. The students were following well-worn scripts that
had been dramatized for them throughout Chinese revolutionary history: the Boxer Rebellion, the May 4th uprising of 1919,
the Cultural Revolution, the funeral of Zhou Enlai, and the other
more minor processions and occupations that had all centered on
Tiananmen. By placing their bodies and their icons in such an
open vulnerable position opposite the picture of Chairman Mao,
they shifted the world's attention from the government to themselves. The Chinese leaders' faces will never look the same. (In his
private speech of 24 June, even Deng Xiaoping admitted that Li
Peng's face was not appealing to the population.)

But it was occupation of the square that really galled the Chinese leadership, not procession through it. While many debate the
folly of the students remaining in the square too long, and thus
precipitating the crackdown, they miss the very crucial nature of
the students' actions: by placing their bodies in the square, the protesters sought to reinsert Tiananmen Square into the public sphere.
Jürgen Habermas' discussion of the structural transformation of
this entity in the rise of the nation-state is entirely appropriate
to China: as self-professed representatives of the people of the
People's Republic, it behooves the Chinese leadership to meet its
people in the public sphere of the square. Otherwise it appears

like a despotic kingship, capriciously refusing dialogue. In a representational nation-state according to Habermas, the public sphere replaces the body of the lordship as the center of authority:

> This publicness [or publicity] of representation was not constituted as a social realm, that is, as a public sphere; rather, it was something like a status attribute, if this term may be permitted. In itself the status of manorial lord, on whatever level, was neutral in relation to the criteria of 'public' and 'private'; but its incumbent represented it publicly. He displayed himself, presented himself as an embodiment of some sort of 'higher' power. (Habermas 1989:7)

This is acutely relevant to China, where the emperor (supposedly dethroned by the People's Republic) embodied the conjunction of divine and human authority in himself as the Son of Heaven. Students parodied the actual state of affairs, however, by such media-oriented slogans as: 'Deng Xiaoping, the Last Emperor of China'. The notion that the embodiment of authority that was vested in the person of the emperor was to be displaced by the people of the People's Republic is part and parcel of China's revolutionary curriculum (Gladney 1990). This discourse of pluralism now plagues China's leaders. It made the popular slogan all the more poignant: 'Why can't Li Peng, the People's Prime Minister, come out to meet the People'. The occupation of Tiananmen Square signified the desire of the Chinese students to no longer take the populist rhetoric of the Communist Party as mere rhetoric. They attempted to reappropriate with their bodies the public sphere.

Just prior to the crackdown, one of the final dramatic acts of the students vividly recalled the opening bodily gestures of *River Elegy* – that of prostration. This time, however, instead of Buddhists, Daoists, and Muslims bowing in supplication to their various gods, it was a lonely student, kneeling on the steps of the Great Hall of the People alongside of Tiananmen Square, knocking his head three times in a classic kowtow, and bearing aloft in his hands the names of thousands of citizens on a petition that called for public dialogue with the leaders of the government. Not unlike the pilgrims pictured in *River Elegy*, they still are waiting for their conversation with the gods of China. Others await their dethronement.

16
CONCLUSIONS

China after 9/11

The economic and political ascendancy of the People's Republic of China at the end of the 20th century has made its neighbors nervous. Indeed, while some have argued the war on terrorism launched in 2001 by the US with Chinese and Russian support has led to increased insecurity for all nation-states, China has been one state that has arguably benefited. Since 2002, China's borders are more secure, its foreign direct investment has skyrocketed, and its international standing has only improved (especially when compared to that of the US). While China's intentions toward the recovery of Hong Kong and Taiwan are clear, much doubt remains about China's other expansionist goals. This book has argued that while China may not have geographic expansionist designs on any of its neighboring territory that is not already considered part of China, cultural and political moves toward China's subaltern groups indicate a gradual but marked increase in Chinese nationalism that will have important implications for China's internal colonialism.

I have argued in this volume that the categorization and taxonomization of all levels of Chinese society, from political economy, to social class, to gender, to ethnicity and nationality indicates a wide-ranging and ongoing project of internal colonialism. Though now long subsided, the debate provoked by Michael Hechter's history *Internal Colonialism: The Celtic Fringe in British National Development, 1536–1966* (1976) had an interesting history of its own. While a few articles had been written on the subject in the mid-1960s and early 1970s, which mainly concerned themselves with the continuing political-economic effects of former colonization in Mesoamerica, Hechter's book was the first to formulate a theoretical approach that had wide application to existing post-colonial Western urban societies. Hechter (1975:8) draws an important theoretical connection between Lenin's *Development of Capitalism in Russia* (1956) and Gramsci's 'Southern Question',[1] arguing that international relations are tied to internal social relationships. In this regard, Hechter suggests that the channeling of certain peoples into 'hierarchical cultural divisions of labor' under colonial administrations led to the development of ethnic identities that superseded class (Hechter and Levi 1979:263). This 'internal colonialism' is predicated upon the unequal rates of exchange between the urban power-centers and the peripheral, often ethnic, hinterlands. In his study of the 'Celtic fringe', Hechter (1975) traces the national development of the post-colonial British state, *as though these areas were still under economic colonial exploitation.*

Hechter's elaboration of the theory of internal colonialism proved incredibly fruitful for studies outside Britain, particularly in post-colonial and socialist societies. An onslaught of more than forty articles and at least two books with the term in their titles appeared in the mid-1970s, culminating in 1979 in a special issue of *Ethnic and Racial Studies* devoted to internal colonialism. The theory was found to be applicable to South Africa, Thailand, the Sudan, Wales, Brittany, Quebec, Austria–Hungary, Scotland, Bangladesh, Cherokee Native Americans and Chicanos in the US, the Palestinians in Israel, and the original intent behind and reason for the success of Stalin's nationalities policy in the Soviet Union (Gouldner 1978:11–14). The majority of these examples stress the exploitation of the many ethnics, who are less culturally literate in the dominant tradition, by the few in the urban power-elite who control access to and distribution of capital. Interestingly, though the theory was later criticized and generally abandoned for being too general and too widely applicable, it was never applied to China. Nevertheless, I would argue that recent shifts in China's policy make the approach even more relevant for understanding China's colonial politic at the beginning of the 21st century.

It is quite ironic that while the People's Republic was founded on an 'anti-imperial nationalism' (Friedman 1994), in the current

1. Gramsci was writing his famous essay when he was arrested in 1926 during Mussolini's crackdown on opposition parties. The essay therefore remained unfinished, and was not published, even in Italian, until 1966 (see Gramsci 1966).

post-colonial world, at a time when most nations are losing territory rather than recovering it, China is busily making good its claims on Hong Kong, Taiwan, and the Spratly Islands. Beijing's claims to the contrary, the removal of the British colonial administration from Hong Kong in 1997 certainly did not mean its liberation. There is something that rings true when one states that Tibet is literally a colony of China, despite any definitional problems with the theory of internal colonialism.

Subaltern perspectives on the Chinese geo-body

As Thongchai Winichakul (1994:15) has argued *Siam Mapped*, modern nations become established through the imposition of borders, boundaries, and categories of configuration upon previously borderless, unbounded, or uncategorized regions, peoples, and spaces. The invention and 'imagined community' (Anderson 1991) of the geo-body of Thailand, Winichakul argues, is effected through the state-sponsored definition of boundaries, peoples, centers, and peripheries. It is clear that parts of China considered to belong to its geo-body, such as Hong Kong, Taiwan, Tibet, and Xinjiang, will never be considered for release from Chinese authority. To do so, most Chinese believe, would be to sever one's limb. Recovery of Hong Kong and Taiwan is merely reconstructive surgery.

Taking inspiration from subaltern studies in South Asian scholarship and studies in cultural criticism, this book has sought to understand the implications of China's increasing internal colonialism and notions of the Chinese geo-body for its subaltern subjects.

As Edward Said notes in his introduction to the 1988 Guha and Spivak collection:

As an alternative discourse then, the work of the Subaltern scholars can be seen as an analogue of all those recent attempts in the West and throughout the rest of the world to articulate the hidden or suppressed accounts of numerous groups – women, minorities, disadvantaged or dispossessed groups, refugees, exiles, etc. (Said 1988: vi)

In China, an indigenous 'subaltern scholarship' has not yet begun to develop. Yet there have been a few studies giving voice to those subalterns who have independent histories and cultural memories that cry out for understanding on their own terms, rather than being placed in a peripheral, subregional, or 'subethnic' position. This is why at the end of the 20th century the plight of China's subalterns becomes increasingly important, for understanding not only China's increasing nationalism, but also the nature of modern internal colonialism. For this book then, 'subaltern subjects' are the very groups, individuals, and subjectivities that continue to be regarded as somehow less authentic, more peripheral, and farther removed from a core Chinese tradition.

Chinese nationalism and its subaltern implications

In an interview with the *Far Eastern Economic Review* (November 1995), Liu Binyan, the former Xinhua journalist and now dissident Chinese writer living in exile in Princeton, clearly indicated that attention to China's ethnic subalterns is critical to our understanding of contemporary Chinese nationalism. 'Nationalism and Han chauvinism are now the only effective instruments in the ideological arsenal of the CCP', Liu declared. 'Any disruption in the relationship with foreign countries or among ethnic minorities can be used to stir "patriotic" sentiments of the people to support the communist authorities'. The outpouring of reports during 2001–02 in the official Chinese media regarding separatist incidents in Xinjiang and elsewhere suggests that Liu Binyan was perhaps correct.

After denying for decades that there were internal conflicts, and stressing instead China's 'national unity', official reports repeatedly now detail Tibetan and Muslim conflicts in the border regions of Tibet, Yunnan, Xinjiang, Ningxia, and Inner Mongolia. Intra-Muslim conflicts and antigovernment protests among the Hui have occurred since 1992 in Xi'an, Yunnan, and Ningxia, China's only autonomous region for its largest Muslim minority.

While much is reported about the policy shifts and reimposed hard line in Tibet, including the prohibition of all public displays of the Dalai Lama's picture and the political re-education of monks, less is known about the extent of the unrest and crackdowns in Xinjiang. Intra-Muslim factionalism and politico-religious killings make the situation in Muslim areas much more complex and volatile than Tibet. Without a Dalai Lama to sort out disputes and impose a restraining hand, China's Muslims, who are riven by political, religious, and local factionalisms, are more susceptible to local and widespread violence. At least thirty international organizations

are working for the independence of Xinjiang (known as East Turkestan), and based in Amsterdam, Munich, Istanbul, Melbourne,
New York, and Washington, DC. Clearly, with Xinjiang representing the last Muslim region under communism, Chinese authorities
have more to be concerned about than just international support
for Tibetan independence.

The real question is, why call attention to these Tibetan and
Muslim activities and external organizations in the past decade,
when during my research in the 1980s the government repeatedly
denied them? The smiling, patriotic Uyghur and Tibetans of the
1980s have given way to the disgruntled, 'backward' terrorists of
the late 1990s. The Istanbul-based groups have existed since the
1950s, and the Dalai Lama has been active since his exile in 1959.
Separatist actions have taken place on a minor but regular basis
since the expansion of market and trade policies in China, and
with the opening of six overland gateways to Xinjiang in addition to the trans-Eurasian railway since 1991, there seems to be no
chance of closing up shop. In his 1994 visit to the newly independent nations of Central Asia, Li Peng called for the opening of a
'new Silk Road'. This was a clear attempt to calm fears in the newly
established Central Asian states over Chinese expansionism, as was
the April 1996 Shanghai communiqué that solidified the existing
Sino-Central Asian borders. This was perhaps the most recent and
clearest example of Chinese government efforts to finally solidify
and fully map its geo-body.

Subaltern separatism and Chinese response

China's geo-body is not threatened by internal dismemberment.
Such as they are, China's separatists are few in number, badly
equipped, loosely linked, and massively outgunned by the army
and police. Local support for separatist activities, particularly in
Xinjiang, is at best ambivalent and ambiguous, given the economic
disparity between these regions and their foreign neighbors, which
are generally much poorer, and in some cases, such as Tajikistan,
formerly riven by civil war. In this region, memories are strong of
mass starvation and widespread destruction during the Sino-Japanese and civil wars of the 20th century, and of the horrific chaos of
the Cultural Revolution. International support for Tibetan causes
has done little to shake Beijing's grip on the region. Rather than

calling for complete separatism or real independence, many local activists are more concerned with environmental degradation, nuclear testing, religious freedom, overtaxation, and limits that were imposed on childbearing in the late 1990s. Many ethnic leaders are simply calling for genuine, legally sanctioned autonomy for the five autonomous regions that are each led by Beijing-controlled Han first party secretaries. Extending the 'Strike Hard' campaign to Xinjiang, Wang Lequan, the Party Secretary for Xinjiang, has consistently declared, 'There will be no compromise between us and the separatists'. He was rewarded for this hardline policy in the fall of 2002 with promotion to the Chinese Politburo. Clearly, Xinjiang policies have become central to China's Communist Party leaders.

[Beijing's official publicizing of the separatist issue may have more to do with domestic politics than any real internal or external threat. Recent moves suggest efforts to promote Chinese nationalism as a 'unifying ideology' that will prove more attractive than communism and more manageable than capitalism. By highlighting separatist threats and external intervention, China can divert attention away from its domestic instabilities of rising inflation, increased income disparity, displaced 'floating populations', Hong Kong reunification, and the post-Deng succession. Perhaps nationalism will be the only 'unifying ideology' left to a Chinese nation that has begun to distance itself from communism, as it has Confucianism, Buddhism, and Daoism in the past. As Bruce Kapferer has noted, nationalism 'makes the political religious'. This is perhaps why religion-based nationalisms, like Islamic fundamentalism and Tibetan Buddhism, are targeted by Beijing, while the rise of shamanism and popular religion goes unchecked. At the same time, a firm lid on Muslim activism in China will send a message to foreign Muslim militant organizations to stay out of China's internal affairs.[In a July 1994 interview with Iran's former ambassador to China in Tehran, I was told Iran would never intervene in a Muslim crackdown in China, despite its support for the training of Kubrawiyya Sufi imams from Gansu and close foreign relations with China.

Any event, domestic or international, can be used as an excuse to promote nationalist goals, the building of a new unifying ideology. As Shen Guofang from the Ministry of Foreign Trade and Economic Cooperation revealed in a statement concerning the 1996 Sino-US trade dispute: 'If the US goes so far as to implement its trade retaliation, China will, according to its foreign trade law, take countermeasures to safeguard its sovereignty and national esteem'. Trade and separatism become obstacles not to economic and political development, but to preserving national esteem. Any action deemed by Beijing to be 'unpatriotic' is quickly interpreted as an attempt to split the country, which runs counter to Chinese efforts at reunification of its entire geo-body. Hong Kong becomes the first example of the attainment of China's historic destiny, with islands such as the Spratlys and Diaoyutai, to say nothing of Taiwan, regarded as impediments to national development and physical reunion. In a perceptive treatment of Chinese nationalism, Zheng Yongnian has argued persuasively that China's 'opening to the West' and capitalist marketization have contributed not only to ethnic nationalism of minorities, but also, in response, an increased Chinese nationalism:

Reform policies [in China] have led to the rise of ethnic consciousness and thus the emergence of ethnic nationalism as exemplified in Tibet … The aim of Chinese nationalism is to pursue national power and wealth through domestic development. As long as the leadership pursues its 'interests,' its nationalistic 'passion' can be constrained and remain rational. (Zheng 1999:35, 147)

China's expanding internal colonialism

In his 1998 visit to the US, then Defense Minister Chi Haotian declared: 'We hope to see a peaceful settlement [regarding Taiwan] yet refuse to renounce the use of force … The entire Chinese history shows that whoever splits the motherland will end up condemned by history'. This follows the Chinese History Project commissioned in 1995 by Song Jian, former Minister for Science and Technology, which aimed at writing a new chronology of China. In a *Science and Technology Daily* editorial, published on 17 May 1998, Song Jian stated that the project's goal was to demonstrates its 6,000-year 'unbroken, unilineal' development. Song declared, 'Unlike those in Egypt, Babylon and India, the Chinese civilization has lasted for 5,000 years without a break'. The project, originally scheduled to be completed by 1 October 1999, clearly took a dim view of anyone accused of separatism. As long as Muslim activism is regarded as 'separatism', it will be regarded as going against not only China's national destiny, but also history itself.

The nationalist rewriting of history, Prasenjit Duara (1995) reminds us, is not unique to China, but accompanies nationalist projects around the globe. The threat of this rewriting is not to China's neighbors, for they do not belong to a nationalist history of China's past or future geo-body. Rather, the rise in nationalist rhetoric in China may have the greatest implications for its internal colonial others, its subaltern subjects. The real question is, what will happen to those Chinese citizens on its borders should a nationalist movement rise up that sees them as more of a threat than as part of a China that is multinational and multi-ethnic? If nationalist sentiments prevail during this time of transition, what will happen to those subaltern subjects currently living in China, but beyond the Great Wall?

BIBLIOGRAPHY

Adams, Kathleen. 1984. ' "Come to Tana Toraja, Land of Heavenly Kings":
Travel Agents as Brokers in Ethnicity.' *Annals of Tourism Research* 11:
469–85.
Allès, Élisabeth. 1994. 'L'islam Chinois: Femmes Ahong.' *Études Oriental*
13/14:163–8.
——. 2000. *Musulmans de Chine: Une Anthropologie des Hui du Henan.*
Paris: Éditions de l'École des Hautes Études en Sciences Sociale.
Alloula, Malek. 1986. *The Colonial Harem.* Minneapolis: University of
Minnesota Press.
Allsen, Thomas T. 1983. 'The Yuan Dynasty and the Uighurs of Turfan in
the 13th Century' in *China among Equals.* Edited by Morris Rossabi.
Berkeley: University of California Press. pp. 243–80.
Allworth, Edward. 1980. 'Ambiguities in Russian Group Identity and
Leadership of the RSFSR' in *Ethnic Russia in the USSR: The Dilemma
of Dominance.* Edited by Edward Allworth. New York: Pergamon Press.
Alptekin, Erkin. 1988. 'Relations between Eastern and Western Turkestan.'
Radio Liberty Research, 30 November.
Alptekin, Isa Yusuf. 1992. *Dogu Türkestan Davasi.* Istanbul: Seha Nesriyat.
Anagnost, Ann S. 1986. 'The Mimesis of Power.' Paper presented at the
conference 'Anthropological Perspectives on Mainland China, Past
and Present', Center for Chinese Studies, University of California,
22 November.
——. 1994. 'The Politics of Displacement' in *State and Religion in East and
Southeast Asia.* Edited by Laurel Kendal and Helen Hardacre. Hono-
lulu: University of Hawai'i Press.
——. 1997. *National Past-Times: Narrative, Representation, and Power in
Modern China.* Durham, NC: Duke University Press.
Anderson, Benedict. 1991. *Imagined Communities: Reflections on the Origin
and Spread of Nationalism.* 2nd ed. (1st ed. 1983). London: Verso Press.
Appadurai, Arjun. 1986a. 'Introduction: Commodities and the Politics of
Value' in *The Social Life of Things: Commodities in Cultural Perspective.*
Edited by Arjun Appadurai. Cambridge University Press. pp. 3–63.

368

———. 1986b. 'Theory in Anthropology: Center and Periphery.' *Comparative Studies in Society and History* 13:745–61.

———. 1990. 'Disjuncture and Difference in the Global Cultural Economy.' *Public Culture* 2(2):1–24.

———. 1993. 'Patriotism and its Futures.' *Public Culture* 5(3):411–30.

'Appealing Call.' 2002. *Tianmu Musilin jianxun* (*Tianmu Muslim Bulletin*) 14 (20 May):3.

Ardener, Shirley. 1987. 'A Note on Gender Iconography: The Vagina' in *The Cultural Construction of Sexuality*. Edited by Pat Caplan. London: Routledge Press. pp. 113–42.

Asian Journal of Social Science. 2002. Special number 'The Internet and Social Change in Asia and Beyond'. Edited by Zaheer Baber. 30(2).

Atwill, David. Forthcoming. 'Blinkered Visions: Islamic Identity, Hui Ethnicity and the Panthay Rebellion in Southwest China, 1856–1873.' *Journal of Asian Studies*.

Bai Shouyi. 1947. 'Sai Dianchi Shan Siding zhuan' (Biography of Sai Dianchi Shans Al-din). *Qingzhen Yuebao* 31. (Reprinted in *Zhongguo Yisilanjiaoshi Cankao Ziliao Xuanbian, 1911–1949* [*China Islamic History Reference Material Selections, 1911–1949*]. 1985. Vol. 1. Edited by Li Xinghua and Fen Jinyuan. Yinchuan: Ningxia People's Publishing Society.)

———. 1951. 'Huihui Minzu de Xingcheng' (The Nature of the Hui Nationality). *Guangming Ribao* 17 February.

Bai Shouyi and Ma Shouqian. 1958. 'Jizhong Huihui Jiapu Zhong Suofanying de Lishi Wenti' (Several Historical Problems Reflected in Huihui Genealogies). *Beijing Normal University Journal* 2. (Reprinted in *Huizu Shilun Ji 1949–1979* [*Hui History Collection 1949–1979*]. 1984. Chinese Academy of Social Sciences Ethnology Department and Central Nationalities Institute Ethnology Department, Hui History Team. Yinchuan: Ningxia People's Publishing Society.)

Bai Shouyi and Yang Huaizhong (eds). 1985. *Huizu Renwu Zhi, Yuandai* (*Annals of Hui Personages, Yuan Dynasty*). Yinchuan: Ningxia People's Publishing Society.

Bakhtin, M. Mikhail. 1981. *The Dialogic Imagination*. Russian edition 1975. Edited by Michael Holquist. Translated by Caryl Emerson and Michael Holquist. Austin: University of Texas Press.

———. 1984. *Problems of Dostoevsky's Poetics*. Russian edition 1963. Edited and translated by Caryl Emerson. Minneapolis: University of Minnesota Press.

Banister, Judith. 1987. *China's Changing Population*. Palo Alto, CA: Stanford University Press.

Bao, Jigang. 1994. 'A study on the distribution of theme parks.' *Ti Li Yan Jiu* (*Geographical Research*) 13(3):83–93.

Barfield, Thomas. 1989. *The Perilous Frontier: Nomadic Empires in China.* New York: Basil Blackwell.

Barmé, Geremie R. 1988. 'TV Requiem for the Myths of the Middle Kingdom.' *Far Eastern Economic Review* 1 September:40–3.

———. 1996. *Shades of Mao: The Posthumous Cult of the Great Leader.* New York: M.E. Sharpe.

Barthold, V.V. 1956. *Four Studies on the History of Central Asia.* Leiden: E.J. Brill.

Bateson, Gregory. 1972. *Steps to an Ecology of Mind.* San Francisco: Chandler Publishing Co.

Baudrillard, Jean. 1981. *Simulacres et Simulation.* Paris: Editions Galilee.

Befu, Harumi. 1993, 'Introduction' in *Cultural Nationalism in East Asia: Representation and Identity.* Edited by Harumi Befu. Berkeley, CA: Institute of East Asian Studies.

Beijing City Sociology Committee *et al.* 1984. 'Beijing Shi Canzaju Xiaoshu Minzu Jiaoyu Wenti Diaocha Baogao' (Research Report on the Problem of Education among Dispersed Minorities in Beijing City). *Central Institute for Nationalities Journal* 1:18–26.

Benedek, Emily. 1996. 'How Circumcision Came Full Circle.' *New York Times* 19 May:B3.

Bentley, G. Carter. 1983. 'Theoretical Perspectives on Ethnicity and Nationality.' *Sage Race Relations Abstracts* 8(2):1–53.

———. 1987. 'Ethnicity and Practice.' *Comparative Study of Society and History* 1:24–55.

Bernstein, Richard. 1989. 'To Be Young and in China: A Colloquy.' *New York Times,* 7 October:11.

Berry, Chris. 1991a. 'Market Forces: China's "Fifth Generation" Faces the Bottom Line' in *Perspectives on Chinese Cinema.* Edited by Chris Berry. London: BFI Publishing. pp. 114–24.

———. 1991b. 'Tian Zhuangzhuang' in *Perspectives on Chinese Cinema.* Edited by Chris Berry. London: BFI Publishing. pp. 194–6.

Bhabha, Hommi K. 1994. *The Location of Culture.* London: Routledge Press.

Blake, C. Fred. 1981. *Ethnic Groups and Social Change in a Chinese Market Town.* Honolulu: University Press of Hawai'i.

Boas, Franz. 1955. *Primitive Art.* First published 1927. New York: Dover Publications.

Borchigud, Wurlig. 1995. 'The Impact of Urban Ethnic Education on Modern Mongolian Ethnicity, 1949–1966' in *Cultural Encounters on China's Ethnic Frontiers.* Edited by Stevan Harrell. Seattle: University of Washington Press. pp. 278–300.

Botham, Mark E. 1924. 'A Saint's Tomb in China.' *Moslem World* 14(2): 185–6.

Bourdieu, Pierre. 1977. *Outline of a Theory of Practice*. Cambridge University Press.

Bowen, John. 1995. 'The Forms Culture Takes: A State-of-the-field Essay on the Anthropology of Southeast Asia.' *Journal of Asian Studies* 54(4): 1004–68.

Brandt, Conrad, Benjamin Schwartz, and John Fairbank. 1952. *A Documentary History of Chinese Communism*. London: Allen and Unwin.

Breckenridge, Carol A. 1990. 'The Work of Leisure, the Culture of Place: The Humble Geographies of Tourism in India.' Paper presented at a seminar at the Institute for Advanced Study, April.

Broomhall, Marshall. 1910. *Islam in China: A Neglected Problem*. New York: Paragon Book Co.

Brownell, Susan. 1995. *Training the Body for China: Sports in the Moral Order of the People's Republic*. University of Chicago Press.

Brudny, Yitzhak. 2000. *Reinventing Russia: Russian Nationalism and the Soviet State, 1953–1991*. Cambridge, MA: Harvard University Press.

Bryant, Lawrence M. 1989. 'Royal Ceremony and the Revolutionary Strategies of the Third Estate.' *Eighteenth-Century Studies* Spring:413–50.

Buck, Elizabeth. 1993. *Paradise Remade: The Politics of Culture in the History of Hawaii*. Philadelphia: Temple University Press.

Bulag, Uradyn Erden. 1998. *Nationalism and Hybridity in Mongolia*. Oxford University Press.

Burhan Shahidi. 1984. *Xinjiang Wushi Nian* (*Xinjiang: Fifty Years*). Beijing: Wenshi Ziliao Chubanshe.

Burras, Laurie. 1989. 'Chinese Students Speak Out.' *World and I* September:100–5.

Buruma, Ian. 1990. 'The Last Days of Hong Kong.' *New York Review of Books* 37(6):41–6.

Cahill, James. 1983. 'Figure, Bird, and Flower Painting in China Today' in *Contemporary Chinese Painting*. Edited by Lucy Lim. San Francisco: Chinese Culture Foundation.

Calhoun, Craig. 1989. 'Tiananmen, Television and the Public Sphere: Internationalization of Culture and the Beijing Spring of 1989.' *Public Culture* 2(1):54–72.

'A Call for Quality, Not Quantity.' 1994. *China Daily* 26 May:3.

Campbell, Joseph. 1983. *The Power of Myth*. New York: Doubleday.

Caplan, Pat. 1987. 'Introduction' in *The Cultural Construction of Sexuality*. Edited by Pat Caplan. London: Routledge Press. pp. 1–30.

Chang, Arnold. 1980. *Painting in the People's Republic of China: The Politics of Style*. Boulder, CO: Westview Press.

Chang Chih-i. 1966. *The Party and the National Question in China*. Translated by George Moseley. Cambridge, MA: MIT Press.

Changji Hui Autonomous Prefectural Situation Committee. 1985.

Changji Huizu Zizhizhou Gaikuang (*Changji Hui Autonomous Prefectural Basic Situation*). Ürümqi: Xinjiang Nationalities Publishing Society.

Chatterjee, Partha. 1986. *Nationalist Thought and the Colonial World: A Derivative Discourse*. London: Zed Books.

Che, Kang. 1996. 'Bomb Explodes in Lhasa, Local Authorities Offer Reward for Capture of Criminals.' *Ta Kung Pao* (Hong Kong), 30 December. FBIS, FTS19970409001371.

Chen Dasheng. 1983. 'Tentative inquiry into the Islamic Sects at Quanzhou and the "Isbah" Disturbance toward the End of the Yuan Dynasty' in *Symposium on Quanzhou Islam*. Quanzhou Foreign Maritime Museum. Quanzhou: Fujian People's Publishing Society.

—— (ed.). 1984. *Islamic Inscriptions in Quanzhou*. Translated by Chen Siming. Yinchuan and Quanzhou: Ningxia People's Publishing Society and Fujian People's Publishing Society.

Chen Erjin. 1984. *China Crossroads Socialism: An Unofficial Manifesto for Revolution*. Translated by Robin Munroe. London: Verso Press.

Chen, Jack. 1977. *The Sinkiang Story*. New York: Macmillan.

Chen Sadong. 1975. 'Li Zhi de Jiashi, Guju ji qi qi Mubei' (Li Zhi's Family, Ancient Residences, and His Wife's Gravestone). *Wenwu* 1. (Reprinted in *Huizu Shilun Ji 1949–1979* [*Hui History Collection 1949–1979*]. 1984. Chinese Academy of Social Sciences Ethnology Department and Central Nationalities Institute Ethnology Department, Hui History Team. Yinchuan: Ningxia People's Publishing Society.)

Ch'en Yüan. 1966. *Western and Central Asians in China under the Mongols: Their Transformation into Chinese*. Monumenta Serica Monograph XV. Los Angeles: Monumenta Serica at the University of California.

Cheng, Allen T. 2003. 'A Surprise Move by the Mainland's Islamic Community.' *South China Morning Post* 25 March.

Cherif, Leîla. 1994. 'Ningxia, l'École au Fémini.' *Études Oriental* 13/14: 156–62.

Chiang Kai-shek. 1947. *China's Destiny*. First published 1943. New York: Roy Publishers.

'China also Harmed by Separatist-Minded Eastern Turkestan Terrorists.' 2001. *People's Daily* 10 October.

'China Increases Suppression in Xinjiang.' 2002. *Oxford Analytica* 20 December.

'China is Taking a Great Leap into the Auto Age.' 1994. *Toronto Globe and Mail* 18 August.

China Islamic Association. 1985. *A Collection of Painting and Calligraphy Solicited for Charity in Aid of the Disabled*. Beijing: China Islamic Association.

'China's Rural Exodus is Threatening Stability of Coastal Regions.' 1994. Agence France Press English Wire, 24 August.

Chinese Nationalities. 1989. Beijing: China Nationality Photography and Art Press.

Chow, Rey. 1990. 'Violence in the Other Country: China as Crisis, Spectacle, and Woman' in *Third World Women and Feminist Perspectives*. Edited by Chandra Mohanty *et al.* Bloomington: Indiana University Press.

———. 1993. *Writing Diaspora*. Minneapolis: University of Minnesota Press.

———. 1995. *Primitive Passions: Visuality, Sexuality, Ethnography, and Contemporary Chinese Cinema*. New York: Columbia University Press.

Christie, Anthony. 1983. *Chinese Mythology*. New York: Peter Bedrick Books.

Christofferson, Gaye. 1993. 'Xinjiang and the Great Islamic Circle: The Impact of Transnational Forces on Chinese Regional Economic Planning.' *China Quarterly* 133:130–51.

Chu Wen-djang. 1955. Ch'ing Policy towards the Muslims in the Northwest. Supplement IV: 'Ma Hua-lung and the "New Sect".' PhD thesis, University of Washington.

Clark, Paul. 1987a. *Chinese Cinema*. Cambridge University Press.

———. 1987b. 'Ethnic Minorities in Chinese Films: Cinema and the Exotic.' *East–West Film Journal* 1(2):15–32.

Cohen, Erik. 1979. 'The Impact of Tourism on the Hill Tribes of Northern Thailand.' *Internales Asienforum* 10(1/2):5–38.

Cohen, Joan Lebold. 1987. *The New Chinese Painting 1949–1986*. New York: Harry N. Abrams.

———. 1988. *The Yunnan School: A Renaissance in Chinese Painting*. Minneapolis, MN: Fingerhut Group Publishers.

Cohen, Myron L. 1991. 'Being Chinese: The Peripheralization of Traditional Identity.' *Daedalus* 120(2):113–34.

Cohen, Ronald, and John Middleton (eds). 1970. *From Tribe to Nation in Africa*. Scranton, PA: Chandler Publishing Co.

Cohn, Bernard S. 1987. 'The Census, Social Structure and Objectification in South Asia' in *An Anthropologist among the Historians and Other Essays*. Edited by Bernard S. Cohn. Delhi: Oxford University Press.

Comaroff, Jean. 1994. 'Epilogue – Defying Disenchantment: Reflections on Ritual, Power, and History' in *Asian Visions of Authority: Religion and the Modern States of East and Southeast Asia*. Edited by Helen Hardacre, Laurel Kendall, and Charles Keyes. Honolulu: University of Hawai'i Press.

Comaroff, John. 1987. 'Of Totemism and Ethnicity: Consciousness, Practice and the Signs of Inequality.' *Ethnos* 52(3–4):301–23.

Connor, Walker. 1984. *The National Question in Marxist–Leninist Theory and Strategy*. Princeton University Press.

Cooper, Richard. 1994. 'Will the Fault Lines Between Civilizations be the Battle Lines of the Future?' *Centerpiece* Winter/Spring:9.

Corbey, Raymond, and Joep Leerssen (eds). 1991. *Alterity, Identity, and Image: Selves and Others in Society and Scholarship.* Atlanta, GA: Rodopi.

Coyajee, Jehangir Colverjee. 1936. *Cults and Legends of Ancient Iran and China.* Bombay: M.J. Karani.

Crapanzano, Vincent. 1973. *The Hamadsha: A Study in Moroccan Ethnopsychiatry.* Berkeley: University of California Press.

Crossley, Pamela Kyle. 1990. 'Thinking about Ethnicity in Early Modern China.' *Late Imperial China* 11(1):1–35.

Cui Wenhua (ed.). 1988. *He Shang Lun* (*Discussions of River Elegy*). Beijing: Wenhua Yishu Press.

Dachang Huizu Zizhixian Gaikuang. 1985. *Dachang Huizu Zizhixian Gaikuang* (*The Situation of the Dachang Hui Autonomous County*). Shijiazhuang: Hebei People's Publishing Society.

'Danger to Economy Lies in Moral Decay.' 1994. *China Daily* 18 May:3.

Debord, Guy. 1983. *Society of the Spectacle.* Detroit, MI: Black and Red.

de Certeau, Michel. 1984. *The Practice of Everyday Life.* Translated by Steven F. Randall. Berkeley: University of California Press.

DeFrancis, John. 1984. *The Chinese Language: Fact and Fantasy.* Honolulu: University of Hawai'i Press.

Deleuze, Gilles, and Felix Guattari. 1987. *A Thousand Plateaus: Capitalism and Schizophrenia.* Minneapolis: University of Minnesota.

Demko, George J. 1969. *The Russian Colonization of Kazakhstan, 1896–1916.* Bloomington: Indiana University Press.

Department of Population Statistics of State Statistical Bureau and Economic Department of State Nationalities Affairs Commission, People's Republic of China. 1994. *Zhongguo Minzu Renkou Ziliao (1990 nian Renkou Pucha Shuju).* (*Population of China's Nationality [Data of 1990 Population Census]*). Beijing: China Statistical Publishing House.

De Rachewiltz, Igor. 1983. 'Turks in China under the Mongols: A Preliminary Investigation of Turco-Mongol Relations in the 13th and 14th Centuries' in *China among Equals.* Edited by Morris Rossabi. Berkeley: University of California Press. pp. 281–311.

Despres, Leo A. 1984. 'Ethnicity: What Data and Theory Portend for Plural Societies' in *The Prospects for Plural Societies.* Edited by David Maybury-Lewis. Washington, DC: American Ethnological Society. pp. 7–29.

Diamond, Norma. 1985. 'Rural Collectivization and Decollectivization in China – A Review Article.' *Journal of Asian Studies* 44(4):785–92.

——. 1988. 'The Miao and Poison: Interactions on China's Southwest Frontier.' *Ethnology* 27.1:1–25.

Dikötter, Frank. 1992. *The Discourse of Race in Modern China.* Stanford

University Press.

—— (ed.). 1997. *The Construction of Racial Identities in China and Japan.* London: C. Hurst & Co.

Dillon, Michael. 1995. *Xinjiang: Ethnicity, Separatism, and Control in Chinese Central Asia.* Durham East Asian Papers 1. University of Durham.

Ding Shaoguang. 1990. Hiestand Gallery portfolio brochure. Oxford, OH: Miami University.

Ding Xiancao. 1990. 'Chendai: The Past and the Present' in *Chendai Huizushi Yanjiu (Research on Chendai Hui Nationality History).* Edited by Chen Guoqiang. Beijing: China Academy of Social Sciences Press. pp. 1–6.

Dittmer, Lowell, and Samuel S. Kim (eds). 1993. *China's Quest for a National Identity.* Ithaca, NY: Cornell University Press.

Dominguez, Virginia R. 1996. *White by Definition: Social Classification in Creole Louisiana.* New Brunswick, NJ: Rutgers University Press.

Drake, F.S. 1940. 'Mohammedanism in the T'ang Dynasty.' *Monumenta Serica* 8:1–40.

Dreyer, June. 1970. 'China's Minority Nationalities: Traditional and Party Elites.' *Pacific Affairs* 43(4):506–30.

——. 1976. *China's Forty Million: Minority Nationalities and National Integration in the People's Republic of China.* Cambridge, MA: Harvard University Press.

Duara, Prasenjit. 1992. 'Book Review: Muslim Chinese.' *Journal of Asian Studies* 53(3):644–6.

——. 1995. *Rescuing History from the Nation: Questioning Narratives of Modern China.* University of Chicago Press.

Dundes, Alan. 1965. 'What is Folklore?' in *The Study of Folklore.* Edited by Alan Dundes. Englewood Cliffs, NJ: Prentice Hall.

Dunlop, John B. 1983. *The Faces of Contemporary Russian Nationalism.* Princeton University Press.

Dyer, Svetlana Rimsky-Korsakoff. 1979. *Soviet Dungan Kolkhozes in the Kirghiz SSR and the Kazakh SSR.* Oriental Monograph Series No. 25. Canberra: Australian National University Press.

——. 1981–83. 'T'ang T'ai-tsung's Dream: A Soviet Dungan Version of a Legend on the Origin of the Chinese Muslims.' *Monumenta Serica* 35: 545–70.

Eberhard, Wolfram. 1965. *Folktales of China.* University of Chicago Press.

——. 1970. *Studies in Chinese Folklore and Related Essays.* The Hague: Mouton.

——. 1982. *China's Minorities: Yesterday and Today.* Belmont, CA: Wadsworth.

Eckholm, Erik. 2002. 'U.S. Labeling of Group in China as Terrorist is Criticized.' *New York Times* 13 September.

Eickelman, Dale F. 1976. *Moroccan Islam: Tradition and Society in a Pilgrimage Center*. Austin: University of Texas Press.

Ekvall, Robert B. 1968. *Fields on the Hoof: Nexus of Tibetan Nomadic Pastoralism*. New York: Holt, Rinehart and Winston.

Elias, Norbert. 1972. *A History of the Moghuls of Central Asia being the Tarikh-i-Rashidi of Mirza Muhammad Haidar, Dughlat*. First published 1895. Translated by E. Denison Ross. Edited by Norbert Elias. London: Curzon Press.

Eliot, Alexander. 1993. *The Global Myths: Exploring Primitive, Pagan, Sacred, and Scientific Mythologies*. New York: Penguin Books.

Emerson, Rupert. 1960. *From Empire to Nation*. Boston: Beacon Press.

Eminov, Sandra. 1972. 'Folklore and Nationalism in Modern China' in *Folklore, Nationalism and Politics*. Edited by Felix J. Oina. Columbus, OH: Slavica Publishers.

Eriksen, Thomas H. 1993. *Ethnicity and Nationalism: Anthropological Perspectives*. London: Pluto Press.

Esposito, John L. 2002. *Unholy War: Terror in the Name of Islam*. Oxford University Press

Evans-Pritchard, E.E. 1940. *The Nuer*. Clarendon: Oxford University Press.

Ewing, Catharine. 1984. 'The Sufi as Saint, Curer, and Exorcist in Modern Pakistan.' *Contributions to Asian Studies* 18:106–14.

'Exile Group Claims Bomb Blast in Xinjiang.' 1997. Agence France Presse (Hong Kong), 1 March. FBIS, FTS19970513001183.

'Explosion Hits Tibet's Capital after China Announces New Regional Leader.' 2000. Agence France Presse (Hong Kong), 9 November. FBIS, CPP20001109000079.

Fabian, Johannes. 1982. 'Six Theses Regarding the Anthropology of African Religious Movements.' *Religion* 11:109–26.

Fallers, Lloyd. 1974. *The Social Anthropology of the Nation-State*. Chicago: Aldine Publishing.

'Family Time in Wealthy China.' 1994. *Christian Science Monitor* 25 August.

Fan Changjiang. 1980. *Zhongguo de Xibei Jiao (China's Northwest Corner)*. First published 1936. Chinese Academy of Social Sciences. Beijing: New China Publishing Society.

Faure, David. 1989. 'The Lineage as Cultural Invention: The Case of the Pearl River Delta.' *Modern China* 15:4–36.

FBIS (Foreign Broadcasting Information Service). 1988a. 'Kazakhstan–Xinjiang Railroad Completion in View.' 18 October:9.

———. 1988b. 'Muslim Pilgrims Leave Xinjiang for Mecca.' 10 June: 13–14.

———. 1988c. 'Protocol Signed.' 24 October:9.

——. 1988d. '600 Uygurs Demonstrate in Xinjiang Capital.' 21 June:61.

——. 1988e. 'Xinjiang Tourism Develops Rapidly.' 10 June:4.

——. 1988f. 'Xinjiang–USSR Volume of Border Trade Increases.' 15 June:6.

Fei Xiaotong. 1981. *Toward a People's Anthropology*. Beijing: New World Press.

——. 1989. 'Zhonghua minzu de duoyuan jiti juge' (Plurality and Unity in the Configuration of the Chinese Nationality). *Beijing Daxue Xuebao* 4:1–19.

——. 1987. 'Minorities Hold Key to Own Prosperity.' *China Daily* 28 April:4.

Feng Jinyuan and Li Xinghua (eds). 1985. *Zhongguo Yisilanjiaoshi Cankao Ziliao Xuanbian, 1911–1949* (*China Islamic History Reference Material Selections, 1911–1949*) 2 vols. Yinchuan: Ningxia People's Publishing Society.

Feng Zenglie. 1985. '"Gedimu" bayi' ('Gedimu' eight opinions) in *Xibei Yisilanjiao Yanjiu* (*Northwest Islam Research*). Gansu Provincial Ethnology Department. Lanzhou: Gansu Nationality Publishing Society.

Fischer, Michael M.J. 1986. 'Ethnicity and the Post-Modern Arts of Memory' in *Writing Culture: The Poetics and Politics of Ethnography*. Edited by James Clifford and George E. Marcus. Berkeley: University of California Press.

——. 1980. *Iran: From Religious Dispute to Revolution*. Cambridge, MA: Harvard University Press.

Fletcher, Joseph F. 1978. 'Ch'ing Inner Asia c. 1800' in *The Cambridge History of China*, vol. 10, *Late Ch'ing 1800–1911*. Edited by John King Fairbank. Cambridge University Press. pp. 35–106.

——. 1979. 'A Brief History of the Chinese Northwestern Frontier' in *China's Inner Asian Frontier*. Edited by Mary Ellen Alonso. Cambridge, MA: Peabody Museum.

——. 1988. The Sufi 'Paths' (*turuq*) in China. Unpublished manuscript, Harvard University. (French version published in 1985 as 'Les "Voies" [*turuq*] a Soufites en Chines' in *Les Ordres Mystiques dans l'Islam, Cheminements et Situation Actuelle*. Edited by Alexandre Popovic and Gilles Veinstein. Paris: EHESS.)

——. 1995. *Studies on Chinese and Islamic Inner Asia*. Edited by Beatrice Manz. London: Valorium.

Fogden, Scott. 2002. Writing Insecurity: The PRC's Push to Modernize China and the Politics of Uighur Identity. MscEcon thesis, University of Wales, Aberystwyth.

Forbes, Andrew D.W. 1976. 'Survey Article: The Muslim National Minorities of China.' *Religion* 6(2):67–87.

———. 1986. *Warlords and Muslims in Chinese Central Asia.* Cambridge University Press.

———. 1987. 'The Role of the Hui Muslims (Tungans) in Republican Sinkiang.' Paper presented at the Second European Seminar on Central Asian Studies, University of London (SOAS), 7–10 April.

Ford, J. 1974. 'Some Chinese Muslims of the 17th and 18th Centuries.' *Asian Affairs* New Series 5(2):144–56.

Foster, Derek. 1997. 'Community and Identity in the Electronic Village' in *Internet Culture.* Edited by David Porter. New York: Routledge Press.

Foucault, Michel. 1972. 'Truth and Power' in *Power/Knowledge.* Edited by Colin Gordon. New York: Pantheon Books, 1972.

———. 1980. *The History of Sexuality.* Vol. 1. Translated by Robert Hurley. New York: Vintage Press.

Fox, Richard. 1990. 'Introduction' in *Nationalist Ideologies and the Production of National Cultures.* Edited by Richard Fox. American Ethnological Society Monograph Series, No. 2. Washington, DC: American Ethnological Society.

———. 1991. 'Introduction: Working in the Present' in *Recapturing Anthropology: Working in the Present.* Edited by Richard Fox. Santa Fe, NM: School of American Research Press.

Francis, E.K. 1976. *Interethnic Relations.* New York: Elsevier.

Franda, Marcus. 2002. *Launching into Cyberspace: Internet Development and the Politics of Five World Regions.* Boulder, CO: Lynne Rienner Publishers.

Frank, Andre Gunder. 1992. 'The Centrality of Central Asia.' *Bulletin Of Concerned Asian Scholars* 24(2):50–66.

Frankenberg, Ruth. 1993. *White Women, Race Matters: The Social Construction of Whiteness.* Minneapolis: University of Minnesota Press.

Fried, Morton. 1969. *Fabric of Chinese Society.* First published 1953. New York: Octagon.

Friedman, Edward. 1993. 'China's North–South Split and the Forces of Disintegration.' *Current History* 92(575):270–4.

———. 1994. 'Reconstructing China's National Identity: A Southern Alternative to Mao-Era Anti-Imperialist Nationalism.' *Journal of Asian Studies* 53(1):67–91.

Fujitani, Takashi. 1993. 'Inventing, Forgetting, Remembering: Toward a Historical Ethnography of the Nation-State' in *Cultural Nationalism in East Asia.* Edited by Harumi Befu. Berkeley: University of California Press.

Fuller, Graham E. 1993. 'Turkey's New Eastern Orientation' in *Turkey's New Geopolitics: From the Balkans to Western China.* Edited by Graham E. Fuller and Ian O. Lesser. Boulder, CO: Westview Press. pp. 37–99.

Furnival, J.S. 1939. *Netherlands India.* Cambridge University Press.

Gansu. 1982. Lanzhou: Gansu People's Publishing Society.

Gao Jun. 1991. 'A Changed Director: Transcription of a Dialogue with Zhang Junzhao' in *Perspectives on Chinese Cinema*. Edited by Chris Berry. London: BFI Publishing. pp. 130–3.

Gao Zhanfu. 1985. 'Guanyu Jiaopai Zhizheng Zai Qingdai Xibei Huimin Qiyi Zhong Xiaoji Zuoyong de Tantao' (Discussion Regarding the Inactive Role of Factional Struggles in the Qing Dynasty Northwest Hui Rebellions) in *Xibei Yisilanjiao Yanjiu* (*Northwest Islam Research*). Gansu Provincial Ethnology Department. Lanzhou: Gansu Nationality Publishing Society.

Garber, Marjorie. 1992. 'The Occidental Tourist: *M. Butterfly* and the Scandal of Transvestism' in *Nationalisms and Sexualities*. Edited by Andrew Parker, Mary Russo, Doris Sommer, and Patricia Yaeger. London: Routledge Press. pp. 121–46.

Garthwaite, Gene R. 1993. 'Reimagined Internal Frontiers: Tribes and Nationalism – Bakhtiari and Kurds' in *Russia's Muslim Frontiers*. Edited by Dale F. Eickelman. London: Routledge Press. pp. 130–48.

Gates, Hill. 1981. 'Ethnicity and Social Class' in *The Anthropology of Taiwanese Society*. Edited by Emily Ahern and Hill Gates. Stanford University Press.

Gaubatz, Piper. 1996. *Beyond the Great Wall: Urban Form and Transformation on the Chinese Frontiers*. Stanford University Press.

Gay, Craig M. 1992. *With Liberty and Justice for Whom? The Recent Evangelical Debate over Capitalism*. Grand Rapids, MI: Eerdmans Publishing Co.

Geertz, Clifford. 1963. 'The Integrative Revolution: Primordial Sentiments and Civil Politics in the New States' in *Old Societies and New States*. Edited by Clifford Geertz. New York: Free Press.

——. 1968. *Islam Observed*. University of Chicago Press.

——. 1988. *Works and Lives: The Anthropologist as Author*. Stanford University Press.

Gellner, Ernest. 1983. *Nations and Nationalism*. Ithaca, NY: Cornell University Press.

Geng Shimin. 1984. 'On the Fusion of Nationalities in the Tarim Basin and the Formation of the Modern Uighur Nationality.' *Central Asian Survey* 3(4):1–14.

Gillette, Maris Boyd. 2002. *Between Mecca and Beijing: Modernization and Consumption among Urban Chinese Muslims*. Stanford University Press.

Gilmartin, Christina K., Gail Hershatter, Lisa Rofel, and Tyrene White (eds). 1994. *Engendering China: Women, Culture, and the State*. Contemporary China Series. Cambridge, MA: Harvard University Press.

Gladney, Dru C. 1987a. 'Muslim Tombs and Ethnic Folklore: Charters for Hui Identity.' *Journal of Asian Studies* 46(3):495–532.

——. 1987b. Qing Zhen: A Study of Ethnoreligious Identity among

Hui Muslim Communities in China. PhD thesis, University of Washington.

———. 1990. 'The Peoples of the People's Republic: Finally in the Vanguard?' *Fletcher Forum of World Affairs* 12(1):62–76.

———. 1993. 'The Muslim Face of China.' *Current History* 92(575): 275–80.

———. 1994. 'Salman Rushdie in China: Religion, Ethnicity, and State Definition in the People's Republic' in *Asian Visions of Authority: Religion and the Modern States of East and Southeast Asia*. Edited by Helen Hardacre, Laurel Kendall, and Charles Keyes. Honolulu: University of Hawai'i Press. pp. 255–78.

———. 1995. 'Economy and Ethnicity: The Revitalization of a Muslim Minority in Southeastern China' in *The Waning of the Communist State: Economic Origins of Political Decline in China and Hungary*. Edited by Andrew Walder. Berkeley: University of California Press. pp. 242–66.

———. 1996a. *Muslim Chinese: Ethnic Nationalism in the People's Republic*. 2nd ed. (1st edition 1991). Council on East Asian Studies. Cambridge, MA: Harvard University Press.

———. 1996b. 'Relational Alterity: Constructing Dungan (Hui), Uyghur, and Kazakh Identities across China, Central Asia, and Turkey.' *History and Anthropology* 9(2):445–77.

———. 1998. 'Introduction: Making and Marking Majorities' in *Making Majorities: Composing the Nation in Japan, China, Korea, Malaysia, Fiji, Turkey, and the U.S.* Edited by Dru C. Gladney. Stanford University Press. pp. 1–24.

———. 1999. 'The Salafiyya Movement in China: An Oppositional Modality among the Muslim Chinese?' in *Islamic Mysticism Contested: Thirteen Centuries of Controversies and Polemics*. Edited by Frederick de Jong and Bernd Radtke. Leiden: Brill.

———. Forthcoming. Decentering Central Asia. Unpublished manuscript.

Gladney, Dru C., and Ma Qicheng. 1996. 'Local and Muslim in China: The Making of Indigenous Identities among the Uygur and Hui.' Paper presented at the Annual Association of Asian Studies Meetings, Honolulu, Hawai'i, 10–14 April.

Glass, Charles. 1990. *Tribes With Flags: A Dangerous Passage through the Chaos of the Middle East*. New York: Atlantic Monthly Press.

Gold, Thomas B. 1989. 'Urban Private Business in China.' *Studies in Comparative Communism* 22(2–3):187–202.

Goldstein, Jonathon (ed.). 1999. *The Jews of China*. 2 vols. Armonk, NY: M.E. Sharpe.

Goldstein, Melvyn C. 1990. 'The Dragon and the Snow Lion: The Tibet Question in the 20th Century' in *China Briefing, 1989*. Edited by Anthony J. Kane. Boulder, CO: Westview Press. pp. 129–67.

Goodman, David S.G., and Gerald Segal. 1994. *China Deconstructs: Politics, Trade, and Regionalism*. London: Routledge Press.

Gong Weiduan. 1987. 'Yongning Xian Na Jiahu Cun Shi Diaocha' (Yong Ning County Na Homestead History Investigation). *Ningxia Shizhi Yanjiu* 1:34–40.

Gormsen, E. 1990. 'The Impact of Tourism on Regional Change in China.' *Geojournal* 21:127–35.

Gouldner, Alvin W. 1978. 'Stalinism: A Study of Internal Colonialism.' *Telos* 34:5–48.

Gramsci, Antonio. 1966. *La Questione Meridionale*. Rome: Editori Ri-uniti.

Grayburn, Nelson. 1977. 'Tourism: The Sacred Journey' in *Hosts and Guests*. Edited by V. Smith. Philadelphia: University of Pennsylvania Press.

Greenfeld, Liah. 1992. *Nationalism: Five Roads to Modernity*. Cambridge, MA: Harvard University Press.

Greenwood, D.M. 1972. 'Tourism as an Agent of Change: A Spanish Basque Case.' *Ethnology* 11:80–91.

'Guanyu 1990 Nian Renkou Pucha Zhuyao Shuju de Gongbao' (Report Regarding the 1990 Population Census Main Statistics). 1991. *Renmin Ribao*. 14 November:3.

Guha, Ranajit, and Gayatri Chakrovorty Spivak (eds). 1988. *Selected Subaltern Studies*. Oxford University Press.

Gulliver, Philip Hugh (ed.). 1969. *Tradition and Transition in East Africa: Studies of the Tribal Element in the Modern Era*. Berkeley: University of California Press.

Gupta, A., and James Ferguson. 1992. 'Beyond "culture": Space, Identity, and the Politics of Difference.' *Cultural Anthropology* 7(1):6–23.

Gürün, Kamuran. 1981. *Türkler ve Türk Devletleri Tarihi*. Ankara: Bilgi Yayinevi.

Habel, Shelley. 1996. 'The "Folklore of a Regime" and Other Minority Tales.' Unpublished seminar paper, University of Hawai'i at Manoa.

Habermas, Jürgen. 1989. *The Structural Transformation of the Public Sphere*. First published 1962. Translated by Thomas Burger and Frederick Lawrence. Cambridge, MA: MIT Press.

Hadi Su Junhui. 1990. *Islamic in Beijing*. Beijing Nationality Pictorial Academic Society.

Haidu, Peter. 1990. 'The Semiotics of Alterity: A Comparison with Hermeneutics.' *New Literary History* Spring:671–91.

Hall, Stuart. 1991. 'The Local and the Global: Globalization and Ethnicity' in *Culture, Globalization, and the World System: Contemporary Conditions for the Representation of Identity*. Edited by Anthony D. King. Binghamton, NY: SUNY Press.

Hamada, Masami. 1978. 'Islamic Saints and Their Mausoleums.' *Acta Asiatica* 34: 79–105.

Handler, Richard. 1988. *Nationalism and the Politics of Culture in Quebec.* Madison: University of Wisconsin Press.

Haneda, Akira. 1978. 'Introduction: The Problems of Turkicization and Islamization of East Turkestan.' *Acta Asiatica* 34:1–21.

Harrell, Stevan. 1990. 'The Invention of Ethnicity: The History of the History of the Yi.' *Comparative Studies in Society and History* 2.

———. 1995. 'Civilizing Projects and Reaction to Them' in *Cultural Encounters on China's Ethnic Frontiers.* Edited by Stevan Harrell. Seattle: University of Washington Press. pp. 3–36.

Harrell, Stevan, and Elizabeth Perry. 1982. 'An Introduction' in *Symposium: Syncretic Sects in Chinese Society.* Edited by Stevan Harrell and Elizabeth Perry. *Modern China* 8(3):283–305.

Harris, Lillian Craig. 1991a. 'China's Middle East Position Damaged by Gulf Crisis.' *Al Ahram Weekly* 28 March:7.

———. 1991b. 'The Gulf Crisis and China's Middle East Dilemma.' *Pacific Review* 4(2):116–25.

———. 1993a. 'Xinjiang, Central Asia and the Implications for China's Policy in the Islamic World.' *China Quarterly* 133:111–29.

———. 1993b. *China Considers the Middle East.* London: I.B. Tauris.

Harumi Befu (ed.). 1993. *Cultural Nationalism in East Asia.* Berkeley, CA: Institute of East Asian Studies.

Harwit, Eric. 2003. 'The Digital Divide of China's Internet Use.' Paper presented at the Association for Asian Studies Annual Meeting, New York, 28 March.

Harwit, Eric, and Duncan Clark. 2001. 'Shaping the Internet in China: Evolution of Political Control over Network Infrastructure and Content.' *Asian Survey* 41(3):377–80.

Hassan, Ihab. 1990. 'Alterity? Three Japanese Examples.' *Meanjin* Spring: 410–20.

Hawkins, John N. 1983. *Education and Social Change in the People's Republic of China.* New York: Praeger Press.

———. 1973. 'The Politics of Intergroup Relations: Minority Education in the People's Republic of China' in *Politics and Education.* Edited by Murray Thomas. New York: Pergamon Press.

Heberer, Thomas. 1989. *China and Its National Minorities: Autonomy or Assimilation?* Armonk, NY: M.E. Sharpe.

Hechter, Michael. 1975. *Internal Colonialism: The Celtic Fringe in British National Development, 1536–1966.* London: Routledge and Kegan Paul.

———. 1976. 'Ethnicity and Industrialization: The Proliferation of the Cultural Division of Labor.' *Ethnicity* 3(3):214–24.

Hechter, Michael, and Margaret Levi. 1979. 'The Comparative Analysis of Ethnoregional Movements.' *Ethnic and Racial Studies* 2(3):260–74.

Helly, Denise. 1985. 'The Identity and Nationality Problem in Chinese Central Asia.' *Central Asian Survey* 3(3):99–115.

Helm, June (ed.). 1968. *Essays on the Problem of the Tribe.* Seattle: University of Washington Press.

Henze, Paul B. 1993. 'Turkey: Toward the Twenty-First Century' in *Turkey's New Geopolitics: From the Balkans to Western China.* Edited by Graham E. Fuller and Ian O. Lesser. Boulder, CO: Westview Press. pp. 1–36.

Hershatter, Gail, Emily Honig, Jonathan N. Lipman, and Randall Stross (eds). 1996. *Remapping China: Fissures in Historical Terrain.* Stanford University Press.

Herzfeld, Michael. 1982. *Ours Once More: Folklore, Ideology, and the Making of Modern Greece.* Austin: University of Texas Press.

Hevia, James. 1989. 'Making China Perfectly Equal.' Paper presented at the American Anthropological Association Annual Meetings, Washington, DC, 20 November.

Hewitt, Giles, 'What Became of the Chinese Hero?' 1994. Agence France Presse, 14 January.

Higashino, Kazunon. 1991. 'Theme Parks in Japan.' *Journal of Japanese Trade and Industry* 10(5):22–35.

Hobbes, Thomas. 1962. *Leviathan.* First published 1651. New York: Fontana Publishers.

Hobsbawm, Eric. 1983a. 'Introduction: Inventing Traditions' in *The Invention of Tradition.* Edited by Eric Hobsbawm and Terence Ranger. Cambridge University Press. pp. 1–14.

——. 1983b. 'Mass-Producing Traditions: Europe, 1870–1914' in *The Invention of Tradition.* Edited by Eric Hobsbawm and Terence Ranger. Cambridge University Press.

——. 1990. *Nations and Nationalism since 1780: Programme, Myth, Reality.* Cambridge University Press.

——. 1992. 'Ethnicity and Nationalism in Europe Today.' *Anthropology Today* 8(1):3–8.

Hobsbawm, Eric, and Terence Ranger (eds). 1983. *The Invention of Tradition.* Cambridge University Press.

Honig, Emily. 1992. *Creating Chinese Ethnicity: Subei People in Shanghai, 1850–1980.* New Haven, CT: Yale University Press.

Honig, Emily, and Gail Hershatter. 1988. *Personal Voices: Chinese Women in the 1980s.* Stanford University Press.

Hoppe, Thomas. 1988. 'Kazakh Pastoralism in the Bogda Range' in *The Kazakhs of China: Essays on an Ethnic Minority.* Edited by Ingvar Svanberg and Linda Benson. Uppsala: Studia Multiethnica Uppsalinensia.

——. 1995. 'Ethnic Composition in Xinjiang.' Paper presented at the Fifth European Seminar on Central Asian Studies, Nordic Institute of Asian Studies, Copenhagen, 21–26 August.

Horowitz, Donald L. 1985. *Ethnic Groups in Conflict*. Berkeley: University of California Press.

Hualong Hui Autonomous County Basic Situation Committee. 1984. *Hualong Huizu Zizhixian Gaikuang (Hualong Hui Autonomous County Basic Situation)*. Xining: Qinghai Nationalities Publishing Society.

Huang Tianzhu and Liao Yuanquan. 1983. 'An Informal Talk on the Moslem Descendants at the Quanzhou Area and Their Heritage' in *Symposium on Quanzhou Islam*. Quanzhou Foreign Maritime Museum. Quanzhou: Fujian People's Publishing Society.

Hudson, Alfred E. 1938. *Kazak Social Structure*. Yale University Publications in Anthropology 20. New Haven, CT: Yale University Press.

Huizu Jianshi Editorial Committee. 1978. *Huizu Jianshi (Brief History of the Hui)*.Yinchuan: Ningxia People's Publishing Society.

Huntington, Samuel P. 1993a. 'The Islamic-Confucian Connection.' *New Perspectives Quarterly* 10(3):19–35.

——. 1993b. 'The Clash of Civilizations?' *Foreign Affairs* 72(3):22–49.

Huo Da. 1992. *The Jade King: History of a Chinese Muslim Family*. Beijing: Panda Press.

——. 1993. *Musilin de Zangli (Muslim Funeral)*. 2nd ed. (1st ed. 1988). Beijing Changpian Xiaoshuo Zhuang Zuo Congshu.

Hutzler, Charles. 2001. 'China–Iraq Policy is Risky for US.' *Asian Wall Street Journal* 10 September.

——. 2002. 'US Gesture to China Raises Crackdown Fears.' *Wall Street Journal* 13 September.

Huxley, Julian S., and A.C. Haddon. 1936. *We Europeans: A Survey of 'Racial' Problems*. New York: Harper.

Hymes, Dell. 1975. 'Folklore's Nature and the Sun's Myth.' *Journal of American Folklore* 88:345–69.

International Monetary Fund. 1990. *Yearbook Review*. Washington, DC: International Monetary Fund.

Isaacs, Harold Robert. 1976. *Idols of the Tribe: Group Identity*. New York: Harper Collins.

Israeli, Raphael. 1978. *Muslims in China*. London: Curzon.

——. 1982. 'Muslim Plight under Chinese Rule' in *Islam in Asia Minor*. Edited by Raphael Israeli. London: Curzon.

——. 1984. 'Muslims in China: Islam's Incompatibility with the Chinese Order' in *Islam in Asia*.Vol. 2. Edited by Raphael Israeli and Anthony H. Johns. Boulder, CO: Westview Press.

Izutsu, Toshihiko. 1983. *Sufism and Daoism*. Berkeley: University of California Press.

Jaschok, Maria, and Jingjun Shui. 2001. *The History of Women's Mosques in Chinese Islam: A Mosque of their Own*. London: Curzon Press.

Jin Binggao. 1984. 'The Marxist Definition of Nationality, Its Origin and Influence.' *Minyuan Xuebao* 3:64–7.

Jin Yijiu. 1985. 'Sufeipai yu Zhongguo Menhuan' (Sufism and China's Menhuan) in *Xibei Yisilanjiao Yanjiu* (*Northwest Islam Research*). Gansu Provincial Ethnology Department. Lanzhou: Gansu Nationality Publishing Society.

Johnson, David. 1985. 'Communication, Class, and Consciousness in Late Imperial China' in *Popular Culture in Late Imperial China*. Edited by David Johnson, Andrew J. Nathan, and Evelyn Rawski. Berkeley: University of California Press. pp. 34–72.

Jones, Steven G. 1997. 'The Internet and Its Social Landscape' in *Virtual Culture: Identity and Community in Cybersociety*. Edited by Steven G. Jones. London: Sage.

Jordan, Tim. 1999. *Cyberpower: The Culture and Politics of Cyberspace and the Internet*. London: Routlege.

Juergensmeyer, Mark. 1993. *The Next Cold War*. Berkeley: University of California Press.

Kanat, Omer. 1986. 'Comments on "The Identity and Nationality Problem in Chinese Central Asia".' *Central Asian Survey* 5(2):113–19.

Kazakh History Editorial Committee. 1987. *Hasakezu Jianshi* (*A Brief History of the Kazakh*). Beijing: People's Publishing House.

Ke Lei, Sang Ya. 1989. *Xing Fengsu* (*Sexual Customs*). Shanghai Chubanshe.

Kessler, Clive S. 1978. *Islam and Politics in a Malay state: Kelantan 1838–1969*. Ithaca, NY: Cornell University Press.

Keyes, Charles F. 1981. 'Introduction: The Dialectics of Ethnic Change' in *Ethnic Change*. Edited by Charles F. Keyes. Seattle: University of Washington Press. pp. 4–30.

———. 1984. 'The Basis of Ethnic Group Relations in Modern Nation-States' in *Ethnic Processes in the USA and the USSR: Material of the Soviet American Symposium*. Edited by V.I. Kozlov. Moscow: INION, the Academy of Sciences.

Kim Ho-dong. 1986. The Muslim Rebellion of the Kashgar Emirate in Chinese Central Asia, 1864–1877. PhD thesis, Harvard University.

Kondo, Dorinne. 1989. *Crafting Selves*. University of Chicago Press.

Kotkin, J. 1993. *Tribes: How Race, Religion, and Identity Determine Success in the New Global Economy*. New York: Random House.

Krader, Lawrence. 1963. *Social Organization of the Mongol Turkic Pastoral Nomads*. The Hague: Mouton.

Kristeva, Julia. 1993. *Nations without Nationalism*. Translated by Leon S. Roudiez. New York: Columbia University Press.

Kristof, Nicholas D. 1993. 'A Muslim Region is Tugging at the Ties that Bind China.' *New York Times* 14 August:1.

Kuhn, Thomas. 1996. *The Structure of Scientific Revolutions*. 3rd ed. (1st ed. 1962.) University of Chicago Press.

Kwong, Julia, and Hong Xiao. 1989. 'Educational Equality among China's Minorities.' *Comparative Education* 25(2):229–43.

LaBelle, Thomas, and Robert E. Verhine. 1975. 'Education, Social Change, and Social Stratification.' *Harvard Education Review* 45:3–71.

Lai Cunli. 1988. *Huizu Shangye Shi (A History of Hui Nationality Mercantilism)*. Beijing: Zhongguo Shangye Chubanshe.

Laing, Ellen Johnston. 1988. *The Winking Owl: Art in the People's Republic of China*. Berkeley: University of California Press.

Lal, Amrit. 1970. 'Sinification of Ethnic Minorities in China.' *Current Scene* 8(4):1–25.

Lapidus, Ira M. 1988. *A History of Islamic Societies*. Cambridge University Press.

Lardy, Nicholas R. 1986. 'Agricultural Reforms in China.' *Journal of International Affairs* 32(2):91–104.

———. 1994. *China in the World Economy*. Washington, DC: Institute for International Economics.

Leach, Edmund R. 1954. *Political Systems of Highland Burma*. Cambridge, MA: Harvard University Press.

Le Coq, Albert von. 1985. *Buried Treasures of Chinese Turkestan*. First published 1928. Oxford University Press.

Lee, Chae-Jin. 1986. *China's Korean Minority: The Politics of Ethnic Education*. Boulder, CO: Westview Press.

Leforte, Claude. 1986. *The Political Forms of Modern Society: Bureaucracy, Democracy and Totalitarianism*. Translated by Roger B. Thompson. Cambridge: Polity Press.

Lenin, Vladimir Il'ich. 1956. *The Development of Capitalism in Russia: The Process of the Formation of a Home Market for Large-Scale Industry*. Moscow: Foreign Languages Publishing House.

Leslie, Donald Daniel. 1981. *Islamic Literature in Chinese, Late Ming and Early Ch'ing: Books, Authurs, and Associates*. Canberra College of Advanced Education.

———. 1986. *Islam in Traditional China: A Short History to 1800*. Canberra College of Advanced Education.

Lewis, Bernard. 1996. *The Middle East: A Brief History of the Last 2,000 Years*. New York: Scribner.

Lewis, Paul. 1993. 'At U.N., Russian Compares Peril of Ethnic Strife to Nuclear War.' *New York Times* 28 September:A4.

Li Shujiang and Karl W. Luckert. 1994. *Mythology and Folklore of the Hui, A Muslim Chinese People*. New York: SUNY Press.

Li Yang and Wu Hsin-i. 1990. 'Status of Grasslands in China: With Special Emphasis on the Qinghai–Tibet Plateau.' Paper presented at the CSCPRC workshop on Grasslands in China, 30 May.

Liao Ping-hui. 1993. 'Commentary as Literature: Reading Taiwan's Newspaper Literary Supplements in 1993.' Paper presented at the 'Symposium on Cultural Studies in Asia, the Pacific, and the US', Program for Cultural Studies, East–West Center, Honolulu, 16–18 September.

Lin Yueh-hwa. 1984. 'Yizu of Liang Shan, Past and Present' in *The Prospects for Plural Societies*. Edited by David Maybury-Lewis. Washington, DC: American Ethnological Society. pp. 88–103.

Lindbeck, J. 1950. 'Communism, Islam and Nationalism in China.' *Review of Politics* 12:473–88.

Linke, Uli. 1990. 'Folklore, Anthropology, and the Government of Social Life.' *Comparative Studies in Society and History* 32(1):117–48.

Linxia Hui Autonomous Prefectural Basic Situation Committee. 1986. *Linxia Huzu Zizhou Gaikuang* (*Linxia Hui Autonomous Prefectural Basic Situation*). Lanzhou: Gansu Nationalities Publishing Society.

Lipman, Jonathan N. 1981. The Border World of Gansu, 1895–1935. PhD thesis, Stanford University.

——. 1984. 'Ethnicity and Politics in Republican China: The Ma Family Warlords of Gansu.' *Modern China* 10(3):285–316.

——. 1988. 'Ethnicity and Economics: The Tibetan–Muslim–Han Trading Network in Northwest China.' Paper presented at the Association for Asian Studies Meetings, San Francisco, 26 March.

——. 1989. 'Ethnic Violence in Modern China: Hans and Huis in Gansu, 1781–1929' in *Violence in China*. Edited by Stevan Harrell and Jonathon Lipman. Albany, NY: SUNY Press. pp. 65–87.

——. 1994. 'The Third Wave: Establishment and Transformation of the Muslim Brotherhood in Modern China.' *Etude Orientales* 13/14: 89–105.

——. 1996. 'Hyphenated Chinese: Sino-Muslim Identity in Modern China' in *Remapping China: Fissures in Historical Terrain*. Edited by Gail Hershatter, Emily Honig, Jonathan N. Lipman, and Randall Stross. Stanford University Press.

——. 1997. *Familiar Strangers*. Seattle: University of Washington Press.

Litzinger, Ralph A. 2000. *Other Chinas: The Yao and the Politics of National Belonging*. Durham, NC: Duke University Press.

Liu Binyan. 1993. 'Civilization Grafting: No Culture is an Island.' *Foreign Affairs* 72(4):19–21.

Liu Shao-ch'i. 1968. 'Internationalism and Nationalism' (1 November 1948). *Collected Works of Liu Shao-ch'i*, vol. 2, *1945–1957*. Hong Kong: Union Research Institute.

Lo Hsiang-lin. 1965. *K'e Chia Shi Liao Hui P'ien* (*Historical Sources for the*

Study of the Hakkas). Hong Kong: Institute of Chinese Culture.

'London Organization – Migrants' Shops Bombed in Tibet.' 1996. Agence France Presse (Hong Kong), 27 December. FBIS, FTS19970409001372.

Löwenthal, Rudolf. 1940. 'The Mohammedan Press in China' in *The Religious Periodical Press in China*. Peking: Synodal Commission in China.

Lufkin, Felicity. 1990. Images of Minorities in the Art of the Peoples Republic of China. MA thesis, University of California, Berkeley.

Lutz, Katherine, and Jane L. Collins. 1993. *Reading National Geographic*. University of Chicago Press.

Ma, Rosey. 2002. 'Chinese Muslims in Malaysia in Different Periods of History' in *Colloquium on Chinese Scholarship on the Malay World: A Reevaluation of a Scholarly Tradition*. Proceedings of conference held at Bilik Senat, Universiti Kebangsaan Malaysia, Baangi, 16–17 September.

Ma Shouqian. 1989. 'The Hui People's New Awakening at the End of the 19th Century and Beginning of the 20th Century.' Paper presented at the conference 'The Legacy of Islam in China: An International Symposium in Memory of Joseph F. Fletcher', Harvard University, 14–16 April.

Ma Tong. 1983. *Zhongguo Yisilan Jiaopai yu Menhuan Zhidu Shilue (A History of Muslim Factions and the Menhuan System in China)*. 2nd ed. (1st ed. 1981). Yinchuan: Ningxia People's Publishing Society.

——. 1989. 'China's Islamic Saintly Lineages and the Muslims of the Northwest' in The Legacy of Islam in China: An International Symposium in Memory of Joseph F. Fletcher. Edited by Dru C. Gladney. Unpublished proceeds of conference, Harvard University, 14–16 April.

Ma Weiliang. 1980. 'Various Aspects of the Nationality Question, Situation Discussed.' Foreign Broadcast Information Service 76883, 25 November:78.

——. 1986. 'Yunnan Daizu, Zangzu, Baizu, he Xiao Liangshan Yizu: Diqu de Huizu' (The Hui of Yunnan's Dai, Tibetan, Bai and Small: Liangshan Yi Areas). *Ningxia Shehui Kexue* 1.

Ma Yin (ed.). 1989. *China's Minority Nationalities*. Beijing: People's Publishing Society.

Ma Yunfu and Yang Zhihua (eds). 1988. *Aizihaer Daxue (Al-Azhar University)*. Changsha: Hunan Educational Publishing Society.

Ma Zheng. 1981. 'Trouble between Han, Uygur Minority Reported in Xinjiang.' Joint Publications Research Service 78873. 1 September: 22–5.

Ma Zikuo. c. 1933. 'Linxia Gongbei Siyuan' (Tracing to the Source Linxia Gongbei). Reprinted in Li Xinghua and Fen Jiuyan (eds). 1985. *Zhongguo Yisilanjiaoshi Cankao Ziliao Xuanbian, 1911–1949 (China Islamic History Reference Material Selections, 1911–1949)*. Vol. 1. Yinchuan:

Ningxia People's Publishing Society.

Mackerras, Colin. 1969. 'Sino-Uighur Diplomatic and Trade Contacts (744 to 840).' *Central Asiatic Journal* 13:215–40.

———. 1972. *The Uighur Empire: According to the T'ang Dynastic Histories.* Columbia: University of South Carolina Press.

———. 1994. *China's Minorities: Integration and Modernization in the Twentieth Century.* Oxford University Press.

McKhann, Charles. 1995. 'The Naxi and the Nationalities Question' in *Cultural Encounters on China's Ethnic Frontiers.* Edited by Stevan Harrell. Seattle: University of Washington Press. pp. 39–62.

McMillen, Donald H. 1979. *Chinese Communist Power and Policy in Xinjiang, 1949–1977.* Boulder, CO: Westview Press.

McNeal, Dewardic L. 2001. *China's Relations with Central Asian States and Problems with Terrorism.* CRS report for Congress RL31213. Washington, DC: Congressional Research Service, Library of Congress.

'Magnificent Paintings: The Murals of the Beijing International Airport.' 1980. *China Pictorial* 1:18–31.

Mair, Walter. 1994. 'Will the Fault Lines between Civilizations be the Battle Lines of the Future?' *Centerpiece* Winter/Spring:10.

Malkki, Liisa. 1992. 'National Geographic: The Rooting of Peoples and the Territorialization of National Identity among Scholars and Refugees.' *Cultural Anthropology* 7.

Mann, Jim. 1985. 'China's Uighurs – A Minority Seeks Equality.' *Los Angeles Times* 13 July.

Marcus, George E. 1994. 'The Modernist Sensibility in Recent Ethnographic Writing and the Cinematic Metaphor of Montage' in *Visualizing Theory.* Edited by Lucien Taylor. London: Routledge Press. pp. 37–53.

Martin, Emily. 1987. *The Woman in the Body: A Cultural Analysis of Reproduction.* Boston: Beacon Press.

Martin, Terry. 2001. *The Affirmative-Action Empire: Nations and Nationalism in the Soviet Union.* Ithaca, NY: Cornell University Press.

Maybury-Lewis, David. 1984. 'Living in Leviathan: Ethnic Groups and the State' in *The Prospects for Plural Societies.* Edited by David Maybury-Lewis. Washington, DC: American Ethnological Society. pp. 220–31.

Maybury-Lewis, David, and Uri Almagor (eds). 1989. *The Attraction of Opposites: Thought and Society in the Dualistic Mode.* Ann Arbor: University of Michigan Press.

Mayer, Iona. 1975. 'The Patriarchal Image: Routine Dissociation in Gusii Families.' *African Studies* 34(4):260–76.

Mengcun Huizu Zizhixian Gaikuang. 1983. *Mengcun Huizu Zizhixian Gaikuang (The Situation of the Mengcun Hui Autonomous County).* Shijiazhuang: Hebei People's Publishing Society.

Menjani, Nikmet. 1989. 'The Spread of Islam among the Kazakh People' in *The Legacy of Islam in China*. Edited by Dru C. Gladney. Conference collection. Cambridge, MA: Fairbank Center, Harvard University.

Menyuan Hui Autonomous County Basic Situation Committee. 1983. *Menyuan Huizu Zizhixian Gaikuang (Menyuan Hui Autonomous County Basic Situation)*. Xining: Qinghai Nationalities Publishing Society.

Mian Weiling. 1981. *Ningxia Yisilan Jiaopai Gaishu (The Islamic Factions of Ningxia)*. Yinchuan: Ningxia People's Publishing Society.

———. 1985. 'Ningxia Huizu Yisilanjiao de Jiaopai Fenhua Qiantan' (Brief Talk on the Distribution of Ningxia Hui Islamic Factions) in *Xibei Yisilanjiao Yanjiu (Northwest Islam Research)*. Gansu Provincial Ethnology Department. Lanzhou: Gansu Nationality Publishing Society.

Miller, Lucien (ed.). 1994. *South of the Clouds: Tales From Yunnan*. Translated by Guo Xu, Lucien Miller, and Xu Kun. Seattle: University of Washington Press.

Millward, Christopher. 1994. 'A New Paradigm for Self in the *Chuang Tzu*.' Paper presented at the 6th Annual SHAPS Graduate Student Conference, University of Hawai'i at Manoa, 4 March.

Millward, James A. 1988. 'The Chinese Border Wool Trade of 1880–1937.' Paper presented at the Association for Asian Studies Meetings, San Francisco, 26 March.

Minhe Hui and Tu Autonomous County Basic Situation Committee. 1986. *Minhe Huzu Zizhixian Gaikuang (Minhe Hui and Tu Autonomous County Basic Situation)*. Xining: Qinghai Nationalities Publishing Society.

'Minorities Hold Key to Own Prosperity.' 1987. *China Daily* 28 April:4.

Moerman, Michael. 1965. 'Ethnic Identity in a Complex Civilization: Who are the Lue?' *American Anthropologist* 67(5):1215–30.

Moore, Rachel. 1994. 'Marketing Alterity' in *Visualizing Theory*. Edited by Lucien Taylor. London and New York: Routledge Press. pp. 126–42.

Morgan, Lewis Henry. 1985. *Ancient Society*. 1st ed. 1878. Tucson: University of Arizona Press.

Morrison, Donald (ed.). 1989. *Massacre in Beijing: China's Struggle for Democracy*. New York: Warner Books and Time Inc.

Mosse, George L. 1985. *Nationalism and Sexuality: Middle-Class Morality and Sexual Norms in Modern Europe*. Madison: University of Wisconsin Press.

Mudimbe, V.Y. 1988. *The Invention of Africa: Gnosis, Philosophy, and the Order of Knowledge*. Bloomington: Indiana University Press.

Muzaffar, Chandra. 1994. Interview in *Third World Network Features*, Penang. Reprinted in 'The Clash of Civilizations? Responses from the World.' *Centerpiece* Winter/Spring:8.

Naby, Eden. 1986. 'Uighur Elites in Xinjiang.' *Central Asian Survey* 5(3/4): 241–54.

Nagata, Judith A. 1981. 'In Defense of Ethnic Boundaries: The Changing Myths and Charters of Malay Identity' in *Ethnic Change*. Edited by Charles Keyes. Seattle: University of Washington Press.

Nakada, Yoshinobu. 1971. *Kaikai Minzoku no Shomondai (Studies on the Hui People)*. Tokyo: Ajia Keizai Kenkyujo.

Naquin, Susan, and Evelyn S. Rawski. 1987. *Chinese Society in the Eighteenth Century*. New Haven, CT: Yale University Press.

Nathan, Andrew. 1985. *Chinese Democracy*. New York: Knopf Press.

'Nationality Identity Can Be Bought.' 1996. *China Focus* 4(2):4.

Nationality Pictorial (Minzu Huabao). 1985. *Minzu Fengmao: 'Minzu Huabao' Qujingzuoping Xuan, 1955–85 (Nationality Special Characteristics: 'Nationality Pictorial' Selected Photographs, 1955–85)*. Beijing: Nationalities Publishing Society.

Ningxia Hui Autonomous Region Population Census Office. 1983. *Ningxia Huizu Zizhiqu Di san ci Renkou Pucha (Ningxia Hui Autonomous Region Third Population Census)*. Beijing.

Norman, Jerry. 1988. *Chinese*. Cambridge University Press.

Oakes, T.S. 1993. 'The Cultural Space of Modernity: Ethnic Tourism and Place Identity in China.' *Environment and Planning Development: Society and Space* 11:47–66.

———. 1995. 'Tourism in Guizhou: The Legacy of Internal Colonialism' in *Tourism in China: Geographic, Political, and Economic Perspectives*. Edited by Alan A. Lew and Lawrence Yu. Boulder, CO: Westview Press.

'Obesity and Stress Becoming the Downside of Economic Boom.' 1994. Agence France Presse English Wire, 5 August.

Oda, Juten. 1978. 'Uighuristan.' *Acta Asiatica* 34: 22–45.

Office of Strategic Services. 1944. Japanese Infiltration among Muslims in China. Unpublished report, Office of Strategic Services, Research and Analysis Branch.

———. 1945. Peoples and Politics of China's Northwest. Unpublished report, Office of Strategic Services, Research and Analysis Branch.

Oi, Jean. 1989. 'Market Reform and Corruption in Rural China.' *Studies in Comparative Communism* 22(2/3):221–33.

Olcott, Martha Bill. 1983. 'Pastoralism, Nationalism and Communism in Kazakhstan.' *Canadian Slavic Papers* Spring.

———. 1987. *The Kazakhs*. Stanford: Hoover Institution Press.

O'Leary, Stephen. 2000. 'Falun Gong and the Internet.' *Online Journalism Review* 15 June. http://www.ojr.org/ojr/ethics/1017964337.php

Orleans, Leo A. 1988. *Chinese Students in America: Policies, Issues and Number*. Washington, DC: National Academy Press.

Paglia, Camille. 1990. *Sexual Personae: Art and Decadence from Nefertiti to Emily Dickinson*. New York: Vintage Books.

Pan, Lynn. 1992. 'A Chinese Master.' *New York Times Magazine* 1 March: 30–7.

Pang Shiqian. 1988. *Aiji Jiu Nian* (*Nine Years in Egypt*). First published 1951. Beijing: China Islamic Association Publishing Society.

Pang Keng-Fong. 1992. The Dynamics of Gender, Ethnicity, and State among Austronesian-speaking Muslims of Hui-Utat of Hainan Island. PhD thesis, University of California, Los Angeles.

Parker, Andrew, Mary Russo, Doris Sommer, and Patricia Yaeger (eds). 1992. 'Introduction' in *Nationalisms and Sexualities*. Edited by Andrew Parker, Mary Russo, Doris Sommer, and Patricia Yaeger. London: Routledge Press. pp. 1–20.

Parks, Michael. 1983. 'Color, Flavor Emerge in Xinjiang Province: China's Minorities Enjoy New Freedom.' *Los Angeles Times*:1–4.

Passell, Peter. 1996. 'Why the Best Doesn't Always Win.' *New York Times Magazine* 5 May:60–1.

Pei Zhi. 1959. 'Hai Rui shi fo Huizu' (Was Hai Rui a Hui?). *Guangming Daily* 26 November. (Reprinted in 1984 in *Huizu Shilun Ji 1949–1979* [*Hui History Collection 1949–1979*]. Chinese Academy of Social Sciences Ethnology Department and Central Nationalities Institute Ethnology Department, Hui History Team. Yinchuan: Ningxia People's Publishing Society. pp. 274–6.)

Peletz, Michael. 1993. '"Ordinary Muslims" and Muslim Resurgents in Contemporary Malaysia: Notes on an Ambivalent Relationship.' Paper presented at the 'Islam and the Social Construction of Identities: Comparative Perspectives on Southeast Asian Muslims' conference, cosponsored by the Center for Southeast Asian Studies at the University of Hawai'i at Manoa, and the East–West Center, 4–6 August.

Pickens, Claude L. 1933. 'Across China in Two Weeks.' *Chinese Recorder* 64:625–28.

——. 1937. 'The Challenge of Chinese Moslems.' *Chinese Recorder* 68: 414–17.

——. 1942. 'The Four Men Huans.' *Friends of Moslems* 16(1).

Picture Album of Turpan Landscape and Custom (*Tulufan Fengqing Huaji*). 1985. Ürümqi: Sinkiang People's Press.

Pillsbury, Barbara L.K. 1973. Cohesion and Cleavage in a Chinese Muslim Minority. PhD thesis, Columbia University.

——. 1976. 'Blood Ethnicity: Maintenance of Muslim Identity in Taiwan.' Paper presented at the Conference on Anthropology in Taiwan, Portsmouth, New Hampshire, 19–24 August.

——. 1978. 'Being Female in a Muslim Minority in China' in *Women in the Muslim World*. Edited by Lois Beck and Nikki Keddie. Cambridge, MA: Harvard University Press.

——. 1981. 'The Muslim Population of China: Clarifying the Question of Size and Ethnicity.' *Journal, Institute for Muslim Minority Affairs* 3(2): 35–58.

Piscatori, James P. 1987. 'Asian Islam: International Linkages and Their Impact on International Relations' in *Islam in Asia*. Edited by John L. Esposito. New York: Oxford University Press.

Pomfret, John. 2003. 'China Executes Tibetan Monk for Alleged Bombings.' *Washington Post Foreign Service* 28 January.

Population Census Office of the State Council of the People's Republic of China and the Institute of Geography of the Chinese Academy of Sciences. 1987. *The Population Atlas of China*. Oxford University Press.

Postiglione, Gerard A., Teng Xing, and Ai Yiping. 1995. 'Basic Education and School Discontinuation in National Minority Border Regions of China' in *Social Change and Educational Development: Mainland China, Taiwan, and Hong Kong*. Edited by Gerard A. Postiglione and Lee Wing On. University of Hong Kong Press.

Price, Sally. 1989. *Primitive Art in Civilized Places*. University of Chicago Press.

Prochaska, David. 1995. 'Viewing Postcards Viewing Others.' Paper presented at the American Historical Association annual meeting, Pacific Coast Branch, Maui, Hawai'i, 6 August.

'Proper Financing May Quash Dodgy Levies.' 1994. *China Daily* 29 April:3.

Pye, Lucien. 1975. 'China: Ethnic Minorities and National Security' in *Ethnicity*. Edited by Nathan Glazer and Daniel P. Moynihan. Cambridge, MA: Harvard University Press. pp. 489–512.

——. 1993. 'How China's Nationalism was Shanghaied.' *Australian Journal of Chinese Affairs* January:130.

Quanzhou Foreign Maritime Museum. 1983. *Symposium on Quanzhou Islam*. Quanzhou: Fujian People's Publishing Society.

Quanzhou Historical Research Society. 1980. 'Ding Clan Genealogy' in *Quanzhou Wenxian Congkan di san Zhong (Quanzhou Documents Collection)* 13. Quanzhou Historical Research Society.

Rabinow, Paul. 1986. 'Representations are Social Facts: Modernity and Post-Modernity in Anthropology' in *Writing Culture: The Poetics and Politics of Ethnography*. Edited by James Clifford and George E. Marcus. Berkeley: University of California Press. pp. 234–61.

Radio Free Asia, Uyghur Service. 2003. 'Separatist Leader Vows to Target Chinese Government (RFA).' 24 January. http://www.rfa.org/service/index.html?service=uyg

Rahim, Syed A. 1994. 'Participatory Development Communication as a Dialogical Process' in *Participatory Communication: Working for Change and Development*. Edited by Shirley A. White, K. Sadanandan Nair, and Joseph Ascroft. New Delhi: SAGE Publications.

Rahman, Fazlur. 1968. *Islam*. New York: Doubleday Anchor Books.

Ramsay, Robert S. 1989. *The Languages of China*. Princeton University Press.

Rayns, Tony. 1991. 'Breakthroughs and Setbacks: The Origins of the New Chinese Cinema' in *Perspectives on Chinese Cinema*. Edited by Chris Berry. London: BFI Publishing. pp. 104–11.

Riftin, Boris. 1989. 'Muslim Elements in the Folklore of the Chinese Huizu and the Soviet Dungans' in The Legacy of Islam in China: An International Symposium in Memory of Joseph F. Fletcher. Edited by Dru C. Gladney. Unpublished proceeds of conference, Harvard University, 14–16 April.

Roff, William R. 1984. 'The Meccan Pilgrimage: Its Meaning for Southeast Asian Islam' in *Islam in Asia*. Vol. 2. Edited by Raphael Israeli and Anthony H. Johns. Boulder, CO: Westview Press

——. 1985. 'Islam Obscured? Some Reflections on Studies of Islam and Society in Asia.' *L'Islam en Indonesie* 1(29):7–34.

——. 1987. *Islam and the Political Economy of Meaning*. Edited by William Roff. Berkeley: University of California Press.

Rosen, Stanley P. 1992. 'The Role of Chinese Students at Home and Abroad as a Factor in Sino-American Relations.' *In Depth* 2(1): 115–53.

Ross, Andrew. 1993. 'Cultural Preservation in the Polynesia of the Latter-Day Saints' in *The Chicago Gangster Theory of Life: Nature's Debt to Society*. University of Chicago Press.

Rossabi, Morris. 1969–70. 'The Tea and Horse Trade with Inner Asia during the Ming.' *Journal of Asian History* 3–4:136–68.

——. 1979. 'Muslim and Central Asian Revolts' in *From Ming to Ch'ing*. Edited by Jonathon D. Spence and John E. Wills Jr. New Haven, CT: Yale University Press.

Rousseau, Jean-Jacques. 1968. *The Social Contract*. Translated by Maurice Cranston. First published 1762. London: Penguin Books.

Rowe, William. 1994. 'Education and Empire in Southwest China, Ch'en Hung-mou in Yunnan, 1733–38' in *Education and Society in Late Imperial China, 1600–1900*. Edited by Alexander Woodside and Benjamin A. Elman. Berkeley: University of California Press. pp. 417–57.

Roy, Olivier. 1994. *The Failure of Political Islam*. Translated by Carol Volk. Cambridge, MA: Harvard University Press.

Ruan Fangfu. 1991. *Sex in China*. Stanford University Press.

Rubenstein, Richard L. 1978. *The Cunning of History: The Holocaust and the American Future*. New York: Harper & Row.

Rudelson, Justin Jon. 1988. Uighur Ethnic Identity Change in the Oases of Chinese Turkestan. Unpublished paper, Harvard University.

———. 1992. Bones in the Sand: The Struggle to Create Uighur Nationalist Ideologies in Xinjiang, China. PhD thesis, Harvard University.

———. 1997. *Oasis Identities: Uyghur Nationalism along China's Silk Road.*
New York: Columbia University Press.

Rushkoff, Douglas. 1994. *Cyberia: Life in the Trenches of Hyperspace.* New
York: Harper Collins.

Saguchi Toru. 1978. 'Kashgaria.' *Acta Asiatica* 34:61–78.

Said, Edward. 1978. *Orientalism.* New York: Random House.

———. 1988. 'Introduction' in *Selected Subaltern Studies.* Edited by Ranajit
Guha and Gayatri Chakrovorty Spivak. Oxford University Press.

Salisbury, Harrison E. 1985. *The Long March: The Untold Story.* New York:
Harper & Row.

Samolin, William. 1964. *East Turkistan to the Twelfth Century: A Brief Political Survey.* The Hague: Mouton & Co.

Saray, Mehmet. 1993. *Kazak Türkleri Tarihi: Kazaklarin Uyanisi.* Istanbul:
YAY Grafik.

Schafer, Edward H. 1967. *The Vermilion Bird: Tang Images of the South.*
Berkeley: University of California Press.

Schein, Louisa. 1990. 'Gender and Oriental Orientalism in China.' Paper
presented at the Annual Meetings of the American Anthropological
Association, New Orleans, 2 December.

———. 2000. *Minority Rules: The Miao and the Feminine in China's Cultural
Politics (Body, Commodity, Text).* Durham, NC: Duke University Press.

Schell, Orville. 1989. *Discos and Democracy: China in the Throes of Reform.*
New York: Anchor Books.

Schlesinger, David. 1994. 'China's Press Raises Spectre of Instability.' Reuters, 4 January.

Schmetzer, Uli. 1994. 'Deng Turns 90, Strong Leader Needed for Reforms.' *Chicago Tribune* 21 August.

Schwartz, Benjamin. 1989. 'Democracy in China.' *Dissent.*

Schwarz, Henry G. 1971. *Chinese Policies Toward Minorities: An Essay and
Documents.* Bellingham: Western Washington State College.

———. 1976. 'The Khwajas of Eastern Turkestan.' *Central Asiatic Journal* 20:
266–96.

———. 1984. *The Minorities of Northern China: A Survey.* Bellingham: Western Washington University Press.

Scott, Charles E. 1990. 'Genealogy and *Différance.*' *Research in Phenomenol-
ogy* 20:55–66.

Selden, Mark. 1971. *The Yenan Way in Revolutionary China.* Cambridge,
MA: Harvard University Press.

Shahrani, M. Nazif. 1984. '"From Tribe to Umma": Comments on the
Dynamics of Identity in Soviet Central Asia.' *Central Asian Survey* 3(3):
26–38.

Sharp, Gene. 1973. *The Methods of Nonviolent Action.* Boston: Porter Sargent Publishers.

Shi, Jinghuan. 1995. 'Cultural Tradition and Women's Participation in Education' in *Social Change and Educational Development: Mainland China, Taiwan, and Hong Kong.* Edited by Gerard A. Postiglione and Lee Wing On. University of Hong Kong Press.

Shichor, Yitzhak. 1984. 'The Role of Islam in China's Middle-Eastern Policy' in *Islam in Asia.* Vol. 2. Edited by Raphael Israeli and Anthony H. Johns. Boulder, CO: Westview Press.

——. 1988. 'Unfolded Arms: Beijing's Recent Military Sales Offensive.' *Pacific Review* 1(3):320–1.

——. 1989. *East Wind over Arabia: Origins and Implications of the Sino-Saudi Missile Deal.* Berkeley: University of California Press.

——. 2002. Virtual Transnationalism: Uyghur Communities in Europe and the Quest for East Turkestan Independence. Unpublished paper.

Shils, Edward (ed.). 1975. *Center and Periphery: Essays in Macro-sociology.* University of Chicago Press.

Shue, Vivienne. 1984. 'The Fate of the Commune.' *Modern China* 10(3): 250–83.

Sinor, Denis. 1969. *Inner Asia: A Syllabus.* Bloomington: Indiana University.

Smedal, Olaf H. 1992. 'Social Anthropology, Radical Alterity, and Culture.' *Canberra Anthropology* 15(1):58–74.

Smith, Mark A., and Peter Kollock (eds). 1999. *Communities in Cyberspace.* London: Routledge.

Smith, Valene (ed.). 1977. *Hosts and Guests: The Anthropology of Tourism.* Philadelphia: University of Pennsylvania Press.

Snow, Edgar. 1938. *Red Star over China.* New York: Grove Press.

Snyder, Louis L. 1951. 'Nationalistic Aspects of the Grimm Brothers' Fairy Tales.' *Journal of Social Psychology* 33:209–23.

Sorkin, Michael (ed.). 1992. *Variations on a Theme Park: The New American City and End of Public Space.* New York: Hill & Wang.

'Special Report: Uighur Muslim Separatists.' 2001. Virtual Information Center, 28 September:6. http://www.vic-info.org

Spivak, Gayatri Chakravorty. 1990. 'Women in Difference: Mahasweta Devi's "Duoloti the Beautiful"' in *Nationalisms and Sexualities.* Edited by Andrew Parker, Mary Russo, Doris Sommer, and Patricia Yaeger. London: Routledge Press. pp. 96–120.

Stafford, Charles. 1992. 'Chinese Nationalism and the Family.' *Man* 27(2): 362–74.

Ståhlberg, Sabira. 1995. 'An Ethnic Melting pot – the Case of the Gansu Corridor.' Paper presented at the Fifth European Seminar on Central Asian Studies, Nordic Institute of Asian Studies, Copenhagen,

21–26 August.

Stalin, J.V. 1953. *Works*, Vol. 11, *1907–1913*. Moscow: Foreign Languages Publishing House.

Stallybrass, Peter, and Allon White. 1986. *The Politics and Poetics of Transgression*. London: Methuen.

Stark, David, and Victor Nee. 1989. 'Toward and Institutional Analysis of State Socialism' in *Remaking the Economic Institutions of Socialism: China and Eastern Europe*. Edited by Victor Nee and David Stark. Stanford University Press. pp. 1–31.

State Commission for Ethnic Affairs (ed.). 1983. *Minzu Lilun yu Minzu Zhengce (Nationality Theory and Nationality Policy)*. Beijing: State Commission for Ethnic Affairs Education Department.

Statistics Bureau of Xinjiang Uyghur Autonomous Region. 2002. *Xinjiang Tongii Nianshu (Xinjiang Statistical Yearbook)*. Beijing: China Statistics Press.

Stoler, Laura Ann. 2002. *Carnal Knowledge and Imperial Power: Race and the Intimate in Colonial Rule*. Berkeley: University of California Press.

Strassberg, Richard E. 1994. *Inscribed Landscapes: Travel Writing from Imperial China*. Berkeley: University of California Berkeley Press.

Su Shaokang and Xia Jun (directors). 1989. *He Shang (River Elegy)*. Six-part film. Beijing.

Sun Yat-sen. 1924. *The Three Principles of the People: San Min Chu I*. Translated by Frank W. Price. Taipei: China Publishing Co.

'Surge in Corruption Threatening China's Reforms.' 1994. Agence France Presse English Wire, 30 August.

'Suspect Detained for Bomb Attack on Tibetan Clinic.' 1999. Agence France Presse (Hong Kong), 14 January. FBIS, FTS19990114000015.

Svanberg, Ingvar. 1989a. 'The Dolans of Xinjiang' in The Legacy of Islam in China: An International Symposium in Memory of Joseph F. Fletcher. Edited by Dru C. Gladney. Unpublished proceeds of conference, Harvard University, 14–16 April.

———. 1989b. *Kazak Refugees in Turkey: A Study of Cultural Persistence and Social Change*. Stockholm and Uppsala: Almqvist and Wiksell International.

———. 1989c. 'Turkistani Refugees.' *Ethnic Groups in the Republic of Turkey*. Edited by Peter Andrews. Heihefte zum Tubinger Atlas des Vorderen Orients: Reihe B, Bd. 60. Wiesbaden: Reichert Publications.

Svanberg, Ingvar, and Linda Benson (eds). 1988. *The Kazakhs of China: Essays on an Ethnic Minority*. Uppsala: Studia Multiethnica Uppsalinensia.

Taussig, Michael T. 1993. *Mimesis and Alterity: A Particular History of the Senses*. New York: Routledge Press.

Thierry, François. 1989. 'Empire and Minority in China' in *Minority Peoples in the Age of Nation-States*. Edited by Gérard Chaliand. London:

Pluto Press.

Thomas, Nicholas. 1992. *Colonialism's Culture: Anthropology, Travel, and Government.* Princeton University Press.

Thompson, Stuart. 1988. 'Death, Food, and Fertility' in *Death Ritual in Late Imperial and Modern China.* Berkeley: University of California Press.

Thurston, Anne F. 1987. *Enemies of the People.* New York: Knopf Publishers.

Tian Xueyuan. 1983. *Xin Shiqi Renkou Lun (On the Population in the New Period).* Harbin: Heilongjiang People's Press.

'Tibet Blames Dalai Lama for Bombing in Lhasa.' 1996. Tibet People's Radio Network (Lhasa), 27 December. FBIS, FTS19970409001370

Ting Shao Kuang. 1990. Hiestand Gallery, Miami University, Oxford, Ohio, 15 September to 12 October. Oxford, OH: Segal Fine Art.

Togan-Aricanli, Isenbike. 1988. 'Islam as a State Power in a Changing Society: The Kwajas of Eastern Turkestan.' Paper presented at the Workshop on Approaches to Islam in Central and Inner Asian Studies, Columbia University, 4–5 March.

Tonkin, Elizabeth, Maryan McDonald, and Malcolm Chapman. 1989. 'Introduction' in *History and Ethnicity.* London: Routledge Press.

Toops, Stanley. 1991. 'Recent Uygur Leaders in Xinjiang.' Paper presented at the Annual Meetings of the Association of Asian Studies, New Orleans, 11–14 April.

Townsend, James. 1996. 'Chinese Nationalism' in *Chinese Nationalism.* Edited by Jonathon Unger. Armonk, NY: M.E. Sharpe.

Trippner, Joseph. 1961. 'Islamische Gruppe und Graberkult in Nordwest China' (Muslim Groups and Grave-Cults in Northwest China). *Die Welt des Islams* 7:142–71.

Tu Weiming. 1989. 'Embodying the Universe: A Note on Confucian Self-Realization.' *World and I* August:475–85.

——. 1991. 'Cultural China: The Periphery as the Center.' *Daedalus* 120(2):1–21.

Tu Weiming, Milan Hejtmanek, and Allen Wacman (eds). 1993. *The Confucian World Observed: A Contemporary Discussion of Confucian Humanism in East Asia.* Honolulu: East–West Center Press.

Turnley, David, and Peter Turnley. 1989. *Beijing Spring.* New York: Steward, Tabori & Chang.

'Twenty-Nine Provinces, Cities, and Autonomous Regions Minority Nationality Population.' 1984. *Minzu Tuanjie (United Nationalities Magazine)* 2:38–9; 3:46–7.

'268 Million without a Job in 2000.' 1994. Agence France Presse, 16 August.

Unger, Jonathan (ed.). 1996. *Chinese Nationalism.* Armonk, NY: M.E. Sharpe.

Vaidyanath, R. 1967. *The Formation of the Soviet Central Asian Republics: A Study in Soviet Nationalities Policy 1917–1936*. New Delhi: People's Publishing House.

Voll, John O. 1985. 'Muslim Minority Alternatives: Implications of Muslim Experience in China and the Soviet Union.' *Journal, Institute for Muslim Minority Affairs* 8(2):332–53.

Wakeman, Frederic. 1989. 'All the Rage in China.' *New York Review of Books* 2 March:19–21.

Wales, Nym. 1952. *Red Dust: Autobiographies of Chinese Communists as Told to Nym Wales*. Stanford University Press.

Wang Jianping. 1996. *Concord and Conflict: The Hui Communities of Yunnan Society in Historical Perspective*. Lund Studies in African and Asian Religions 11. Stockholm: Almquist and Wiksell International.

Wang Shoujie. 1930. 'Niu jie Huimin Shenghuo Tan' (Discussion of the Lifestyle of the Oxen Street Hui). *Yue Hua* 25 May; 5 July.

——. 1937. 'Beiping shi Huimin Gaikuang' (A Survey of the Hui People of Beiping). *Li Gong* 1 May.

Wang Yiping. 1985. 'Najiahucun de Zongjiao Zhuangkuang' (The Religious Situation in Najiahu Village). *Ningxia Shehui Kexue* 9:7–9.

Wang, Yuejin. 1989. 'Mixing Memory and Desire: *Red Sorghum* a Chinese Version of Masculinity and Femininity.' *Public Culture* 2(1):31–53.

Warikoo, K.B. 1985. 'Chinese Turkestan during the Nineteenth Century: A Socio-Economic Study.' *Central Asian Survey* 4(3):75–114.

Wasserstrom, Jeffrey N. 1989. 'Student Protests in the Chinese Tradition, 1919–1989.' *Perspectives on the Chinese People's Movement: Spring 1989*. Edited by Tony Saich. New York: M.E. Sharpe.

Watson, Burton (trans.). 1968. *The Complete Works of Chuang Tzu*. New York: Columbia University Press.

Weber, Max. 1952. *Ancient Judaism*. Translated and edited by Hans H. Gerth and Don Martindale. Glencoe: Free Press.

——. 1958. *The Protestant Ethic and the Spirit of Capitalism*. Translated by Talcot Parsons. New York: Charles Scribner.

——. 1978. *Economy and Society*. Vol. 1. First published 1956. Translated by Guenther Roth and Claus Wittich. Berkeley: University of California Press.

Weigert, Andrew. 1991. *Mixed Emotions: Certain Steps toward Understanding Ambivalence*. Albany: SUNY Press.

Whiting, Allen S. 1957. '"Contradiction" in the Moscow–Peking Axis.' ASTIA Document No. AD 133049. Santa Monica: Rand Corporation.

Whiting, A.S., and Sheng Shih-tsai. 1958. *Sinkiang: Pawn or Pivot?* Lansing: Michigan State University Press.

Williams, Brackette. 1989. 'A Class Act: Anthropology and the Race to Nation across Ethnic Terrain.' *Annual Review of Anthropology* 18: 401–44.

Wilson, William A. 1976. *Folkore and Nationalism in Modern Finland.* Bloomington: Indiana University Press.

Wimbush, S. Enders. 1985. 'The Politics of Identity Change in Soviet Central Asia.' *Central Asian Survey* 3(3):69–78.

Wingrove, David. 1989. *Chung Kuo, Book 1, The Middle Kingdom.* London: New English Library.

Winichakul, Thongchai. 1994. *Siam Mapped: A History of the Geo-Body of a Nation.* Honolulu: University of Hawai'i Press.

Wittfogel, Karl A. 1957. *Oriental Despotism: A Comparative Study of Total Power.* New Haven, CT: Yale University Press.

Wolf, Arthur P. 1978. 'Gods, Ghosts, and Ancestors' in *Studies in Chinese Society.* Edited by Arthur P. Wolf. Stanford University Press.

Woodside, Alexander, and Benjamin A. Elman. 1994. 'Introduction' in *Education and Society in Late Imperial China, 1600–1900.* Edited by Alexander Woodside and Benjamin A. Elman. Berkeley: University of California Press. pp. 1–15.

Worsley, Peter. 1984. *The Three Worlds.* University of Chicago Press.

WuDunn, Sheryl. 1991. 'China Opposes Oscar Nomination of Film it Suppresses at Home.' *New York Times* 25 February:B1, B3.

Yang Hongxun. 1985. ' A Preliminary Discussion on the Building Year of Quanzhou Holy Tomb and the Authenticity of its Legend' in *The Islamic Historic Relics in Quanzhou.* Committee for Protecting Islamic Historical Relics in Quanzhou and Research Center for the Historical Relics of Chinese Culture. Quanzhou: Fujian People's Publishing House.

Yang Huaizhong. 1981. 'Lun Shiba Shiji Zhehlinye Musilin di Qiyi' (On the 18th-Century Jariyya Muslim Uprisings) in *Qingdai Zhongguo Yisilan jiao Lunji (Essays on Islam in China During the Qing Period).* Ningxia Philosophy and Social Science Institute. Yinchuan: Ningxia People's Publishing Society.

—— (ed.) 1988. 'Lüe Lun Sufeipai Zai Zhongguo Neidi Yisilanjiao Zhong de Fazhan' (A Discussion of the Development of Sufism in Internal China's Islam) in *Zhongguo Yisilanjiao Yanjiu Wenji (Compendium of Chinese Islamic Research).* Chinese National Research Committee. Yinchuan: Ningxia People's Publishing Society.

——. Forthcoming. 'Sufism among the Muslims in Gansu, Ningxia, and Qinghai' in *Minority Nationalities of China: Language and Culture.* Edited by Charles Li and Dru C. Gladney. Amersterdam: Mouton Press.

Yang Kun. 1992. *Minzu Xue Diaocha Fangfa (Nationality Studies Research Methodology).* Original dedication 1984. Beijing: CASS.

Yang, Mayfair Mei-Hui. 1989. 'The Gift Economy and State Power in

China.' *Comparative Studies in Society and History* 31(1):25–54.

Yang Ping. 1991. 'A Director Who is Trying to Change the Audience: A Chat with Young Director Tian Zhuangzhuang' in *Perspectives on Chinese Cinema*. Edited by Chris Berry. London: BFI Publishing. pp. 127–30.

Yanov, Alexander. 1987. *The Russian Challenge and the Year 2000*. Translated by Iden J. Rosenthal. Oxford: Basil Blackwell.

Yasuo Yuan (ed.). 1987. *The Body*. Albany: State University of New York.

Ye Zhengang. 1981. 'Ningxia Yihewanyi Zhuming Jingxuejia Hu Gaoshan' (The Renowned Scriptural Scholar of the Ningxia Ikwan, Hu Gaoshan) in *Qingdai Zhongguo Yisilan jiao Lunji (Essays on Islam in China during the Qing Period)*. Ningxia Philosophy and Social Science Institute. Yinchuan: Ningxia People's Publishing Society.

Yeo, Kwang-Kyoon. 1996. The Koreans in China: The Most Educated Minority and its Ethnic Education. Unpublished seminar paper, University of Hawai'i at Manoa.

Yin Xiao-huang. 1994. 'China's Gilded Age: Part 2.' *Atlantic Monthly* April.

Yokoyama, Hiroko. 1988. 'Ethnic Identity among the Inhabitants of the Dali Basin in Southwestern China.' Paper presented at the 87th Annual Meeting of the American Anthropological Association, Phoenix, Arizona, 16–20 November.

Yoshino, Kosaku. 1995. *Cultural Nationalism in Contemporary Japan*. 2nd ed. (1st ed. 1992). London: Routledge Press.

Young, Robert J.C. 1995. *Colonial Desire: Hybridity in Theory, Culture, and Race*. London: Routledge Press.

Zhang Chengzhi. 1991. *Xinling Shi (A History of the Soul)*. Beijing: Huacheng Publishing Society.

Zhang Yuzhi and Jin Debao. 1940. 'Dao Chendaixiang Qu – Baogao' (Trip to Chendai Xiang – Report). Unpublished report, Quanzhou, February.

Zheng, Yongnian. 1999. *Discovering Chinese Nationalism in China: Modernization, Identity, and International Relations*. Cambridge University Press.

Zhongguo Shaoshu Minzu (ed.). 1981. *Zhongguo Shaoshu Minzu (China's Minority Nationalities)*. Beijing: People's Publishing Society.

Zhu Yuntao. 1985 'Najiahucun Chanye Jiegou de Diaocha' (Najiahu Village Industrial Production Structure Research). *Ningxia Shehui Kexue* 9:1–6.

Zhuang Jinghui. 1993. 'Chendai Dingshi Huizu Hanhua de Yanjiu' (Research on Han Assimilation of the Ding Lineage in Chendai). *Haijiaoshi yanjiu* 34(2):93–107.

Zipes, Jack. 1979. *Breaking the Magic Spell: Radical Theories of Folk and Fairy Tales*. Austin: University of Texas Press.

INDEX